G000001692

Trusts in Prime Jurisdictions

Fifth Edition
Volume II

General Editor **Alon Kaplan**
Advisory Editor **Barbara R Hauser**

General editor
Alon Kaplan

Advisory editor
Barbara R Hauser

Managing director
Sian O'Neill

Trusts in Prime Jurisdictions, Fifth Edition
is published by

Globe Law and Business Ltd
3 Mylor Close
Horsell
Woking
Surrey GU21 4DD
United Kingdom
Tel: +44 20 3745 4770
www.globelawandbusiness.com

Printed and bound by CPI Group (UK) Ltd, Croydon CR0 4YY, United Kingdom

Trusts in Prime Jurisdictions, Fifth Edition

ISBN 9781787422988
EPUB ISBN 9781787422995
Adobe PDF ISBN 9781787423008
Mobi ISBN 9781787423015

Table of contents

Volume II

Trusts and estate planning in Israel

Alon Kaplan
Alon Kaplan Advocate & Notary
Meytal Liberman
Herzog, Fox & Neeman

1. Introduction: the legal, demographic and economic environment

Israel has a mixed legal system, which incorporates elements from both common law and civil law.[1] Its civil law influences derive from the Ottoman Empire era, while the UK government introduced English principles of common law and equity during the British Mandate (1923–1948). These were gradually replaced by new independent *Knesset* (Parliament) legislation and decisions of the Supreme Court of Israel on the establishment of the Israeli state.[2]

Israel is a country of immigration. Formal statistics[3] show that at the time of its establishment, Israel's population was only 872,700, of whom 716,700 (82%) were Jews and 156,000 (18%) were Muslims, Christians and Druze. Formal statistics[4] further show Israel's phenomenal population growth: at the end of 2018, the population stood at 8,955,300, of whom 6,554,700 (73%) were Jews, 1,874,800 (21%) Muslims and 525,800 (6%) others, all of whom enjoy equal legal rights in all areas of life. From the establishment of the state of Israel up to 2017, approximately 110,000 immigrants were born in the United States.[5]

Israel is also known as a 'start-up nation' in relation to high-tech and technology. This sector of the economy is a source of tremendous wealth and has created a new generation of rich families. *Israel 21c* magazine reported that in 2017,[6] the value of Israeli high-tech exits totalled $7.44 billion – an increase of 9% on 2016 – and 9% of those deals were each worth $400 million to $1 billion.

---

1   This chapter is based upon the following publications by the authors: "The Israeli Trust", 17(2) *Trusts Quarterly Review* 11 (June 2019); "Trusts and Estate Planning in Israel", *The US-Israel Legal Review* 30 (2019), https://lp.landing-page.mobi/index.php?page=landing&id=248533&token=fb100c5136180ae 03b01d7b703d6856b; and "The Use of Real Estate Trust for Holding of and Management of Property in Israel", 25(1) *Trusts & Trustees* 135 (1 February 2019), https://academic.oup.com/tandt/advance-article/doi/10.1093/tandt/tty182/5258080?searchresult=1.
2   The Library of Congress, "Introduction to Israel's Legal System", bit.ly/2HMYJJZ.
3   Central Bureau of Statistics, *Population, by Religion and Population Group*, www.cbs.gov.il/he/publications/ DocLib/2004/2.%20Shnaton%20Population/st02_01.pdf.
4   Central Bureau of Statistics, *Population, by Population Group*, www.cbs.gov.il/he/publications/ doclib/2019/yarhon1218/b1.pdf.
5   Central Bureau of Statistic, *Immigrants, (1) By Period of Immigration, Country of Birth and Last Country of Residence*, www.cbs.gov.il/he/publications/doclib/2018/4.%20shnatonimmigration/st04_04.pdf.
6   *ISRAEL21c* staff, "Israeli high-tech exits in 2017 totaled $7.44 billion", *Israel21c* (31 December 2017), www.israel21c.org/israeli-high-tech-exits-in-2017-totaled-7-44-billion.

This legal, demographic and economic environment is a fertile ground for the growth of family businesses and high-net-worth individuals, as well as for investment by foreign persons – whether foreign nationals residing in Israel or Israeli nationals residing abroad – in assets in Israel. This is in turn creating a growing need for estate planning for the purpose of transferring family businesses or other assets to the next generation efficiently and successfully.

Such estate planning often proves difficult, as high-net-worth individuals and families often have ties to multiple jurisdictions worldwide. Consider the example of Sir Frank Lowy, a well-known billionaire and holocaust survivor: he was born in 1930 in what is now Slovakia, where he worked as a plumber, spent some time in Hungary before serving as a soldier in the days of the establishment of the state of Israel, immigrated with his mother and father to Australia in 1952 and then – at the age of 88 – immigrated back to Israel, having sold his shopping centre company in Australia in December 2017 for $33 billion.[7]

Over the course of his life, Lowy accumulated assets in Australia, Israel, the United Kingdom and the United States.[8] He has family members in Sydney, New York, Los Angeles and other locations in the United States.[9] Lowy has always valued his family: his sons have always been an integral part of the business[10] and today he lives in a in a nine-story seaside building in Tel Aviv, where he can entertain his entire family.[11]

In addition to the complexity of estate planning for international families, costly family disputes should also be taken into consideration.

This chapter describes the main laws governing estate planning in Israel.

2. Inheritance in Israel

One of the main instruments through which to transfer assets to the next generation is under the inheritance procedure. Inheritance in Israel is governed by the Succession Law.[12] According to Section 2 of the Succession Law, the estate of a deceased passes to his or her heirs in accordance with the law (intestate inheritance), unless the deceased has left a valid will, in which case the estate is bequeathed in accordance thereof.

---

7   *Times of Israel* staff, "Australian billionaire Sir Frank Lowy makes Aliyah", *Times of Israel* (29 May 2019), www.timesofisrael.com/australian-billionaire-sir-frank-lowy-makes-aliyah.

8   Swati Pandey and Byron Kaye, "With Westfield sale, Frank Lowy calls time on rags-to-riches story", *Reuters* (12 December 2017), www.reuters.com/article/us-westfield-m-a-unibail-rodamco-lowy/with-westfield-sale-frank-lowy-calls-time-on-rags-to-riches-story-idUSKBN1E619J; Gili Izikovich, "The Story of the Jewish Child Who Survived Holocaust to Become a Billionaire Real Estate Baron", *Haaretz* (23 June 2019), www.haaretz.com/israel-news/.premium.MAGAZINE-escaping-nazis-at-13-australian-billionaire-frank-lowy-looks-back-in-new-biography-1.7397015.

9   "Frank Lowy retires to live in Israel", *Jmedia.online* (30 May 2019), https://jmedia.online/2019/05/30/frank-lowy-retires-to-live-in-israel/.

10 Jill Margo, "2018 AFR Rich List: What Frank Lowy and sons will do after Westfiel", *Financial Review* (23 May 2018,) www.afr.com/rich-list/2018-afr-rich-list-what-frank-lowy-and-sons-will-do-after-westfield-20180413-h0yqnm.

11 Izikovich, *supra* note 8.

12 Succession Law, 5725-1965, 19 SH 215 (1964-65) (Isr).

The Israeli court has jurisdiction over a person's estate, provided that his or her centre of life at the time of his or her death was in Israel, or he or she left assets in Israel.[13] Accordingly, the Israeli court has jurisdiction, for example, over the estate of a US resident who passes away leaving assets in Israel or that of a US person who immigrated to Israel.

2.1 Intestate inheritance

In the absence of a valid will, the Succession Law provides a mechanism that determines the order of inheritance and the portion to be inherited by each heir. Accordingly, the first right of inheritance is divided equally between the spouse of the deceased and his or her children. The spouse receives one-half of the estate and the children divide the remaining half between them in equal shares.[14]

2.2 Inheritance under a will

Alternatively, the estate can be distributed as set out in the testator's will. Under the Succession Law, a will can be made in one of four ways:[15]

- Handwritten will:[16] This must be written entirely in the testator's own hand and dated and signed by the testator.
- Will made in the presence of witnesses:[17] This must be written and dated, and signed by the testator before two witnesses after the testator has declared before them that the will is the testator's own. The witnesses must attest by their signature on the will that the testator has declared and signed the will as stated.
- Will made before an authority:[18] This is made by the testator stating its provisions orally before a judge, a court registrar, the registrar of inheritance or a member of a religious court, or by the deposit of a written will by the testator with any of these authorities. For this purpose, a notary is equivalent to a judge.
- Oral will:[19] People who are on their deathbeds or who in all circumstances reasonably regard themselves as facing death may declare a will orally before two witnesses. The testator's directions and the circumstances of the making of the will must be recorded in a memorandum signed by the two witnesses and deposited with the Registrar of Inheritance. An oral will becomes invalid within one month if the circumstances which warranted its making change and the testator is still alive.

---

13   Succession Law, §§ 135–136.
14   Succession Law, §§ 11, 12.
15   Succession Law, §§ 18–23.
16   Succession Law, § 19.
17   Succession Law, § 20.
18   Succession Law, § 22.
19   Succession Law, § 23.

Despite the formal requirements mentioned above, the court is authorised to validate a will even if it is defective or missing certain formal requirements, provided that the court is satisfied that it reflects the true and free will of the testator.

2.3 Freedom of testation

The principle of freedom of testation is a cornerstone of Israeli inheritance law. Section 27, entitled "Freedom of Testation", provides as follows: "(a) An undertaking to make, to change or to revoke a will – or to abstain from doing any of these things – is of no effect; (b) A testamentary provision that negates or restricts the testator's right to change or revoke the will is void."

The principle of freedom of testation is also evident in Section 8 of the Succession Law, entitled "Transactions with future inheritances", which provides as follows: "(a) An agreement about a person's estate and a waiver of his estate, made while that person was alive, is void; (b) A gift made by a person with the intention that it be vested in the donee only upon the donor's death is not valid, except if made by a will under the provisions of this Law."

Justice Cheshin stressed the importance of freedom of testation in *Lishitzky*:[20]

> *If there is a foundation principle, if you will, a super-principle, in inheritance law, there is none but the principle that instruct us that a person, any person, is at liberty to bequeath his estate, and the principle that derives from it, whereby the living are obliged to keep the deceased's wishes. The freedom of testation and the obligation to keep the deceased's wishes – two sides of the same coin – the two as one derive from the human dignity, and the personal autonomy derived from the dignity.*

2.4 Maintenance out of the estate

An exemption to the principle of freedom of testation is the right to receive maintenance from the estate.[21] Section 56 of the Succession Law provides that where the deceased leaves a spouse, children or parents who are in need of maintenance, they shall be entitled to such maintenance, regardless of whether the deceased has made a valid will.

Moreover, Section 63 of the Succession Law provides a 'claw-back' rule, which provides that if the estate is insufficient to provide maintenance to all those entitled to it, the court is authorised to view transfers of assets carried out without proper consideration in the two years prior to the death of the deceased as part of the estate, except for gifts and donations made as customary under the circumstances.

---

20   CA 4660/94 *Attorney-Gen v Lishitzky* 55(1) PD 88, 115 [1999] (Isr).
21   Succession Law, §§ 56–65.

Section 57 defines the scope of the right for maintenance from the estate and, among other things, provides that a child of the deceased under the age of 18 who is disabled, mentally ill, or cognitively disabled is entitled to maintenance.

In *Levitt*[22] Chief Justice Shamgar clarified that it is insufficient to belong to a class of persons who are entitled to maintenance from the estate; a need for maintenance must also be established. Where this need is not properly established, the testator may bequeath his or her entire estate to another. Shamgar further held that this need exists only where the applicant for maintenance cannot properly satisfy his or her basic needs. According to Shamgar, the wishes of the testator should be enforced to a certain extent only. The limit lies where a first-degree relative of the testator becomes an unreasonable burden on society. The maintenance from the estate reflects the notion that the existence of a family relationship justifies the imposition of a maintenance obligation on the estate, in specific instances.

2.5   Inheritance procedure in Israel

Under the Succession Law, the rights of the heirs in the estate are created only upon the issuance of an order with respect to the estate by a competent authority. If the deceased left a will, an application should be made for a probate order; only upon the issuance of this order does the will become valid and enforceable. Only a probate order issued in Israel in accordance with the Succession Law is regarded as valid; probate orders issued by foreign authorities are invalid.[23] However, if the deceased left a will relating to only a part of his or her estate, or did not leave a will at all, an application should be made for an inheritance order.[24]

Both an application for a probate order and an application for an inheritance order are made to the Registrar of Inheritance, which is authorised to declare the rights of the heirs accordingly.[25] However, in the circumstances described in Section 67A of the Succession Law, the Registrar of Inheritance must forward the application to the Family Court. These circumstances include where:

- the application is contested;
- the will is defective; or
- the administrator general represents a minor in the application.

The Family Court is authorised to issue the relevant order accordingly.[26]

---

22   CA 393/93 *Doe v the estate of Israel Levitt* (3 April 1994), Nevo Legal Database (by subscription) (Isr).
23   Succession Law, § 39.
24   Succession Law, § 66.
25   Succession Law, § 66.
26   Succession Law, § 67A(b).

Probate procedure in Israel requires that the original will be submitted to the Registrar of Inheritance, except in the case of an oral will. In the absence of an original will, such as where the original has already been submitted in another jurisdiction, a separate application should be made to the Family Court to approve submission of a copy.[27]

Section 54 of the Inheritance Regulations[28] provides that a copy of any application, including an application for a probate or inheritance order, shall be submitted to the review of the administrator general, who may, at his or her discretion, conduct an additional inspection of the application and require further information and documents.

Section 17 of the Inheritance Regulations requires that a notice with respect to the application for the inheritance or probate order be published in one daily newspaper and in the formal publication of the state of Israel (*Reshumot*). The notice includes an invitation to contest the application.

Section 14 of the Inheritance Regulations provides that an application for a probate or inheritance order shall be dismissed, unless notifications are sent with respect thereto as follows:

- in the case of an application for an inheritance order, notifications to the heirs under law listed in the application; and
- in the case of an application for a probate order, notifications to the beneficiaries under the will, together with a copy of the will itself. If the beneficiaries under the will do not include children of the deceased or their children, parents of the deceased or their children, or the deceased's spouse, then such notifications should be delivered to the deceased's children and spouse at the time of his or her death. If none of those is alive, the notifications should be delivered to the deceased's parents or, if none of those is alive, to the deceased's siblings.

As is evident from the above, the inheritance procedure in Israel is complex and cumbersome. It may also be uncomfortable for the deceased's family members, due to the requirement to disclose the contents of the will.

3. A corporate structure as an instrument of estate planning

Another possible avenue through which to transfer assets to the next generation is in accordance with the applicable law of contracts,[29] the Succession Law and the Companies Law.[30]

In this context, the articles of association of a company can be regarded as a contract between the shareholders and the company, as well as a contract

---

27   Succession Law, § 68(b).
28   Inheritance Regulations, 1998, KT 5923 (Isr).
29   Contracts Law (General Part), Contracts Law (Remedies), and case law.
30   Companies Law, 5759–1999, 1711 SH 189 (1999) (Isr).

between the shareholders among themselves, in accordance with the well-known theory of 'nexus of contracts', which views the company as a collection of contracts between different parties.[31]

The articles of association of a company holding assets or operating a family business can therefore be drafted to better meet the needs of the family and, in effect, constitutes the family constitution[32] within a company framework. This allows the shareholders to protect their rights and to ensure the implementation of the family constitution through the Companies Law and the corporate documents of the company.

For example, the articles of association can provide for several classes of shares, thereby allowing the founder to hold the management while assigning dividend shares, which do not grant voting rights, to other family members. The management shares can subsequently be bequeathed to selected family members. This separation of classes is also possible in the United Kingdom.[33]

Other relevant mechanisms can be added to the articles of association, such as alternative dispute resolution clauses under the Arbitration Law.[34]

4. A trust as an instrument of estate planning

Another efficient instrument of estate planning is a trust under Israeli law, as it allows for the holding of assets under central management and the regulation of its activities. The Israeli Trust Law[35] defines a 'trust' as "a relationship to property by virtue of which a trustee is bound to hold the same or to act in respect thereof in the interest of a beneficiary or for some other purpose". Section 2 of the Trust Law further provides that "a trust is created Law, by a contract with the trustee or by an instrument of *Hekdesh*", as set out below.

4.1 A trust created by law

A trust that is created in accordance with the law is a relationship that complies with the definition in Section 1 that its terms and conditions are determined in legislation. Section 42 of the Trust Law provides that the provisions of the Trust

---

31   Williamson, "Corporate Governance", 93 *Yale LJ* 1197 (1984); Uriel Procaccia, *New Company Laws in Israel* 14 (1989) (Hebrew).
32   A family constitution is a formal document which sets out the rights, values, responsibilities and rules applying to stakeholders in the family business and provides plans and structures to deal with situations which arise in the course of the family business. Such a document may assist the family in dealing with unexpected events; keeping it focused on the matters that are most important to it; managing disputes; and creating a common language and values to serve as the guidelines for the family business – even for future generations that were not involved in the business when it was first established. A family constitution tends not to be legally binding on family members (Taryn Hartley, "Family Constitutions – What, When and Why", *Lexology* (2 November 2015), www.lexology.com/library/detail.aspx?g= e5d5c264-e453-4d03-b1a6-b93f958f9f17).
33   Spencer Summerfield and Beliz McKenzie, "Shareholders' Rights in Private and Public Companies in the UK (England and Wales): Overview", *Thomson Reuters Practical Law* (1 June 2015), https://uk.practicallaw. thomsonreuters.com/5-613-3685?transitionType=Default&contextData=(sc.Default)&firstPage=true& bhcp=1.
34   Arbitration Law, 5728-1968, 22 LSI 210 (1967–1968).
35   Trust Law, 5739-1979, 33 LSI 41 (1966–1967) (Isr).

Law shall apply where no other Israeli law contains special provisions on the matter in question. It therefore follows that, in the case of a trust relationship subject to a specific law, the Trust Law can be viewed as a complementary mechanism only.

(a) Trustees appointed by a judicial authority

Scholar Shlomo Kerem[36] sets out the four main characteristics of a trustee appointed by a judicial authority as follows:

- The scope of the trustee's powers to act is determined by the legislation. The trustee receives control over the property by way of law and does not need any other legal means in order to execute his or her duties, such as a licence, ownership or any other right in the property.
- A special law sets out the modus of the appointing body and the powers, duties and obligations conferred on the trustee.
- The trustee's demise terminates the powers of the acting trustee.
- The appointing authority may replace the trustee without the need to transfer any right of ownership.

A good example of such a trustee is an estate executor appointed in accordance with the Succession Law. Under Sections 77 and 78, the court may appoint an executor who, under Section 82, is subject to the instructions of the court, and must assemble the assets of the estate, manage the estate, discharge the debts of the estate and distribute the balance of the estate among the heirs, in accordance with a succession order or a probate order, and do anything else necessary for execution of the succession order or the probate order. Further, under Section 86, the executor must keep accounts and file regular reports with the administrator general.

(b) Administrative statutory bodies acting in the captivity of a trustee

These are bodies of the state that effectively act in the capacity of a trustee on behalf of the state in matters of need, such as those listed below:

- The administrator general as the public trustee: Section 36 of the Trust Law provides that the minister of justice shall appoint a public trustee, who may be appointed by the court as a trustee of trusts. Accordingly, the administrator general was appointed to act in the capacity of public trustee in 1985. In *Public Trustee v Agmon*,[37] Justice Barak held that the court holds the authority to supervise the public trustee's activity and to give instructions where necessary to uphold the purposes of the trust, including instructions regarding the appropriate time to release the public trustee from office.

---

36   Shlomo Kerem, *Trust Law*, 5739–1979, 144 (4th ed, 2004).
37   PCA 9420/04 *Pub Tr v Agmon* 59(1) PD 627 (2005) (Isr).

- The administrator general as the administrator of abandoned assets: according to Section 2(b) of the Administrator General Law,[38] the administrator general is responsible for the administration of abandoned assets. Section 1 defines an 'abandoned asset' as an asset without a known owner, or without a person entitled to or capable of administering the asset, which has a connection to Israel: the asset is either situated in Israel or belongs to an Israeli resident, citizen or corporation.

(c)   Trustees appointed with the consent of a governmental regulatory body

Kerem[39] points out the mutual characteristics of such consensual trustees as follows:

- Legislation is limited to the minimum required to ensure the proper operation of the trustee.
- Subject to the minimum legislation, the parties are free to agree between themselves on the powers, rights and obligations of the trustee.
- The parties must confer on the trustee power and authorities by transferring the proprietary rights in the assets to the trustee, or by granting the trustee control and power over the assets.

Debenture trustees, whose *modus operandi* is governed by the Securities Law,[40] and trustees of employee stock option incentive programmes, whose *modus operandi* is governed by the Income Tax Rules (Tax Relief in the Allocation of Shares to Employees),[41] are good examples of such trustees.

4.2   A trust created under a contract

A trust created by contract is governed by the Contracts Law[42] and accordingly requires an agreement between the settlor and the trustee. Under this framework, a trust contract can be viewed as being established for the benefit of a third party in accordance with Section 34 of the Contracts (General Part) Law, 1973, thereby granting the beneficiary a right to enforce the trust contract.

Section 23 of the Contracts Law provides that a contract may be made orally, in writing or in some other form, unless a form is a condition of validity by virtue of law or agreement between the parties. Since the law does not require the fulfilment of any formal conditions and applies to any trust relationship that complies with the definition set forth in Section 1, it therefore follows that in order to determine whether a contract can be regarded as a trust contract, the nature of the relationship between the parties should be examined.

---

38   *Administrator General Law*, 5738–1978, 883 SH 61 (1978) (Isr).
39   *Supra* note 36.
40   Securities Law, 5728–1968, 541 SH 234 (1968) (Isr).
41   Income Tax Rules (Tax Relief in the Allocation of Shares to Employees), 5763–2003, KT 6222, 448 (Isr).
42   Contracts (General Part) Law, 5733–1973, 27 SH 117 (1972–1973) (Isr) and Contracts (Remedies for Breach of Contract) Law, 5731–1970, 25 SH 11 (1970–1971) (Isr), and relevant case law relating thereto.

Justice Goren affirmed this in *Arnon v Pieutrekovsky*,[43] stating: "A transaction shall be regarded as a trust transaction subject to the provisions of the Trust Law if the conditions of the definition stipulated in the Law have been materially fulfilled. The applicability of the definition of a trust on a transaction is not subject to the mere wishes of the parties, and despite using the phrase 'trust' in the transaction between them, the transaction shall not be a trust transaction and subject to the provisions of the law if its contents do not go in line with the definition of the trust in the Law."

As mentioned above, Section 23 of the Contracts Law provides that a contract may be entered into orally (ie, without a written document). Therefore, a trust relationship may be created by the mere behaviour of the parties. This is commonly known as an 'implied trust'. Shamgar addressed this issue in *Wallas v Gat*,[44] stating the following: "The Implied Trust was created in the Common Law to deal with circumstances where the behavior of the parties and their actions imply that they intended to create a trust, but for some reason, this intention was not explicitly expressed … It is implied from their relationship and behavior, that although the asset is registered under the name of one of them, the beneficial ownership belongs to the other."

4.3 A trust created by deed of *hekdesh* (endowment)

Section 17 of the Trust Law deals with the creation of a *hekdesh* and provides in Section 17(a) that a *hekdesh* is created when a property is dedicated in favour of a beneficiary or for some other purpose by a written document, in which the *hekdesh*'s creator expresses his or her intention to create the *hekdesh* and determines its objectives, property and conditions. The written document should take one of the following forms:

- a written document signed by the *hekdesh*'s creator before a notary. A trust created in this manner is commonly known as an *inter vivos* trust under Israeli law;
- a written will from the *hekdesh*'s creator, created in accordance with the Succession Law, which provides that a written will can be made before two witnesses, the court or a notary, or in the handwriting of the testator. A trust created in this manner is commonly known as a testamentary trust under Israeli law; or
- a payment instruction in accordance with Section 147 of the Succession Law, which provides that payments made to beneficiaries under an insurance policy are not included in one's estate. Accordingly, the setting out of beneficiaries in an insurance policy is regarded as a *hekdesh*.

---

43   File 548/06 District Court (Tel Aviv), *Arnon v Pieutrekovsky* (30 June 2013), Nevo Legal Database (by subscription) (Isr).
44   CA 3829/91 *Wallas v Gat* 48(1) PD 801, 810 [1994] (Isr).

(a) Commencement of a hekdesh

Section 17(b) of the Trust Law provides that the *hekdesh* shall become effective upon the transfer of control of the *hekdesh* property to the trustee. Accordingly, an *inter vivos* trust commences on the transfer of the trust assets to the control of the trustee and a testamentary trust commences on the issuance of a probate order with respect to the will, which effectively transfers the assets to the control of the trustee.

While the transfer of assets to a trustee during the lifetime of the settlor does not usually give rise to any special difficulties, this may not be the case where a testamentary trust is concerned. Section 54 of the Succession Regulations[45] provides that a copy of an application for a probate order shall be submitted for the review of the attorney general,[46] who may, at his or her discretion, conduct additional inspection of the application and request further information and documents. Further to that inspection, the attorney general may also intervene in the probate procedure and effectively alter the terms and conditions of the testamentary trust set forth by the testator.

The Trust Law does not set a perpetuity period for the *hekdesh* and once commenced, it can last forever.

(b) A declaration of a hekdesh by the court

Section 17(c) further provides that, when any property is *de facto* a *hekdesh*, but no instrument of *hekdesh* exists with respect thereto, the court may declare the existence of a *hekdesh* and may determine its objectives, property, conditions and date of commencement.

In *Weinstein v Fox*[47] the testator bequeathed his entire estate to his children, who were resident in the United States, on the provision that they immigrate to Israel and that all assets of the estate and the income derived therefrom remain in Israel. Under these circumstances, the executor of the estate, Advocate Fox, applied to the court to release him from his position of executor of the estate, but simultaneously appoint him as trustee with respect to the assets under his control for the period until the children of the deceased immigrated to Israel. Ultimately, the Supreme Court approved his appointment as trustee and declared the existence of a *hekdesh* under Section 17(c).

4.4 The charitable trust: the public *hekdesh*

As regards charitable trusts, Section 26 of the Trusts Law provides that:

A trustee of a trust, the objective or one of the objectives of which, is the furtherance of a public purpose (hereinafter: public hekdesh) shall, within three months from

---

45   Succession Regulations, 1998 KT 5923 (Isr).
46   A governmental department within the Ministry of Justice, which supervises inheritance guardianship and charity procedures in Israel, among other things.
47   CA 5717/95 *Weinstein v Fox* 54(5) PD 792 [2000] (Isr).

the date on which he becomes a trustee, inform the Registrar of the existence of the hekdesh and of the particulars enumerated hereunder, unless notification thereof has been made previously, and he shall inform the Registrar of any change in those particulars within three months of the date thereof. Notification of the existence of a public hekdesh shall be accompanied by a copy of the instrument of hekdesh.

As evident from the wording of this section, such a public *hekdesh* need not meet the conditions of Section 17 of the Trust Law. Hence, a trust pursuant to contract, where one of its objectives is the furtherance of a public purpose, will be considered a public *hekdesh* and will therefore be subject to registration with the registrar.

4.5 Use of companies

The trust, including the *hekdesh*, is not recognised as a legal entity in Israel.[48] Therefore, a common practice of trustees is to hold the assets of a trust via an underlying company incorporated in accordance with the Income Tax Ordinance,[49] thereby creating a designated legal entity to hold the *hekdesh* assets on behalf of the trustee.

According to Section 75C of the Income Tax Ordinance, such an underlying company is defined as set forth below:

a company that directly or indirectly holds trust assets for a trustee and for which all the following hold true:

(1) it was set up only in order to hold trust assets;

(2) in respect of a company that holds trust assets of Israel residents, or of an Israel resident beneficiary trust, or assets of a trust under a will in which there is an Israeli resident beneficiary, or trust assets that are in Israel, notice of its incorporation and status as such shall be communicated to the Assessing Officer within 90 days after the incorporation.

(3) the trustee directly or indirectly holds all its shares; for purposes of this paragraph, "holding indirectly" – only holding through another company to which the provisions of paragraphs (1) and (2) apply and all the shares of which the trustee holds.

4.6 Recognition of foreign trusts and trust-like structures in Israel

Several different wealth management and legacy structures can be found in operation in Israel. These structures include not only common law trusts, but also foundations, establishments and settlements made under the laws of other jurisdictions. Evidence on the operation of foreign trust-like entities in Israel can be found in the records of the Israeli Registrar of Companies as foreign corporations.[50]

---

48   PCA 46/94 *Zacks-Abramov v Land Registry Officer* 50(2) PD 202 [1996] (Isr).
49   Income Tax Ordinance (New Version), 5721–1961, 6 DMI 120 (1961) (Isr).
50   A review of the records of the Registrar of Companies shows, for example, a company named 'Favorit Establishment', which was incorporated on 19 November 1987 in Liechtenstein.

Further, Section 75C of the Income Tax Ordinance (New Version), 5721-1961 (the 'Income Tax Law')[51] defines a 'trust' as an arrangement according to which a trustee holds the trust's assets in favour of a beneficiary, whether established in Israel or outside Israel, and whether it is defined under the law applicable to it as a 'trust' or is otherwise defined.

The Income Tax Law further provides that a 'trustee' is "a person to whom assets or income of assets are attributed, or who holds assets in trust ... For this purpose, ... a legal entity listed in the First Schedule A shall be regarded as a trustee; the Minister of Finance may, by order, add corporate bodies to First Schedule A".

The legal entities listed in First Schedule A are the following:

- a foundation under the laws of Liechtenstein, Panama, the Bahamas or the Netherlands Antilles (Curaçao);
- an establishment under the laws of Liechtenstein; or
- a registered trust enterprise (trust reg) under the laws of Liechtenstein.

The fact that foreign trusts are recognised under Israeli law was demonstrated in *Lnl Reg Trust v Levine*,[52] in which a trust entity litigated in the Israeli District Court. In this case, the trust entity, Lnl Reg Trust, was established in 1965 to hold assets and administer thereof for a family. A dispute arose with respect to the validity of a certain document executed by the founder, where he left instructions to the trustee, since it was not probated as a will.

The importance of this case lies in the fact that the legal capacity of a Liechtenstein trust reg entity was effectively recognised by the Israeli District Court, since it was able to file a claim and litigate in Israel. Further, the district court reviewed the bylaws of the trust entity and other legal arrangements within the trust and determined the rights of the beneficiaries accordingly

4.7 Real estate trusts

A real estate trust (RET) is a legal structure under which real estate is purchased by a trustee or is transferred to a trustee, which acts as a nominee – that is, a 'bare trustee' – for an identifiable beneficiary. This legal structure is governed by the Taxation of Real Property Law[53] and the Trust Law.

Under such a structure, the trustee is recorded in the Land Register[54] as the legal owner of the real property either directly in its name or indirectly via a

---

51   Income Tax Ordinance (New Version), 5721–1961, 6 DMI 120, Fourth Chapter: Trusts (1961) (Isr) (the Income Tax Law).
52   File 1327/96 District Court (TA) *Lnl Reg Trust v Levine* (2 January 2008) Nevo Legal Database (by subscription) (Isr).
53   Taxation of Real Property Law (Capital Gains and Purchase), 5723–1963, 17 SH 193 (1963) (Isr).
54   Under the Land Law, 5729–1969, 23 SH 293 (1968-1969) (Isr), the Ministry of Justice keeps and manages a public record of property rights – the Land Register. Under Section 125 of the Land Law, Land Register records are regarded as conclusive evidence of the rights prescribed therein.

company incorporated for this purpose (ie, a special purpose vehicle), whose shares are wholly held by the trustee.

Accordingly, real property may be registered in the name of a trustee to hold and manage in accordance with the terms of a trust contract or a *hekdesh*, whereas the transfer of the real property to the trustee can be executed during the lifetime of the settlor under a trust contract or an *inter vivos* trust (*hekdesh*), or upon the death of the settlor under a testamentary trust (*hekdesh*).

The merits of the relationship are to determine the existence of the trust with respect to the real property, as evident in the following cases.

In *RG*,[55] the apartment in dispute was purchased and registered in the name of the daughter, while her father provided most of the funds required for the purchase. The apartment was used alternatively for the parents and the daughter upon her visits to Israel. After the demise of the mother, the daughter filed a claim against the father demanding the eviction of the father from the apartment, claiming that she had ownership of the apartment. The court dismissed the claim, recognising the ownership rights of the father, who provided evidence that the apartment was his property held by the daughter as a trustee for the father.

The Supreme Court's decision in *Amster* is also interesting.[56] A trustee was registered in the Land Register as the owner of a real property. The registration did not reference the fact that the property was held in trust.[57] The trustee was declared bankrupt and a creditor tried to attach the property for the satisfaction of his claim against the trustee. The court was presented with evidence that the property was held in trust for beneficiaries and, upon accepting this evidence, ruled that the creditor had no right against the real property, even though the Land Register included no reference to the rights of the beneficiaries. This was an important precedent reconfirming the concept of holding real estate in trust for a beneficiary and ensuring beneficiaries' rights against third parties.

Separate from the RET described above, the 'Israeli-made constructive trust' is a RET which have been declared as such by the court, such as *Tzimbler*.[58] In this case, the Tzimbler spouses purchased an apartment, but before the rights were registered under their name, the seller passed away, leaving the apartment to his widow, who refused to register the apartment under the name of the Tzimbler spouses. The Supreme Court held that the Tzimbler spouses had a beneficial right in the apartment, which was a semi-proprietary right, recognised under Israeli law; therefore, a trust relation existed under law

---

55   File 19831-04-10 Family Court (TA) *RG v MP* (7 July 2013) Nevo Legal Database (by subscription) (Isr).
56   File 5955/09 Supreme Court, *Amster (Receiver) v Tauber Tov* (19 July 2011), Nevo Legal Database (by subscription) (Isr).
57   Such a reference is possible under a procedure named 'caveat' under Section 4 of the Trust Law, and Land Law, 5729–1969, 23 SH 293, §127 (1968–1969) (Isr).
58   CA 1559/99 *Tzimbler v Turgeman* 57(5) PD 49 [1993] (Isr).

between them and the widow held the title of the apartment for the benefit of the Tzimbler spouses as beneficiaries.

Under the Taxation of Real Property Law[59] and a tax ruling issued in 2012,[60] the holding of real property under a RET does not create adverse tax consequences.

5.   Tax considerations

There is no gift tax or estate tax in Israel. Should a person decide to transfer his or her assets by way of inheritance in accordance with the Succession Law, or by way of will, the transfer will not be considered a tax event, regardless of the nature of the assets. However, such transfer of assets in Israel may be regarded as a tax event under non-Israeli law.

Should a person decide to transfer his or her assets by way of creating a trust – an *inter vivos* trust or a testamentary trust – there may be applicable reporting and tax obligations in accordance with the law on the taxation of trusts from 2006, as subsequently amended in 2014.[61] Although the transfer of assets to a trustee in a testamentary trust is not considered a tax event, reporting and tax obligations may be imposed upon the trustee and the beneficiaries under the Law for the Taxation of Trusts.[62]

Israel is a party to many double tax treaties,[63] although these do not usually regulate estate tax.

6.   Conclusion

Israel's legal system allows for a significant degree of flexibility through the use of various estate planning instruments, aligning Israel suitable with other modern jurisdictions when it comes to sophisticated estate planning.

This chapter further demonstrates that estate planning in Israel is a complex task, which requires high-level expertise in inheritance law, company law, contract law, trust law and legal capacity law, among others. In addition, this task usually involves multiple jurisdictions, as assets and some family members are often situated outside Israel. Therefore, cooperation with foreign professionals is also of upmost importance.

The Israeli trust is an efficient instrument for estate planning, as it both minimises the need for inheritance procedures and allows for greater control over the assets, provided that it is approached properly. It can also be

---

59   Taxation of Real Property Law (Capital Gains and Purchase), 5723–1963, 17 SH 193 (1963) (Isr).
60   Tax Ruling 3324/12, *The Establishment of a Hekdesh – Tax Ruling in Agreement*, www.misim.gov.il/ tmmisuyweb/frmShowLinkedAbs.aspx?num=20120030 (Hebrew).
61   Income Tax Ordinance [New Version], 5721–1961, 6 DMI 120, §§ 75C-75R (1961) (Isr).
62   A comprehensive review of the taxation of trusts in Israel can be found in section 2.4. of the chapter on Israel.
63   All of Israel's treaties for the avoidance of double taxation are available at https://mof.gov.il/en/ InternationalAffairs/InternationalTaxation/Pages/AvoidanceDoubleTaxationTreaties.aspx.

advantageous for those who wish to ensure that their assets are managed in accordance with their instructions for a relatively long period following their death. However, tax implications should be taken into consideration when deciding on the best course of action.

For this purpose, it is recommended to set up a trust in accordance with the procedure set out in Section 17 of the Trust Law – preferably an *inter vivos* trust that does not require probate proceedings. It is also recommended to use an underlying company to hold the trust assets, thereby holding them through a designated separate legal entity.

Trusts in Switzerland: core implications for the Swiss estate planning environment

Dominique Jakob
Peter Georg Picht
University of Zurich

1. Introduction: 'implanting' the trust

Switzerland's ratification of the Hague Trust Convention[1] enhanced the potential for trusts to become an important estate planning instrument within the Swiss legal system. The bedrock of this potential is the recognition of the trust under Article 11 of the Hague Trust Convention and Articles 149a and following of the Swiss Private International Law Act. 'Recognition' means that the Swiss legal system accepts the trust as an existing, independent legal structure which is (in principle) governed by a foreign law and whose provisions are (in principle) given legal effect within the Swiss law system.[2] It seems, however, important to point out two consequences that arise from this basic principle. First, recognition does not mean that a trust can be set up according to Swiss law provisions – at least for the time being,[3] there is no Swiss substantive law allowing for the creation of a trust and there is no such thing as a Swiss law trust or a Swiss trust law. In fact, in Switzerland, a trust can exist only as a legal entity under a foreign jurisdiction that has a trust law of its own.[4] Second, to accept the independent nature of the trust concept means to desist from any tendency of equating the trust with Swiss law legal concepts. In particular, a trust is not the same as a Swiss law corporation or foundation. As follows from the common law trust concept, it is not the trust itself that holds – as some kind of legal person – rights or obligations; it is the trustee.

---

1   The Hague Convention on the Law Applicable to Trusts and on their Recognition came into effect for Switzerland on 1 July 2007, cf SR 0.221.371.

2   For the practical impact of this recognition, see P M Gutzwiller, "*Trusts für die Schweiz*", *Anwaltsrevue* 2007, at 156. For a review of the practical importance of the Hague Trust Convention in Swiss courts, see L Thévenoz, "*Les trust sont-ils effectivement reconnus en Suisse? Un bilan sept ans après la ratification de la Convention de La Haye sur les trusts*", *Schweizerische Zeitschrift für Wirtschafts- und Finanzmarktrecht* 2014, at 161 onwards.

3   In fact, political efforts are being made to change that; cf section 7.3.

4   The applicable trust statute is defined under Articles 6 and following of the Hague Trust Convention and principally depends on the choice of the settlor. When no applicable law has been chosen, the law that has the closest connection to the trust is applicable. In ascertaining the relevant law, criteria such as the place of administration, the situs of the assets of the trust, the place of residence or business of the trustee and the objects of the trust are particularly relevant.

It follows that the law under which the trust is set up (the proper law of the trust) and Swiss law apply to the trust in combination. The proper law of the trust, determined under Articles 6 and following of the Hague Trust Convention and Article 149c of the Swiss Private International Law Act, governs issues such as the creation of the trust, its validity, its termination and its administration by the trustee.[5] However, the transfer of assets to a trust property, transactions on behalf of the trust and succession matters are examples of issues that are governed not by the proper law of the trust, but by the law of a jurisdiction determined under the choice of law rules of the Swiss Private International Law Act.[6]

Estate planning by means of a trust must therefore take all relevant laws into account. The issue of whether the intended trust is valid and operative under the proper law of the trust must be examined. But it is also necessary to examine which other laws come into play in relation to trust operations, and how their specific provisions and limitations can be reconciled with the intentions of the settlor.

Delineating the scope of application of the respective laws and securing an effective interaction of their provisions can be challenging – in general as well as for an individual estate planning process. This chapter sets out a select sample of core issues that are particularly relevant from an estate planner's perspective.

2. The creation of a trust in a will under Swiss inheritance law

Testamentary trusts are part and parcel of the trust concept and represent an important means of estate planning in trust jurisdictions. It may therefore be surprising that in Switzerland, there is some debate as to whether a testamentary trust can be created in a will under Swiss inheritance law. The discussion deals with cases where a decedent to whom Swiss inheritance law applies[7] sets up a will that complies with the formal requirements of Swiss law. In this will – perhaps alongside other provisions – he or she creates a trust. Since no Swiss law trust exists, the intended trust must comply with the legal requirements of a jurisdiction that allows for the formation of a trust, which will therefore form the proper law of the trust. Even if the requirements of that law for the creation of a trust are met, it is a matter of debate as to whether this combined construct of a Swiss law will and a foreign law trust can be accepted.

The courts have not yet ruled on this point and the explanatory memorandum accompanying the ratification of the Hague Trust Convention[8] –

---

5   Cf Article 8 of the Hague Trust Convention.
6   It may be that the Swiss choice of law rules lead to the application of the law which is also the proper law of the trust.
7   According to Articles 86 and following of the Swiss Private International Law Act, Swiss inheritance law applies in principle if the decedent was a Swiss citizen and/or domiciled in Switzerland. However, Swiss citizens living abroad and foreign persons domiciled in Switzerland may choose the application of a different inheritance law.
8   *Botschaft zur Genehmigung und Umsetzung des Haager Übereinkommens über das auf Trusts anzuwendende Recht und über ihre Anerkennung*, 2 December 2005, BBl 2006, 551. The memorandum can be accessed at www.bj.admin.ch/bj/de/home/wirtschaft/gesetzgebung/archiv/trust.html.

although it seems to favour the possibility of a testamentary trust under Swiss inheritance law – does not take a clear stand.

Many scholars oppose such legal constructs. Their core concern relates to the limited set of testamentary dispositions (the so-called *numerus clausus*) a testator can make under Swiss inheritance law. Whereas he or she is allowed – for instance – to appoint an heir or to bequeath a legacy, there is no Swiss provision envisaging the creation of a trust by will. Although this can easily be explained by the fact that Swiss law has never recognised the concept of a trust, according to those who oppose the idea, it makes the creation of a testamentary trust under Swiss inheritance law inadmissible.[9]

Other authors are ready to accept the creation of a 'testamentary trust' in a will under Swiss law. They either exempt the creation of a trust from the *numerus clausus* by limiting the *numerus clausus* to testamentary provisions in a narrow sense, or equate the testamentary trust with the 'testamentary foundation', which is recognised in Swiss inheritance law (Article 493 of the Swiss Civil Code),[10] and therefore hold it to be compatible with the *numerus clausus*.[11]

In the authors' opinion, this discussion is somewhat beside the point, as we regard the creation of a testamentary trust as a matter to be judged by the proper law of the trust, not the law governing inheritance. This follows from Articles 2 and 8 of the Hague Trust Convention, which include the testamentary trust. Consequently, the *numerus clausus* does not apply to the trust, so that a testamentary trust can be accepted. Only if the *numerus clausus* (or parts thereof) were to be considered as a law whose application is mandatory (*loi d'application immédiate*) or as an issue of public policy – a feature that not even the most ardent Swiss opponents of testamentary trusts suggest – would the law governing inheritance be applicable.[12] In any case, with respect to the intentions of the Hague Trust Convention, the recognition of trusts should include such an important element as the testamentary trust.

---

9   See, among others, F Guillaume, *"Trust, réserves héréditaires et immeubles"*, Aktuelle Juristische Praxis 2009, 33, at 38; L Thévenoz, *Trusts en Suisse: Adhésion à la Convention de La Haye sur les trusts et codification de la fiducie – Trusts in Switzerland: Ratification of the The Hague Convention on Trusts and Codification of Fiduciary Transfers* (Zurich, 2001), at 215.

10   Article 493 of the Swiss Civil Code:
       1 *The testator is entitled to bequeath all or part of the disposable portion of his or her property to a foundation for any purpose of his or her choosing.*
       2 *However, the foundation is valid only if it conforms to the legal requirements.*
       (The official – albeit non-binding – English version of the Swiss Civil Code can be found at www.admin.ch/opc/en/classified-compilation/19070042/index.html).

11   See, among others, P Eitel and S Brauchli, *"Trusts im Anwendungsbereich des Erbrechts"*, successio 2012, at 116 onwards; S Wolf and N Jordi, *"Trust und schweizerisches Zivilrecht – insbesondere Ehegüter-, Erb- und Immobiliarsachenrecht"* in S Wolf, ed, *Der Trust – Einführung und Rechtslage in der Schweiz nach dem Inkrafttreten des Haager Trust Übereinkommens* (Bern, 2008), at 60.

12   For further detail, see D Jakob and P Picht, *"Trust und Nachlassplanung in der Schweiz nach Ratifikation des HTÜ"* in M Martinek, P Rawert and B Weitemeyer, eds, *Festschrift für DIETER REUTER zum 70. Geburtstag am 16. Oktober 2010* (Berlin, 2010), at 146; see also T Meyer, *"Trusts und Schweizerisches Erbrecht"*, successio 2017, 159, at 163 onwards.

As long as the current uncertainties persist, it may nonetheless be advisable – if Swiss inheritance law is to govern the inheritance – to prefer a trust made during the settlor's life to a testamentary trust if such a planning option is possible.

3. The trust and Article 335 of the Swiss Civil Code

3.1 The meaning of Article 335 of the Swiss Civil Code
Article 335 of the Swiss Civil Code[13] is directed against certain ways of linking separate estates to a family. Article 335(1) prohibits foundations that grant maintenance payments to the members of a family without tying them to particular purposes. Article 335(2) forbids entailments (ie, settlements which perpetually tie up assets as special property of a particular family). By introducing those rules, the legislature intended to prevent the establishment or perpetuation of feudal structures, and to keep potential beneficiaries of separate family estates from idleness.[14]

3.2 Impact on trusts?
Trusts can be set up in a way that is contrary to these prescriptions – in particular, if they grant maintenance benefits without tying them to special purposes and if the beneficiaries belong to one family. Hence, Article 335 of the Swiss Civil Code could prevent the recognition of such trusts in Switzerland.

As Article 335 will not be part of the applicable proper law of the trust which, in principle, governs the existence of the trust, its possible prohibiting impact would need to be based on a provision that is allowed to interfere with the law governing the trust. Article 16 of the Hague Trust Convention could be such a provision, since it allows for the application of those provisions of the law of the forum which must be applied even to international situations, irrespective of rules of conflict of laws (so-called *'lois d'application immédiate'*).

However, the discussion seems to lead to a different outcome. Scholars have criticised Article 335 of the Swiss Civil Code for the outdated purposes it pursues; the legislature is considering abolishing the provision; and the Swiss

---

13   Article 335 of the Swiss Civil Code:
> *1 A body of assets may be tied to a family by means of a family foundation created under the law of persons or inheritance law in order to meet the costs of raising, endowing or supporting family members or for similar purposes.*
>
> *2 It is no longer permitted to establish a fee tail.*

14   For a taxonomy of the current debate on the suitability of Article 335 of the Swiss Civil Code in a contemporary legal system and a differentiated set of possible solutions, see D Jakob, "*Ein Stiftungsbegriff für die Schweiz*", *Zeitschrift für Schweizerisches Recht* 2013, 185, at 322; further see by the same author, "*Freiheit durch Governance – Die Zukunft des Schweizer Stiftungsrechts mit besonderem Blick auf die Familienstiftung*" in D Jakob (ed), *Stiftung und Familie* (Basel, 2015), at 61; and with a slightly different view G Studen, "*Die Familienstiftung und der gesellschaftliche Wertekanon im Wandel der Zeiten*" in D Jakob (ed), *Stiftung und Familie* (Basel, 2015), at 89.

Federal Court held in 2009[15] that Article 335 cannot be considered as a *loi d'application immédiate* under Article 18 of the Swiss Private International Law Act (a provision that parallels Article 16 of the Hague Trust Convention).

Against this background – although scholars still want Article 335 of the Swiss Civil Code to have an impact on trusts in exceptional cases – it can and should be held that the provision does not limit the creation or recognition of trusts in Switzerland.[16]

4. The trust and Article 488 of the Swiss Civil Code

4.1 The meaning of Article 488
Article 488(1) of the Swiss Civil Code[17] permits the appointment of a reversionary heir, but Article 488(2) limits this capacity to one succession of a first and reversionary heir. A decedent can therefore, for instance, make a bequest to his son as first heir and his granddaughter as reversionary heir, but he cannot appoint his granddaughter's daughter to be his (third) heir after his granddaughter's death.

4.2 Article 488(2) of the Swiss Civil Code as *loi d'application immédiate*
As in the case of Article 335 of the Swiss Civil Code, the potential of trust deeds to contradict Article 488(2)[18] raises the question of whether the Swiss provision may, based on Article 16 of the Hague Trust Convention, limit the recognition of trusts. As attention thus far has centred on Article 335, this question still needs to be finally settled.

In the authors' opinion, Article 488(2) should not be regarded as a *loi d'application immédiate* under Article 16 of the Hague Trust Convention. One main goal of the provision – the prevention of quasi-feudal estates – is close to the intentions of Article 335 of the Swiss Civil Code and therefore debatable. Moreover, a testamentary foundation under Article 493 of the Swiss Civil Code can also be shaped in ways that conflict with Article 488(2). However,

---

15 See Swiss Federal Court Decision 4A_339/2009 of November 17 2009, E 4.3. Although the object of the decision was a Liechtenstein law foundation and not a trust, the conclusion that Article 335 of the Swiss Civil Code is not a *loi d'application immédiate* also applies to trusts. Swiss scholars almost unanimously agreed with the Federal Court, but see T Geiser, *"Familienfideikommiss und Trusts"* in H Honsell and others (eds), *Liber amicorum Nedim Peter Vogt, Privatrecht als kulturelles Erbe* (Basel, 2012), 89, at 100 onwards.
16 For a detailed discussion see D Jakob and P Picht, *"Der trust in der Schweizer Nachlassplanung und Vermögensgestaltung"*, Aktuelle Juristische Praxis 2010, 855, at 860 onwards; see also T Meyer, *op cit*, at 165 onwards.
17 Article 488:
   1 The testator is entitled in his or her dispositions to require the named heir, as provisional heir, to deliver the estate to a third party, as remainderman.
   2 No such obligation may be imposed on the remainderman.
   3 The same provisions apply to legacies.
18 A settlor may, for example, designate as successive beneficiaries first his or her spouse, then his or her child and then his or her grandchildren.

testamentary foundations are held to be valid even if they contradict Article 488(2). A legal instrument that conflicts with Article 488(2) (here a trust) therefore cannot be totally unacceptable to the Swiss legal system.[19]

4.3 Abuse of rights – exemption

Even if a future majority of authors comes to interpret Article 488 of the Swiss Civil Code as a provision that falls under Article 16 of the Hague Trust Convention, this cannot mean an automatic ban on all trusts foreseeing multiple reversionary beneficiaries. The second main goal of Article 488 is to ensure that a testator cannot order the treatment of his or her estate in perpetuity. Trusts constituted under a governing law that includes an effective rule against perpetuities do not run contrary to this intention and should generally be admissible. Where the trust is not subject to an effective rule against perpetuities, its deed still expresses the settlor's autonomous will, and this expression deserves to be respected as far as possible. The application of Article 488(2) of the Swiss Civil Code to trusts should therefore be limited to cases involving abuse of rights. An abuse may in particular be constituted by an accumulation of factors that aggrieve the beneficiaries, such as the lengthy duration of the trust, a high degree of discretion for the trustee, a lack of inherent structures for securing any control or protection for the beneficiaries, the intent of the settlor to harm the beneficiaries and so on.

5. Trusts and forced heirship

5.1 Reduction of transfers to the trust property

In Switzerland, the spouse or registered partner, the progeny and the parents of a decedent are entitled to a compulsory portion of the deceased's estate (Article 471 of the Swiss Civil Code). If the future decedent alienates assets (whether during his or her life or on death) to an extent that the remaining property is too small to cover (all of) the compulsory portions, the entitled persons can (under certain conditions) have the alienations reduced and thereby have the decedent's property augmented until the compulsory portions can be covered (Articles 522 and following of the Swiss Civil Code). Article 82 of the Swiss Civil Code[20] extends these rules to transactions which transfer assets to a foundation. The applicable aspects of the law of inheritance, determined by Articles 86 and following of the Swiss Private International Law Act, include those relating to compulsory portions.[21] Hence, if Swiss law constitutes the applicable law of

---

19   See D Jakob and P Picht, *op cit*, at 864 onwards, and the differentiated analysis by the same authors in D Jakob and P Picht, *"Der Einsatz von trusts in Vor- und Nacherbschaftskonstellationen"* in H Honsell and others, *Liber amicorum Nedim Peter Vogt, Privatrecht als kulturelles Erbe* (Basel, 2012), at 177 onwards.
20   Article 82: "A foundation may be challenged by the founder's heirs or creditors in the same manner as a gift."
21   See, among others, A K Schnyder and M Liatowitsch, in H Honsell and others (eds), *Basler Kommentar, Internationales Privatrecht*, third edition (Basel, 2013), Article 86 note 4.

inheritance, its rules determine whether a disposal by the bequeather violates the compulsory portion rules and which mechanisms are applicable to correct such a violation.

If the transaction that violates the rules on compulsory portions lies in a transfer of assets to a trust property made during the settlor's life, unanimous opinion favours the application of forced heirship provisions in order to secure close relatives of the decedent a minimum share of the inheritance.[22] The transaction in question can therefore be reduced under Article 527[23] in conjunction with Article 82 of the Swiss Civil Code.[24] Referring to Articles 527(3) and (4) of the Swiss Civil Code, alienations to a revocable trust, alienations within the five years preceding the settlor's death and alienations made with the obvious intention of evading forced heirship rules may in consequence have to be reversed.

The reduction may deprive the trust of all or a large part of its assets. Whether the trust nevertheless stays valid and (if so) whether its decreased property requires a modification of the trust should be judged by the law governing the trust and not – as some authors propose – by the (Swiss) law of inheritance. Hence, from a practical perspective, this ought not to lead to an automatic demise of the trust, especially if there are some assets left and the 'three certainties' are still fulfilled. Rather, the autonomous intention of the settlor should be considered and the trust adapted accordingly.

5.2 Installing entitled persons as beneficiaries

The wish to organise one's estate planning by means of a trust does not necessarily imply an intention to violate compulsory portions. It may therefore be interesting to reconcile a trust with existing rights to a compulsory portion by installing the entitled persons as beneficiaries. However, to be entitled to a compulsory portion under Swiss law implies in principle the certainty of receiving the full value of one's portion at one's free disposal. Whether the recipient's position as a beneficiary meets these requirements – and can therefore satisfy the statutory rights – will depend on the circumstances of each individual case. The beneficial position might only amount to a compulsory

---

22 This position should be based on Article 15(c) of the Hague Trust Convention. Therefore, an application of Article 16 of the Hague Trust Convention is not necessary.

23 Article 527:
    The following are subject to abatement in the same manner as testamentary dispositions:
    1 advances against a person's share of an inheritance made in the form of wedding gifts, settlements or assignments of assets, to the extent these are not subject to hotchpot;
    2 compensation payments in settlement of future rights of inheritance;
    3 gifts that were freely revocable by the deceased or made in the five years prior to his or her death, with the exception of customary occasional gifts;
    4 assets alienated by the deceased with the obvious intention of circumventing the limitations on his or her testamentary freedom.

24 The doctrine argues for the combined application of Articles 527 and 82 of the Swiss Civil Code because the transfer to a trust in some ways resembles the transfer to a foundation.

portion if the trust satisfies certain general criteria. First, the trust must be irrevocable and non-discretionary. Second, the equitable title must embody the full value of the compulsory portion and the allotment of this value may not be subject to undue delays, procedures or other restrictions. And finally, it must be established that the appointment as beneficiary was meant to satisfy the right to a compulsory portion.

In order to avoid legal uncertainties regarding the satisfaction of these complex criteria, it may be advisable that the trust beneficiaries waive their forced heirship rights by way of contract with the settlor and decedent.

6. The conveyance of Swiss real estate to a trust property

6.1 The legal structure of a real estate transfer

As regards the validity and the administration of a trust, it is the proper law of the trust that establishes the consequences of transferring assets to the trust property (Article 8 of the Hague Trust Convention). Whether an asset has effectively been transferred depends on the relevant law of property (Articles 4 and 15 of the Hague Trust Convention). For real estate located in Switzerland, it is Swiss law – the law of the place where the property is located – that forms the property statute (Article 99 of the Swiss Private International Law Act).[25] Thus, the rules of Articles 656 and 657 of the Swiss Civil Code must be considered. Article 656 draws a fundamental distinction between transfers of real estate that are based on contract and those that are not, which include cases of testate or intestate succession. In the former case, registration in the land register has constitutive effect on acquisition of the real estate; whereas in the latter, registration is only declaratory, but gives the acquirer the power of disposal over the property. In consequence, the estate planner will have to distinguish not only cases where the real estate is conveyed to the trust within the life of the settlor from cases where this is done on death, but also whether the real estate transfers are contractual.

---

25 Article 99:
　　1 Interests in real property shall be subject to the law of the place where the property is located.
　　2 Claims arising from nuisances emanating from real property shall be governed by the provisions of this Code concerning torts (Article 138).
　　(All translations of Swiss Private International Law Act provisions refer to the translation by Umbricht Attorneys at Law, Zurich; the translation can be accessed at www.umbricht.ch.)

26 Article 657:
　　1 In order to be binding, a contract to transfer land ownership must be executed as a public deed.
　　2 Testamentary disposition and marital contracts require the forms prescribed by the law of succession and marital property law.

27 Article 656:
　　1 The acquisition of land ownership must be recorded in the land register.
　　2 In the case of appropriation, inheritance, compulsory purchase, debt enforcement or court judgment, the acquirer becomes the owner even before registration in the land register but obtains the power of disposal over the immovable property only once he or she has been recorded as the owner in the land register.

(a)   Conveyance of real estate during the settlor's life

Under Swiss law, the transfer of real estate during the transferor's life requires an authenticated legal instrument (eg, a contract – see Article 657 of the Swiss Civil Code)[26] and registration in the land register (Article 656(1) of the Swiss Civil Code).[27]

Article 119 of the Swiss Private International Law Act: The law governing legal instruments under Article 657 of the Swiss Civil Code is determined not by Article 99 of the Swiss Private International Law Act, but by Article 119 of the Swiss Private International Law Act,[28] because the legal instrument itself is governed not by the law of property, but by the law of obligations. Article 119(1) of the Swiss Private International Law Act states that Swiss law applies to contracts concerning Swiss real estate;[29] and Article 119(3) adds that in that case, the form shall be governed by Swiss law too. The parties can choose a different law according to Article 119(2). However, a choice of law that leads to the law of property and the law of obligations being governed by the laws of two different jurisdictions might not be advantageous.

The trust deed as 'legal instrument': After the enactment of the Hague Trust Convention, it was debated whether a trust deed could by itself constitute an authenticated legal instrument and which documents needed to be produced to the administration of the land register for the registration of the trustee.

Some authors argued that a special contract was needed between trustee and settlor declaring the transfer of the asset. This contract should – in their opinion – be produced to the administration of the land register.

The official – although not binding – guidelines on the administration of the land register with regard to trusts[30] did not require an additional contract. However, for the trustee to be registered, they demanded a certificate from a Swiss notary public confirming that:

- the trust has been effectively created;
- the trustee has been appointed as such; and
- the estate has been designated as trust property.[31]

---

28   Article 119:
    1 Contracts concerning real property or its use shall be governed by the law of the State in which it is located.
    2 A choice of law by the parties is permitted.
    3 The form of the contract shall be governed by the law of the State in which the real property is located unless that law permits the application of another law. In the case of real property located in Switzerland, the form shall be governed by Swiss law.

29   This corresponds to most analogous regulatory decisions, such as Article 4, paragraph 1, litera c of the Rome I Regulation, which states: "a contract relating to a right in rem in immovable property or to a tenancy of immovable property shall be governed by the law of the country where the property is situated."

30   *Wegleitung zur grundbuchlichen Behandlung von Trustgeschäften* as of 28 June 2007. These guidelines were introduced in order to fill existing gaps in the previous Land Register Ordinance. Hence, after the introduction of the new Land Register Ordinance of 23 September 2011, in force since 1 January 2012, their relevance dwindled, as most of the decisions taken in the guidelines were overridden by the legislation.

31   Trust guidelines, at 3.

This dispute has since been clarified somewhat through the enactment of the new Land Register Ordinance on 1 January 2012. According to Article 67(1)(a) of the Land Register Ordinance, a publicly authenticated contract is sufficient legal title for the transfer of real estate when the real estate is transferred into a trust during the settlor's lifetime. This underpins the authors' opinion that there is no need for an asset-transferring contract in addition to the trust deed, provided that the trust deed declares the transfer of the real estate and follows the formal rules on real estate transfers by being publicly authenticated. However, it should remain possible for the settlor to establish an additional instrument, for example, to clarify the legal situation. As it may be difficult for a Swiss notary public to judge a foreign law trust, we consider it sufficient for the registration of a trustee to produce the trust deed, declaring the transfer of the real estate, to the administration of the land register. If the real estate is transferred by the settlor to an existing trust, the transfer is effected by a unilateral legal act and this legal act must be produced to the register.

Foreign authentication: As regards the authentication requirement, some scholars question whether an authentication under foreign law can conform to the authentication required under Article 657 of the Swiss Civil Code. However, most authors favour such a possibility. The authors concur with this view, provided that the foreign authentication can be shown to be equivalent to the authentication required by Swiss law.

(b)   ***Transfer on the settlor's death***
A transfer as a result of the settlor's death takes effect by testate or intestate succession and a declaratory registration in the land register (Articles 656(2) and 657(2) of the Swiss Civil Code). With regard to a trust, it can take effect by appointing the trustee as either an heir or a legatee. The new Article 67(1)(b) of the Land Register Ordinance states that in the case of a transfer as a result of death, legal title must be rendered through a certificate of succession or a certification of the competent authority.

If the trustee is one of several heirs, he or she belongs to the community of joint heirs within the meaning of Articles 602 and following of the Swiss Civil Code. As the co-heirs own the estate assets jointly, until partition, the transfer to the trust property is completed and the trustee acquires sole proprietorship only after partition of the estate.

If the trustee is a legatee, he or she has a personal claim for delivery of the bequeathed asset against the heirs (Article 562 of the Swiss Civil Code).

From the estate planning viewpoint, a legacy may be the best solution, because it avoids the need to integrate a trustee into the community of joint heirs and the subsequent (potentially complicated and time-consuming) partition issues.

6.2 The implications of Article 149d of the Swiss Private International Law Act

Real estate that forms part of a trust property is registered in the name of the trustee – who is the holder of the legal title – in the land register. However, Article 149d(1) of the Swiss Private International Law Act provides that the fact that real estate belongs to a trust can be made apparent by a 'mention' in the land register. According to Article 149d(3), if such a mention is omitted, the trust relationship cannot be enforced against a person without notice thereof. As regards a purchaser acting in good faith or a creditor of the trustee, the asset is therefore treated as property of the trustee without any restrictions relating to the trust.

In the case of a purchaser acting in good faith, Article 149d(3) interacts with Article 973 of the Swiss Civil Code[32] protecting reliance in good faith on the land register. In consequence, a purchaser acting in good faith[33] can validly acquire the estate and – provided that no mention has been made – is protected from claims for restitution of the estate to the trust property. A creditor of the trustee can take hold of the estate by way of execution.

The lack of mention can therefore impair the trust property and prejudice the beneficiaries. A settlor who wants to avoid such undesired effects has basically three options – he or she can (at least according to the trust guidelines):

- initiate inclusion of the mention himself or herself at the time the asset is transferred to the trust;[34]
- oblige or call on the trustee to initiate inclusion of the mention; or
- vest the beneficiaries or third parties with the right to include the mention.[35]

However, in order for the mention to be made upon the application of the beneficiaries or third parties, the trust guidelines require either the assent of the trustee or a judgment authorising the mention.[36] If the trustee, according to the trust deed and the circumstances, is obliged to assent to the mention, the beneficiaries should have the right to force his or her assent by way of a legal action.

Prudent estate planning should take into account the settlor's possibilities to ensure a mention and may enable the beneficiaries to initiate inclusion of a mention themselves.[37]

---

32 Article 973:
   1 Any person who, relying in good faith on an entry in the land register, has acquired property or any other right in rem in reliance thereon, is protected in such acquisition.
   2 This rule does not apply to boundaries of land in areas designated by the cantons as being in permanent danger of ground displacement.
33 Some scholars advocate, however, that the transfer of property must be reversed if it was made without consideration.
34 Trust guidelines, at 3.
35 *Ibid.*
36 *Ibid.*
37 From a practical perspective, such a mention may entail legal consequences for the notary involved if he or she fails to observe the obligation to examine the trustees' right of disposal; see D Pannatier Kessler, *"Die Anmerkung des Trustverhältnisses und die Pflichten des Notars"*, *Zeitschrift für Beurkundungs- und Grundbuchrecht* (2011), 73, at 84 onwards.

6.3 Conveyance by way of an underlying company

If a settlor wants real estate to be held in trust, he or she can either transfer the relevant real estate asset directly to the trust property by conveying it to the trustee, or transfer the asset to the trust in an indirect way by conveying it to an underlying company whose shares are held by the trustee. Even though this often happens in practice, the current discussion in Switzerland (and, in consequence, this chapter) focuses on the direct method of putting real estate in trust. However, the use of an underlying company may – depending on the circumstances – be a viable alternative, as some of the difficulties explained above relate to the direct conveyance of the asset to the trustee and can arguably be avoided if a company acts as acquiring entity.[38]

6.4 The implications of the *Lex Koller*

One of the least settled aspects of the recognition of trusts in Switzerland is the treatment of real estate transfers to a trust property under the federal law on acquisition of real estate in Switzerland by non-residents[39] – the so-called *Lex Koller*.[40] This uncertainty is all the more unsatisfactory as the *Lex Koller* currently has a significant influence on trust-related estate planning, especially as its possible liberalisation or abolition is becoming an increasingly remote prospect.[41] The relevance of the *Lex Koller* is due to the fact that any trust is necessarily established under a law other than Swiss law, and that the transfer of real property to the trust will therefore always imply a foreign element which triggers an examination under the *Lex Koller*. The main problems in this examination relate – as will be shown – to the fact that the transfer of assets to a trust property cannot easily be interpreted as a direct act of transmission from the settlor to the beneficiary. The trust, being itself a legal construct and not a physical person (although linked to the person of the trustee), sits in between the settlor and the beneficiary, which makes it difficult to say who 'acquires' the asset in terms of the *Lex Koller*.[42]

(a) Loi d'application immédiate

Designed to limit foreign infiltration,[43] the *Lex Koller* in principle makes the

---

38 However, the creation of an underlying company, besides the effort and expense involved, may have implications with regard to the *Lex Koller* situation; see section 6.4.
39 *Bundesgesetz vom 16. Dezember 1983 über den Erwerb von Grundstücken durch Personen im Ausland (BewG)* as of 1 January 1985.
40 For a general review of the treatment of trusts under the *Lex Koller*, see T Meyer, "*Die Behandlung des Trusts im Rahmen der Lex Koller*", *Aktuelle Juristische Praxis* 2017, 45–49.
41 A government proposal to abolish the *Lex Koller* was remitted by Parliament in 2008. On 12 November 2012, the Federal Council published a statement recommending the retention of the law; and on 21 November 2013, it adopted a corollary message on the retention of the *Lex Koller*. The current status of the legislative procedure can be reviewed at www.bj.admin.ch/bj/de/home/themen/wirtschaft/gesetzgebung/lex_koller.html. Recently, however, there have been signs that Switzerland might once again tighten the laws on the acquisition of real estate by non-residents.
42 See, however, Decision 2C_409/2009 of 15 January 2010 of the Swiss Federal Court discussed under section 6.4(d).
43 Article 1 of the *Lex Koller*.

purchase of Swiss real estate by a foreign person subject to official authorisation and prohibits some kinds of real estate transactions altogether. As the act can be regarded as a provision requiring application within the meaning of Article 16 of the Hague Trust Convention (ie, a *loi d'application immédiate*), it can apply to trusts – although they are governed by foreign law (ie, the proper law of the trust).

(b) No automatic prohibition for transfer of non-commercial property

In principle, the transfer of commercial property to a trust does not require authorisation, according to Article 2(2)(a) of the *Lex Koller*.[44] However, if an estate is serving as place of residence or as holiday home, the *Lex Koller* and its accompanying regulation[45] could be interpreted in such a way as to create an insurmountable obstacle to any transfer of that estate to a trust property: it follows from Article 2(2)(b), Article 9(1)(c) and Article 9(2) of the *Lex Koller* that only physical persons can acquire places of residence or holiday homes. Article 8 of the *Lex Koller* Regulation clarifies this requirement by stating that the physical person must acquire directly and under his or her own name. If neither the trustee (because he or she is only a kind of fiduciary) nor the beneficiaries (because they are not parties to the transfer) are seen as an acquirer, such transfers could be inadmissible due to the lack of a physical person acting under his or her own name. Some initial administrative decisions took this position and refused authorisation. However, such a reading would run contrary to the intention and wording of the Hague Trust Convention, which encompasses the transfer of real estate to trust properties.[46] It must therefore be appreciated that recent administrative decisions and statements do not seem to consider the transfer of non-commercial estates as necessarily prohibited.[47]

(c) Acquisition under Articles 4, 10 of the Lex Koller

When a settlor transfers real property to a trustee, this act is quite clearly an 'acquisition' under Articles 4 and 10 of the *Lex Koller*. This is mainly due to the sweeping approach of the *Lex Koller*, which does not look at the legal construction of a transfer, but considers only whether, economically, the property comes under different ownership.

---

44 For commercial property, the trustee may therefore be inscribed in the Land Register without the cantonal administration having reviewed the transfer; in all other cases the trustee must pass through an authorisation procedure; see Articles 15 and following of the *Lex Koller*; and the trust guidelines at 1.

45 *Verordnung vom 1 Oktober 1984 über den Erwerb von Grundstücken durch Personen im Ausland (BewV)* as of 1 October 1984 (hereinafter referred to as the '*Lex Koller* Regulation').

46 See, for instance, Articles 4, 12, and 15 of the Hague Trust Convention.

47 Having regard to the underlying company solution (see section 6.3), however, it is not clear whether this position also applies where the real estate asset is acquired by an underlying company, which is even less of a physical person than a trust. Among other factors, it may be relevant whether the company is considered to be transparent, so that the beneficiaries are the relevant parties rather than the company.

(d) ***Acquiring person under Article 5 of the* Lex Koller**

Even if the acquisition requirement is fulfilled, it is far from clear how to determine which person[48] makes the acquisition (Article 5 of the *Lex Koller*). However, it is necessary to determine this in order to assess whether that person is foreign. The administrative decisions on this point were inconsistent for a long time. Some focused on the seat of the trust;[49] some on the trustee; and some on the 'protagonists' – that is, the settlor, the trustee and the beneficiaries.

In a 2010 decision the Swiss Federal Court clarified this matter to a certain extent. It held that upon the acquisition of real estate through a trust, the question of whether authorisation is needed depends not on the seat of the trust, determined by analogy to Article 5(1)(b) of the *Lex Koller*, but rather on whether the trustees or the beneficiaries are deemed to be foreign under Article 5 of the *Lex Koller*.[50]

(e) ***Foreign person under Article 5 of the* Lex Koller**

Having identified the relevant person, the next step is to decide whether that person is a foreign person under Article 5 of the *Lex Koller*. In principle, a person is not foreign if he or she:

- has Swiss citizenship;
- is a citizen of a member country of the European Union or of the European Free Trade Association and lives in Switzerland; or
- is a citizen of a country not belonging to the European Union or the European Free Trade Association, but has acquired the right to reside permanently in Switzerland and is effectively residing in Switzerland.

(f) ***Waiver of authorisation under Articles 2 and 7 of the Lex Koller***

Even if the transfer constitutes an acquisition by a foreign person, the need for authorisation can be waived under Articles 2 and 7 of the *Lex Koller*, especially where:

- the property is used commercially (Article 2(2)(a));
- the acquirer – being a physical person – takes up residence (Article 2(2)(b));
- the acquirer is the spouse or direct relative of the transferor (Article 7(b)); or
- the acquirer qualifies as potential heir of the transferor in the event of the latter's intestacy (Article 7(a)).[51]

---

48   We limit the present analysis to situations where settlor, trustee and beneficiaries are physical persons. As regards corporations, see Articles 5 and 6 of the *Lex Koller*.
49   This seems to mean the place where the trust is administered.
50   Swiss Federal Court Decision 2C_409/2009 of 15 January 2010. Also, see D Jakob, K Messmer, P Picht and G Studen, *Verein – Stiftung – Trust, Entwicklungen 2010, njus.ch* (Bern, 2011), at 134 onwards.
51   An heir under a will who, in the absence of a testamentary provision, would not be an heir in the event of intestacy can acquire an estate, but must resell it within two years if there are no other reasons for (the waiver of) authorisation; see Article 8(2) of the *Lex Koller*.

Here again, it is not certain who should be looked at in order to decide whether Articles 2 and 7 of the *Lex Koller* apply to a trust. Some decisions have looked at the connection between settlor and beneficiaries and applied Articles 7(a) and (b) of the *Lex Koller* to that connection. The *Lex Koller* guidelines advocate a similar perspective.[52] Nevertheless, this approach cannot yet be regarded as firmly established.

(g)   ***Conditions for authorisation under Articles 8 to 13 of the* Lex Koller**

Articles 8 to 13 of the *Lex Koller* determine whether an authorisation will be granted or denied. Those provisions are very restrictive, and therefore the only chance to obtain authorisation in a trust context may be through proof of a particularly close relationship between the relevant person and the property (Articles 8(2) and 9(1)(c) of the *Lex Koller*) or the allocation of a cantonal quota for holiday apartments (Article 9(2) of the *Lex Koller*).

An authorisation, or a declaration that an authorisation is not required, can be made subject to certain conditions (Article 14 of the *Lex Koller*) – for example, the condition that any changes in the structure or among the beneficiaries of the trust be notified to the administration.

(h)   ***Perspectives after Swiss Federal Court Decision 2C_409/2009***

Even years after the implantation of the trust into the Swiss legal landscape, the *Lex Koller* still causes legal uncertainty with regard to real estate held by trusts. At the same time, mentions under Article 149d of the Swiss Private International Law Act that real property forms part of trust remain rare. However, although the legislature has failed to resolve the issue, the Swiss Federal Court – in the 2010 decision mentioned above[53] – has provided some trust-friendly guidance on how to apply the law to trusts; and some legal scholars have also been able to identify at least some types of cases in which real estate can be acquired without authorisation.[54]

7.   Recent developments

7.1   The recognition of trusts under Swiss matrimonial property law

(a)   **Rybolovlev**

Although trusts established under the proper law of the trust as determined by Articles 6 and following of the Hague Trust Convention are recognised in

---

52   *Lex Koller* guidelines, 3. According to the guidelines, authorisation is not required where the settlor is the (only?) beneficiary of the trust.

53   See note 48 above.

54   See, among others, G Nater-Bass and M Seiler, *"Die Anmerkung des Trustverhältnisses im Grundbuch aus praktischer Sicht", successio* 2013, 220, at 221.

Switzerland under Article 11 of the Hague Trust Convention, they still face considerable legal uncertainty. This is primarily since Swiss courts seem to feel far less confident when dealing with cases involving trusts than they do when tackling cases involving legal entities created under domestic law.

An example of this effect is *Rybolovlev v Rybolovleva*,[55] which involved interim measures under Swiss matrimonial property law, but with regard to a trust.[56] In 2005 Russian billionaire Dimitri Rybolovlev and his wife Elena failed to agree on a marital settlement which would have declared substantial parts of their multi-billion fortune to be the individual property of Dimitri under Article 199 of the Swiss Civil Code. As their marital difficulties worsened, Dimitri established two irrevocable discretionary Cyprus trusts and transferred the fortune into those trusts without Elena's consent.

Elena filed for divorce in 2008 and requested the Geneva Court of First Instance to freeze assets in Switzerland and abroad as an interim measure. However, the court refused to do so and an appeal ensued. In the following proceedings, the Geneva Court of Justice (appellate court) pierced the veil of the trusts and froze the assets in an interim measure under Article 178 of the Swiss Civil Code. In its decision, that court completely ignored the Hague Trust Convention and the applicable Cyprus trust law, and resolved the case by applying exclusively Swiss domestic law. In doing so, it reasoned that the husband's actions were an attempt to diminish the property acquired during marriage to the disadvantage of his wife. Therefore, the assets were subject to an addition under Article 208 of the Swiss Civil Code and the attempt to circumvent precautionary measures under Article 178 of the Swiss Civil Code was held to be abusive. The court added that such measures should be allowed even if the assets were only in the beneficial ownership of the husband.

Applying a restricted standard of review, the Swiss Federal Court upheld the decision as not manifestly unlawful and thus non-arbitrary. It further added that although, in principle, decisions on whether to pierce the veil should be decided under the proper law of the trust (the law governing its constitution), the application of Swiss law is justified when considering interim measures, as specific private international law principles come into play under Article 62 of the Swiss Private International Law Act.

This decision drew sharp criticism from both national and international scholars,[57] and may paint a discouraging picture for the recognition of trusts in

---

55 Swiss Federal Court Decision 5A_259/2010 of 26 April 2012.
56 For an overview of the fairly complex *Rybolovlev* case, see D Jakob, D Dardel and M Uhl, *Verein – Stiftung – Trust, Entwicklungen 2012*, njus.ch, (Bern, 2013), at 175 onwards.
57 T Graham, "The Hague Trusts Convention five years on: the Swiss Federal Supreme Court's decision in Rybolovlev v Rybolovleva", *Trusts & Trustees* 2012, at 746 onwards; D W Wilson and J Wynne, "*Trusts et divorce: La salade russe de Rybolov c Rybolovleva*", *Not@lex* 2013, at 14 onwards; J Perrin and M Shayle, "*Trusts et restrictions au pouvoir de disposer dans le cadre d'un divorce en Suisse*", *Jusletter* of 16 September 2013; T Bersheda, "*Quelques questions de droit international privé en relation avec la reconnaissance de trusts en Suisse*", *Aktuelle Juristische Praxis* 2013, at 45 onwards; and, with a more differentiated view, L Thévenoz, *op cit* at note 2, at 161 onwards.

Swiss legal practice. However, this negative impression should be qualified; *Rybolovlev* is a typical example of a bad case producing bad law, as it encompassed a quite blatant attempt to evade marital property rules – a fact that is underscored by the overly strong control on the trusts that the husband retained throughout. Additionally, as previously mentioned, the Swiss Federal Court's decision was limited to an appeal on interim measures and its specific principles.

The latter caveat appeared to have lost some of its force in 2014, when the first instance court rendered its decision on the substance of the case. The court seems to have ignored the establishment of the two Cyprus trusts and thus considered the total value of the assets at the time of the legal dispute in 2008 (about CHF 8 billion), and not the value the assets had in 2005, when the trusts were established. Elena Rybolovleva was therefore allowed to avail herself of the considerable growth of the trusts' assets (around CHF 6.8 billion),[58] and was awarded a record sum of about CHF 4 billion. However, the second instance court reversed.[59] It applied, as it seems, the rules of the Hague Trust Convention and recognised the establishment of the two Cyprus trusts under Cypriot trust law. However, as the wife did not consent to the transfer of the assets into the two trusts, it also applied the rules under Article 208 of the Swiss Civil Code, under which the total value of the assets is considered at the time of their disposal. The court therefore took into account a value of about CHF 1.2 billion and subsequently awarded a 'mere' CHF 564 million to Elena.

The decision of the Geneva Court of Justice – which is final, as the parties settled in October 2015 – shed a more positive light on the prospect of trusts being recognised under the law applicable according to the conflict rules following the application of the Hague Trust Convention.

(b)   *The intertwining of trusts and Swiss marital property law*

In reading *Rybolovlev*, one might wonder how such a situation ought to have been solved under Swiss marital property law.[60]

The proper solution depends on whether the assets of the trusts are still to be considered part of the property acquired during marriage under Articles 197 and following of the Swiss Civil Code. If so, an array of interim measures will be taken and the spouse's assets at the time of the dissolution of the marital property regime will be defined and calculated at the time of the division (Article 214(1) of the Swiss Civil Code). If not, there is only the possibility of an addition under Articles 208 and 220 of the Swiss Civil Code, whereby the

---

58   Mainly due to the very successful initial public offering of Rybolovlev's potash enterprise, Uralkali, and the subsequent sale of its shares.

59   Unpublished decision of the Geneva Court of Justice of 5 June 2015.

60   For the following, see D Jakob, *"Stiftung und Familie"* in K Hilbig-Lugani and others, *Zwischenbilanz, Festschrift für Dagmar Coester-Waltjen zum 70. Geburtstag* (Bielefeld, 2015), 123, at 126 onwards.

valuation of the added assets is calculated on the date of their alienation (Article 214(2) of the Swiss Civil Code). In order to determine whether the assets of the trust should be considered part of the property acquired during marriage, one must focus on the validity of the establishment of the trust, which should be assessed under the applicable trust law.

If the transfer of assets into the trust is legitimate, the assets are no longer part of the property acquired during marriage under Articles 197 and following of the Swiss Civil Code and thus the applicable protective mechanisms of Swiss marital property law are only those in Articles 208 and 220 of the Swiss Civil Code. This means that, if the establishment of the trust and the asset transfers into it are legitimate under the trust statute (according to Articles 11 and 8 of the Hague Trust Convention respectively), Swiss marital property law does not prejudice the establishment of the trust, and its assets can be claimed only by a virtue of an addition through Articles 208 and 220 of the Swiss Civil Code.[61] From that, it follows that the value of dispositions made without consideration by one spouse without the other's consent during the last five years preceding divorce, as well as the value of assets disposed of by one spouse with the intent to diminish the other's share, are added to the property acquired during marriage. If there is a shortfall in assets as a result of such a claim, the entitled spouse has a claim against third parties, such as trusts, to demand the return of assets from the beneficiaries. These protective measures are qualified somewhat by the fact that the value of the added assets will be calculated at the date on which the assets were transferred to the trust, hence alienated in the sense of Article 214(2) of the Swiss Civil Code.

If, on the other hand, the establishment of the trust is found to be flawed and, consequently, the trust is deemed to be void, the trust assets are to be considered an integral part of the property acquired during marriage. Under Article 8 of the Hague Trust Convention, the law governing the trust must be used to establish whether the trust is a sham or whether it is possible to pierce the veil. The only instance where Swiss law can lead to a trust established under foreign law being void is in situations of a manifest abuse of a right; in this instance, Article 2(2) of the Swiss Civil Code applies as a *loi d'application immédiate* (under Article 16 of the Hague Trust Convention) or as a norm of Swiss public policy (under Article 18 of the Hague Trust Convention).

In conclusion, the Swiss courts seem to have gained a robust understanding of the interplay between the Hague Trust Convention, the relevant proper law of the trust and Swiss marital property law. Cases in which courts have enforced

---

61   As these provisions interfere with the relevant trusts, a justification for limiting of the scope of application of the law governing the trust must be found. This is the case with Article 15(1)(b) of the Hague Trust Convention, as Articles 208 and 220 of the Swiss Civil Code cannot be derogated from by voluntary act and fulfil an important protective function; see in detail D Jakob and P Picht, *"Das Haager Trust-Übereinkommen und seine Geltungseinschränkungen – ein Fass der Danaiden?"* in F Lorandi and D Staehelin, *Innovatives Recht, Festschrift für Ivo Schwander* (Zürich and St Gallen, 2011), at 552 onwards.

public policies by entirely disregarding matters of trusts remain isolated instances that should not overshadow the positive attitude towards trusts in the Swiss legal landscape.[62]

7.2 A trust law for Switzerland?

On 13 March 2019 the Swiss National Council (*Nationalrat*) adopted a motion titled "Introduction of the Trust into the Swiss Legal System".[63] The motion effectively mandates the Federal Council – Switzerland's seven-member executive council – to take the lead on a legislative project to introduce the trust into substantive Swiss law. This is the latest iteration of a series of parliamentary proposals to consider the adoption of a Swiss trust, the last three of which were successful.[64] In response to these proposals, the Federal Department of Finance has appointed an expert commission to devise a list of desired legal effects and to develop regulatory models for a Swiss trust law. In parallel, an external commission is examining the likely socioeconomic impact of the project. However, opinions on the desirability of a substantive Swiss trust law are split among both academics and practitioners. Supporters expect this will have a positive effect on the Swiss financial market, whereas opponents have pointed out the numerous incompatibilities between the common law trust and the Swiss legal system, and favour the liberalisation of the (existing) family foundation.[65] Although the outcome of this legislative project cannot be predicted at this stage, the idea has garnered unprecedented political support and there is a real chance that Switzerland might join the growing list of civil law countries to adopt its own trust law.

8. Conclusion

Even this short chapter has revealed considerable interplay between the foreign laws under which trusts may be constituted and Swiss law. Further issues have not even been discussed. The ongoing process of the recognition of trusts will have to analyse areas where the laws (seem to) conflict and find viable solutions. In our view, these solutions must be trust friendly, but they must also try to protect essential third-party interests. If the Swiss legal order manages to reconcile those aspects and gain further familiarity with the trust concept, it can – and, in the authors' opinion, will – take on board important advantages of the trust as an additional estate planning instrument.

---

62   A recent analysis of the most recent case law confirms this finding; see Thévenoz, *op cit* at note 2, at 161 onwards.

63   Cf Motion 18.3383 *"Einführung des Trusts in die schweizerische Rechtsordnung"* of 26 April 2018.

64   Cf Postulate 15.3098 *"Prüfung einer allfälligen gesetzlichen Regelung von Trusts"* of 11 March 2015 and Parliamentary Initiative 16.488 *"Aufnahme des Rechtsinstituts des Trusts in die schweizerische Gesetzgebung"* of 13 December 2016.

65   For an overview of the various arguments for and against a Swiss trust law, see M Ferber, *"Braucht es einen Schweizer Trust?"*, Neue Zürcher Zeitung of 1 March 2019; D Jakob and M Kalt, *"Ein Trustrecht für die Schweiz?"*, ExpertFocus 2019, at 630 onwards.

The use of US trusts in international estate planning

Stanley A Barg
Kozusko Harris Duncan

Individuals who are subject to US taxation can realise substantial savings by doing proper estate planning, especially if they are not citizens or residents of the United States. Not only does the United States recognise a broad range of trusts, but its tax and other laws combine to encourage the use of trusts in achieving important estate planning goals. It is particularly important to consider the use of trusts for non-US persons who are moving to the United States and who will become subject to US tax as residents of the United States. Important opportunities may be lost if advice is not taken prior to the time one becomes a US resident. This is because there are planning opportunities that are available only when one is not a US person, and if a person takes advantage of those opportunities, he or she can then be in a substantially more advantageous position upon the commencement of US residency.

It is also important to remember that US citizens are subject to both worldwide federal income tax on their worldwide incomes, irrespective of where they live; and to US federal estate and gift tax on their worldwide assets, again irrespective of their place of residence. Although this subject has received substantial publicity in recent years, a considerable degree of misunderstanding and lack of knowledge remains as to how the US tax system works.

In looking at US taxes, particularly from outside the United States, one generally first considers federal income tax, which includes a tax on capital gains. There is also a federal estate and gift tax – sometimes referred to as a transfer tax – which applies to gratuitous transfers during lifetime and to transfers at death. These transfers are subject to US tax in the case of transfers by non-US persons with respect to any property located in the United States and, as stated previously, for US citizens and individuals who are regarded as domiciled in the United States with respect to their worldwide assets.

In doing estate planning, it is important to remember that the individual states of the United States also have their own tax systems which apply to residents of those states and sometimes to property located in the state, and which vary widely among the 50 US states. In some instances the individual state taxes may mirror the federal tax system, but other states have their own system of tax which bears little relationship to the federal system. Although some states have no income tax, others have a substantial rate of income tax, but may have lower rates that apply to other transactions. In certain circumstances there are also municipal taxes which can apply with respect to income earned locally and transfers of real estate in those jurisdictions, such as New York, irrespective of the residence of the individuals. These taxes can be quite substantial and must be carefully considered in any decision with respect to the acquisition, holding and disposition of assets in the United States. All of these taxes are important to keep in mind when doing any planning for individuals and families who have, or will have, a connection with the United States.

Trusts play an important part in the estate plan of virtually every person of means in the United States. It is important to consider issues with respect to control of assets, asset protection and tax efficiency in every US estate planning situation. In particular, in considering the establishment of trusts, it is important to remember that, where international families are subject to tax in other jurisdictions, one must consider the tax consequences in each relevant jurisdiction. The establishment of trusts may be viewed in very different ways in other countries and, when individuals are residing and subject to tax in other countries, the tax consequences in each respective country must also be carefully considered. In the case of double taxation the availability of treaty relief should also be considered.

There are other types of entities, referred to hybrid trusts, which can have varying consequences under US law. For example, in many states of the United States one can form what are referred to as business trusts. Although these are trusts for state law purposes, they are generally regarded as corporations for US tax purposes because they are formed for business rather than family purposes. In addition, in many jurisdictions purpose trusts can be formed. A purpose trust is a trust established for a particular purpose rather than for specific named individuals. Again, the characterisation of these trusts for US tax purposes can sometimes be difficult to determine. In this regard, one may also consider how foundations are treated for US purposes. Foundations have typically been problematic for US purposes because it can be difficult to ascertain whether foundations as such are regarded as corporations or trusts for US tax purposes. Accordingly, although foundations are frequently used, particularly in some civil law jurisdictions, it is sometimes difficult to utilise foundations where there is any US connection, through either beneficial ownership or the types of assets owned, because of the difficulty knowing how the foundation will be taxed in the United States. In 2009 the Internal Revenue Service (IRS) issued a memorandum dealing with Lichtenstein *Stiftungs* and *Anstalts* and their classification for US tax purposes. This memorandum was issued by the IRS Office of Chief Council on 16 October 2009.[1] After describing the nature of the

---

1   Memorandum AM2009-012.

alternative forms of Liechtenstein foundations, the ruling concluded that in most instances, *Anstalts* will generally be classified as business entities rather than trusts, but *Stiftungs* will more likely be classified as trusts rather than business entities, unless they are created primarily for commercial purposes. In all instances it is important to look at and carefully consider the individual facts and circumstances which, in appropriate circumstances, can change the result dramatically. Accordingly, although the ruling provides some degree of guidance, it is far from definitive with respect to how such entities will be classified. Nevertheless, because of its issuance, it has provided some additional measure of comfort in using these entities for US purposes, knowing at least the preliminary view of the IRS as to how they should be classified.

In considering whether a trust is a US trust, it is important to think about what it means for a trust to be a US trust. Trusts are created under a particular state's law in the United States, so although a trust may be created under the laws of a particular state, that does not determine how it will be taxed or classified for US federal tax purposes. Thus, there is no such thing as a 'US trust' when one is talking about the creation of that trust: there are trusts created in the United States which can be regarded as US trusts for US tax purposes, and there are trusts created under US state law which are regarded as foreign trusts for US tax purposes.

Specific rules defining the residence of trusts for US tax purposes are set out in Section 7701(a)(30) of the Internal Revenue Code. Under those rules, a trust is regarded as a US trust for tax purposes only if it satisfies both the so-called 'court' test and the 'control' test. A trust that does not satisfy both of these tests is a foreign trust for US tax purposes, irrespective of its place of creation. Thus, in many instances a trust can be established under the laws of a particular US state, such as Delaware, Wyoming or South Dakota, and can nevertheless be a foreign trust for US tax purposes irrespective of its place of creation.

Under the court test, a US court must be able to exercise primary supervision over the administration of the trust.[2] The Treasury Regulations include a safe harbour providing that the court test will be satisfied if:

- the trust instrument does not direct that the trust be administered outside the United States;
- the trust is actually administered exclusively in the United States; and
- the trust is not subject to an automatic migration provision moving the trust to another jurisdiction under any circumstances.[3]

In connection with the court test, it is important that the actual administration of the trust take place in the United States, and that a court be

---

2 Internal Revenue Code, §7701(a)(30)(E)(i) .
3 Treasury Regulations, §301.7701-7(c)(1).

able to assume jurisdiction over the administration of the trust. It is sometimes possible to get a court specifically to assume such jurisdiction in certain states, which is helpful in demonstrating that that court does in fact have jurisdiction over the trust.

Under the control test, one or more US persons must have the authority to control all 'substantial' decisions of the trust.[4] US Treasury Regulations provide a very inclusive list of what matters are included within 'substantial' decisions.[5] These include:

- whether and when to distribute trust income or principal;
- the amount of any distributions;
- the selection of a trust beneficiary;
- whether a receipt is allocable to income or principal of the trust;
- whether to terminate the trust;
- whether to compromise, arbitrate or abandon claims relating to the trust;
- whether to sue on behalf of the trust or to defend suits against the trust;
- whether to remove, add or replace a trustee; and
- investment decisions.

Accordingly, if any non-US person can exercise authority over the trust and can make any of the decisions relating to the listed issues with respect to the trust, a US person will not be regarded as having control of all substantial decision of the trust and the trust will be regarded as a foreign trust.

As one can readily see, it is relatively easy to ensure that a trust is a foreign trust should one wish to achieve that. On the other hand, it is frequently harder to make a trust a US trust if there is any foreign participation in the trust administration. When there are multiple trustees and some of those trustees are US persons and some of them are foreign persons, the US trustees must be able to control all of those decisions of the trust to ensure that the trust will be a US trust. As referenced previously, it is not unusual to establish a trust in the United States that is not a US trust for US tax purposes, and in certain circumstances this can be very effective in planning in the international context.

In addition, we are seeing many circumstances where trusts that are classified as foreign for US tax purposes are later domesticated to the United States, and become US trusts for US tax purposes. There are many reasons one may choose to domesticate a trust to the United States, but when foreign trusts have US beneficiaries or own US assets it is increasingly difficult to maintain a foreign presence, in large part because of the concerns of banks and other financial institutions outside the US when dealing with trusts that have a US

---

4   Treasury Regulations, §301.7701-7(a)(1)(ii).
5   Treasury Regulations, §301.7701-7(d)(1)(ii).

"involvement". In particular when trusts acquire US assets such as US real estate, it is frequently advantageous to use US trusts rather than foreign trusts because the income relating to the ownership of that real estate will be regarded as US source income in any event, so that the income will be subject to US tax. In addition, although subject to current US taxation, the use of a US trust avoids the harsh taxation rules that otherwise can apply to foreign trusts with US beneficiaries.[6]

In addition to trusts, there are business entities that are frequently used in estate planning. These can include, for example, family limited partnerships, which are frequently organised as either partnerships or limited liability companies and which are used to facilitate the transfer of interests in those entities among members of the family. These entities are frequently used with trusts to facilitate planning within a family. Again, all of the relevant non-US tax issues must be considered in using these entities.

Given the variety of trusts and other entities that can be used, it is also important to consider the operation of the 'check the box' rules in relation to these entities, under which various entities can be classified in different ways for US tax purposes.[7] Under these rules, although there are some business entities that are regarded as *per se* corporations and, as such, automatically classified as corporations for US tax purposes, most business entities can choose how they will be classified for such purposes. These rules do not apply to entities that are regarded as trusts for US tax purposes, and, in some instances, it may be difficult to distinguish between an entity classified as a trust and a business entity. There is very little guidance on this distinction, and, if the entity is a trust, these rules have no application, but, on the other hand, if the entity is a business entity and is not a *per se* corporation, it is regarded as an 'eligible' entity and can then elect its tax classification.

If a joint undertaking is considered an entity separate from its owners for federal tax purposes and is an eligible entity, it may elect how it will be classified under these rules. Eligible entities can make a classification election. An eligible entity with at least two members can choose to be classified as either an association taxable as a corporation, or a partnership. An eligible entity with a single member can choose to be classified as an association taxable as a corporation, or to be disregarded as an entity separate from its owner. Once an election is made, the status cannot be changed for 60 months after that election takes place.

For example, in certain circumstances limited liability companies in the US

---

6   Although it is beyond the scope of this chapter, a so-called throwback tax, together with a special interest charge, can apply where a distribution is made to a US beneficiary from a non-grantor foreign trust that has historically distributed less than all of its income on a current basis, resulting in a punitive penalty; see Internal Revenue Code, §§665-668.
7   Treasury Regulations, §§ 301.7701-1–301.7701-3.

that are owned by one individual are actually disregarded for all federal tax purposes. Corporations, on the other hand, are generally regarded as separate business entities. In many circumstances, one can elect a classification different than that which is otherwise applicable. For example, a limited liability company that is disregarded or treated as a partnership, where it has multiple earners, can elect instead to be treated as a corporation. Similarly, if a limited liability company is foreign, its default classification will be that as a corporation, but, if eligible, it may elect out of that status by filing a form with the Internal Revenue Service.[8] The form includes a list of various entities around the world which are treated as *per se* corporations, in which case one may not elect an alternative entity classification. The IRS Form 8832 is generally effective when filed, although one may make an election that is effective retroactively up to 75 days or prospectively up to 12 months. In other circumstances one can make an election which has further retroactive effect, or one can apply to the Internal Revenue Service for a ruling to the effect that an election be even further retroactive. The availability of these rulings varies depending on the facts and circumstances of each individual case.

In conclusion, it can be seen that US trusts can play an important role in international estate planning. In the implementation of such trusts it is important to understand the priorities of our clients, and, where there are relevant US issues, the flexibility afforded by US trusts can be very effective.

---

8   IRS Form 8832.

Trusts, trustees and family businesses

Christian Stewart
Family Legacy Asia (HK) Limited

1. Introduction

In the world of family-owned businesses a well-known 'three circle model'[1] is often referred to; yet this model is largely unknown in the world of trusts. When trustees own a family business, it is the thesis of this chapter that this three circle model holds the key to increasing the chances of family business success. Further, trustees of trusts that hold a controlling stake in a family business and advisers who are involved in the structuring of such trusts can enhance the chances of family business continuity through promoting and designing governance structures, policies and processes intended to:

- help clarify the boundaries between family, ownership and business;
- ensure there are communication and decision-making forums for each of the three circles;
- ensure an ongoing balance is maintained between the competing interests of:
  - family and business; and
  - ownership and business;[2]
- ensure that the management circle is professional;
- ensure that the business has an effective board that includes one or more non-family, non-executive directors; and
- preserve the family's emotional commitment to the family business.

Emotional commitment means that family member stakeholders who are not engaged in the management of the business (those who are outside the business) are willing to continue to provide 'patient capital' for the business and to support the family's continued ownership of the business. Emotional commitment means ensuring that family member stakeholders who are outside the business have a voice, have meaningful roles to participate in, are educated to be effective owners and are free to go if they wish to.

---

1   R Tagiuri and JA Davis.
2   As each of the three circles is always changing, the balancing act required needs to be an ongoing one – or at least there needs to be a mechanism whereby the balance can be reset periodically.

2.   Defining the family-owned business

What is a family-owned (or controlled) business? In the academic world there are many definitions, but one important characteristic is an intention to keep ownership of the business within the family beyond the current generation. Hence, trusts seem to be a perfect tool in this regard.

Another key characteristic is that a family business is one in which the family dynamics, the family culture or the family emotional system has a significant impact on the business system. Family values (eg, that every family member is entitled to equal love and attention) are often in conflict with business values (eg, if you are the top performer this year, you deserve top pay). These kinds of value conflicts are one reason why it is actually very hard to preserve the family business, not to mention the impact of unhealthy family dynamics such as bitter sibling rivalries.

Another key theme in looking at the family business is that such a business will typically go through a number of distinct ownership stages. The basic model is that a family business starts with a first-generation founder, and in this first generation configuration ownership and management are united in the one person. A second generation business, in terms of ownership configurations, is the 'sibling partnership', where the owners or controlling owners are a group of siblings. In a sibling partnership you might still have the same group both owning and managing – or you might not. You can start to see a divergence between those who own the shares and those who manage the business by this second stage. The next stage of the family business is the 'cousin consortium'. By this third stage, you would expect there to be a wide divergence between ownership and management.

Putting the above themes together, the family-owned business is often looked at in terms of a complex system made up of the overlap between the family system, an ownership system and a business system.[3] This model of the family business is often represented as three overlapping circles; hence the three circle model of family business.[4]

Figure 1. Three-circle model

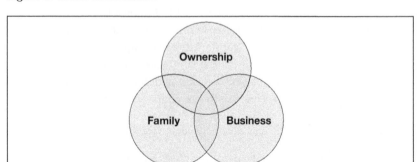

2.1 Family business continuity is challenging

Around the world, only 33% of family firms will continue into the second generation of ownership control and only between 6% and 12% into the third generation of ownership control. The three circle model helps to explain these statistics by showing the complexity of the family business system, which increases exponentially as the number of family members grows with each new generation of the family.

For example, family-owned businesses can fail:

- as a result of conflict caused by confusion as to roles;
- as a result of conflict caused by poor boundaries between family and business;
- as a result of predictable conflicts between family members in the ownership circle and family members in the management circle – for example, over dividends versus reinvestment of profits;
- simply because the business has reached the end of its own lifecycle and cannot be renewed or taken in a new direction; or
- because the family stops supporting the business, which happens when emotional commitment to the business runs out.

As an aside, destructive conflicts can also be interpersonal in nature. Structural and governance-based solutions cannot address interpersonal conflicts.[5] Family culture will eat structure for breakfast.

2.2 The use of trusts to strengthen family businesses

Does setting up a trust to own the business really help to increase the chances of a business continuing beyond 33% for the second generation of a family and beyond a chance of between 6% and 12% for the third generation? Does setting up a trust really help to avoid predictable family firm conflicts?

If there were no trust used to hold the business, the ownership of the business would start to fragment and to pull away from the management of the business. It might become hard to make decisions at the ownership level. By putting the shares in the business into a trust structure, this prevents the share ownership from fragmenting and might ensure that ownership-level decisions can always be made by the trustee(s). However, addressing the ownership level alone does not fully address all of the reasons for family business failures listed

---

3 Each of these three systems goes through its own predictable developmental stages.
4 One question is whether the three circle model is the best model for analysing family firms. Dennis Jaffe notes that, in terms of capturing different perspectives, the model does not easily accommodate the perspective of directors, if you take the view that the role of the board is both to represent the interests of the owners and to strike a balance between ownership and management. However, while one can debate whether there are better models for the purpose of this chapter, the three circle model is a good place to start.
5 Therapeutic interventions are required to address such interpersonal conflicts or a helping relationship that can work at the level of the family culture.

above. In particular, trust ownership does not guarantee that the beneficiaries will remain emotionally committed to the business.

Rather, it is suggested that the way to increase the odds of success (in terms of both business continuity and reducing the possibility of destructive family conflicts)[6] lies in developing a better, more professional governance system[7] for both the trust and the business; and that it should be in the best interests of the trust creator, the beneficiaries and the trustee(s) to work towards the implementation of an effective governance system. What does an effective governance system look like? The six elements listed in the introduction to this chapter represent the core components of an effective governance system for a family business.

3.   The three circle model

3.1   The three circles in more detail

(a)   The family circle
The family circle is concerned with family rules, dynamics, emotions and values. The way that the family members communicate together (or not), the flexibility of the family, the values of the family, the way the family members deal with stress and anxiety and how the family deals with conflict are all elements of the family circle. Typical values or rules of the family circle include the desire to protect and support family members, the desire to protect people's feelings and the need to treat family members equally. The family circle is inward looking and it tries to avoid change.

(b)   The management circle
The management circle is focused on making profits; it must adapt and deal with change; it is competitive; and its decision making is rational. It is focused outwards and, especially for founders, it defines their identity.[8] A fundamental goal for the management circle is to ensure that the business is managed in a professional manner.

(c)   The ownership circle
The ownership circle is concerned with questions of return on investment, dividends, share valuation, liquidity, ease of exit and the need to provide capital for the business. Ownership is also ultimately about who has control.

---

6   See note 5; structural solutions such as improving the governance system will not address family conflicts that are interpersonal in nature; such conflicts require therapeutic interventions and similar.

7   The word 'professional' needs further consideration. Family firms are emotional systems. Approaches that are purely structural are bound to fail. Perhaps a better term would be to refer to a governance system that helps to provide clearer boundaries between the three circles and brings clarity to the roles involved.

8   Professor Dennis T Jaffe of Wise Counsel Research Associates.

3.2   Principles derived from the model

The three circle model offers the following insights into and general predictions about family firms, before considering the impact of trust ownership:

- A change in any one circle will impact on, and be impacted by, the other circles.
- The health of the overall system requires that the interests of all three circles be kept in balance.
- The three circle model can be subdivided into seven different discrete subsections. Family members who are located within the same section of the model can be expected to have similar perspectives and concerns. Family members who are located in different sections of the model can be expected to have different perspectives and concerns.
- One of the classic family firm conflicts is the conflict between family members who are 'inside shareholders' and family members who are 'outside shareholders'. Inside shareholders are family members who are owners and are also involved in the management of the firm. Outside shareholders are family members who are owners, but who are not involved in management. For example, inside shareholders will typically favour the reinvestment of profits and expansion of the business. Inside shareholders can draw remuneration from the company. Outside shareholders will typically want to maximise dividend payments and liquidity.
- Over time, it is the family members in the ownership role who will be more important to family firm continuity than the family members in management roles. A family firm can fail by the third generation (if not before then) because the family member outside shareholders cannot make joint decisions together concerning the firm.
- The three circle model predicts that over time, the ownership circle and the management circle will start to disconnect. The family member outside shareholders will start to lose their emotional commitment to the firm and stop supporting the management. However, continuity of a family firm requires either maintaining the emotional commitment of family member outside shareholders or a process of 'pruning the tree'. 'Pruning the tree' means having a mechanism in place to buy out family member shareholders who cease to be interested in supporting the management of the business.
- Family businesses are very complicated. This complexity naturally leads to role confusion. A common cause of family firm conflicts is role confusion.
- One way to minimise role confusion and family business conflicts is to ensure that there are good boundaries in place between family and management, and between ownership and management. A good

boundary is neither too rigid nor too porous. One way to have good boundaries is to ensure that there is role clarity. In a family firm context, the principle of ensuring fair process in decision making is also very important. It can be helpful to be clear about who has the vote on each major decision and who has a voice in relation to that decision.

- To keep this complex system in balance, it is important that each of the three circles has its own communication and decision-making forums. In the family circle this can mean holding periodic family meetings, or it might mean forming a family council and a family assembly. The ownership circle needs an effective board of directors to represent it, but it also needs to have its own forum, away from the boardroom, where the interests of the owners can be discussed.
- There needs to be communication and information flows between each of the three circles, while still respecting roles and having good boundaries.

3.3   Where does a trust fit into this?

The three circle model represents the big picture of the whole complex system. A trust is a tool for the ownership circle. If there is a corporate trustee exercising the voting rights on the shares in the business, these are ownership-level rights. If these rights are exercised at the direction of an investment committee constituted under the terms of the trust, then that committee is the party exercising ownership-level rights. To create a sustainable family business and avoid the destructive conflicts that so often cause the demise of family firms, the relationships among the three circles must be addressed. Providing for ownership of a family business by a trust, insofar as it deals only with one of the three circles, will not be sufficient on its own to help increase the chances of success – that is, unless the trustee and the other parties to the trust structure can be used to support governance structures, policies and processes that are aimed at addressing the interactions between family and business, and between the beneficial ownership (ie, the beneficiaries) and management, and are designed to encourage a sense of balance among the three circles.

4.   A trust to own the family business

This chapter should be read as exploring the scenario where:
- all of the shares in a family business (or a controlling stake therein) are transferred to the trustee of a single trust;
- the settlor of the trust is the founder of the business and was the controlling shareholder before setting up the trust;
- the trust will be a traditional discretionary trust, in the sense that each beneficiary who is of age and who has full capacity will have the right to enforce the due administration of the trust, but will have no fixed interest in the trust fund; and

- the beneficiaries of the trust will be defined as a class comprising the settlor, his or her children and grandchildren, and any more remote issue of the settlor born prior to the expiration of the trust period. In other words, it is a single pot trust with multiple beneficiaries and multiple family branches present.

4.1 Trustee options

This chapter assumes that there are four basic options for the trustee role, and that in practice the second of these options (or some variation on the second option) is the most common scenario. These four options concern the question of who has investment control and responsibility for the trust. This goes to the question of who has control of the voting rights over the shares in the family business.

(a) *A corporate trustee*

One possibility, the first option, is that the trustee of the trust is a professional corporate trustee, and that the terms of the trust instrument leave the corporate trustee with full control and responsibility for exercising the voting rights on the shares in the family business.

(b) *An investment committee*

The second option is that the trustee is a professional corporate trustee, but the terms of the trust instrument are drafted to provide that the trustee must exercise all voting rights on the shares in the business in accordance with the directions given to the trustee by an investment committee constituted under the terms of the trust. The initial composition of the investment committee will be determined by the settlor of the trust. In some cases this approach will be preferred by the settlor, who may like the idea of using a corporate trustee for distribution decisions and general administration of the trust, but wants to be able to decide who will exercise the voting control over the shares in the family business. In other cases, the corporate trustee will suggest such an approach on the basis that it does not want to assume responsibility for the investment performance of the family operating business.

(c) *A private trustee company*

A third scenario is where the trustee is a private trustee company established specifically for the owning family, the initial board of which shall be determined by the settlor of the trust. With respect to the exercise of the voting rights on the shares in the business, it can be assumed that the private trustee company is essentially acting as an incorporated form of an investment committee. Therefore, comments in this chapter about the investment committee for a trust should also be read as applying to the board of directors of a private trustee company.

(d)   Special company provisions

A fourth common scenario is that again the trustee is a corporate trustee, but the terms of the trust contain strong special company provisions and the trustee is required to keep its hands off the special companies. The corporate trustee holds the shares in a special company. The special company holds the shares in the family business. The board of the special company in effect operates as a holding-level board supervising the operating board of the family business.

If the trustee can be given directions with respect to the exercise of the voting rights on the shares in the special company by, for instance, a protector committee, then for the purposes of this chapter that protector committee can be regarded as being an investment committee for the trust. The other alternative is that the board of the special company might be regarded as effectively being an investment committee, as it will have control over the voting rights on the shares in the family business that are vested in the special company. Again, therefore, references in this chapter to the investment committee for a trust should also be considered to apply generally to a trust with special company provisions.

4.2   The benefits provided by trust ownership

Clearly, there are some ways in which the kind of trust structure that has been described will be beneficial:

- The trust will provide the usual general benefits of asset protection for the beneficiaries, avoidance of probate, protection for incapacitated beneficiaries, commercial privacy and the ability to tailor a distribution plan to the goals and objectives of the family.
- In addition, the trust structure can help to create and maintain a voting bloc. It helps to prevent the family control over the family business from being diluted and prevents legal ownership from becoming fragmented.
- The trust structure means that beneficiaries might view themselves collectively as being stewards of the family assets, rather than owners.

Where the trust is created with an investment committee that can direct the corporate trustee, this provides the following further benefits:

- The investment committee arrangement allows the settlor to distinguish between those individuals who get to control the voting rights on the shares in the family business and those who get to enjoy the economic benefits from the family business.
- In practice, the exercise of setting up the trust should allow the perfect opportunity for clear rules to be written into the trust instrument as to how the investment committee will vote and what the mechanism is for dealing with any deadlocks. There is an opportunity to spell out the role of the investment committee and how ownership-level decisions will be made.

- It is also an opportunity to write clear rules into the trust instrument spelling out how one qualifies for membership of the investment committee and how succession to the investment committee is dealt with. As such, setting up the trust structure is the perfect exercise to draw up a clear (legal) ownership succession plan.
- As will be explained later, there is also an opportunity to draft the terms of the investment committee as requiring a certain number of seats to be reserved for inside beneficiaries and a certain number to be reserved for outside beneficiaries.
- Members can be added to and removed from the investment committee without having to change the ownership of the underlying shares, which remain registered in the name of the corporate trustee.
- Trusted non-family members can be appointed to the investment committee to represent the interests of the beneficiaries – for example, if one branch of the family feels that it is not capable of properly understanding the family business operations.

4.3   The disadvantages of trust ownership

The first and main disadvantage of trust ownership has already been alluded to. This is that a trust is only a tool for the ownership circle, while creating a sustainable family-owned business and avoiding destructive family conflicts requires a holistic approach that addresses the entire three circle model as it applies with respect to the relevant business.

Other disadvantages include the following:

- It is all too possible to design a trust structure that is controlled by the members of the management circle and therefore has a built-in bias in favour of those in management circle roles.
- Trust ownership can arguably hasten the demise of family emotional commitment to the business.
- As a discretionary trust creates no fixed beneficial interests that can be disposed of by a beneficiary who wishes to exit from the trust, there is no easy way to create a mechanism to 'prune the tree'.

The suggested remedies for these potential disadvantages is the subject matter of the rest of this chapter.

4.4   Creating a mechanism to allow pruning of the tree

Again, one of the advantages of using a trust is that it helps to consolidate voting control and to mitigate the impact of fragmentation of the shares. On the other hand, pruning the tree is actually a proven pathway to family business continuity. Yet how do you prune the tree with family members who are only discretionary beneficiaries? Ideally, a well-designed structure for ownership of a family firm must find a way both to consolidate voting control and to provide a right to exit. One approach to achieve this might be to establish separate trusts for each branch of the family – so that a compensated exit can at least occur on a branch basis.

5. Working with two levels of ownership

If there is no trust, then those in the ownership role within a family firm will be concerned with issues such as liquidity, capital allocation, assuring succession, providing strategic direction and monitoring performance, and so on.[9] It is a fundamental point that where the shares in a family firm are all held in trust, in practical and non-technical terms,[10] there will be two levels of ownership to work with. The first level will be referred to as that of legal ownership and the second that of beneficial ownership. When considering how to design an effective governance system for a trust-owned family firm, it is critical to be mindful of, and to address, each of these two levels. The discretionary beneficiaries cannot be ignored in designing the governance structure.

5.1 Legal ownership rights

The level of legal ownership is concerned primarily with the question of who has the power and the responsibility to exercise the voting rights on the shares in the family firm. These legal voting rights will be vested in the trustee. As previously noted, in this chapter it is assumed that the trustee will be either a corporate professional trustee company or a private trustee company; or alternatively these voting rights will be carved out and reserved to an investment committee constituted under the terms of the trust instrument. In this last case the investment committee will be exercising ownership-level rights. Most likely, the powers reserved to the investment committee will be fiduciary powers.[11]

5.2 Beneficial ownership

The second level of ownership – that of beneficial ownership of the shares in the business – will in non-technical terms be with the beneficiaries of the trust. It is suggested that in terms of planning for the trust structure using the three circle model, those beneficiaries (even if they are purely discretionary

---

9   Craig Aronoff and John L Ward, *Family Business Governance* (Palgrave Macmillan).
10   In a trust with fully discretionary dispositive provisions, it might be that each beneficiary individually, and the beneficiaries as a whole, have no proprietary interest in the assets comprising the trust fund or in the trust fund as a whole.
11   Even if the investment committee includes members who are also beneficiaries, unless they comprise the only beneficiaries for the trust, the investment committee will be making investment decisions on behalf of other people: the rest of the class of beneficiaries. In addition, if the investment committee is drafted as an office, which is to say that committee members can come and go but the office continues, then this will also support the fiduciary nature of the powers of the investment committee.

beneficiaries or objects) should be regarded for these purposes as being situated within the ownership circle, and should be regarded as being the stakeholders having an interest in the ownership of the business.[12] As discussed above in relation to the three circle model, part of the governance system for the structure will be to ensure that there is a communication forum created for the adult discretionary beneficiaries.

5.3   Inside and outside beneficiaries

If a beneficiary is also engaged in a role within the management circle of the business, then that beneficiary will be referred to here as an 'inside beneficiary', because he or she is inside the management circle of the business. For these purposes, being a member of the investment committee or a non-executive director on the board will not of itself qualify a beneficiary as being an inside beneficiary – because these are (legal) ownership and board roles, respectively. If, on the other hand, a family member is a beneficiary, but is not engaged in a role that puts him or her in the management circle for the business, then he or she will be referred to here as an 'outside beneficiary', because he or she is outside the management of the business.

Family firms have predictable conflicts and one of the traditional areas of predictable conflict (in the context of a trust-owned firm) is between the outside beneficiaries and the inside beneficiaries. The classic example is that inside beneficiaries want to accumulate and reinvest profits (after all, they can take compensation directly out of the business), while outside beneficiaries will want to see greater dividend distributions being paid.

Where a family firm is controlled by a trust, the trustee should be concerned to minimise the possibility of conflicts that could become destructive. Accordingly, to help preserve the value of the trust's shares in the family business, the trustee should also be concerned to see that the interests of ownership (and in particular, the interests of the beneficial owners) can be balanced with the interests of management.

5.4   Three tools to balance ownership and management

Creating a sustainable family business requires finding ways to strike a balance between the interests of beneficial ownership (in particular the outside beneficiaries) and the interests of management (in particular the inside beneficiaries). There are three key ways in which the interests of beneficial ownership and management can be balanced:

- having an effective board for the business;

---

12   After all, if the trust fund suffers an investment loss, each adult beneficiary will have the right to enforce the due administration of the trust and thereby to enquire as to whether that loss was the result of a breach of trust.

- considering the design of the investment committee; and
- ensuring that there is a communication forum for the beneficiaries.

An additional element is to have clarity of roles, so that all beneficiaries are on the same page as to the meaning of the legal ownership role in the business – what powers are exercised by the investment committee with respect to the business – and are educated so that they understand that the beneficial owners have no formal voting powers and authorities with respect to the ownership or management of the business.

6. Ensuring the relationship between family and business is professional

While there will be advantages of making use of a trust to own the shares in a family business, especially in terms of protecting the ownership of the shares and ensuring that ownership fragmentation is avoided, another critical dimension of ensuring family business continuity is to address the nature of the boundary between the family emotional system (the family circle) and the management system of the business. Due to the different goals and rules of these two systems, tensions and family conflicts at the intersection are inevitable.

Conflicts between the family system and the business system can be reduced to the extent that the management of the business can be made professional, and to the extent that a clear boundary between family issues and business issues can be developed. A 'clear boundary' means that family members know which topics are family issues and which topics are business issues.

6.1 Trustees should be concerned about the family/management boundary

Where the family business is owned by a trustee, the trustee is in the legal ownership role. Good governance of a family business requires that the owners not interfere in management issues. To the extent to which we are considering the relationship between family and management, it might be said that these issues do not concern the trustee. However, the nature of the relationship between family and business will impact on the value of that business; if it gives rise to a disruptive family conflict, it could even destroy the business. Therefore, assuming that the trustee is responsible for maintaining the real value of the trust fund, the trustee will want to protect the value of the ownership stake in the business. If the trustee is a corporate trustee that is directed as to investment matters, then the investment committee for the trust will likewise be responsible for protecting the value of that ownership interest.

6.2 Questions trustees should be asking

As an interested stakeholder, either the corporate trustee or the investment committee (as the case may be) should ask the board and senior management of the business questions designed to ascertain the following:

- What ongoing work is being done to ensure the business is managed professionally?
- Is there a clear and healthy boundary between family and management?
- Is there an agreed statement of the family business philosophy?[13]
- Is there a fair process for making decisions that require a balancing act to be struck between doing what is fair from a family perspective and what is fair from a business perspective?
- Is there is an agreed process for ensuring that conflicts among family members are addressed and not left to simmer?
- Are appropriate written policies in place to help regulate the relationship between the family and the business – for example, a family employment policy?
- Are the family members united around a shared set of values and a shared vision for the future?
- Are the family members committed to helping to preserve the golden goose that the business represents?
- Is there an effective family forum that meets periodically?

Trustees that own a controlling stake in a significant family business should consider developing a review checklist of effective family firm governance practices. Given that conflicts between the family circle and the management circle are a common source of family firm conflicts, and can lead to the destruction of a family firm, it makes good sense for the prudent trustee/investment committee to assessing on an annual basis the degree to which these more formalised governance practices and processes can be implemented in the business.

7. The critical role of the board in family firms

It has been said that one of the two most effective practices that can be implemented to protect and preserve a family business is to build an independent board to strengthen the business.[14] The board[15] is a critical tool in ensuring that the interests of beneficial ownership are kept in balance with the interests of management. The board in a family firm has been called a balancing point[16] and therefore represents another essential tool to help preserve balance among the three circles.

---

13   A family may agree that as a general principle, when called to make a decision that requires balancing family system rules with business system rules, members will 'do what is good for the family', or 'do what is good for the business' or 'look for a win/win solution'. This can be referred to as their family business philosophy.
14   John L Ward and Daniela Montemerlo, *The Family Constitution* (Palgrave Macmillan). The other practice is to draft a family agreement to strengthen the family.
15   This chapter proceeds on the basis of a unitary (or single tier) board model.
16   *Family Enterprise* (The Family Firm Institute).

7.1 Questions trustees should be asking about the board

Given the pivotal role that can be played by the board of a family business, the trustee of a trust that owns a family firm should always enquire whether that firm has a board that can act effectively – a board that is adding value to the governance and strategic thinking of the business. Trustees should ask the following questions:

- Are there processes in place periodically to assess board performance and effectiveness?
- Is the question of board effectiveness being addressed by the board chairman or by other members of the board (eg, a committee of the board)?
- Are board meetings being facilitated so that all of the board members have a chance to contribute their thinking?
- Is someone responsible for addressing the question of board succession?
- Is the role of the board clearly defined in a board charter or other similar document?
- Does the board include one or more non-family, non-executive directors, who can bring objectivity and perspective to board discussions?
- Does the board seek to strike a balance between the interests of the ownership and management of the business – for example, in ensuring that dividend pay-outs take into account the interests of both the outside beneficiaries and the inside beneficiaries?

Where the trust's investment powers have been reserved to an investment committee, the investment committee should be addressing these questions. Even where the corporate trustee has no control over the exercise of the voting rights on the shares in the business, the corporate trustee can still consider incorporating these kinds of questions into its annual review meetings with the settlor, the protectors or the members of the investment committee.

7.2 The critical task of holding the board accountable

If the voting rights on the shares in the business are controlled by the corporate trustee, then the trustee has the power (subject to the terms of the trust instrument and the constitutional documents for the company) to appoint and remove directors. The trustee in this case also has the ability to hold the board accountable for its performance. If the composition and role of the board has been set out in a board charter or a family constitution or other document, then the trustee will have the capacity to hold the board members accountable to the standards and processes expressed in such document. Given the importance to a family firm of having an effective board to oversee the governance of the business, the corporate trustee will be adding considerable value to the entire system by acting to police the agreed corporate governance arrangements.

When it comes to selecting the trustee of the trust, if considering the appointment of an independent corporate trustee, it should be ascertained whether the trustee would be willing to hold the board accountable for its performance and to help police the agreed corporate governance arrangements. If a corporate trustee cannot be identified that would be willing to assume this role, then this would be a reason either to consider a private trustee company arrangement or to carve out the investment control on the trust, including the voting rights on the shares, and vest them in an investment committee.

If the trustee is a private trustee company, then the board of the trustee company will be responsible for holding the board of the business accountable.

If the trust has been drafted with an investment committee, then the role of the investment committee includes holding the board of the business accountable.

7.3 Appointing and removing directors

The trustee, especially an independent corporate trustee, will be interested to see that there is a board charter in place (so the role of the board as a whole is clear), and that the criteria and process for the selection of new directors are clearly documented. Subject to compliance with its fiduciary obligations to act independently and to safeguard the trust fund, it would be reasonable to expect that a corporate trustee will seek to rely on the recommendations for new directors that come from the board's nominating committee. In terms of preserving the emotional commitment of the beneficiaries, it would also be prudent if, as part of the process of selecting new members of the board, the beneficiaries have some input into the proposed selection of new directors through a beneficiaries' forum.

8. Designing the composition of the investment committee

One of the benefits of trust ownership is the ability to ensure separation between economic rights and control (voting) rights. Settlors might like the idea of creating an investment committee because they might see it as a way to allow the family members who currently work in the management circle (the inside beneficiaries) to control the voting rights on the shares in the business. At first glance, this appears to be similar to the non-trust approach of giving all of the voting shares in the family business to the family members who work in management roles (and sharing ownership of the non-voting, dividend-paying shares between all family members, whether they work in management or not). However, the difference is that with a trust arrangement, members of the investment committee will likely be regarded as fiduciaries who can be held accountable for any breach of trust that they commit.

Remember that the concept of finding balance among the three circles is important in designing a sustainable family business system. When designing the composition of the investment committee, it is critical to consider the question of how to ensure that the interests of beneficial ownership and the interests of management are balanced.

8.1 Being out of balance with a bias in favour of management

If the approach is taken of populating the investment committee entirely with inside beneficiaries (ie, those working in and controlling the management circle), then this composition of the investment committee is likely to create a scenario where the trust is out of balance, with a bias in favour of management. If a family business is out of balance because the management circle overrides or overpowers the beneficial ownership circle,[17] this may have the following results:

- a risk profile for the business that is set solely by those who play a management role;
- critical decisions, such as setting the strategy, being set solely by those who play a management role;
- a bias towards reinvestment of surplus profits in the business;
- managers who rely on remuneration from the business and who are less inclined towards having the company pay dividends to the trust;
- lack of voice for outside beneficiaries;
- outside beneficiaries who have no emotional commitment to the business;
- strained family relationships with a lack of harmony; and
- outside beneficiaries who are forced to resort to legal remedies to vent their frustration and unhappiness with the trust and with those in management roles.

The obvious danger where the investment committee is populated entirely with inside beneficiaries is that they use their control over the voting rights of the shares to have decisions made that reflect only their inside (ie, management) perspective. As an example, in this scenario, the investment committee members might use their powers to block or minimise the payment of any dividends from the business, rather than approving dividends that seek to balance the reasonable reinvestment needs of the business with the income and diversification needs of the beneficial owners as a whole.

8.2 Where ownership overrides management

On the other side of the coin, if a family business is out of balance because the beneficial ownership circle overrides or overpowers the management circle,

---

17   This theme is elaborated on in Christian Stewart, "Finding the Harmonious Pathway", *Offshore Investment Magazine*, April 2014.

then as the outside beneficiaries grow in number, they will want to extract resources from the business – for example, they might demand more and more dividend income from the business and refuse to support adequate capital investment. The lack of an easy exit mechanism for discretionary beneficiaries and an ever-increasing number of beneficiaries can also result in conflicts. This alternative out-of-balance scenario could arise either where the trust has a corporate trustee (and there is no investment committee) and the corporate trustee is responding to the demands of an ever-increasing number of outside beneficiaries, or alternatively where the trust does have an investment committee, but that committee is dominated by outside beneficiaries.

8.3 Designing balance into the investment committee

When designing a trust structure to own control of a family business, if that trust is designed with an investment committee, then the question of whether the system will be balanced should be considered when planning the membership of the investment committee.

First, one way to avoid the out-of-balance scenarios described above would be to ensure that the investment committee includes representation from both inside beneficiaries and outside beneficiaries.

Second, regardless of composition, the members of the investment committee need to learn how to 'manage their hat collection' properly and remember that the investment committee is both a representative role and an ownership-level role, and that the members of the investment committee must communicate and consult with the beneficiaries' forum and listen to the voice of the outside beneficiaries before exercising their voting powers. That is, the members of the investment committee have the right (collectively) to exercise the voting rights on the shares in the family business, but should give the members of the beneficiaries' forum (collectively) a voice on how the shares are to be voted.

Third, the independent directors on the board of the business should help by reminding the members of the investment committee to consider the perspective of the outside beneficiaries, as might the protector.

9. Preserving emotional commitment

In family businesses, the concept of preserving the emotional commitment of the owners to the business is an important one. Emotional commitment means that the family members, in particular those who do not work in management circle roles, are willing to support the decisions of the family members who manage the business. Where there is emotional commitment, the family outside shareholders (or beneficiaries) are willing to provide patient capital for the business. Emotional commitment is similar to 'family glue'. This is something that is important to the business founder. It flows naturally from proximity to the business founder and from family members working side by side together in management roles. However, it is also natural that both family glue and emotional commitment to the business will start to fade as the family members move out of management roles and as beneficial ownership starts to become separated from management. In the majority of family firms, emotional commitment and family glue will have dried up by the time the business starts to pass into the third generation of ownership. To preserve family glue and emotional commitment to the business, both need to be intentionally cultivated and nurtured.

9.1   **What happens when emotional commitment fades and there is no trust?**
What happens when emotional commitment dries up, assuming the business is not owned by a trust structure – that is, where the family members are directly holding shares?

- The outside shareholders will have a differing perspective from those who are in management roles.
- The outside shareholders will stop supporting the management of the business.
- The outside shareholders will tend to want to maximise dividends and to minimise any reinvestment in the business.
- It can be difficult to get the outside shareholders to make or approve major decisions concerning the business.
- In a privately owned company, it is common to find that the outside shareholders are stuck with no mechanism in place to allow them to sell their shares – there is no way to prune the tree.
- Small minority shareholders can feel frustrated as they cannot influence decision making and they cannot sell their shares.
- The outside shareholders can become suspicious of the compensation and benefits enjoyed by those who are in management roles.
- Family relationships, trust and communication can deteriorate.
- Family glue can fail and the system end up in entropy, if not in conflict.

9.2   **What happens when emotional commitment fades and there is a trust?**
What happens when emotional commitment dries up in the case where the business is owned by a trust structure? Assume that the trust has been drafted so that the voting control is with an investment committee which entirely comprises family members who are working in the management circle – so that the investment committee has a built-in bias towards the management circle:

- The outside beneficiaries will have a different perspective from those who are in management roles.
- The outside beneficiaries (who possess no voting rights) will want to maximise dividends, minimise reinvestment in the business and, if they could, sell out of the ownership of the business (which they cannot).

- The outside beneficiaries can become suspicious of the compensation and benefits enjoyed by those who are in management roles.
- The outside beneficiaries can start asking the members of the investment committee, based on the fiduciary nature of the investment committee's role, questions such as the following:
  - Do the members of the investment committee have a conflict between their duties as members of the committee and their own personal self-interest, having regard to the benefits they are receiving as a result of their involvement in the management of the business?
  - Is it in the best financial interests of all beneficiaries for the trust to continue to own this business?
  - Is this business a prudent investment for a trust?
  - Should the trust assets not be more diversified?
  - Would it not be in the best interests of the beneficiaries of the trust for a larger portion of the annual income of the business to be distributed?
- Family relationships, trust and communication can deteriorate;
- The family glue can fail and the system end up in entropy, if not in conflict.

Therefore, loss of emotional commitment to the business is a topic that is just as important to the long-term sustainability of the business, whether it is owned by a trust or not. Arguably it might even be of greater importance given the fiduciary nature of the powers of the investment committee.

9.3 How do you preserve emotional commitment to the business?

Preserving emotional commitment to the business is an important concept for the family business, whether it is owned by a trust or not. The natural trend, as mentioned, is that emotional commitment will fade with time – it is simply the law of entropy at work. To counter this trend, the family leaders and family elders[18] must take active, intentional steps to cultivate and grow family emotional commitment. How is this to be done?

- Planning for family participation is an important part of preserving emotional commitment. This means participation, based on family members' skills and interests, in the joint affairs of the family.
- Hand in hand with planning for family participation is the education and development of family members so that they have a baseline of competence to contribute to the effective governance of the family and to be effective owners.

---

18 For a discussion of family elders see James E Hughes Jr, Susan Massenzio and Keith Whitaker, *The Cycle of the Gift* (Bloomberg Press). Also see Christian Stewart, "The Wisdom of Elders", *STEP Journal*, July 2014.

- Participation in the family's affairs and in the ownership of the shared family assets is voluntary. This means that there is a way to exit and that family members know what that mechanism is. In the context of a single discretionary trust as owner of the business, this element of the right to exit cannot easily be satisfied.[19]

9.4 Does trust ownership automatically hinder emotional commitment to the business?

As mentioned, it is natural that emotional commitment will start to fade away, whether or not there is ownership by a trust, unless it is intentionally cultivated through the practices listed above. Ownership by a trust does add an additional level of complexity and can allow those in management roles to use the trustee, or the investment committee, as a buffer or shield to insulate themselves from the outside beneficiaries. Wherever a large distance is maintained between the outside family stakeholders and the leadership and management of the business, with no attempt to engage with the outside stakeholders, this will hasten the breakdown in emotional commitment.

To overcome the extra layer that a trust structure can add between the beneficial owners and the business, it is suggested that the antidote is:

- to ensure that there is a communication forum for the adult beneficiaries of the trust;
- to adopt the other practices for cultivating emotional commitment listed above; and
- to treat the beneficiaries as collectively being the ultimate beneficial owners (or stewards) of the business.

10. Creating a communication forum for the beneficiaries

Under the three circle model, the ownership circle should have its own forum so that the interests and concerns of ownership can be voiced, and so that the owners can come together to make joint decisions about the ownership of the business. Where the business is owned by a trust, even if they have no voting rights the beneficiaries should be regarded as being the persons located within the ownership circle for the purposes of the three circle model; they need a forum. In addition, providing a forum for the beneficiaries gives them a voice and helps to preserve emotional commitment to the business. Finally, a forum for the beneficiaries is another mechanism to help ensure that there is balance in the system between ownership and management.

---

19   Hence there is a role for the structuring lawyer to seek to design an ownership structure that can combine trust ownership and a mechanism for a compensated exit of a beneficiary's interest in that trust.

10.1 Benefits of having a beneficiaries' forum

Other reasons for creating a communication forum for the beneficiaries include providing a platform:

- to educate the beneficiaries on the roles and responsibilities under the trust, on the governance system and on the structure of, and roles and responsibilities in, the business, which might also include being educated on best practices for families in business and learning skills such as communication and joint decision-making skills together;
- to share information on the terms of the trust;
- to share information on the strategy and performance of the business;
- where the beneficiaries may get introduced to the independent directors, and to the trusted advisers and non-family 'family elders';
- to help get the beneficiaries all on the same page, and so that any differences can be worked out behind closed doors;
- to provide a platform for the exploration of a shared family mission, vision and values; and
- to encourage the representatives of the corporate trustee, or the members of the investment committee, to develop their relationship with the beneficiaries that they represent so that they can understand the goals, needs and concerns of the beneficiaries.

10.2 Structuring the forum

The degree of formality required around the beneficiaries' forum will be a function of the size and complexity of the family.[20] It assumes that the beneficiaries of the trust already include multiple adult beneficiaries. In its simplest form, the forum could be an annual family meeting of the beneficiaries. The key factor, however, will be to emphasise the communication and educational nature of the forum, and that the beneficiaries have no decision-making power. To preserve the integrity of the trust structure, it will be important to ensure that in practice the beneficiaries are not giving directions to the corporate trustee or to the members of the investment committee. The terms of the trust structure have to be respected.

11. The protector role

In practice, the core protector role is that of being a party to the trust that has the power to appoint and remove the trustee. The protector can step in and remove the trustee in the event that the beneficiaries are unhappy with the administration of the trust by the trustee, or in the event of a conflict between the beneficiaries and the trustee. The protector is often also talked about in terms

---

20   For a discussion of family councils, family assemblies and other committees, see Barbara R Hauser, *International Family Governance, A Guide for Families and Their Advisors* (Mesatop Press).

of acting as a bridge between the beneficiaries and the trustee, interpreting and facilitating two-way communication between these two parties.

11.1 The relationship between the protector and the investment committee

In some trusts the power to give binding directions to the trustee as to the investment of the trust fund and the exercise of the voting rights on the shares in the family business (the investment committee function) is combined into the office of the protector. To ensure a good system of checks and balances, and clarity of roles, it is suggested that the better drafting approach would be to have the role of protector defined as a separate and discrete role from that of the investment committee.

11.2 The relationship between the protector and the beneficiaries' forum

The protector will have those powers that are expressly reserved to the protector under the terms of the trust instrument. It is a decision-making role. The scope of that role should be expressly described in the trust instrument. The beneficiaries' forum, on the other hand, is a family communication and education forum; it is not a decision-making role. The terms defining the beneficiaries' forum can be contained in the family constitution or other non-binding governance documentation. It is again recommended that these two functions be kept conceptually separate.

11.3 A recommended approach to the composition of the protector committee

In terms of designing an effective governance system for a family trust, it is suggested that the protector role should be seen as one of acting as the judicial branch of the governance system that the trust represents, and that the role of the protector includes stepping in to help resolve conflicts between the trustee and the beneficiaries.[21] With this approach, the protector committee would be populated with non-family, non-beneficiary, trusted advisers or with family elders.

By populating the protector committee with trusted advisers or family elders who are not beneficiaries, who are not on the board of the private trustee company and who are not members of the investment committee, this allows the protector committee to maintain some distance from the beneficiaries, the investment committee and the trustee. The protector committee can then keep an eye on the nature of the relationship and the communication between the beneficiaries and the investment committee, and between the beneficiaries and the trustee (eg, with respect to dispositive functions), and even between the investment committee and the corporate board of the family business.

---

21   See Hartley Goldstone, James E Hughes Jr and Keith Whitaker, *Family Trusts, a Guide for Beneficiaries, Trustees, Trust Protectors and Trust Creators* (Bloomberg Press).

While the protector role should be kept separate and distinct from the investment committee role, the protector should be mindful of questions such as whether the members of the investment committee can avoid personal conflicts of interest and whether they can 'wear the right hat' when they attend investment committee meetings.

The protector should also be mindful of questions such as whether the beneficiaries' forum is being convened in practice and whether the voice[22] of that forum is being heard by the trustee, the investment committee and the corporate board.

12. Conclusion

A trust can be a very useful tool for the ownership circle of a family business, but it is important not to forget that there is a wider context which must also be addressed. It has been said that a trust structure cannot be used to bottle up family emotions. Trusts do involve two levels of ownership, and the level of beneficial ownership must be acknowledged and given a voice; the emotional commitment of the beneficial owners to the business must be preserved. Trustees can play a vital role in directing attention to issues such as the effectiveness of the board, the boundary between family and management and the need to help balance the perspective of the outside beneficiaries with that of the inside beneficiaries. If all of the principles summarised here are followed, a trust structure can be immensely helpful for the sustainability of a family business.

---

22 While appreciating that voice is not the same thing as authority.

International family governance: integration with family trusts

Barbara R Hauser
Independent family adviser

This chapter presents an innovative proposal about ways in which family governance could be integrated with family trusts.[1] The author always had a strong trust background[2] as a private client lawyer, and later developed a focus on family governance as the key to building cohesive families and avoiding family fights over wealth transfers.[3] This chapter contains ideas about how family governance could now be integrated with family trusts.

1. Importance of family governance

The term 'family governance' refers to the way in which a family makes decisions as a family. Key questions range from the initial and often delicate question of 'who is in the family?' for these purposes, to the question of 'how are these decisions enforced?'

I am now a firm believer that good family governance is more valuable than good trust documents. My test criterion for 'valuable' is whether something will enable a family to avoid the bitter fights that can result in the disintegration of its wealth and even of the family itself.

My point of view is a result of a learning process over a 35-year period of working with wealthy families in many countries. It was certainly not my view at the beginning of my career. I began my career as a traditional trusts and estates lawyer for wealthy clients. I would advise the patriarch and then I would draft trust documents to carry out his wishes. Our focus was on writing clear and tightly drafted conditions in the trust agreement.

I eventually realised that bitter family fights can and do take place no matter how carefully the trust document is drafted. I became intrigued by a growing field of family system professionals (largely from a psychology or business background)[4] who were working on ways to preserve harmony among family members. As I now say to groups of lawyers: "If the most carefully drafted trust

---

1   Many of these ideas are likely to appear in forthcoming articles by the author, perhaps even in a book.
2   See, for example, her chapter in this book on trusts in the United States.
3   See her book *International Family Governance: A Guide for Families and their Advisors* (Mesatop Press, 2011).

documents can end up in court if the family members want to fight … why don't we all pay more attention to helping families learn to avoid those fights?"

Now, I encourage families to begin with family governance. The implementing documents can follow after the family has completed its work on its internal policies and governance. After the family has agreed upon its goals for the future, the choice of associated legal documents becomes much easier. One former banker summarised this approach succinctly: process first, then product.

I asked to have this chapter included in our 2010 edition of *Trusts in Prime Jurisdictions* in the hope that trust advisers around the world would read about family governance and would think about how those successful concepts could be integrated into trust documents. I am pleased that it is included again in the fifth edition of this book.

This chapter will address four primary topics: family governance, traditional trusts, the gap between them and a proposed model of integration.

2. Key elements of family governance

We begin with an executive summary of family governance.[5] Although every family is unique in the development of its own governance system and families in different cultures will have their own differences, there are several common elements, which include the following.

2.1 Family councils

A family council (perhaps with a different name) is a smaller group chosen to act on behalf of the larger family. The family council is given authority to make certain decisions and to communicate them to the larger family. Some major decisions might need ratification by the larger family. Vacancies in the family council may be filled by the remaining members or by the larger family. In many ways they have a role that is similar to boards of companies.

An effective family council will have regular formal meetings, often on a quarterly basis. There are written agendas and decisions will be recorded in writing after the meeting.

2.2 Purpose

The purpose of family governance is to support the continuing, multi-generational wellbeing of the larger family. The family council is created for this purpose and has the responsibility of acting on behalf of the larger group. The

---

4   James E Hughes, Jr is a notable exception, having begun as a partner at the Coudert law firm and then devoting his counselling efforts to the family governance field. His first book, *Family Wealth: Keeping it in the Family*, is often regarded as the seminal book in the field.

5   See generally, Barbara R Hauser, "Family Governance: Who, What and How?" in the *Journal of Wealth Management*, Fall 2002.

larger group participates in the formation of the family governance system, which is required in order for the system to be truly adopted by all of the members of the larger family.

2.3   Written document – the family constitution

Most families around the globe who are engaged in family governance work to create a written document that will contain the key elements of their family governance system.[6] Often called a family constitution, it is also sometimes called a protocol, a family charter or a code of conduct.

The family constitution might include a summary of the history of the family and the reasons that the family has decided to write a constitution.[7] It will describe the range of issues that are to be decided by the rules in the constitution, and which issues will remain personal. The constitution is where the family council will be formed. The document will include the method of voting by the family council and by the larger family. The voting procedures will also address the position of spouses and the voting ages for children. It may also address whether various family branches need proportionate representation.

Family constitutions are extremely flexible documents. Sometimes they are long enough to resemble a rule book to cover every possible situation. Other times they are very short and just establish the procedure by which the rules will be made. If they create a family council, for example, they may delegate all decision-making discretion to the council.

It is often said that a family constitution is not a binding document, but that might be changing. I am aware of at least one family that has obtained the equivalent of a private court ruling that its constitution would be enforced. If the family controls a business that generates income, it is also possible for penalty provisions in the constitution to include a reduction in dividend payments. One could make an argument under contract law that the constitution is a binding contract because each member has given a form of consideration in the exchange of promises.[8]

The final point in putting together a written constitution is addressing the need for future flexibility. I always recommend that some provision be included to allow a procedure for amendments. This is especially important to accommodate future generations.

---

6   For a template of a family constitution (including a two-tier proposal), see Barbara R Hauser, "International Family Governance: A Proposal for 'Two-tier' Family Constitution" in *STEP Journal* (June 2010).

7   For example, the beginning of the preamble to the US Constitution could apply to families: "We the people, in order to form a more perfect union, to establish justice, insure domestic tranquility ..."

8   See Barbara R Hauser, "Family Constitutions: Are they (or should they be) Binding?" in *STEP Journal* (April 2012).

2.4 Administration

To carry out its purpose, the family council will often create sub-groups. These can include investment committees, budget projection committees, education committees, annual gathering committees and committees to prepare written family histories.

2.5 Distribution of benefits

The family council, acting in its role to benefit the larger family, may be charged with responsibility for the decisions relating to the distribution of dividends from family companies. The council may be entitled to a position on the company boards, to represent the interests of the entire family.

The council may create a family venture fund to support entrepreneurial projects presented by individual family members. This would allow a family member to make a formal funding proposal to the family venture fund. The family committee would have to approve of the business plan, and would normally monitor the success or failure of the funded project.

It may create a philanthropic committee to make contributions to various charities selected by the family. Family members could make formal proposals to contribute funds to an existing charity or to create a new charity. There might be requirements that the charities be consistent with the stated values of the family.

In some cases, the council might provide an emergency fund for special needs by family members. The family member could present a request for special funding, such as for a catastrophic illness, which could be approved by the council.

Realising that the skills and competencies of the younger family members are crucial to the continuing success of the family, the council may create a family educational fund to ensure that every family member receives the highest possible education. In some cases the family will form an additional learning academy, to be sure that the subjects that are important to the family will be included and will be taught in a consistent manner to the entire family.

If these core functions sound familiar, that was deliberate – they have been written to mirror the core elements of a family trust.

3. Elements of family trusts

The core elements of family trusts can be broken into very similar categories, as follows.

3.1 The trustees

The trustees are those persons chosen by the settlor to act for the benefit of the larger family (the beneficiaries). The settlor may direct the manner in which vacancies are filled or may give that function to the current trustees. Their legal responsibility is to be fiduciaries for present and future beneficiaries. Although the trustees have legal control over the trust assets, they are under strict fiduciary rules to manage those assets for the larger family, and not for their personal benefit.

3.2 Purpose

The purpose of a family trust is for the trustees to manage (and distribute) the trust assets for the continuing (multi-generational) wellbeing of the larger family (of beneficiaries). The entire trust fund is dedicated to this purpose. Courts will enforce compliance with the purpose of the trust.

3.3 Written document – the family trust

In the trust field, there is a nearly universal requirement that there be a written document. The settlor will create the document, which is referred to as a trust agreement (US practice) or a trust deed or settlement (English practice). The written document can be very long (US practice could include as many as 150 pages) or very short (some offshore jurisdictions have standard trust deeds that are only two pages long). In the longer documents, the settlor has tried to address every possible situation. In the shorter documents, the trustees are given complete discretion, including the discretion to add or remove beneficiaries.

Whether or not the trust document can be amended is a serious issue. Generally speaking, the trust document, which is written at the direction of the settlor, cannot be changed. The settlor generally requires that his or her wishes will be carried out. In some jurisdictions a practice has developed of using a letter of wishes written by the settlor, who thereby retains some ongoing sense of having an ability to change the terms of the trust document if he or she has changed his or her mind since the document was originally written, even though as a matter of law the letter of wishes is not a legally binding document.

In the United States there is also a heavy use of trusts that can be amended directly by the settlor, at any time and for any reason. These trusts are primarily written in order to avoid a probate proceeding. Even these trusts provide that upon the death of the settlor, the terms of the document cannot be changed.

Recently, as referred to in many chapters of this book, procedures have been developed that will allow someone besides the settlor to make changes to the terms of the trust document. One example is the position of a protector, who is often given the right to make changes in a variety of areas.

The above comments relate to the trust practices of England and the United States, where the lawyer or solicitor is actively involved in tailored drafting to suit the wishes of the client. In parts of Asia and some offshore jurisdictions, the use of trusts is more confined to a bank-generated form document.[9]

---

9   This caution was added by Christian Stewart, based in Hong Kong, a former banker who founded Family Legacy Asia (HK) Ltd to focus on family governance approaches.

3.4 Administration

To carry out its purpose, the trust may include sub-groups. These can include investment committees, budget projection committees, charitable committees and so on. Modern trust law is permitting an increasing amount of delegation of the administrative functions.

3.5 Distribution of benefits

Traditionally the trustees are directed to distribute assets of the trust to the beneficiaries at the times and for the reasons that are stated in the trust document. In the longer trust documents, the reasons for distributions could be listed in some detail. Examples would be allowing, or directing, distributions for "health, education, support and maintenance" (a standard taken from the tax provisions in the Internal Revenue Code of the United States), to purchase a home or to start a business. They are also often authorised to make loans to beneficiaries.

The trustees, acting in their role to benefit the larger family, in accordance with the terms of the trust agreement, may (although these are admittedly not very common provisions, at least not yet) create a family venture fund to support entrepreneurial projects presented by individual family members. They may create a philanthropic committee to make contributions to various charities selected by the family. They may create a family educational fund to ensure that every family member receives the highest possible education. Some trusts contain funds to pay for annual family reunions.

Most likely, though, the trustees will simply make outright distributions of trust funds as directed by the written directions in the trust document.

4. The key differences between family governance systems and family trusts

Before moving on to the positive proposals for the integration of family governance with family trusts, it is helpful to point out some of the key differences between family governance (as described in section 2 above) and family trusts (as described in section 3 above).

In the author's opinion, these differences are the root causes of litigation by beneficiaries against their trustees.

Some of the key differences between family governance systems and family trusts are as follows:

- The single biggest difference between family governance systems and family trusts is the matter of who creates them. The successful family governance system is one that is created by the larger family, including all of those who will be affected by it. The family trust is created by one individual senior (and wealthier) family member, usually with no input from any other family member, including any of the beneficiaries.[10]

- There is little or no input from the family members (beneficiaries) on the ongoing operation of the trust administration and investment decisions.
- There is little or no input from the family members (beneficiaries) on distributions of the trust assets. When, why and to whom distributions are made are terms that the settlor would have included in the trust document. The terms might be very specific, as in the longer documents, or might be given to the trustees in their broad discretion. The beneficiaries would rarely have been given any control over the distribution decisions.
- No changes are allowed by the family members (beneficiaries) in the terms of the trust document, which must be followed as it was written and in accordance with the original intent of the settlor (disregarding the English use of letters of wishes, which are intended only for the use of the settlor anyway).
- The family members (beneficiaries) usually have no right to determine who will act as successor trustees.

5. Proposed integration of family governance with family trusts

The field of family governance is increasingly being recognised as the critical success factor in maintaining family harmony and wealth from one generation to another. The use of trust documents to control the passage of wealth from one generation to another continues to increase globally, even in countries that have not had the concept of a trust in their domestic law. Yet there is a serious gap between these two very different tools.

I am convinced that finding ways to integrate family governance concepts into family trusts would create better trusts and more competent and fulfilled family members (beneficiaries), and would help families to avoid much harmful trust litigation. The question of how these can be integrated has been on my mind for several years. My initial thought was that a copy of the family constitution could be attached as an exhibit to a trust agreement. This would allow the trustees to have a sense of the family. But there would not be any real impact on the administration of the trust and the exhibit would not be a legally binding document.

Recently I have been thinking of ways in which the important and effective family governance concepts can be integrated into the actual trust document. This chapter has been an initial attempt to persuade trust advisers and drafters, and settlors also, to consider including some innovative provisions in trust documents. Some examples follow.

---

10   See Barbara R Hauser, "Appreciating Beneficiaries" in *Trusts & Estates*, June 2007, for an argument to include the beneficiary in the planning process.

If we consider the list of differences between family governance concepts and traditional trust concepts, I would argue that the common element of the differences between family trusts and family governance systems is the element of control.

In country governance terms, the typical family trust is a governance system of a dictator, albeit usually of the benevolent type, with no participation allowed ('taxation without representation'). Successful family governance systems, on the other hand, succeed because they are based on the initial and ongoing participation by all of the affected members of the family ('taxation with representation').

Without a means of active participation in the governing system (or trust agreement) that impacts on their individual lives, family members (beneficiaries) either develop a passive, dependent role – or there is rebellion and litigation.

Here then are some proposals as to how successful family governance concepts can be integrated into family trusts.

5.1 The trustees

The trustees could be chosen by a representative of the entire group of beneficiaries, such as a family council, if they have one. That same group could remove and replace the trustees. They could also name one or more of themselves to serve as a co-trustee or as a liaison between the trustees and the larger family group. The family could form its own trustee advisory committee, to hold regular meetings with the trustees.

5.2 Purpose

The purpose of a family trust could still be to manage and distribute the trust assets for the continuing, multi-generational wellbeing of the larger family of beneficiaries. But the control over the management and distribution would be shared with the larger family of beneficiaries, all of whom would be expected to exercise a fiduciary type responsibility on behalf of the larger family, including future generations.

In other words, instead of saying that the purpose is to carry out the wishes of the settlor, the written purpose could be to provide for the general wellbeing of the multi-generational family based on their input from time to time. As in the preamble to the US Constitution, this purpose would be "to promote the general welfare" of the family.

5.3 Written document – the family trust

Instead of leaving the selection of the terms of the trust to the settlor and his or her lawyer, the beneficiaries could be included in the planning. The process, for example, could include the participation of representatives of all of the intended beneficiaries in the formation of the trust document.

There could be formal family meetings to discuss the selection of suitable trust provisions. There could be a requirement that there would be official family approval of any final trust document.

5.4 Administration

To carry out its purpose, the trust – written with the input of the beneficiaries – may include sub-groups. These can include investment committees, budget projection committees and so on. Those groups could be constituted by the family council or by other members of the family. The more groups, the more opportunity there is for the family to feel involved in the trust administration. This would alleviate the common complaint of beneficiaries that they lack information about the trust administration.

5.5 Distribution of benefits

In addition to the traditional distribution of income and principal, the trust agreement could authorise a number of creative family-based uses of the trust funds.

For example, the trust agreement could provide that the family council, acting in their role to benefit the larger family, would have the power to create a family venture fund to support entrepreneurial projects presented by individual family members.

The family council could also create a philanthropic committee to make contributions to various charities selected by the family.

The family council could create a family educational fund to ensure that every family member receives the highest possible education. The funding for these ongoing funds would be provided by the trust assets, upon approval of the trustees. The trust agreement would authorise the trustees to make such decisions, for the ongoing multi-generational benefit of the larger family.

5.6 Dispute resolution

If a beneficiary is dissatisfied, for example with the amount of a distribution or with the investment policy of the trustees, the traditional process that is followed is for the beneficiary to make claims in court. In this new integrated model, though, dispute resolution provisions could be included in the document. For example, the trustees could meet with the family council to determine the reasons for the dissatisfaction. The trust document could provide that a determination by the family council would be final.[11]

---

11   This section was added at the urging of Alon Kaplan, and raises intriguing questions about whether the beneficiary could be denied redress to the court system. It is different from an *'ad terrorem'* or 'no contest' clause, because the contest would be considered just by an internal family council instead of the public judiciary system. Indeed, it could be seen as a form of binding arbitration.

6.   Conclusion

This proposed integration would be a radical change, but it can be done. I will close with a poignant example of how that change can occur.

I met with a patriarch who had included some particular provisions in his trust documents that would impose his views on his children's access to funds for a significant period of time. I suggested that he review those terms with his children, all of whom were adults. At first he was adamantly against the idea. He said that how his wealth would be administered was his personal decision to make and it was a private matter.

Later I was invited to his home to meet with the whole family. To my amazement, after social talk, the patriarch said, "So, Barbara, go ahead and tell them about the plan." I did so, with a careful eye on the patriarch. His own contribution, from time to time, was to explain his caring motives to them. They in turn expressed their appreciation. At the end of the discussion he said to his children, "You know, I feel happy that we can talk about this."

This illustrates how a process of family governance might begin. It is likely now that the trust plan for the future will be redesigned with the input and cooperation of the adult children. This will be an integrated trust, and as such is likely to benefit the family for many generations and without disruptive conflict.[12]

In sum, my argument is that the integration of successful family governance principles into family trusts – would remove the root causes of conflict and ensuing trust litigation, and would instead strengthen the intended positive benefits of family trusts. Family trusts that integrate family governance principles should provide positive support for the family for many generations of beneficiaries.

---

12   While thinking about integrating family governance into trust agreements, I ended up writing another article suggesting that all of the succession planning be handled in a family governance model.

Asset protection trusts

Gideon Rothschild
Moses & Singer LLP

1. Introduction

Although the use of the so-called offshore trust as a vehicle to protect assets from creditors has often been cited as a relatively recent phenomenon, in fact offshore jurisdictions have long been favoured over domestic jurisdictions for various asset protection purposes. Most notably, offshore trusts have been used to escape domestic political strife, exchange controls, forced heirship provisions or confiscatory government action, or to obtain favourable tax benefits – all of which can, to some extent, be considered to be asset protection purposes.

Today's offshore asset protection trusts, however, are at least as likely to be created for the purpose of obtaining leverage against future private creditors as for these other purposes, since such trusts can provide significant procedural, substantive and psychological barriers which impact upon a private creditor's ability to attach a debtor's assets. For individuals resident in stable political and economic jurisdictions, such as the United States, leverage against private creditors is probably the most common use of the offshore asset protection trust today.

The offshore trust is unique to asset protection planning since, if established in one of a number of jurisdictions that have repealed the common law prohibition against self-settled spendthrift trusts, the settlor can name himself or herself as a discretionary beneficiary of the trust while at the same time protecting the trust corpus from the claims of future creditors. Thus the settlor is relieved from the traditional dilemma inherent in having permanently and completely to divest himself or herself of property in order to protect it from potential future creditors.

Although a not insignificant number of domestic jurisdictions have followed suit in repealing the self-settled trust rule, the US Constitution makes it questionable whether trusts established under the law of such domestic jurisdictions by non-resident settlors will provide significant asset protection in the event of an aggressive creditor challenge. Of course, as an asset protection device, the more traditional domestic trust (as well as an outright transfer of property) remains viable where the settlor, for whatever reason, desires irrevocably to transfer his or her property for the benefit of another. Where the named beneficiaries include the settlor's spouse, the transferred property can potentially be used for the indirect benefit of the settlor – provided, of course, that neither a divorce nor the spouse's untimely death intervenes. In the past, such asset protection planning techniques were used because no viable alternative existed. Today, those who are at substantial risk (eg, real estate developers, corporate directors, doctors, lawyers, and others who may be viewed as having 'deep pockets'), and who are willing to incur the greater costs associated with the offshore trust settlement, have the viable alternative of protecting their assets in an offshore self-settled spendthrift trust.

As the use of offshore trusts for asset protection purposes has become increasingly prevalent in recent years, a basic understanding of the law governing such entities has become essential for professionals practising and advising across a broad spectrum of disciplines. This chapter provides the reader with such a grounding in the law relating to offshore and domestic asset protection trusts.

2. Benefits of offshore asset protection trusts

2.1 Creditor protection

A trust, foreign or domestic, is uniquely geared to provide asset protection to its beneficiaries since the very concept of the trust involves a division between the legal (administrative or managerial) and the beneficial ownership of property. Specifically, a trust imposes a fiduciary relationship with respect to property, subjecting the title holder (the trustee) to equitable duties to deal with the property for the benefit of another (the beneficiary). Pursuant to this important distinction, and in accordance with the legal maxim of *cujus est dare, ejus est disponere* (meaning that the person who gives a thing may decide how it is disposed), most courts will recognise as effective a trust provision purporting to restrain the alienation of the beneficial trust interest, either voluntarily by the trust beneficiary or involuntarily by his or her creditors.

Such a provision is called a 'spendthrift provision' and such a trust is called a 'spendthrift trust', although whether the beneficiary is actually a spendthrift is immaterial to the protection afforded. Notwithstanding the wide recognition of spendthrift trust protections where one individual establishes a trust for the benefit of another, however, an exception is often made on public policy grounds for the so-called 'self-settled' spendthrift trust, which is a trust in which the settlor retains for himself or herself an interest as a beneficiary, even if it is only a potential to receive distributions from the trust within the discretion of an independent third-party trustee.

The principle underlying this limitation (where it exists) is that it is against public policy to allow an individual to tie up his or her property in such a way that he or she can still enjoy it, but can prevent creditors from reaching it.

Significantly, this is the case whether the settlor's creditors are present or future, reasonably anticipated or impossible to foresee, as an intent in the settlor to defraud creditors is not required to invalidate a self-settled spendthrift trust in such jurisdictions.

The settlor of a trust, however, may designate the law of any jurisdiction as governing the administration of the trust, and hence may designate a jurisdiction that recognises self-settled spendthrift trusts as valid even if the settlor's domicile does not. Moreover, under established rules relating to conflicts of law, including the Hague Convention on the Law Applicable to Trusts and their Recognition, and the American Law Institute's Restatement (Third) of the Law of Conflict of Laws, the settlor's designation of governing law should be respected, both domestically and internationally, regardless of venue. Notwithstanding the foregoing, however, case law indicates that particularly egregious cases (generally those which implicate fraudulent conveyance or sham trust arguments) are unlikely to withstand a spirited attack on public policy grounds in the settlor's domicile.

Beyond having repealed the self-settled spendthrift trust rule, however, an offshore trust geared towards asset protection should be sited in a jurisdiction that has also statutorily modified the Statute of Elizabeth. The Statute of Elizabeth, enacted in England in 1571 and which now forms the basis of fraudulent transfer law throughout most of the common law system, renders void any transfer made with an intent to defeat, delay or hinder any creditor. Since the Statute of Elizabeth sets a very low threshold relating to the imputation of fraudulent intent and contains no set period of limitations within which a creditor must bring a fraudulent conveyance claim, no real asset protection can be obtained in a jurisdiction in which the Statute of Elizabeth is in force. In contrast, a jurisdiction that has statutorily repealed the Statute of Elizabeth will typically provide for a short limitation period and will limit the potential to impute, from the circumstances surrounding the transfer, the intent required for finding that the settlor has made a fraudulent conveyance.

It is also important that an offshore asset protection trust be sited in a jurisdiction that denies judicial comity to foreign judgments that conflict with the substantive law of the jurisdiction. In the absence of this facet of asset protection law, a judgment rendered in the trust settlor's domicile on fraudulent conveyance grounds could potentially be filed and then enforced in the offshore jurisdiction without ever implicating the otherwise protective asset protection laws of that offshore jurisdiction.

Finally, aside from the United States, most common law jurisdictions:

- do not allow attorneys to take matters based on a contingency fee; and
- provide that the losing party to a lawsuit must pay all of the victor's expenses, including attorneys' fees.

Combined with an evidentiary standard in some asset protection jurisdictions which requires proof beyond a reasonable doubt on fraudulent conveyance claims, assets held in trust may in the end be unreachable. At a minimum, the process of litigating such a claim in an offshore jurisdiction may prove prohibitively expensive for a creditor when the potential reward is so uncertain. The aggregate of these factors will likely provide the settlor of an offshore asset protection trust with significant leverage against his or her creditors.

2.2   Estate planning

Since the settlor of an offshore asset protection trust will almost always be named as a discretionary beneficiary of the trust (since preservation of the trust estate would generally be as well served onshore if the trust were not, in fact, self-settled), the trust will normally be structured so that its funding is an 'incomplete gift' for US transfer tax purposes. As an incomplete gift, no transfer tax is imposed upon the funding of the trust. A gift to the trust will be deemed complete for transfer tax purposes if the settlor has parted with dominion and control over the gifted property, so as to leave in the settlor no power to change the disposition of the trust property. Conversely, US Treasury regulations provide that a gift will be deemed incomplete if and to the extent that a reserved power gives the settlor the power to name new beneficiaries or to change the interest of the beneficiaries as between themselves (provided, however, that the power is not a fiduciary power limited by a fixed or ascertainable standard).

Pursuant to this guidance, a self-settled spendthrift trust structured so that its funding constitutes an incomplete gift will typically reserve a power of appointment to the settlor. The retained power should, however, be carefully circumscribed so that its existence does not have the inadvertent effect of opening up the trust to claims of the settlor's creditors. Therefore, the power should be limited to a select class of beneficiaries (eg, the settlor's descendants) and to a testamentary exercise, so as to avoid the potential argument that the settlor retained an excessive amount of control over the trust during life. If the trustee has discretion to distribute to other beneficiaries as well as the settlor, then the settlor should also reserve a veto power over such distributions. Additionally, if the settlor is not the sole beneficiary during his or her lifetime, the settlor should retain a veto power over distributions.

In the alternative, if it is unlikely (although not impossible) that the settlor will ever need a distribution from the trust, the offshore asset protection trust would be better structured if its funding were a completed gift, albeit at a current gift tax cost for transfers exceeding the tax-exempt amount, which is currently $10 million (indexed for inflation). As a completed gift, the trust corpus, as well as any post-transfer appreciation thereon, will not be included in the settlor's estate when the settlor dies, notwithstanding that the settlor can, in the interim, receive distributions from the trust within the discretion of the trustees. Aside from the estate planning benefit, however, a trust structured in this manner gains an additional asset protection benefit, since the settlor can then defend against a creditor's fraudulent conveyance attack by demonstrating that the trust was funded for an estate tax benefit rather than to hinder, delay or defraud the settlor's creditors.

Most domestic trusts, however, cannot confer this estate planning benefit, because the US estate tax regime will deem a trust includable in the settlor's estate to the extent that the settlor's creditors can access the trust. This is because the settlor is considered to have retained to himself or herself, at least indirectly, the 'use and enjoyment' of the transferred assets, since his or her creditors can look to the trust corpus in satisfaction of their claims against the settlor. In the same vein, however, if the trust is sited in a jurisdiction where the settlor's creditors cannot reach the trust assets (a jurisdiction that has repealed the self-settled spendthrift trust rule), then the gift will be complete for US federal transfer tax purposes notwithstanding the fact that the trustees have discretion to make distributions to the settlor.

Since many offshore trust jurisdictions have also repealed the common law rule against perpetuities, an additional estate planning benefit can be obtained by creating a perpetual offshore asset protection trust and then allocating a sufficient amount of the settlor's unused generation-skipping transfer tax exemption to the trust. Properly structured, such a 'dynasty' trust will preserve the transferred assets, as well as any accumulations thereto, free from creditors of both the settlor and the settlor's descendants, including all tax authorities. Generally, such a trust will provide that, to the extent possible, the trust corpus will be preserved for the benefit of the beneficiaries rather than being distributed to the beneficiaries; for example, the trust could purchase a home for a beneficiary to live in rent free rather than distribute capital to that beneficiary so that the beneficiary could purchase a home in his or her own name. In this manner, the home would never be subject to the beneficiary's creditors (including an ex-spouse of the beneficiary), and would not be taxed as a part of the beneficiary's estate when the beneficiary ultimately dies.

2.3 Foreign investment

As noted in the previous section regarding estate planning, the question of whether an offshore asset protection trust will be able to withstand creditor attack will depend, in part, on the strength of the creditor's fraudulent conveyance claim, which in turn will depend, in part, on the settlor's intent in creating the trust. In this regard, any evidence the settlor can proffer that demonstrates an intent other than to avoid creditors may prove critical to preserving the trust.

To the extent that the settlor cannot afford (or otherwise does not wish) to structure the offshore asset protection trust as a completed gift, the estate tax benefits of the trust may be insignificant. Therefore, the settlor may have to look to the unique opportunities which an offshore trust provides for foreign investment (which may not be available to US residents) in order to provide the 'good' intent necessary to defend against a fraudulent conveyance claim. The vast majority of offshore investment opportunities are unavailable to onshore entities because those who structure such investments choose not to meet the relatively strict US regulatory requirements relating to public investments. In consequence, certain offshore investments are arguably more attractive than domestic investments, in part because they have the potential to earn higher returns than similar onshore investments that must bear the substantial costs of complying with domestic regulation of public investments.

2.4   Confidentiality

A legitimate offshore asset protection trust need not operate by means of secreting assets. In fact, it is questionable whether any asset protection benefit is obtained by secreting assets, since concealment of assets from creditors is one of the badges of fraud that may be used to impute fraudulent conveyance intent. Notwithstanding the foregoing, however, confidentiality is often an important consideration in choosing to create an offshore asset protection trust or in choosing the particular jurisdiction in which to settle the trust. To the extent that a settlor's legitimate desire for confidentiality can be distinguished from an impermissible effort to secrete assets from creditors, this beneficent aspect of the offshore asset protection trust should not be deemed a badge of fraud.

An offshore asset protection trust provides confidentiality to its beneficiaries primarily by reason of the natural division between the beneficial and legal ownership of the trust structure; since assets are held in the name of the trustees in a fiduciary capacity, rather than in the name of any one or more of the beneficiaries, the beneficial ownership of the assets is hidden from casual observance. In order for the beneficial ownership of the assets to be discovered, generally, a copy of the trust document must be reviewed – and the trust document is not a public document. Onshore, the use of revocable living trusts as a substitute for a will is a common example of how a trust provides confidentiality to the settlor. Additional confidentiality can be obtained if the trust assets are held by a nominee on behalf of the trustees, or in the name of a corporation or other business entity which, in turn, is wholly owned by the trust.

In fact, the trust instrument could legitimately provide that the trustees have no obligation to furnish even the trust beneficiaries with any information relating to the trust's holdings (although it may be deemed to violate public policy to limit the trustees' obligation to provide such information to the settlor). Certainly, however, the trustees are under no obligation to reveal information concerning the trust to any non-governmental third party (eg, the settlor's creditors). In addition, offshore asset protection trusts will likely provide greater confidentiality than onshore trusts, since most offshore centres that wish to attract significant trust business have made it a criminal offence to divulge information relating to the establishment, constitution or business affairs of an offshore trust.

2.5 Avoidance of forced heirship

'Forced heirship' (including a right of election in a surviving spouse) is the legal right of a family member to claim an interest in the estate of a decedent despite the fact that the decedent desired to exclude that family member under his or her dispositive testamentary documents. Although property held in trust is, for most purposes, not considered to be part of the decedent's probate estate, many domestic jurisdictions will deem the trust a testamentary substitute subject to the jurisdiction's forced heirship provisions as though the trust assets were in fact a part of the decedent's probate estate. Although an offshore asset protection trust will also likely be deemed a testamentary substitute in the decedent's domicile, assets held in an offshore trust may avoid a forced heirship if neither the trust nor the property held therein can be claimed to be subject to the jurisdiction of the domestic court. In addition, the law of the offshore jurisdiction will likely override the forced heirship claim in the deceased settlor's domicile.

3. Jurisdictional issues

3.1 Common law versus civil law

The trust concept, rooted in equity, is a product of the common law legal system and is alien to the civil law system, which does not generally recognise the trust concept. For this reason, the vast majority of asset protection trusts are created within a jurisdiction governed by common law principles. Notwithstanding the fact that the trust is not native to the civil law, several civil law jurisdictions have enacted legislation that attempts to append the trust concept to their legal system. Although these civil law jurisdictions will ostensibly recognise an offshore asset protection trust, complications that are likely to arise by reason of a general unfamiliarity with the trust concept inherent in a civil law jurisdiction will likely warrant the use of a similarly protective jurisdiction with a common law tradition.

3.2 Effect of retained interests and powers

For various reasons, including an innate distrust of an unknown offshore trustee, retained interests and powers are often made a prerequisite to the settlor's agreement to settle the trust. Unfortunately, retention of control has a direct inverse relationship to asset protection: the more control is retained (eg, the settlor retaining the assets in his or her own name), the less asset protection is provided. At the other extreme, were the settlor to transfer his or her assets to a non-self-settled trust with an independent corporate fiduciary overseen by an independent corporate protector, he or she would obtain the most asset protection.

Between these two extremes, the settlor's creditors are afforded various arguments with which to attack either the validity of the trust or the settlor himself or herself. In this regard, to the extent that the settlor remains within the jurisdiction of the domestic court, rather than expatriating at the first sign of a creditor attack, the settlor must rely upon the trust's anti-duress clause and his or her own impossibility of performance to protect him or her from the spectre of being held in contempt for failing to repatriate the trust's assets. Since the burden of proving impossibility of performance is upon the settlor, case law has demonstrated that to the extent the settlor has exercised control over the trust until entry of the court's order, the settlor will be hard pressed to prove a current inability to the court in an effort to avoid punishment for contempt.

3.3   Effect of Statute of Elizabeth

The Statute of Elizabeth was enacted in England in 1571 as a compilation of prior English common law on fraudulent conveyance. More than four centuries later, the Statute of Elizabeth still provides the basis for the prohibition on fraudulent conveyances throughout the entire common law system, including the United States. The Statute of Elizabeth provides that transfers made with the intent to hinder, delay or defraud creditors of the transferor are voidable. Although the statute requires that the debtor's actual intent be proved, it was recognised early on that very few debtors would admit to such an intent. The courts have therefore deemed a number of facts as so-called 'badges of fraud' which, when aggregated in sufficient number, will be deemed to provide proof of the debtor's intent. Some badges of fraud so far recognised by the courts are that:

- the transfer was to an insider;
- the debtor retained possession or control of the transferred property;
- the transfer was concealed;
- the debtor had been sued or threatened with suit prior to the transfer;
- the transfer consisted of all or substantially all of the debtor's assets;
- the debtor absconded;
- the debtor removed or concealed assets;
- the value of the consideration received by the debtor was not reasonably equivalent to the assets transferred;
- the debtor was insolvent at the time of the transfer or was thereby rendered insolvent; and

- the transfer occurred at the same time that a substantial debt was incurred.

The Statute of Elizabeth does not distinguish between existing creditors and future creditors, provided that the requisite fraudulent intent exists and can be sufficiently proved.

Similarly, the Uniform Voidable Transactions Act (the successor to the Uniform Fraudulent Transfer Act), which forms the law of fraudulent conveyance in the United States, allows a fraudulent conveyance claim by a future creditor (again, provided that the transfer was made with the actual intent to hinder, delay or defraud, which is likely a more difficult proposition for future creditors to prove). A major difference between pure Statute of Elizabeth jurisdictions and Uniform Voidable Transactions Act jurisdictions exists, however, with regard to the limitation period within which a creditor must bring his or her claim: to wit, no limitation period exists under the Statute of Elizabeth, while Uniform Voidable Transactions Act jurisdictions generally provide for a limitation period of four years or one year from discovery, whichever is greater.

4. Comity issues

Under principles of judicial comity, the courts of one jurisdiction will often give effect to the judicial decisions of another jurisdiction as a matter of deference and mutual respect. The 'full faith and credit' clause of the US Constitution – which provides, in pertinent part, that "Full Faith and Credit shall be given in each State to the public Acts, Records and judicial Proceedings of every other State" – is a clear example of a codification of the principle of judicial comity. Since the principle of judicial comity is effective both domestically and internationally, its potential application by an offshore asset protection jurisdiction in favour of the jurisdiction of the settlor's domicile would vitiate any certainty that asset protection can be achieved through the creation of an asset protection trust in such jurisdiction.

Therefore, it is important that the trust be settled in a jurisdiction that has negated the potential application of judicial comity through a statute providing that foreign judgments are unenforceable to the extent that the foreign judgment conflicts with the substantive law of that jurisdiction. For example, the International Trusts Act 1984 of the Cook Islands provides that no proceedings for or in relation to the enforcement of a foreign judgment against a trust may be brought in a Cook Islands court if the judgment is based upon the application of law inconsistent with that act.

5. Tax laws and exchange controls

In the increasingly competitive market for offshore asset protection business, most (but not all) offshore asset protection jurisdictions exempt trusts settled by non-residents from taxation; those jurisdictions recognise that the local services which such trusts necessarily use provide a much more lucrative benefit to the local economy than does a direct tax on the trusts themselves. Therefore, the offshore asset protection trust should be settled in a no-tax jurisdiction. Similarly, the trust should be settled in a jurisdiction that does not impose exchange controls.

6. Selected offshore jurisdictions with favourable asset protection laws

Many offshore jurisdictions have adopted legislation to obtain a piece of the asset protection trust pie, but considerable differences exist among jurisdictions. The first jurisdiction to enact such legislation was the Cook Islands (in the South Pacific), when it passed the International Trusts Act 1984. With subsequent amendments to the act made in 1985, 1989, 1991, 1995 to 1996 and 1999, the Cook Islands is generally considered to remain the foremost offshore asset protection jurisdiction, notwithstanding that its notoriety in this regard may, in the eyes of some planners, be considered to detract from the asset protection that a Cook Islands asset protection trust can provide.

At least 22 jurisdictions have either statutory or common law that encourages the use of trusts to protect assets from creditors, those jurisdictions being Anguilla, Antigua, the Bahamas, Barbados, Belize, Bermuda, the Cayman Islands, the Cook Islands, Cyprus, Gibraltar, Guernsey, Jersey, Labuan, Liechtenstein, the Marshall Islands, Mauritius, Niue, Nevis, St Vincent and the Grenadines, St Lucia, Seychelles and the Turks and Caicos Islands.

The planner should select the jurisdiction in which to establish the trust by analysing numerous factors, including:

- the jurisdiction's legal system and specific trust law;
- political and economic stability;
- tax laws;
- the existence of exchange controls;
- the availability of professional services;
- the presence of modern telecommunications facilities; and
- the existence or lack of language barriers.

7. Funding the trust

7.1 Revocable and irrevocable trusts

Although a revocable trust with a spendthrift provision can provide asset protection to non-settlor beneficiaries, the settlor's retention of such direct control over the trust will vitiate any asset protection with respect to the settlor's own creditors even if the settlor is not named as a beneficiary of the trust. This is because the right to revoke the trust is tantamount to the retention of a general power of appointment over the trust's assets. In fact, an irrevocable self-settled trust (in the appropriate jurisdiction) provides a greater degree of asset protection since the settlor cannot, by his or her action alone, receive back the trust assets.

7.2 Control issues

Even though it is almost universally recognised that a settlor should not retain control of assets transferred to an offshore asset protection trust either by naming himself or herself as co-trustee of the trust or as trust protector, or by establishing an underlying entity such as a limited partnership in which the settlor is the general partner or a limited liability company in which the settlor is the manager, there are a number of other ways in which a settlor can be made comfortable with the idea of the trust.

In the first instance, it should be understood that the named trustee need not be adverse to the settlor's wishes in order to be deemed 'independent'. Even a corporate fiduciary should prove amenable to the settlor's wishes, provided that the settlor's wishes are not unreasonable or in violation of the trust agreement. Further, a corporate fiduciary will likely be especially receptive to acting in accordance with the settlor's requests where the settlor's counsel has a longstanding relationship with the corporate fiduciary and a track record of making valuable referrals.

Finally, where a trust protector has authority to remove and replace the trustee with or without cause, not only can a more compliant trustee be substituted in the unlikely event of intransigence on the part of the current trustee, but the likelihood of such intransigence is almost certainly reduced. And although the trust protector should also be an independent, offshore corporate body, the same factors that suggest that an offshore corporate trustee will be amenable to the settlor's wishes should also prove relevant in assuaging concerns about the trust protector acting in the desired fashion, according to the settlor's best interests and receptive to the settlor's reasonable requests.

7.3 Asset situs and related issues

Since most offshore asset protection jurisdictions do not require any local investment by the trust, an offshore asset protection trust need not invest its assets in the jurisdiction of the governing law of the trust. Moreover, although an offshore investment might strengthen the settlor's defence against allegations that the trust was funded to avoid creditors, many settlors wish to have the trust retain their original domestic investments following settlement of the trust.

However, since conflict of laws rules are generally considered too esoteric to engender a consistent favourable application by the domestic courts, it is highly advisable to have the trustees position assets outside the jurisdiction of the domestic courts at the earliest possible opportunity and, in all events, prior to any creditor problem. Provided that the trust's assets are located offshore (whether in the jurisdiction of the trust's governing law or an established financial centre such as Switzerland or Luxembourg), a creditor with a domestic judgment will still be faced with significant hurdles before actually being able to levy on any of the trust's assets. In fact, since most offshore asset protection jurisdictions will not recognise foreign judgments, the creditor may be forced to re-litigate its entire case against the trust if the trust's assets are appropriately sited in a timely manner.

8. Protective trust clauses

8.1 Discretionary distributions

A provision in the trust agreement giving the trustees sole discretion to distribute any amount, or all or none, of the trust assets to any one or more of a number of beneficiaries is deemed protective of the trust assets since no one beneficiary (or his or her potential creditors) has any vested interest in them. In the alternative, were the settlor entitled to a set amount of the trust assets, a court could potentially order the distribution of that vested amount to the settlor's creditors. Even if the settlor were not necessarily entitled to a set amount of the trust assets, but was the sole trust beneficiary entitled to them within the discretion of the trustees, a court might mistakenly deem all the trust as assets to be vested in the settlor and command their distribution to the settlor (or his or her creditors).

Therefore, a trust provision allowing the trustees to distribute trust assets, within their discretion, to one or more of the settlor and one or more other persons is most protective. Such a discretionary distribution provision can provide unfettered discretion to the trustees, for example, as follows:

The Trustees may pay to, appropriate or apply for the benefit of one, more or all of the Beneficiaries so much of the net income and/or capital of the Trust Fund as the Trustees in the Trustees' sole and absolute discretion may think fit for any purpose.

Alternatively, such a discretionary distribution provision can limit the trustees' discretion to distribute trust assets.

A provision limiting the trustees' discretion to make distributions might be desirable if the interest of a particular beneficiary (eg, the settlor) is particularly likely to be the subject of a creditor attack, since a distribution in satisfaction of a creditor's claim might be outside of the trustees' discretion and hence less likely to be compelled by a court with jurisdiction over the trustees.

An example of a discretionary distribution provision which limits the trustees' discretion might read as follows:

The Trustees may pay to, appropriate or apply for the benefit of the Settlor, the net income or capital of the Trust Fund only to the extent reasonably necessary or appropriate, as determined in the sole and absolute discretion of the Trustees, for the Settlor's needs for health, support or maintenance in the Settlor's accustomed standard of living, after considering the Settlor's other income or resources.

8.2 Spendthrift provision

Asset protection is not exclusively within the domain of foreign trusts. There are currently 18 states in the United States whose laws provide for the validity of self-settled spendthrift trusts. Even outside those states, however, one of the more common uses of trusts in the United States is for protection from creditors (albeit a protection afforded only to non-settlor beneficiaries). Consider, for example, the spendthrift trust provision included in most trust agreements. Such provisions have been upheld in most jurisdictions, except where the settlor retains excessive control over the trust or benefits from the trust.

A sample spendthrift clause might read as follows:

Subject to the Applicable Law, no Beneficiary shall have any right, power, or authority to sell, assign, pledge, mortgage or in any other manner to encumber, alienate or impair all or any part of his interest in the Trust Fund or otherwise under this Settlement. The beneficial and legal interest in, and the capital and income of, the Trust Fund and every part of it shall be free from interference or control of any creditor of any Beneficiary, and shall not be subject to the claims of any such creditor, including claims for the payment of alimony, nor liable to attachment, execution, bankruptcy, or any other legal or equitable process. No creditor of any Beneficiary shall be entitled to obtain an order for attachment of the Trust Fund or any part thereof either by way of execution, in bankruptcy proceedings or otherwise. No benefit devolving on any Beneficiary under this Settlement shall be subject to seizure, attachment or lien by any creditor.

8.3 Anti-duress provision

If an offshore asset protection is drafted so that the settlor retains certain powers (eg, the power to remove and replace trustees), a creditor may attack the trust by moving to compel the settlor to exercise that retained power so as to discharge the foreign trustee and repatriate trust assets held offshore into the hands of a domestic receiver appointed as trustee. Accordingly, an anti-duress clause should be included in the trust, so as to direct the foreign trustee to ignore any order or instructions given by the settlor if made under duress. The purpose of such a clause is to protect the settlor against acts of coercion by a domestic court since impossibility of performance, if proven, should be an absolute defence to coercive civil contempt.

The following is a sample anti-duress clause:

The Settlor directs that this Settlement be administered consistent with its terms, free of judicial intervention and without order, approval, or other action of any court. To the extent any person is granted the power hereunder to compel any act on the part of the Trustee, or has the authority to render advice to the Trustee, or to otherwise approve or compel any action or exercise any power which affects or will affect this Settlement, the Trustee is directed, to the extent the Trustee would not be subject to personal liability or personal exposure (for example, by being held in contempt of court or other such sanction by a court having jurisdiction over the Trustee): (i) to accept or recognise only instructions or advice, or the effects of any approval or compelled action or the exercise of any power, which are given by or are the result of persons acting of their own free will and not under compulsion of any legal process or like authority; and (ii) to ignore any advice or any directive, order, or like decree, or the results or effects thereof, of any court, administrative body or any tribunal whatsoever, or of past or present Trustees, or of any Protector hereunder, or of any other person, where (a) such has been instigated by directive, order, or like decree of any court, administrative body or other tribunal, or where (b) the person attempting to compel the act, or attempting to exercise the authority to render advice, or otherwise attempting to compel any action or exercise any power which affects or will affect this Settlement, is not a person either appointed or so authorised or the like pursuant to the terms and conditions of this Settlement.

8.4 Change of situs provision

There may come a time when a change of situs (legal location) may be desired to protect assets from the claims of creditors, the threat of political instability or a change in the law. The trust agreement can include various provisions to permit a change of trustees, the situs of the trust or the situs of the trust's assets. These provisions (often referred to as flee clauses) can give the trustee or a trust protector a discretionary power to change the situs by appointing new trustees, removing trust assets to another jurisdiction or amending the trust to comply with the laws of a new jurisdiction.

A sample flee clause follows:

The Trustees may by a signed declaration in writing, at any time or times and from time to time, during the Trust Period, as the Trustees shall deem advisable in the Trustees' discretion for the benefit or security of this Trust Fund or any portion hereof, remove (or decline to remove) all or part of the assets and/or the situs of administration thereof from one jurisdiction to another jurisdiction and/or declare that this Settlement shall from the date of such declaration take effect in accordance with the law of some other state or territory in any part of the world and thereupon the courts of such other jurisdiction shall have the power to effectuate the purposes of this Settlement to such extent. In no event, however, shall the law of some other state or territory be any place under the law of which: (i) substantially all of the powers and provisions herein declared and contained would not be enforceable or capable of being exercised and so taking effect; or (ii) this Settlement would not be irrevocable. From the date of such declaration the law of the state or territory named therein shall be the Applicable Law, but subject always to the power conferred by this paragraph and until any further declaration be made hereunder. So often as any such declaration as aforesaid shall be made, the Trustees shall be at liberty to make such consequential alterations or additions in or to the powers, discretions and provisions of this Settlement as the Trustees may consider necessary or desirable to ensure that the provisions of this Settlement shall (mutatis mutandis) be so valid and effective as they are under the Applicable Law governing this Settlement at the time the power contained herein is exercised. The determination of the Trustees as to any such removal or change in Applicable Law shall be conclusive and binding on all persons interested or claiming to be interested in this Settlement.

8.5 Trust protector provision

The use of a trust protector (alternatively called a trust adviser or a trust enforcer) is common among foreign trusts, although it is only recently becoming commonplace among domestic trusts. This person (or a committee of such persons) generally has the power to replace trustees and, perhaps, to veto certain discretionary actions by the trustees. With the exception of the power to remove and replace trustees, the protector's powers should generally be drafted as negative powers so as to protect against an order compelling the protector to exercise his or her control over the trust in a manner adverse to the beneficiaries' interests.

A sample trust protector provision might provide:

Notwithstanding anything to the contrary herein contained, and in particular anything conferring an absolute or uncontrolled discretion on the Trustees hereof, all and every power and discretion vested in the Trustees by this Settlement and incorporated herein by this reference shall only be exercisable by the Trustees subject always to the power of the Protector to veto any exercise by the Trustees of such power or discretion, and accordingly the Trustees shall be required to provide the Protector with reasonable prior notice before any such powers or discretions may be exercised so as to allow the Protector reasonable advance opportunity within which to veto or refrain from vetoing the exercise of the power or discretion. The Protector's exercise or non-exercise of this veto power shall be communicated in writing to the Trustees and failure to so communicate in a timely fashion provided notice is actually received by the Protector shall be treated by the Trustees as a veto by the Protector of the proposed exercise of the power or discretion; however, if one or more of the Trustees reasonably believe that failure by the Protector to so communicate is due to the Protector being restrained or enjoined from doing so, then such failure to communicate shall be treated by the Trustees and deemed for all purposes hereof as acquiescence by the Protector to the proposed exercise of the power or discretion. It is further provided that, notwithstanding anything to the contrary otherwise herein expressed or implied, no discretion or *power conferred upon the Protector, or upon any other person by this Settlement, or by any rule of law, or arising in consequence of the exercise of any power conferred upon the Protector, or any other person by this Settlement, shall be exercised, and nothing contained herein shall operate, so as to cause the Protector to be successful in ordering any action or causing any result which is not of the Protector's own free will, or which is otherwise the result of the Protector acting under the duress or influence of an outside force.*

9. Selective jurisdictional reviews

9.1 The Bahamas

The Bahamas is a group of islands located in the western Atlantic Ocean just off the east coast of Florida. Although completely independent of the United Kingdom since 1973, the Bahamas remains a member of the British Commonwealth.

The Bahamas has strict bank secrecy laws. Under Bahamian secrecy laws, it is a crime for a banker (or other person) who, in a professional capacity, has acquired information about the identity, assets, liabilities, transactions or accounts of a customer to reveal such information to another person unless such disclosure is required by Bahamian law or unless the customer consents to the disclosure. Moreover, although the Bahamas requires the reporting of large currency transactions in certain situations, it excepts customers who have an existing relationship with a Bahamian bank, as well as transactions by customers who have the recommendation of a reputable party.

Fraudulent dispositions are addressed in the Bahamas under the Fraudulent Disposition Act 1991. Under that statute, dispositions are voidable by the creditor prejudiced by the disposition if the transferor made the disposition with an intent to defraud. Under the statute, an 'intent to defraud' means an intention wilfully to defeat an obligation owed to a creditor. The burden of proof for establishing such intent is on the creditor and the statute of limitations is two years from the date of the applicable disposition.

The Trusts (Choice of Governing Law) Act 1989 (as amended in 1996) provides, in pertinent part, that if Bahamian law is designated as the trust's governing law, such designation will be binding and effective regardless of any other circumstances. The Trust (Choice of Governing Law) Act 1989 gives protection to Bahamian trusts and their settlors in civil law countries against forced inheritance claims. The act makes Bahamian law the proper law of a trust if the deed so declares, and makes the trust immune to foreign judgments. The Trustee Act (1998) provides that a trust shall not be invalidated by the settlor's having retained any powers to revoke the trust, power to appoint the property, power to remove the trustees, protectors or beneficiaries, right to be appointed protector or retain a beneficial interest. The Perpetuities (Amendment) Act

(2004) increased the period for trusts from 80 years to 150 years. Pursuant to general principles of trust law, a settlor may name himself or herself as a discretionary beneficiary of his or her trust and the settlement will be protected against the settlor's creditors provided that it does not violate the provisions of the Fraudulent Disposition Act 1991.

Finally, the Bahamas is essentially a no-tax jurisdiction. It has no personal income tax, corporate income tax, value added tax, capital gains tax, withholding tax, gift tax, estate tax or employment tax, and does not tax offshore trusts in any manner.

9.2   Bermuda

Bermuda is a group of islands in the Atlantic Ocean approximately 1,000 kilometres (km) east of North Carolina. It is an English-speaking dependent territory of the United Kingdom and has a common law legal system. Strict privacy laws prevail with regard to Bermuda trusts. Significantly, Bermuda trusts need not be registered or filed with any public agency. The Statute of Elizabeth does not apply in Bermuda. However, certain types of transfer are likely to be recognised as fraudulent in Bermuda and therefore may defeat a transfer of assets to a trust. These transfers generally equate to recognised badges of fraud – for instance, the following are all recognised badges of fraud under Bermuda law:

- the transfer of most of the settlor's assets;
- the settlor's continued possession of the assets or continued enjoyment of their use or income;
- the settlor's secrecy or haste in disposing of the assets;
- the settlor's disposition of assets while litigation is pending; and
- the settlor retaining an advantage under the trust.

In addition, there must be a two-year period after the trust's creation, or after any transfers are made to the trust, during which the settlor has no knowledge or reasonable notice of any creditor or action. If there is a problem during that two-year period, the creditor has six years to bring an action to declare a transfer to a trust void or fraudulent. Bermuda law recognises the settlor's choice of governing law expressed in a trust, as well as the trust's ability to change its governing law to or from that of Bermuda. Questions of capacity and the validity of the trust are therefore determined under the law of Bermuda. Bermuda law allows full delegation of powers of investment and management of the trust fund. A Bermuda trust may accumulate income and the trust term can extend to 100 years. The trust laws in Bermuda protect a trust from application of the laws of another jurisdiction with respect to marital rights, forced heirship claims and creditors' rights. Similarly, subject to the Judgments (Reciprocal Enforcement) Act 1958, whereby judgments rendered in the United

Kingdom and certain other Commonwealth nations may be enforced in Bermuda, Bermuda courts generally do not recognise foreign court awards. A Bermuda trust may be validly self-settled.

9.3 Cayman Islands

The Cayman Islands is located in the western Caribbean Sea, approximately 750 km south of Miami, Florida. The Cayman Islands is an English-speaking dependent territory of the United Kingdom and has a common law legal system strongly influenced by English case law. The Cayman Islands has strict secrecy laws which provide for substantial penalties for revealing confidential information. In general, a foreign government cannot obtain assistance from the Cayman Islands in pursuing criminal matters unless the offence is also an offence under Cayman Islands law. Notwithstanding the foregoing, however, the United States and the Cayman Islands entered into a Mutual Legal Assistance Treaty in 1988 under which the Cayman Islands promised to provide US authorities with information in investigations involving either drugs or certain white-collar crimes, including bank fraud. However, the person who is required to give evidence or make a disclosure must still receive permission for such action from the Cayman Islands Grand Court.

As it relates to fraudulent transfers, Cayman Islands law provides that a disposition is voidable by a creditor prejudiced by the disposition only if the disposition was made with an intent to defraud. An 'intent to defraud' is defined as an intention of the transferor wilfully to defeat an existing obligation owed to a creditor. The burden of proof for establishing an intent to defraud is on the creditor. If a fraudulent disposition is proved, it will set aside the disposition only to the extent necessary to satisfy the claim of the creditor bringing the action. Finally, the statute of limitations on proving a fraudulent disposition is six years from the date of the disposition. The trust law of the Cayman Islands comprises the Trusts Law (2011 Revision), the Trusts (Foreign Element) Law 1987 and the Fraudulent Dispositions Law (1996 Revision).

As it relates to asset protection, Cayman Islands trust law provides that the Cayman Islands will use the choice of governing law provision which the settlor sets forth in the trust instrument so that all questions regarding the trust will be determined by the laws of the Cayman Islands (unless and until amended under the trust instrument). Moreover, a Cayman Islands trust may not be set aside because the laws of a foreign jurisdiction prohibit or do not recognise the trust concept, or because the trust defeats certain rights conferred by foreign law. In addition, there is no limitation on the accumulation of income within the trust and no restriction on permissible investments by trustees. A settlor may name himself or herself as a discretionary beneficiary of the trust and the settlement will be protected against the settlor's creditors (except in the case of a bankruptcy), provided that the settlement does not violate the Fraudulent

Dispositions Law (1996 Revision). The Cayman Islands imposes no taxes whatsoever.

9.4 Cook Islands

The Cook Islands, located in the Pacific Ocean east of New Zealand and south of Hawaii, is a self-governing democracy with a parliamentary system of government and a common law legal system. The Cook Islands' closest link is with New Zealand, which retains responsibility for defence and foreign affairs since the islands became self-governing in 1965. English is the official language.

The Cook Islands enacted the world's first comprehensive asset protection trust legislation with the International Trusts Act 1984. The legislation addresses 'international trusts' and the effect thereon of fraudulent dispositions and bankruptcy. With respect to fraudulent dispositions, a creditor seeking to set aside a disposition must prove beyond reasonable doubt that the disposition was made with an intent to defraud that particular creditor, and that the transferor was rendered insolvent by the transfer. As a bright-line rule, if the fair market value of the settlor's property after the transfer to the trust exceeds the value of the creditor's claim at the time of the transfer, an intent to defraud necessarily cannot be found. Even if the creditor meets the heavy burden necessary to prove a fraudulent disposition, the transfer is not void or voidable; instead, the transferor must pay the creditor's claim from property which would have been subject to its claim but for the transfer.

Further, the statute expressly states that an international trust will not be deemed void by virtue of the settlor's bankruptcy. Another section of the legislation sets out certain circumstances which will not be deemed badges of fraud: fraudulent intent cannot be imputed from a transfer to an international trust within two years of the accrual of a creditor's cause of action or the retention of powers or benefits by the settlor, or the designation of the settlor as a beneficiary, trustee or protector. With regard to fraudulent conveyance claims, if a creditor's cause of action accrues more than two years before a transfer to an international trust, the transfer will not be deemed to be fraudulent. If a creditor's cause of action accrues less than two years before a transfer to a trust, the creditor must bring an action within one year of the date on which the transfer to an international trust occurs, unless an action has been commenced in a court of competent jurisdiction before the expiry of one year from the date of transfer.

Further, if the transfer (whether initial or subsequent) to an international trust occurs before a creditor's cause of action accrues, such a disposition will not be fraudulent as to that creditor. A 'cause of action' is defined as the first cause of action capable of assertion against a settlor. Finally, as regards redomiciled trusts, the limitation period commences at the time of original transfer, even though the transfer was to an offshore centre other than the Cook

Islands. An international trust cannot be declared void or be affected in any way because the settlor:

- has the power to revoke or amend the trust, to dispose of trust property or to remove or appoint a trustee or protector;
- retains, possesses or acquires any benefit, interest or property from the trust; or
- is a beneficiary, trustee or protector.

The rule against perpetuities has also been repealed in the Cook Islands. Other provisions of trust legislation in the Cook Islands:

- make selection of Cook Islands law binding and conclusive;
- ensure that an international trust is not subject to forced heirship laws of other countries; and
- mandate the non-recognition of a foreign judgment against an international trust, its settlor, trustee and protector.

The Cook Islands is a no-tax jurisdiction.

9.5   Gibraltar

Gibraltar is a British territory located at the southern tip of the Iberian Peninsula. Gibraltar generally follows the English common law system. The Trusts (Recognition) Ordinance 1989 incorporates the 1984 Hague Convention on the Law Applicable to Trusts and their Recognition, which expressly provides that a trust shall be governed by the law chosen by the settlor. In conjunction with its trust law, Gibraltar's Bankruptcy Ordinance provides that a creditor cannot reach the assets of a trust properly registered in Gibraltar (as an asset protection trust is required to do, in any event) by claiming that the settlement was a fraudulent conveyance if, at the date of settlement of the trust, the settlor:

- was solvent;
- did not render himself or herself insolvent by reason of the transfer of property to the trust; and
- was not then subject to any outstanding litigation.

However, Gibraltar does not provide for the non-recognition of foreign judgments; nor does it provide for a statute of limitations on fraudulent conveyance claims. It should also be noted that the registration requirement of an asset protection trust in Gibraltar is required, upon criminal offence, to be kept confidential.

Offshore trusts established in Gibraltar are not subject to Gibraltar income tax, notwithstanding the fact that the trustees are resident in Gibraltar, provided that the trust has no Gibraltar residents as beneficiaries.

9.6 Jersey

Jersey is the largest of the Channel Islands, a group of islands located in the English Channel. Jersey, together with the other Channel Islands, is a possession of the British Crown and is self-governing for all internal matters, including all tax matters. Jersey is a common law jurisdiction with a number of civil law aspects by dint of historical ties to France (in particular, relating to inheritance and family rights).

As a partially civil law jurisdiction, Jersey had no trust law until 1984 when it enacted the Trusts Law, codifying English common law principles relating to trusts. The Trusts Law specifically allows the settlor to be a beneficiary of the trust. The 2006 amendments to the Trusts Law protect Jersey trusts from foreign laws being applied to issues of forced heirship and creation of marital rights. Also, the amendments allow Jersey trusts of unlimited duration. Jersey does not, however, have an asset protection trust law, but instead provides that the law of another jurisdiction (which does have an asset protection trust law) may be validly designated as controlling.

Trust information is kept confidential by Jersey law which provides that, in the absence of a court order, no one is entitled to information about the trust if he or she does not have an interest in the trust. A trust established by a non-resident of Jersey for the benefit of a non-resident of Jersey is taxed only on local source income (excluding local bank deposits and excluding capital gains).

9.7 United States

Of the 50 states comprising the United States, 18 have enacted legislation providing spendthrift protections to a settlor-beneficiary of a discretionary trust. Those states are Alaska, Connecticut, Delaware, Hawaii, Indiana, Michigan, Mississippi, Missouri, Nevada, New Hampshire, Ohio, Rhode Island, South Dakota, Tennessee, Utah, Virginia, West Virginia and Wyoming. A 19th state, Oklahoma, permits the creation of a protective revocable trust for the benefit of the settlor's spouse and dependants worth up to $1 million.

In all cases, however, 'foreign' trusts will likely offer more substantive barriers to creditors than domestic trusts, at least where the trust fund is invested outside the United States, since a US judgment should not be enforceable offshore, whereas the full faith and credit clause of the US Constitution may result in a court's enforcement of a sister state's judgment against a settlor's US situs trust. Nevertheless, domestic trusts remain relevant, in particular where illiquid US assets exist. A few of the more well-known asset protection states are described briefly below.

(a) Alaska

The Alaska Trust Act (1997) modified Alaska's previously undistinguished body of trust law in an effort generally touted as making Alaska an onshore alternative to offshore asset protection trusts. In contrast to the general state of domestic spendthrift trust law at the time the Alaska statute was enacted (as exemplified by the Restatement (Second) of Trust Section 156(2)), Alaska law permitted a settlor to create a trust for his or her own benefit which would be protected from the settlor's future creditors. As subsequently amended, the law provides for protection as long as:

- the settlor has not retained the right to revoke or terminate the trust;
- the settlor has not been in default by 30 days or more in making a child support payment;
- the settlor's ability to receive distributions from the trust is within the discretion of the trustees rather than mandatory. However, the trustee may permit a beneficiary the use of property and the settlor may retain an annuity or unitrust interest in a charitable remainder trust. The settlor may also retain the right to receive a percentage of the trust each year not to exceed the unitrust amount provided under Internal Revenue Code Section 643(b); and
- the transfer of property to the trust was not intended to hinder, delay or defraud creditors (which would be a 'fraudulent conveyance').

Moreover, under Alaska law, a creditor of the settlor existing at the time the trust is created must bring suit on a fraudulent conveyance claim within the later of four years from the transfer or one year after the transfer is, or reasonably could have been, discovered. A creditor arising after the transfer to the trust must bring suit within four years of the transfer.

Furthermore, the law requires that:

- at least one trustee be a trust company or bank in Alaska or an individual resident of Alaska;
- some of the trust assets be deposited with a bank in Alaska;
- the Alaska trustee's duties include the obligation to maintain the trust's records and to prepare or arrange for the preparation of the trust's income tax returns (although neither of these requirements must be exclusive to the Alaska trustee); and
- part or all of the trust administration occur in Alaska.

Alaska law prohibits a challenge to a trust on the grounds that it defeats a claim against the settlor relating to a personal, business or marital relationship. Alaska law also prohibits claims against trustees and others involved in the preparation or funding of the trust for conspiring to commit a fraudulent conveyance, aiding or abetting a fraudulent conveyance or participating in a trust transaction.

(b)   *Delaware*

The avowed purpose of the Delaware self-settled trust law is to allow settlors to reduce estate tax by excluding creditors' claims against self-settled trusts. Under the Delaware law, a trust must be irrevocable and have a trustee resident in Delaware. It can include one or more of the following provisions, whereby the settlor:

- may retain the power to veto distributions;
- may retain a special power of appointment and a lifetime limited power of appointment;
- may receive income, principal or both in the sole discretion of a trustee who is neither the settlor nor a related or subordinate party;
- may retain the power to remove and replace trustees and advisers, and to appoint additional trustees and advisers; and
- may even retain:
  - current income distributions;
  - payments from a charitable remainder trust;
  - annual payments of up to 5% of the initial value of the trust or of its value as determined from time to time;
  - principal distributions under an ascertainable standard (eg health, maintenance, education or support);
  - the right to use a residence held in a qualified personal residence trust; and
  - the right to direct the trustee to pay the income tax of the trust.

Provided that the transfer of property to the trust was not intended to hinder, delay or defraud creditors, no action to enforce a judgment can be brought for attachment against such transfer. Under Delaware law, a creditor existing at the time a transfer to a trust is made must commence an action to enforce a judgment within the later of four years or one year after the transfer was, or could reasonably have been, discovered by the creditor. If the creditor's claim arose after the transfer, the action must be brought within four years of the transfer. Moreover, a trust that is redomiciled to Delaware will tack on the time during which it was located elsewhere for purposes of the statute of limitations regarding creditor claims.

Finally, addressing the full faith and credit clause problem, the trustee's authority will be immediately terminated upon the occurrence of another state court's attempt to exercise jurisdiction over a trustee if that other state's court declines to apply Delaware law with respect to the validity, construction or administration of the trust. If the trust instrument does not provide for a successor trustee, the Delaware Court of Chancery will appoint a successor trustee (and presumably one who would be subject to the Delaware court's jurisdiction only).

(c) *Nevada*

Similar to the Alaska and Delaware laws, Nevada law provides that a person may create a spendthrift trust for his or her own benefit (or for the benefit of the settlor and another), provided that the writing establishing the trust:

- is irrevocable;
- does not mandate the distribution of income or principal to the settlor; and
- was not intended to hinder, delay or defraud known creditors.

The settlor of a spendthrift trust may:

- retain the power to veto distributions;
- hold a testamentary special power of appointment or similar power;
- serve as a co-trustee of the trust;
- direct investments;
- remove and replace a trustee;
- retain an interest in a charitable remainder trust, a grantor-retained annuity trust or grantor-retained unitrust, and a qualified personal residence trust; and
- use real or personal property owned by the trust.

Unlike in Alaska and Delaware, however, Nevada law provides for a substantially shorter period within which a creditor must commence a fraudulent transfer claim against the trust. If the creditor existed at the time the transfer to the trust was made, the creditor must commence an action within two years of the transfer or within six months of the date on which it discovered or reasonably should have discovered the transfer; if, however, the creditor's claim arose after the transfer to the trust, the action must be brought within two years of the transfer to the trust.

In order to prevail on a fraudulent transfer claim against the trust, the creditor must prove "by clear and convincing evidence" that the transfer of property to the trust was fraudulent or "violates a legal obligation owed to the creditor under a contract or a valid court order that is legally enforceable by that creditor". Proof by one creditor that the transfer of a specific asset was fraudulent or wrongful does not constitute proof as to any other creditor or any other asset.

(d) *New Hampshire*

Under New Hampshire's Qualified Dispositions in Trust Act, a self-settled trust must:

- appoint at least one qualified trustee (a New Hampshire resident other than the settlor or a bank or trust company with a place of business in New Hampshire);

- expressly incorporate New Hampshire law as the governing law of the trust;
- be irrevocable; and
- contain a spendthrift clause.

The settlor may serve as a trust adviser, although the settlor's authority in that role will be limited to vetoing distributions and consenting to trustee action in investing trust assets. Regardless of whether the settlor chooses to act as trust adviser, the settlor may retain:

- the power to veto distributions;
- the power to replace a trustee or trust adviser;
- a special power of appointment and a limited lifetime power of appointment;
- the right to receive distributions of income and principal;
- the right to receive payments from the trust for income taxes attributable thereto; and
- an interest in a qualified personal residence trust or annuity.

New Hampshire's statute extends to trusts formed in other states (including states that do not provide for self-settled asset protection trusts) if they are transferred to New Hampshire. These trusts need not be governed by New Hampshire law, but they must meet all other requirements of the Qualified Dispositions in Trust Act. A qualified disposition is deemed to have been made at the time of the original transfer into the trust rather than the subsequent transfer to New Hampshire.

Creditor claims against such self-settled trusts are only allowed for:

- tort claims for injury suffered before the date of the qualified disposition:
- claims for support or alimony by the settlor's spouse or former spouse who was married to the transferor at or before the date of the qualified disposition;
- claims for child support; and
- fraudulent transfers under the Uniform Fraudulent Transfer Act.

(e)   *South Dakota*

The Act to Authorize Qualified Dispositions, effective for trusts settled on or after 1 July 2005, permits self-settled spendthrift trusts to be created under the law of South Dakota. In order to qualify, the trust must meet the following requirements:

- The governing law must be that of South Dakota;
- The trust must be irrevocable; and
- The trust must prohibit voluntary or involuntary assignment.

In addition to the receipt of income, principal or both, in the discretion of a trustee who is neither the settlor nor a related or subordinated party within the meaning of Section 672(c) of the US Internal Revenue Code, the settlor may also retain the following rights and powers:

- the power to veto trust distributions;
- a limited testamentary power of appointment;
- the right to receive distribution of current income;
- the right to receive payments under a charitable remainder trust;
- the right to receive annual payments of up to 5% of the initial value of the trust, or of its value as determined from time to time;
- the right to receive principal distributions under an ascertainable standard (eg, health, maintenance, education or support);
- the power to remove and appoint trustees; and
- the right to the use of a residence in a qualified personal residence trust.

The trustee must be either an individual resident of the state of South Dakota or a South Dakota bank or trust company. In either case the trustee is required to:

- maintain or arrange for custody of some or all of the property in the state of South Dakota;
- maintain records on an exclusive or non-exclusive basis;
- prepare or arrange for the preparation of the trust's tax returns; and
- otherwise materially participate in the administration of the trust.

The act also permits the appointment of a non-resident trust adviser, including a trust protector, who may hold one or more trust powers. The settlor may even be designated as the trust adviser.

Transfers are subject to the provisions of South Dakota's version of the Uniform Fraudulent Transfer Act. Moreover, certain additional creditors can avoid qualified dispositions even though these may not be a fraudulent transfer. They are:

- any person to whom the settlor is indebted on account of an agreement or court order for support, alimony or property distribution in favour of a spouse, former spouse or children; and
- any person who suffers death, personal injury or property damage on or before the qualified disposition, which was caused by the transferor or another person for whom the transferor is liable.

(f) Wyoming

Wyoming's Uniform Trust Code provides for the creation of a qualified spendthrift trust if:

- the trust instrument expressly states that it is a qualified spendthrift trust under Wyoming law;

- the trust instrument expressly incorporates Wyoming law to govern the validity, construction and administration of the trust;
- the trust contains a spendthrift provision; and
- the trust is irrevocable.

The trust must also have at least one Wyoming qualified trustee (a Wyoming resident or regulated financial institution) and transfers to the trust must not violate the Wyoming Uniform Fraudulent Transfers Act. Once these requirements have been satisfied, creditor protection is immediate.

(g)   *Section 548(e) of the US Bankruptcy Code*
Under Section 548(e) of the US Bankruptcy Code, the power of the trustee of the bankruptcy estate to avoid transfers is extended to encompass transfers made in the 10 years before the date of filing of the bankruptcy petition if the debtor made the fraudulent transfer to a 'self-settled trust or similar device'.

10.   Legal challenges to asset protection trusts

Although a self-settled spendthrift trust that is valid under the law designated by the settlor as governing the trust should be held similarly valid by all courts, wherever situate, a self-settled spendthrift trust may yet be tested against concepts of fairness and good faith if the settlor is ultimately forced to obtain judicial sanction of the trust in a jurisdiction that does not, under its own law, recognise self-settled spendthrift trust protections as valid.

Although the heavy costs of litigation, when weighed against the likelihood of a successful recovery against assets held in an offshore asset protection trust, have severely limited the number of cases that have been decided in this area, a few reported decisions do exist which may provide insight into how the courts, both in the United States and internationally, are likely to view the offshore asset protection trust.

More recently, a few decisions involving domestic asset protection trusts have similarly applied public policy considerations to invalidate the trusts. *In re Mortensen (Battley v Mortensen)*[1] was the first reported case to deal with a domestic asset protection trust. In that case, Mortensen, a resident of Alaska, without the aid of counsel, drafted a trust document in 2005 called the "Mortensen Seldovia Trust (An Alaska Asset Preservation Trust)" intending for the trust to qualify as an asset protection trust under Alaska law. Following his creation and funding of the trust, Mortensen's financial condition deteriorated, his income became sporadic and he ultimately filed for bankruptcy. Although the bankruptcy court concluded that Mortensen was not insolvent when he established and funded the trust, due to the specific circumstances of the case it

---

1   2011 WL 5025249 (Bankr D Alaska).

held that his funding of the trust nevertheless fell under Section 548(e) of the Bankruptcy Code as a fraudulent transfer to a self-settled trust made in the 10 years prior to his bankruptcy filing.

In re Huber[2] involved the creation of an Alaska asset protection trust by a Washington developer at a time when he "was or had to be aware of the 'gathering storm clouds'", including "the threat of a collapsing housing market", and when his prospects for repayment of several substantial loans were "fragile at best". The court in *Huber* held the trust invalid under a conflict of laws analysis which, if correct, would invalidate every self-settled spendthrift trust created by a Washington resident, irrespective of circumstances. Whether this analysis was correct, however, is subject to dispute. It is unfortunate that the first case to address the conflict of laws issue with regard to a domestic asset protection trust involved fraudulent transfers that seemingly influenced the court's decision on the conflict of laws issue.

The court in *Huber* cited Section 270 of the Restatement (Second) of Conflict of Laws (1971), which speaks to the validity of an *inter vivos* trust in movables. After finding that the trust had its most significant relationship with Washington, partially based on the debtor's residence, the court held without real analysis that Washington had a strong public policy against asset protection trusts. Indeed, it is not clear why the court even felt compelled to address the conflict of laws issue, since the same result was obtainable by reference to the fact that the trust's funding was a fraudulent transfer. Thus, the question left after *Huber* is whether another court would rule similarly on the conflict of laws question absent the fact of the fraudulent transfer.

Ultimately, however, whether a domestic court gives credence to the application of offshore trust law is unlikely to affect the asset protection which such trust provides. Provided that the trust's assets are located offshore (whether in the jurisdiction of the trust's governing law or in an established offshore financial centre such as Switzerland), a creditor with a domestic judgment will still be faced with significant hurdles before actually being able to levy on any of the assets of an offshore asset protection trust. For example, notwithstanding the bankruptcy court having denied the respective debtors their desired discharge in bankruptcy, reliable sources have reported that the creditors in *Brooks*[3] settled for approximately $0.50 on the dollar and that the creditor in *In re Portnoy*[4] settled for approximately $0.20 on the dollar. Contrast, however, *Nastro v D'Onofrio*,[5] in which the US district court, in order to maintain jurisdiction over at least some of the assets of a foreign asset protection trust pending a decision on the merits, entered a preliminary injunction against a US

---

2   493 BR 798 (Bankr WD Wash 2013).
3   1998 Bankr lexis 60 (DCT, 1998).
4   201 BR 685 (SDNY 1996).
5   263 F Supp 2d 446.

corporation with respect to stock in the corporation that was held in the name of the trust. In any event, these reported cases obviously represent a tiny fraction of all offshore asset protection trust controversies; based on the author's experience, most controversies are never reported because a favourable settlement is entered into prior to judgment.

The fact that the determination by the courts of the settlor's domicile may ultimately not impinge upon the asset protection afforded by an offshore trust does not mean, however, that the trust should not be structured with an eye towards obtaining a favourable domestic judicial decision should the need arise. In this regard, the reported cases provide some important guidance. First, the trust should be as separate as possible from its settlor. This requires an independent, if friendly, trustee who has control of the trust's assets exclusive of the settlor. Additionally, it would be advisable to give the trustee discretion to distribute trust assets to persons in addition to the settlor (called a 'sprinkling power'), such as the settlor's spouse and descendants. Finally, the circumstances surrounding the creation or funding of the trust must be as distant as possible from a potential creditor's claim. This means that the trust should be set up as early as possible for the purpose of guarding against future, rather than current, creditors.

11. Ethical considerations with asset protection planning

There is little force behind the argument that asset protection planning is in itself unethical. In this regard, there are at least two US estate bar association advisory opinions that provide that asset protection planning, in the appropriate circumstances, is ethical. In fact, it can be argued with some merit that an attorney or other professional adviser who fails to counsel his or her clients as to opportunities to structure their planning in a manner which maximises asset protection has committed malpractice.

Whether asset protection planning in any particular situation is an ethical pursuit depends primarily upon the application of local fraudulent conveyance law. For example, the American Bar Association's Model Rules of Professional Conduct provide that an attorney "shall not counsel a client to engage, or assist a client, in conduct that the lawyer knows or reasonably should know... is fraudulent". Therefore, if an offshore asset protection trust is established while litigation is pending, it may result in disciplinary claims against the attorneys who assisted in the establishment of the trust, since the trust's funding will likely be seen locally as a fraudulent conveyance. The best way for an adviser to avoid violating applicable disciplinary rules and engaging in unethical behaviour in the practice of asset protection planning is to perform a due diligence check on each client who requests such planning. If an appropriate due diligence check is made prior to any planning, the adviser should be insulated from liability even if the client's transfer does, in fact, constitute a fraudulent conveyance, since the scienter (knowledge) requirement necessarily cannot be met.

12. Conclusion

The concept of 'hiding' assets is no longer a viable one. The ever-expanding adoption of laws enabling settlors to shield their assets from future creditors demonstrates the increased level of interest among both professional advisers and their clients. And while the developed countries are pursuing greater tax transparency with the US Foreign Account Tax Compliance Act and common reporting standards, clients will still have available to them myriad options to protect their wealth from government expropriation, divorce or other forms of risk. As noted above, clients have many jurisdictions to choose from in settling a trust. But given the negative perceptions of such trusts by US courts (even where justly so given the facts), utilising an offshore jurisdiction will still provide the utmost protection in most cases.

The author gratefully acknowledges Daniel S Rubin, a partner at Moses & Singer LLP, for his assistance in preparing this chapter.

International trust litigation: jurisdiction and enforcement

David Faust
Gallet Dreyer & Berkey LLP

This chapter will explore choices of jurisdiction, forum and law, as well as issues of enforcement in international trust litigation. As used in this chapter:

- 'international trust' means a trust in which one or more of the trustee(s), protector(s), grantor(s) or beneficiary(ies) ('affected parties') are from different countries or where the purported jurisdiction of formation or the designated governing law is different from the residence or domicile of one or more of the affected parties;
- 'international trust litigation' means a lawsuit involving an international trust in which either:
  - one or more of the parties are residents or domiciliaries of different countries; or
  - one or more of the parties are residents or domiciliaries of countries other than the forum in which the suit is pending and/or the country the law of which governs the case;
- 'jurisdiction', when used in the context of choice of jurisdiction, means the country the laws of which should apply to disputes; and
- 'forum' means the tribunal with authority to resolve disputes, such as a a court or arbitrator(s).

1.   General observations

As trusts have become more common, so has trust litigation. As international trusts have become more common, so has international trust litigation. Trust litigation, domestic or international, can be about contesting the purpose of the trust or about how investments and/or distributions were made, or not made – that is, about trust administration. This chapter will explore the choice of jurisdiction in which to form a trust, choice of forum and governing law provisions, and the increasing use of equity jurisdiction by judges to frustrate law, jurisdiction and forum shopping.

The first question to be addressed by counsel and client in considering the creation of any trust is: what is the objective? Trusts are formed for a wide variety of purposes, including general asset protection, asset protection specifically intended to protect assets in the event of marital discord, general estate planning, avoidance of forced heirship and minimisation of various taxes. The next question is whether a trust is the best way to accomplish the relevant objective. If a trust seems to be the most appropriate vehicle by which to achieve the objective, the next question is: where? For some purposes, the home jurisdiction of the settlor or the intended beneficiary may be most appropriate – a subject for another day. For the specific objectives initially noted above, another jurisdiction may well be more appropriate. This is most obviously the case where the main, or even only, purpose of the trust is to avoid or circumvent the laws of the settlor's domicile or residence or the location of his or her assets. If, for example, the objective is to protect assets from prospective creditors while retaining economic benefits from such assets, or to avoid the rules of forced heirship – limits on the free disposition of property which require that at least minimal amounts or percentages of an estate go to designated persons – in the settlor's domicile or residence, then the drafter of a trust must be sure that the chosen jurisdiction will respect trust provisions which are inconsistent with the laws of the settlor's nationality, domicile or residence even if the settlor is not a national, domiciliary or resident of the chosen jurisdiction. A more difficult question is whether those choices will be respected elsewhere.

Common to all litigation are threshold issues of jurisdiction and governing law. Just as the outcome of battles by armies or navies are dictated, and often decided, by the terrain or place of the fight, so too with litigation. Effective designations of jurisdictions for the resolution of disputes, the forum (courts or mediation/arbitration) and choice of governing law can be dispositive of the outcome of a dispute.

Trusts are contractual arrangements between one or more settlors and one or more trustees. Even testamentary trusts require the trustee to accept appointment and the terms of the trust as set forth in a will. Ordinarily, parties to a contract can avoid litigation by agreeing to have disputes settled by mediation or arbitration under a designated set of laws. The key here is that, with few exceptions, such methods of alternative dispute resolutions require the express written consent of the parties.[1] In New York, the Court of Appeals has held that because a party who agrees to arbitrate waives many of his or her normal rights under the procedural and substantive laws of the state, a waiver

---

1   See, for example, Section 2 of the Federal Arbitration Act, 9 USC: "A written provision in any... contract...or an agreement in writing to submit to arbitration...shall be valid, irreversible and enforceable, save upon such grounds as exist at law or in equity for the revocation of any contract;" New York Civil Practice Law and Rules § 7501: "A written agreement to submit any controversy...to arbitration is enforceable...and confers jurisdiction on the courts of the state to enforce it and to enter judgment on an award;" London Court of International Arbitration, Article 1, § 1.1(b): "Any party wishing to commence an arbitration under these Rules...shall send to the Registrar of the LCIA Court...a written request for arbitration... containing or accompanied by...a copy of the written arbitration clause or separate written arbitration agreement invoked by the Claimant...together with a copy of the contractual documentation in which the arbitration clause is contained or in respect of which the arbitration arises".

of such rights will not be inferred "on the basis of anything less than a clear indication of intent".[2]

Trust litigation often involves litigants who are not parties to the creation of the trust. The most obvious examples of such non-party litigants are creditors of the settlor or of a beneficiary (private or governmental), beneficiaries themselves and persons who claim rights of forced heirship which are being denied or frustrated by the trust. If a trust agreement or deed contains an arbitration provision, it is not likely to be enforced against such claimants who object to arbitration, mediation or other alternative dispute resolution methods, since they did not agree to such methods. An exception is court-ordered mediation (or arbitration), which can be ordered notwithstanding the lack of prior agreement. For example, New York has adopted regulations (22 NY Code of Rules and Regulations, Part 28) requiring mandatory but non-binding mediation to resolve small claims involving monetary disputes below specified amounts, as well as mandatory binding arbitration of fee disputes between attorneys and their clients in most civil matters at the client's election pursuant to 22 NYCRR, Part 137.

Since trust creditors and beneficiaries are not party to the creation of the trust and did not agree to any of its terms, much less to jurisdiction, choice of law or choice of forum, their challenges to jurisdiction and/or choice of law should have greater weight than such challenges by a party to the trust deed or agreement.[3]

Courts are generally reluctant to take a case in which an essential party is not within its jurisdiction or where the subject matter has no meaningful relation to the jurisdiction. This not only is a basic issue of both personal and subject-matter jurisdiction, but also a matter of judicial economy, as well as familiarity or lack thereof with foreign laws and practice. Courts in places such as Jersey (Channel Islands), with a robust trust caseload and a high degree of international trust law experience, are more likely to be willing to hear such a case than a state court in the United States without such background and experience. Some jurisdictions, such as New York, are actively seeking to establish themselves as jurisdictions for the settlement of international disputes, generating business for their legal communities. The New York International Arbitration Center is but one example of this effort.

In choosing a jurisdiction, counsel should consider practical as well as strictly legal issues. For example, if English language documents are to be the subject of a dispute heard in a French-speaking country, even though

---

2   *Marlene Industries Corp v Carnac Textiles, Inc*, 45 NY 2d 327, 334 (1978). But see *Aceros Prefabricados, SA v TradeArbed, Inc*, 282 F 3d 92, 99-100 (2d Cir NY 2002) (in 'battle of the forms' case involving interstate commerce, New York rule imposing enhanced burden of proof on issue of party's intent to arbitrate is pre-empted by the Federal Arbitration Act).

3   See discussion of *Crociani v Crociani, infra*.

documents may be translated into the language of the forum, will nuances be lost? Will the judge, arbitrators or their staff be as comfortable with such translations, much less with laws and jargon from other legal systems?

Before selecting a law and jurisdiction or forum which has no connection to the parties or trust assets, but is chosen solely because it has a statute with provisions not available in the settlor's place of domicile or residence, some practical issues should be considered, such as the following:

- Is the settlor fluent in the language of the chosen jurisdiction? What about potential witnesses?
- Does the designated forum permit proceedings in a language other than that of the place in which it is located?
- Will translations of documents or testimony be required? If so, might a literal translation miss nuances, usage or other subtleties which could distort the meaning of the document or testimony? If translations are not required, how confident can the settlor be that the judges or arbitrators and their staff are fully fluent in the language of the documents as well as in their ability to understand the colloquialisms of witnesses who do not speak the language of the chosen jurisdiction?
- Could travel time and expenses, for both the parties and lawyers, be a factor for the potential plaintiff? The settlor or trustees?

If an objective is to avoid forced heirship, prudence dictates keeping assets out of the jurisdiction whose laws are sought to be avoided. The reason is evident from the following case. The author is counsel to the estate of a US citizen who died a domiciliary of Switzerland. His wife was French; he had three children, one of whom is a ward of the state in Switzerland. The decedent elected to have his estate probated in the United States, the country of his citizenship, even though he had not lived in the United States for decades. This is a valid election under Article 90(2) of Switzerland's Federal Code on Private International Law. However, the decedent owned real estate in France, which does not provide for such a right to elect non-French law to govern the succession of French real estate. France has strict laws about the rights of children to inherit from parents. The will in question did not leave the child, who is a ward of the state, the share of the estate required by French law, or under Swiss law but for Article 91 of Switzerland's Federal Code on Private International Law. Under French law, the French real estate cannot be sold without the signature of, or on behalf of, all the children. Even if the authorities in Switzerland would be willing to sign a deed on that child's behalf, will the French authorities accept the deed without assurances that the proceeds of the French property are being settled in accordance with French laws of forced heirship? This is an open question, as of the writing of this chapter.

2.   The British Commonwealth

The Privy Council judgment in *Crociani v Crociani*, UKPC 40 (2014) is a warning of two things – not only to lawyers in those jurisdictions throughout the world for which the Privy Council is the highest appellate forum, but for trust practitioners everywhere:

- the care with which choice of jurisdiction, law and forum provisions – often considered 'boilerplate' – should be drafted; and
- the ingenuity and creativity with which judges can use their equitable jurisdiction to reach the result they think appropriate notwithstanding the text of agreements before them.

This case arose in Jersey, where the plaintiffs sued present and former trustees for, among other things, breach of trust. The defendants sought a stay based on what they contended was an exclusive jurisdiction clause in favour of Mauritius.

Crociani is a quintessential example of both law and jurisdiction shopping. The trust at issue was formed in 1987 in and under the laws of the Commonwealth of the Bahamas. The settlor was apparently an Italian national resident in Mexico. There were three trustees: the settlor herself, an Italian individual and a Bahamian corporate trustee. Beneficiaries included the settlor's two daughters, neither of whom was Bahamian. The trust was initially funded with a secured term note; the Privy Council decision does not indicate the identity or jurisdiction of the maker of the note or the nature or jurisdiction of the assets securing it. Other assets not specified in the Privy Council decision were added to the trust from time to time. By October 2007, the corporate trustee had been changed to BNP Paribas Jersey Trust Corporation (BNP) and the governing law had been changed to the law of Jersey, Channel Islands. In 2010 all assets of the trust, other than the original note, were decanted to another trust, misnamed the Fortunate Trust, of which the settlor was a trustee and a beneficiary, together with her daughters and their children; BNP was co-trustee. In 2011 the settlor purported to revoke the Fortunate Trust and withdraw all of its assets for herself. One daughter, whose relations with her mother had deteriorated to the point where the mother revoked the trust, threatened to take action against BNP. In February 2012 BNP resigned and appointed Appleby Trust (Mauritius) Ltd as sole trustee of the Fortunate Trust, the settlor presumably having resigned as well, purportedly moving the trust to Mauritius. It is not clear from the Privy Council decision what assets remained to constitute the corpus of the trust after the mother/settlor's purported revocation and withdrawal of all assets. In any event, after further objections from the daughter's lawyers, in August 2012 both BNP of Jersey and Appleby of Mauritius purported to decant the assets previously decanted to the Fortunate Trust (whatever they may have been in 2012) to yet another new trust (the Agate

Trust), this one back in Jersey, with Appleby and an individual – not the settlor – as co-trustees. The Privy Council does not discuss how or why BNP could act in August 2012, having resigned in February 2012, or why Appleby of Mauritius (rather than a Jersey affiliate) would create the new Agate Trust in Jersey.

The disenfranchised daughter and her two children brought suit in Jersey to revoke the 2010 and 2012 decantings and for damages.

The trustees sought to stay the litigation on the basis that Mauritius was the exclusive forum in which to hear claims relating to the trust. This, of course, assumes the validity of the first February 2012 deed, moving the trust to Mauritius, but not the August 2012 deed moving the trust back to Jersey.

The trust instrument provision – from the original 1987 deed – relied on by the appellants as empowering the trustees to appoint a replacement trustee and to move the trust to a new jurisdiction (Mauritius), where its courts and law would govern, provided:

> *and upon such appointment being made the then Trustee or Trustees shall immediately stand possessed of the Trust Fund upon trust for the new Trustee or Trustees as soon as possible so that the Trust Fund shall continue to be held upon the trusts hereof but subject to and governed by the law of the country of residence or incorporation of such new Trustee or Trustees and thereafter the rights of all persons and the construction and effect of each and every provision hereof shall be subject to the exclusive jurisdiction of and construed only according to the law of the said country which shall become the forum for the administration of the trusts hereunder (but so that nonetheless the then Trustee or Trustees or the new Trustee or Trustees may by deed declare that the trusts hereof shall continue to be read and take effect according to the laws of the said Commonwealth of The Bahamas as provided by Clause 15 hereof) and Clause 15 hereof shall take effect and be subject to the provisions hereinbefore declared by this clause.*[4]

The Privy Council decision did not address the anomalies noted above, especially the assumptions and inconsistencies regarding the efficacy of the various deeds and decantings, but focused on the proper forum for resolving the substantive issues. In doing so, it first parsed the above-quoted trust language. The Privy Council determined that the meaning of this language was that the trust may be administered in Mauritius and even that Mauritius law may be the exclusive law under which disputes should be resolved; but that when it came to the situs of litigation, the courts of Mauritius had no exclusivity. If the decision had rested solely on the phrase "forum for the administration of the trusts hereunder" and the omission of specific language such as "the exclusive forum for the litigation of any and all disputes arising under or relating to...", the case would be of little note, other than as an admonition against arguably imprecise draftsmanship. However, there is much more to the Privy Council's decision.

---

4   *Crociani*, para 7 at p3.

The Privy Council began what may turn out to be the most important part of its decision, albeit dicta, by reiterating that, "in the context of contractually exclusive jurisdiction claims", the law is, as described in *Donohue v Armco Inc* [2001] UKHL 64, that a party commencing litigation in the non-contractual form must carry the burden of showing "strong reasons" for doing so: "Thus, where a claim has been brought in a court in breach of a contractual exclusive jurisdiction clause, the onus is on the claimant to justify that claim continuing, and to discharge the onus, the claimant must normally establish 'strong reasons' for doing so."[5]

Of particular interest to trust practitioners is what follows:

The question of principle which arises in this case is whether the same test applies to an exclusive jurisdiction clause in a deed of trust. Contrary to the appellants' argument, the Board is of the opinion that it should be less difficult for a beneficiary to resist the enforcement of an exclusive jurisdiction clause in a trust deed than for a contracting party to resist the enforcement of such a clause in a contract. The Board is of the opinion that in the case of a trust deed, the weight to be given to an exclusive jurisdiction clause is less than the weight to be given to such a clause in a contract. Given that a balancing exercise is involved, this could also be expressed by saying that the strength of the case that needs to be made out to avoid the enforcement of such a clause is less great where the clause is in a trust deed.[6]

The Privy Council made this determination even though the claimants were not challenging the establishment or purpose of the trust, but rather its administration by the trustees. Thus, the Privy Council decision did not rest on whether the beneficiaries were parties to the trust instrument, but rather on the broad equity power of the courts in dealing with trusts.

Having unlocked the door to the lower burden to be carried by a challenger to a trust instrument's choice of jurisdiction or choice of law provisions, the Privy Council opened that door and walked through it: "In the case of a trust, unlike a contract, the court has an inherent jurisdiction to supervise the administration of the trust – see eg, *Schmidt v Rosewood Trust Ltd* [2003] UKPC 26, [2003] 2 AC 709 para 51, where Lord Walker of Gestingthorpe referred to 'the court's inherent jurisdiction to supervise, and if necessary to intervene in, the administration of trust.'"[7]

In upholding the Jersey Court of Appeals' exercise of the "inherent jurisdiction" to permit the proceedings to continue in Jersey, the Privy Council referred to several factors, each of which may be useful as guides to both the formation and the administration of trusts in jurisdictions with only tenuous ties to the parties likely to challenge it:

---

5   *Crociani*, para 34 at p11.
6   *Crociani*, para 35 at p4.
7   *Crociani*, para 36 at p12.

- Most of the substantive claims in *Crociani* alleged improprieties from October 2007 to February 2013, when the trust was housed in Jersey, and Jersey law was then the applicable law. "The Jersey Courts have very extensive experience of dealing with trust litigation, and are plainly more familiar with Jersey law than any other court would be."[8]
- Since Jersey courts and Jersey law were, at least for some period, the clearly agreed venue and law, there could be no objection to the abilities or fairness of the Jersey courts or the nature or substance of Jersey law.
- Documentation and witnesses would likely be in Jersey.
- The prescribed purpose of choice of jurisdiction clauses, especially in trusts which permit shifting jurisdiction, is that proceedings should be brought where the trustee is/was based. The Privy Council did not discuss the fact that jurisdictional choices may be primarily dictated by substantive laws (eg, in the case of trusts established to avoid forced heirship) or by procedural laws (eg, statutes of limitations and related provisions designed to shield asset protection trusts), and that the choice of trustee generally follows the choice of law.
- The settlor visited Mauritius for long holidays, but had no other significant contacts there and neither did any other member of her family. This last point may well be the most pregnant in the Privy Council's decision. If choices of law and jurisdiction must be supported, if challenged, by more than mere preference, then counsel may well be obligated to consider advising clients to establish connections long before a challenge arises. For example, if enough money is involved and available, a residence in the chosen jurisdiction and spending significant time there should help. Keeping some significant assets there should also help.

The argument that a beneficiary who accepts the benefit of a trust accepts the terms thereof as well was noted by both the Jersey Court of Appeals and the Privy Council in support of the rule that there must be strong reasons to depart from a jurisdiction clause in a trust instrument, assuming the relevant language deals with choice of jurisdiction as well as choice of law. This reasoning may have some merit, assuming *prima facie* the validity of the claims, in a case such as *Crociani*, where the substantive issues involved the administration of the trust and whether the trustee fulfilled or violated its fiduciary duties. In *Crociani*, the daughter did in fact receive benefits under the trust for years, before the estrangement from her mother. This point was given little weight in *Crociani* and has little or no merit if a claimant is not seeking benefits under a trust, but is rather seeking to attack a trust because it is allegedly being used to frustrate a

---

8   *Crociani*, para 41 at 13.

statutory right, such as rights of forced heirship or of the right by a creditor to enforce a judgment or of a spouse to recover assets moved without consent to trust outside easy reach. The Privy Council upheld the Jersey Court of Appeals by determining that while choice of jurisdiction claims are entitled to *prima facie* respect, the weight to which they are entitled is less in cases where the party contesting the claims was not a party to the trust document.

The Privy Council decision does not indicate why Mauritius law was chosen, other than consistency with the choice of jurisdiction. Since there were no apparent significant ties between the settlor or her family or the trust assets and the Bahamas, Jersey or Mauritius, and no analysis of any differences in the respective laws on any relevant issues, one might assume that the changes in jurisdiction, if not the initial choice, were less a matter of the substance of the law of the various jurisdictions and more a matter of relative convenience – or inconvenience – to the settlor and challengers.

The fate of candour remains to be tested. What would the Privy Council, the Supreme Court of the United States or the highest court of any of its states or the highest court of any other jurisdiction do faced with the following facts?

- A settlor with no personal, family or business ties to Country X, and no assets in Country X, forms a trust in Country X.
- The trust documents clearly provide that the courts of Country X are the exclusive forum for adjudication of any and all challenges to the formulation, funding and administration of the trust and all claims against the trust, its trustees or assets, and that all such challenges and claims must be decided in Country X under the laws of Country X, excluding its choice of law rules. The trust is a self-settled asset protector trust (ie, the settlor is a beneficiary) which is permitted in Country X but not in the settlor's domicile or the trust is explicitly inconsistent with forced heirship laws of the settlor's domicile.
- A challenge is made against the choices of jurisdiction and law by a creditor or disinherited heir, seeking to force the trustee or settlor to justify the choices.
- The challenge is brought in the settlor's domicile.
- The trustee defends the choices by asserting that Country X's laws were chosen for the sole and explicit purpose of taking advantage of its trust statute which permits self-settled trusts, which has strong asset protection provision and specifically permit trusts to ignore forced heirship requirements in the settlor's domicile.

Query: Is this enough for the challenge to overcome the reduced weight given to jurisdiction and choice of law provisions of a trust deed under the principles of *Crociani*?

3.   European Union

In 2012 the European Union enacted Regulation 1215/2012, dealing in part with jurisdiction clauses. The relevant section is Article 25, which provides in pertinent part:

> *1. If the parties, regardless of their domicile, have agreed that a court or the courts of a Member State are to have jurisdiction to settle any disputes which have arisen or which may arise in connection with a particular legal relationship, that court or those courts shall have jurisdiction, unless the agreement is null and void as to its substantive validity under the law of that Member State. Such jurisdiction shall be exclusive unless the parties have agreed otherwise.*

> *3. The court or courts of a Member State on which a trust instrument has conferred jurisdiction shall have exclusive jurisdiction in any proceedings brought against a settlor, trustee or beneficiary, if relations between those persons or their rights or obligations under the trust are involved.*

> *The validity of the agreement conferring jurisdiction cannot be contested solely on the ground that the contract is not valid.*

The general provision in favour of an exclusive jurisdiction clause, Article 25(1), has two conditions:

- The agreement must be substantively valid under the law of the designated jurisdiction; and
- The parties must have agreed to the provision.

The first hurdle should be no barrier at all. The laws of the chosen jurisdiction are generally chosen precisely because they provide for the settlor's objective, whereas the laws of the settlor's domicile may not. However, Regulation 1215/2012 deals only with designations of member states of the European Union in jurisdiction clauses. Such a designation may not be appropriate if the objective is to avoid forced heirship, since that could violate the substantive laws of the designated country.

The second hurdle may be insurmountable if the plaintiff, the claimant or any affected beneficiary, vested or contingent, is not a party to the trust document and therefore cannot be held to have agreed to the jurisdiction clause. Failure to meet this condition may arguably deprive the jurisdiction clause of any presumptive validity whatsoever. Article 25(1) could be read to mean that if both of its conditions are not met, there is no presumptive validity of a jurisdiction clause.

The specific provision of Article 25(3) dealing with trust instruments is even more problematic. It unambiguously provides that where a trust instrument has jurisdiction clauses, the courts of that designated jurisdiction have exclusive jurisdiction in any proceeding brought against a settlor, trustee or beneficiary if a dispute between that party or his or her rights or obligations under the trust is involved. This seemingly straightforward rule is anything but.

First, this rule provides only for a proceeding brought against a settlor, trustee or beneficiary. It does not, by its terms, apply to a proceeding brought by a beneficiary against a trust or its assets, claiming that the trust is itself is invalid because, for example, it violates the plaintiff's right of forced heirship. Second, the rule applies only if the litigation is about the relations between those persons, settlor, trustee or beneficiary or his or her rights or obligations under the trust. This language may not apply if the plaintiff claims a right to trust assets, either as a creditor or as an heir with rights of forced heirship. Under the latter circumstances, the settlor may well be deceased. One could argue that the obligations of the trustee are involved and that the rights of other beneficiaries would be affected if the right of the disinherited heir or a creditor were to be disrespected. However, I suggest that a better interpretation of that clause is that it is intended to apply to claims that the trust has been improperly administered, and that either investments or distributions have been improperly made. The alternative interpretation is that a clause confirming jurisdiction absolutely confers exclusive jurisdiction if the right or obligations of a settlor or trustee are involved would bar any challenge, even if *Crociani*-like hurdles could be surmounted.

The interpretation of Article 25 remains to be clarified.

4. The Hague Convention

In considering the enforceability of trust provisions in jurisdictions other than where a trust was formed, there is the Hague Convention of July 1985 on the Law Applicable to Trusts and on their Recognition – for what it is worth. In the author's judgement, it is not worth much. The United States signed the convention in 1988. Twenty-seven years later, it remains unratified by the US Senate and therefore is not effective as US law. Currently 13 signatories have ratified this convention. Panama is the latest.

The convention defines the applicable law of the trust essentially to be the law designated by the settlor or, failing that, the law determined with reference to four factors specified in the convention:

- the place of administration designated by the settlor;
- the location of the trust assets;
- the place of residence or business of the trustee; and
- the objects of the trust with reference to where they are to be fulfilled.

The convention deals more with the rights and duties of the trustees than with the challenges to trusts from the various sources indicated above.[9] However, the convention expressly provides as follows:

Article 15: The Convention does not prevent the application of provisions of the

---

9   See Articles 8 and 9.

law designated by the conflicts rules of the forum, in so far as those provisions cannot be derogated from by voluntary act, relating in particular to the following matters –

> *(a) the protection of minors and incapable parties;*
> *(b) the personal and proprietary effects of marriage;*
> *(c) succession rights, testate and intestate, especially the indefeasible share of spouses and relatives;*
> *(d) the transfer of title to property and security interests in property;*
> *(e) the protection of creditors in matters of insolvency;*
> *(f) the protection, in other respects, of third parties acting in good faith.*

If recognition of a trust is prevented by application of the preceding paragraph, the court shall try to give effect to the objects of the trust by other means.

Article 16: The Convention does not prevent the application of those provisions of the law of the forum which must be applied even to international situations, irrespective of rules of conflict of laws.

If another State has a sufficiently close connection with a case then, in exceptional circumstances, effect may also be given to rules of that State which have the same character as mentioned in the preceding paragraph.

Any Contracting State may, by way of reservation, declare that it will not apply the second paragraph of this Article.

Article 18: The provisions of the Convention may be disregarded when their application would be manifestly incompatible with public policy (order public).

The rather convoluted language of Article 15 seems to provide that a choice of jurisdiction or law can be disregarded if its purpose is to avoid or circumvent the laws of the settlor's domicile regarding, among other things, asset protection or:

- the personal and proprietary effects of marriage;
- succession rights, testate and intestate, especially the indefeasible share of spouses and relatives.

The Hague Convention on the Recognition of Trusts is of little practical help either to plaintiffs or defendants in litigation where:

- a plaintiff is seeking to obtain satisfaction from the trust of a judgment against the settlor or a beneficiary;
- a claimant is seeking to proceed directly against trust assets; or
- the claimant is a government – either the government of the forum jurisdiction or some other sovereign state.

In any event, it is applicable only where the convention has been adopted.

5.   United States

In the United States, trust law is a matter of state, not federal law. The 50 different state laws vary substantially regarding substantive trust issues, resulting in significant forum shopping within the United States.

Some non-US jurisdictions have enacted legislation specifically providing that trusts created under their laws can have provisions inconsistent with the succession or forced heirship laws of the domicile of the settlor, and that the inconsistent provisions should nevertheless be respected. See, for example, Section 83A of the British Virgin Islands Trustee Act and the Trusts (Choice of Governing Law) Act of 1989 of the Bahamas. In the United States, some states have followed suit.

Delaware changed its law to improve its attraction as a place to form asset protection trusts in light of aggressive competition from offshore jurisdictions and some other states. In Delaware, qualified dispositions to trusts now provide some protection against creditors beyond that previously available. A 'qualified disposition' is defined to include a transfer to a trustee of a Delaware trust with at least one Delaware trustee. The trust must be irrevocable, but the settlor can have veto power over distributions, retain a special power of appointment, and be a beneficiary of income and principal at the discretion of an unrelated and unsubordinated trustee. The definitions of 'related' and 'subordinate' are by reference to Section 672 of the US Internal Revenue Code. These definitions are of questionable practical reality. For example: a grantor father asks a trustee, who is one of his children and a beneficiary of the trust as well – that is, an adverse party – to consent to a distribution from a trust to the father. The child can refuse – with the threat (implied or implicit) of being cut out of the father's will. Suppose the 'unrelated and unsubordinated' trustee is the grantor's attorney or accountant. How 'unsubordinated' is he in fact?

In a classic example of statutory exceptions to exceptions, the Delaware Qualified Dispositions Act at §3573 provides that:

the *"limitations on actions by creditors to avoid a qualified disposition shall not apply:*

(1) to any person to whom the transferor is indebted on account of an agreement or order of court for the payment of support or alimony in favor of such transferor's spouse, former spouse or children, or for a division or distribution of property incident to a separation or divorce proceeding in favor of such transferor's spouse or former spouse, but only to the extent of such debt ..." 12 Del. C. § 3573

However, the statute also states "Paragraph (1) of this section [i.e. the limitations on actions by creditors] shall not apply to any claim for forced heirship, legitime or elective share." 12 Del. C. § 3573(1) (emphasis and bracketed clause added)

Thus, a clear distinction is drawn under the Delaware statute between child support and both pre and post-divorce spousal support on the one hand, and the rights of a spouse to inherit on the other. 'Forced heirship' is not defined in the Delaware statute, though it is customarily used to mean the inheritance rights of children. In the United States, children generally do not have rights of inheritance unless a parent dies without a will (ie, intestate). The use of term in the same section as 'elective share' – a term generally used to refer to spousal rights of inheritance – could be read to mean that qualified Delaware trusts can be used, as far as Delaware is concerned, to defeat both spousal inheritance rights (unless contained in a separation or divorce decree) and any forced heirship rights of children. However, under New York law, a transfer to a self-settled trust is a 'testamentary disposition' which is subject to a surviving spouse's right of election.[10]

The author is unaware of a decision in either Delaware or New York testing the use of a Delaware trust to defeat a surviving New York spouse's right to an elective share of deceased spouse's estate. Whenever that decision comes and whatever the decision of a Delaware court, one may expect a constitutional challenge under the 'full faith and credit' clause of the US Constitution. *Imo Daniel Kloiber Dynasty Trust*, 98 A 3d 924, 928 (Del Ch 2014) approaches this issue, but is not close enough to give definitive guidance. *Kloiber* involved divorce proceedings in Kentucky in which the wife claimed her husband fraudulently transferred over $200 million to a Delaware trust and sought to prevent her husband as the beneficiary and 'special trustee' of the trust from distributing or otherwise disposing of its assets which she claimed was marital property. The trustee sought a temporary restraining order in Delaware, asserting that Delaware had exclusive jurisdiction and control over the assets of the trust.

The trustee relied on a provision of the Delaware Qualified Dispositions in Trust Act, which provides that: "The [Delaware] Court of Chancery shall have exclusive jurisdiction over any action brought with respect to a qualified disposition."[11] The chancellor held this provision does nothing more than allocate jurisdiction among the various courts in Delaware, but is not a restriction on the ability of courts of other states to hear cases under the Delaware Qualified Disposition in Trust Act.[12] The Delaware chancellor also held that: "The United States Supreme Court has interpreted the *Full Faith and Credit Clause* as requiring the state courts not only respect the laws of their sister states but also entertain claims under their laws."[13] Nevertheless, the Delaware Chancery Court retained jurisdiction over the trust.[14]

At least three lessons pertinent to the issues dealt with in this chapter may be taken from *Kloiber*. First, *Kloiber* deals with the division of assets in a divorce, not with the right to an elective share of a deceased spouse's estate. There is a clear distinction between these two types of rights in the Delaware statute quoted above and noted in passing.[15] Second, this case differs from the situation

---

10   New York Estates, Powers and Trusts Law § 5-1.1-A(b)(1)(F).
11   12 Del C § 3572(a).
12   *Id* at 939.
13   *Id* at 940.
14   See Amended Status Quo Order by Vice Chancellor Laster. 2014 Del Cts LEXIS 196 (3 September 2014), affirmed by the Supreme Court of Delaware 100 A3d 1020.
15   *Kloiber* at 941.

where parties have voluntarily agreed to an exclusive forum.[16] Third, the chancellor upheld the right of non-Delaware courts (under both the full faith and credit clause of the US Constitution and the text of the Delaware Code) to hear cases under the Delaware Qualified Dispositions in Trust Act, so long as Delaware law is applied. This principle does not provide useful guidance as to how to predict whether a New York (or other) court would held that the substantive provisions of the Delaware Code cited above violated New York public policy regarding a surviving New York spouse's right to an elective share of a deceased New York State spouse who put substantial assets in a Delaware trust. The chancellor did note, in *dicta*, that "just as this court has no interest in the conduct of judicial proceedings before courts of a different state, *this court* also has no interest in having Delaware law deployed to defeat the marital property laws of another state".[17] Will this principle also be applied to elective share laws of other states, though Delaware law distinguishes between marital property disputes and election share rights – a distinction made by the Delaware legislature?

The Delaware Qualified Dispositions in Trust Act remains to be clarified by the courts.[18]

6. Enforcement

As a general, and perhaps overly gross, simplification: if choices of law and jurisdiction are respected, a challenger of a trust is likely to lose; if the choices of law and jurisdiction were well made to serve the objectives of the settlor, the trust should survive the challenge. However, if the choices of law and jurisdiction is not respected by a court willing to accept the case notwithstanding the stated choices of jurisdiction and law, and if the plaintiff is therefore successful, where and how can the judgment be enforced?

Especially with offshore trusts, the costs and uncertainties of dealing with foreign laws often result in creditors accepting low settlements. Even trusts which would not stand sustained attack in a sophisticated forum work quite well when the creditor is unwilling or unable to stay the course of foreign litigation. They can be effective in giving a settlor powerful leverage in negotiations. Some advocates and marketers of these trusts are quite open in stating that obtaining negotiating leverage is their real purpose. The fact that there are relatively few reported decisions dealing with the enforcement of judgments against offshore asset protection trusts, because most cases settle, is proof that they are effective. This exhibits a variant of the well-established legal principle, "Possession is nine-tenths of the law."

---

16   *Id* at 940.
17   *Id* at 950 (emphasis added).
18   See *Trustco Bank v Mathews*, 2015 Del Ch LEXIS 18 (Del Ch 2015).

Those cases in the United States which have gone to decision often turned less on the specific terms of the trust than on such things as:

- whether an order to either a trustee who is not before the court or a settlor/beneficiary/ defendant to use ostensible retained powers to cause the trust to pay a debt of the settlor/beneficiary can be enforced;
- the public policy of the jurisdiction; and
- the sense of equity of the court.

The ability of any court to issue an order to a trustee who is not a party, especially one who is outside the jurisdiction of the court, is problematic. Therefore, the critical question becomes: can (or should) a court issue an order to a trustee or a settlor/creditor to get the money from his or her trust to pay the creditor or to satisfy inheritance rights of a spouse or children? Aside from the legal defence of 'impossibility of performance', judges are generally reluctant to issue orders, even to persons over whom they may have jurisdiction, which are effectively directed to persons outside their jurisdiction. This is especially the case when issues of foreign laws are involved which are inconsistent with their own and involve questions of whether a settlor can in fact comply by getting a trustee to make the payment. Yet US courts are increasingly willing to force the question from a practical point of view where the settlor is a beneficiary of the trust he or she created and where the judge is convinced that the settlor has the power to cause the trustee to act so as to provide the funds needed to pay the judgment. The essence of a trust is the separation of legal and beneficial ownership of assets. If a settlor has truly and timely divested himself or herself of legal title – that is, the right/ability to invest and/or make discretionary distributions – then, in the absence of fraud or a law like those of many states dealing with self-settled trusts, it is unlikely that a judge will order payment to a creditor, a spouse or an ex-spouse out of trust assets. However, US courts are increasingly willing to look beyond the text of the trust document to see whether the settlor has in fact retained practical control over the trust assets. Cases on this issue tend to be fact specific and rely on an analysis of whether, in fact, the settlor/creditor practically divested himself or herself of effective control, or whether such authority and control was retained, thereby violating the very essence of a trust separation of legal and beneficial interests.

This evolving trend reflects a growing scepticism regarding offshore asset protection trusts both in judicial circles and among academics. As one judge put it:

> 'Asset protection planning' has become more problematic in recent years. As noted in a recent law review article [which discussed the Lawrence case], 'Stephan Lawrence's efforts to avoid his creditors – euphemistically called "asset protection planning" by its practitioners – have become increasingly common in recent years.

Although determining with any precision the value of assets that debtors have transferred offshore to avoid creditor claims is nearly impossible, conservative estimates exceed one trillion dollars. One lawyer, prominent in the asset protection business, represented that his firm alone in the 1990s had clients with more than three billion dollars in asset protection trusts." Stewart E Sterk, *"Asset Protections Trusts: Trust Law's Race to the Bottom?" 85 Cornell L Rev 1035, 1036 (2000) footnotes omitted). See also Randall J Gingiss, "Putting a Stop to 'Asset Protection' Trusts", 51 Baylor L Rev 987 (1999), In re Lawrence, 251 B.R. 630, 635 (S.D. Fla. 2000), aff'd, 279 F.3d 1294 (11th Cir. 2002).*

In *Breitenstine v Breitenstine*[19] the Supreme Court of Wyoming did not recognise a self-settled offshore trust for various reasons, among which was "Husband has named a 'protector' over the trust assets who is a long-time friend of Husband's who even Husband agreed would act in Husband's best interests, not necessarily the children's".[20] As to a court's ability to direct actions affecting property outside of its jurisdiction, the *Breitenstine* court carefully distinguished jurisdiction (and practical power) over assets from jurisdiction over parties, as follows:

Lastly, Husband claims that, in an effort to punish him, the district court exceeded its jurisdiction by ordering territories outside Wyoming to take action on assets held by Husband. We have said: We think the issue settled, at least since Fall v. Eastin, *215 U.S. 1, 30 S.Ct. 3, 54 L.Ed. 65 (1909), 23 L.R.A., N.S., 924 that the court of one state has no power to directly affect title to land located wholly within the borders of another. Decrees and judgments purporting to this effect are void, and to the extent the decree before us purports to so do it must fail. However, we consider it equally well established that a court of equity having authority to act upon the person may indirectly act upon real estate located in another state, through the instrumentality of its equity power over the person.* Fall v. Eastin, *supra;* Rozan v. Rozan, *49 Cal.2d 322, 317 P.2d 11 (1957), reh. Denied;* Weesner v. Weesner, *168 Neb. 346, 95 N.W.2d 682 (1959);* McElreath v. McElreath, *162 Tex. 190, 345 S.W.2d 722, 1961 reh. Denied; 34 A.L.R.3d 962.* Kane v Kane, *577 P.2d 172, 175-76 (Wyo.1978). One equitable function of the court is the disposition of property. When the court has jurisdiction over the parties in a divorce action, the court has the power to settle property matters even if the property is not located in the jurisdiction. Id. We distinguish between a judgment directed at the property itself and one directed against the owner of the property. Id. at 176. The district court's judgment does appear to attempt to direct judgment on both the property itself and the owner of the property. The former cannot stand, but the later can. Id. We, therefore, recognize that the judgment can properly operate upon Husband ...* Id. at 594.

---

19   2003 WY 16, ¶ 4, 62 P 3d 587, 589 (Wyo 2003).
20   *Id* at 593.

In New York, the trend is also to substance over form. In *Alvares-Correa v Alvares-Correa*[21] the Supreme Court, Appellate Division (which hears appeals from the trial term of the Supreme Court) had before it trusts in the British Virgin Islands. The defendant husband was not the settlor of the trusts; they were settled by his grandmother for his benefit and the benefit of his brother. However, the defendant was held to have had control of, and access to, those trusts by virtue of his powers of appointment, permitting him to direct distributions of all or any part of the trusts' assets. He was ordered to make substantial payments to his wife which, the court determined, he was able to make or cause to be made.

Judges who determine that a settlor-creditor does in fact have the power to direct or cause the trust to make designated payments are increasingly willing to force the exercise of that power by using the judicial weapon of a civil contempt citation. The power to pressure a party before a court to cause action by a party outside the court's jurisdiction is nothing new. The key is the willingness of a court to do so:

> Courts have a responsibility to remedy wrongful conduct, and have, recently, cast a discerning eye at the substantiality of off-shore spendthrift trusts in order to find the proverbial 'chink in the armor'. See, eg, Lawrence v Goldberg (In re Lawrence), 279 F.3d 1294 (11th Cir. 2002) (affirming bankruptcy court's contempt citation against settlor of an off-shore spendthrift trust, which was created two months prior to the issuance of an arbitration judgment of $20.4 million against him, who refused to repatriate the trust assets to the bankruptcy estate despite retaining control over the trust); F.T.C. v Affordable Media, LLC, 179 F.3d 1228, 1238 to 1244 (9th Cir. 1999) (affirming district court's contempt citation against perpetrators of a fraud scheme who refused to repatriate assets held in an off-shore spendthrift trust on the grounds that the perpetrators retained enough control over the trust so that they could be ordered to repatriate the assets). Here, the presence of the Connecticut corporations before this court is a sufficient connection to allow the court to provide relief. See generally 12 Charles Alan Wright, Arthur R. Miller, & Richard L. Marcus, Federal Practice and Procedure § 3021, at 167 (2d ed. 1997) ('However, a court may compel action outside of its jurisdiction by its order with regard to persons and property within its jurisdiction. Equity courts have known for a long time how to impose onerous alternatives at home to the performance of affirmative acts abroad as a means of getting those affirmative acts accomplished: Nastro v. D'Onofrio, 76 Conn. App. 814, 815 (2003).

In exercising its civil contempt power, a court can jail someone until that person complies with a court order to do something. This is a power which any responsible judge will use with the greatest caution and reluctance. It is the use

---

21   726 NYS 2d 668 (1st Dep't 2001).

of an essentially criminal sanction, incarceration, where no crime has been committed. It is a highly discretionary remedy. It is justified, as a civil remedy, only as long as the judge believes that incarceration might have the desired effect – that is, to cause the person who is jailed to do something specific. Most, but not all, people who face the threat of jail, even the 'tough nuts' who spend a night or two behind bars, end up doing what they were ordered to do. However, if it is apparent that this simply will not work – that is, that the person is willing to sit in jail indefinitely – courts will likely release the disobedient party and hope to compel compliance by fines or by the pursuance of assets.

Additional tools which can be used to enforce judgments include levying on tax refunds and taking away drivers' licences and other privileges. Courts willing to enforce judgments have weapons between the extremes of oral admonitions and jail if only they are willing to exercise some creative judgement.

Other than obstinate intransigence, the typical defence to the threat of jail for civil contempt is 'impossibility of performance.' Generally, courts should not and will not order someone to do something – much less jail someone to force obedience with such an order – if compliance by that person is impossible (not difficult, expensive or inconvenient, but impossible). The burden to prove the defence of impossibility of performance is on the person who asserts it:

> Once a prima facie *showing of a violation has been made, the burden of productions shifts to the alleged contemnor, who may defend his failure on the grounds that he was unable to comply.* CFTC v Wellington Precious Metals, Inc., *950 F.2d 1525, 1529 (11th Cir. 1992); U.S. CFTC v. S. Tr. Metals, Inc., 1:14-CV-22739-JLK, 2019 WL 1900463, at *4 (S.D. Fla. Apr. 29, 2019);* United States v. Rylander, *460 U.S. 752, 757, 103 S.Ct. 1548, 1552, 75 L.Ed.2d 521 (1983) ('Where compliance is impossible, neither the moving party nor the court has any reason to proceed with the civil contempt action. It is settled, however, that in raising this defense, the defendant has a burden of production.');* United States v. Roberts, *858 F.2d 698, 701 (11th Cir.1988);* United States v. Hayes, *722 F.2d 723, 725 (11th Cir.1984). The burden shifts back to the initiating party only upon a sufficient showing by the alleged contemnor;* U.S. v. D'Argenio, *01-00010-CR, 2019 WL 297091, at *10 (S.D. Fla. Jan. 3, 2019), report and recommendation adopted, 01-00010-CR, 2019 WL 296534 (S.D. Fla. Jan. 23, 2019) (party with present inability to comply has the initial burden of production to prove such inability). CFTC, 950 F.2d at 1529. The party seeking to show contempt, then, has the burden of proving ability to comply. Id. In re Laurence, 251 BR 630, 651.*

In dealing with international trusts in US courts, the burden of proof on the defence of impossibility of performance is particularly high. In *SEC v Bilzerian*[22] the court was, to say the least, highly sceptical about assertions that Mr Bilzerian had actually relinquished control over the assets of the trust he created. The

---

22   112 F Supp 2d (DDC, 2000).

trust instrument apparently was, inexplicably, not before the court. The court ruled: "Thus, even if Bilzerian's claim that he is no longer beneficiary or trustee of the trust is true, the trust instrument may provide him the power to reinstate himself ... at any time he chooses. Also, the trust's current trustees and trust protector – all Bilzerian's family members – may have the authority under the trust instrument to reinstate Bilzerian as a trustee and beneficiary."[23]

Since a contempt citation was on the horizon and the impossibility defence had been raised, the court held that: "Where assets are held in an offshore trust, the 'burden of proving impossibility as a defense to a contempt change will be especially high'. See *F.T.C. v Affordable Media, L.L.C.*, 179 F.3d at 1241. By providing only incomplete disclosure ... and refusing to provide the trust instrument, Bilzerian clearly has not met this high burden."[24]

One of the best-known cases in this area is *Anderson*, actually titled *FTC v Affordable Media, LLC*.[25] The Florida Federal District Court in *In re Lawrence* referred to *Affordable Media* as follows:

> The court finds that these actions do not constitute sufficient steps to purge the contempt finding. The Ninth Circuit's holding in F.T.C. v Affordable Media, LLC, 179 F.3d 1228 (9th Cir.1999) is instructive. Affordable Media involved an attempt by a couple, the Andersons, to hide money in an offshore trust based in the Cook Islands, claiming that they had willingly relinquished all control over millions of dollars to unaccountable overseers. The trust was set up with the Andersons as co-trustees, together with a trustee company, and contained a provision that revoked their trustee status in the event of duress, such as the court's order to turn over the trust's assets. In finding that the Andersons' burden of proving impossibility could not be met, the Ninth Circuit set forth language that is particularly relevant in this case:
>
> 'In the asset protection context, moreover, the burden on the party asserting the impossibility defense will be particularly high because of the likelihood that any attempted compliance with the court's order will be merely a charade rather than a good faith effort to comply. Foreign trusts are often designed to assist the settlor in avoiding being held in contempt of a domestic court while only feigning compliance with the court's orders. Affordable Media, 179 F.3d at 1241. The court went on to explain that: With foreign laws designed to frustrate the operation of domestic courts and foreign trustees acting in concert with domestic persons to thwart the United States courts, the domestic courts will have to be especially chary of accepting a defendant's assertions that repatriation or other compliance with a court's order concerning a foreign trust is impossible. Consequently, the burden on the defendant of proving impossibility as a defense to a contempt charge will be especially high. Id. See also, In re Lawrence 251 BR at 653.

---

23   *Id* at 25.
24   *Id* at 26.
25   179 F 3d 1228 (9th Cir 1999).

In the context of the matters considered in this chapter, a settlor who might be ordered to cause a trust he or she created, in which he or she is a beneficiary, to pay an ex-spouse either a portion of the assets or a portion of income or both, will rely on the trust documents and on the law of the situs of the trust, to say: "I cannot do it; it's impossible." Depending on the specific trust, that might mean: "Even though I am a trustee or a protector, or though the protector is my brother or friend, I have no power to order the trustee to do anything." The issue of whether the settlor has the power to direct a payment out of trust funds even if he or she is a protector may be further complicated by whether that power is 'fiduciary' or individual – a topic for another day and another chapter. Depending on the law of the trust and the terms of the trust document, the argument might go further – to wit, the trustee must disregard any 'instructions' from the settlor, the protector or anyone else who might otherwise have authority to instruct the trustee if such instructions are not the product of 'free will', but rather result from legal process outside the jurisdiction of the situs of the trust. Such a provision is common in Cook Islands trusts and is explicitly supported by Cook Islands legislation.

Section 13D of the Cook Islands International Trust Act of 1984, as amended (most recently in 1999), specifically provides for the non-recognition of foreign judgments if, among other things, it "relates to a matter or particular aspect that is governed by the law of the Cook Islands". Thus, a claimant seeking to enforce a judgment from a court in the United States or elsewhere against a self-settled Cook Islands trust might well, at the least, have to litigate *de novo* in Rarotonga after hurdling the jurisdictional and statute of limitations obstacles discussed elsewhere herein. Other haven jurisdictions have similar rules.

However, just as a Cook Islands court need not recognise a decision of other courts, those other courts are not bound to recognise impediments to their authority created under the umbrella of Cook Islands law. The Cook Islands may permit a trust agreement to have an 'anti-duress' provision and Cook Islands courts may well give effect to such provisions, but a non-Cook Island court need not be so deferential. A US bankruptcy court in Florida held: "Debtor's proposed defense of impossibility is invalid in that the law does not recognize the defense of impossibility when the impossibility is self-created."[26] As the US District Court for the Southern District of Florida put it:

> *It appears that Clause 16 of the January 21, 1993 Supplemental Deed was carefully worded so as to avoid permanently revoking the powers of the Settlor. The divestiture is episodic in nature and vests with the Settlor and his hand-picked off-shore trustees the subjective ability to determine which instances of alleged duress or coercion will render the Settlor's powers inoperative. The effect of such a clause,*

---

[26] *In re Coker*, 251 BR 902, 905 (Bankr MD Fla 2000) (upholding a contempt citation; the jurisdiction of the offshore trust was not apparent from the decision).

if validated, is to permit the trustees to ignore each and every action requested or demanded by the Debtor that may aid or satisfy the claims of creditors or advance the processes of law issued by courts of the United States against the Debtor in respect to the Trust. As the Ninth Circuit has recognized, debtors commonly design offshore asset protection trusts to assist the settlor in attempting to avoid being held in contempt of court while only feigning compliance with the court's orders: '[A] clause could be inserted in the trust contract which specifically directs the trustee to ignore any instruction, exercise of a power, and the like where the direction is given under the compulsion of a court order. Thus, the settlor could comply with the court order and "order" his trustee to turn over the funds, knowing full well that the trustee will not comply with his request'. F.T.C. v Affordable Media, LLC, 179 F.3d 1228, 1241 (9th Cir.1999) (quoting James T. Lorenzetti, The Offshore Trust: A Contemporary Asset Protection Scheme, 102 Com. L.J. 138, 158–59 (1997)). In this case, Lawrence's attempts to employ such a strategy contravenes the clear public policy against allowing a debtor to shield money placed in a trust for his or her own benefit from creditors, defies common sense, and is undermined by the language in the Trust granting the Settlor power to remove and appoint trustees. In re Lawrence, 251 BR at 645.

The US Court of Appeals for the Eleventh Circuit strongly affirmed that decision as follows:

We also find that the district court did not clearly err when it determined that the 1993 Duress Amendment is void as to current and future creditors under Florida law where the settlor creates a Trust for his own benefit and inserts a spendthrift clause. ... The bankruptcy court and the district court both concluded that Lawrence clearly established this Trust for his own benefit and to shelter these assets from an anticipated adverse arbitration judgment. Further, this provision was specifically designed to prevent permanent revocation of the settlor's powers. Rather, it leaves to the settlor and the Trustees the discretion to determine when an event of duress has occurred. The sole purpose of this provision appears to be an aid to the settlor to evade contempt while merely feigning compliance with the court's order. We agree with our colleagues in the Ninth Circuit, and with the district court herein, that validation of such a provision would contravene public policy proscribing a debtor from shielding money placed in a Trust for his or her own benefit and to the prejudice of legitimate creditors.[27]

US courts are increasingly willing to face this question from a practical point of view, especially in dealing with asset protection trusts where the settlor is a beneficiary of the trust he or she created and where the judge is convinced that the settlor in fact has the power to cause the trustee to act so as to provide the funds needed to pay a creditor.

In *Federal Trade Commission v Affordable Media, LLC*, the Ninth Circuit held

---

27   *In re Lawrence*, 279 F 3d 1294, 1299 (11th Cir, 2002).

that the district court did not err in finding that the contemnors' compliance was not impossible because they remained in control of an offshore trust. In that case the contemnors, the Andersons, created a trust in the Cook Islands which contained a duress clause providing that in the event of duress, the Andersons would be terminated as co-trustees and, accordingly, control over the trust assets would appear to be exclusively in the hands of a foreign trustee. After the Andersons were ordered to repatriate the trust assets to the United States, they, as protectors of the trust, sent a notice to the foreign trustee ordering it to repatriate the funds based on the court order. The trustee then removed the Andersons from their positions as co-trustees and refused to comply with the order to repatriate, basing the decision on the duress provision of the trust.

The Andersons claimed that compliance with the court's order would be impossible because they no longer had control over the trust. Our appellate colleagues found that the protectors' powers over an offshore trust were significant when given 'affirmative' powers such as the power to appoint a new Trustee. The Andersons recognised this power and attempted to resign as the protectors. The appellate court found this to be compelling evidence demonstrating their ability to control the trust. The court held that the 'asset protection trust' was designed to frustrate the power of the courts to enforce judgments, and found that there was "little else that a district court judge can do besides exercise its contempt powers to coerce people like the Andersons into removing the obstacles they placed in the way of a court". The court also pointedly observed that, "While it is possible that a rational person would send millions of dollars overseas and retain absolutely no control over the assets, we share the district court's scepticism."[28]

Koehler v The Bank of Bermuda,[29] a New York Court of Appeals decision decided on 4 June 2009, did not deal with trusts. It did, however, arise in an interesting context and it indicates the views of the highest court of New York State on the question of a New York court's powers to order a defendant over which it has personal jurisdiction to transfer assets which were outside the court's jurisdiction.

The case arose in the federal court of Maryland, where a creditor obtained an award against a former partner. The victorious creditor then registered the judgment in the District Court for the Southern District of New York. The defendant owned stock in a Bermuda corporation. The certificates evidencing the stock were held by the Bank of Bermuda Limited in Bermuda. The Bank of Bermuda Limited had a subsidiary in New York (the Bank of Bermuda (New York) Ltd), which was alleged to be not only a subsidiary, but also an agent of

---

28   *In re Lawrence* 279 F3d at 1297.
29   12 NY 3d 533.

its parent – the Bermuda bank which held the shares of a Bermuda corporation in Bermuda. The creditor filed a petition against the Bermuda bank in the federal court in New York by serving the New York subsidiary/agent, demanding delivery of the shares of the Bermuda corporation belonging to the judgment debtor or their cash equivalent. (An aside for those who are not students of the esoterica of federal jurisprudence in the United States: when a federal court is hearing a non-federal law case, it is supposed to follow state law; on procedural/judicial matters, it should follow the law of the state in which it sits.) The federal district court sitting in New York dismissed the petition on the grounds that under New York law, a New York court cannot attach property that is not in New York. On appeal, the Second Circuit Court of Appeals determined that "New York law does not make clear whether a court sitting in New York has the authority... to order a defendant, other than the judgment debtor himself, to deliver assets into New York, when the court has personal jurisdiction over the defendant but the assets are not located in New York". The Second Circuit certified this question to the New York Court of Appeals – that is, it sought the opinion of the highest court in New York on this question of New York law. The New York Court of Appeals answered: "While pre-judgment attachment is typically based on jurisdiction over property, post-judgment enforcement requires only jurisdiction over persons."[30] This decision should be of interest not only to trustees in New York who may be directed by a New York court to pay over trust assets which are in other jurisdictions, but also to trustees in other jurisdictions which might follow this principle. Although not cited in the New York decision, this principle was evident in various cases referred to above dealing with trusts. *Koehler* has been criticised in some states,[31] but remains good law in New York.

7.   Tax enforcement and trusts

The lack of any federal trust law or federal property law in the United States creates particular issues when the federal government seeks to enforce the tax liability of a taxpayer against the assets of a trust in which the taxpayer may have an interest, particularly if that interest is discretionary or contingent rather than quantifiable and vested.

Assuming that the federal government has a valid and established claim against a taxpayer and seeks to enforce that claim against a trust, the threshold question is whether the taxpayer has a sufficient interest in the trust assets to warrant enforcement against the trust. The federal government may have a lien for the taxes due to it, but must first establish what rights the taxpayer has in

---

30   *Id* at 537.
31   See, for example, *Sargeant v Al-Saleh*, 1370 So 3d 932 (4th Cir Fl 2014; see also *Cioffari v Wells Fargo Bank, NA*, 18 CV 4650 (VB), 2019 WL 130577, at *2 (SDNY 8 January 2019).

the trust assets. The nature and extent of the taxpayer's rights in the trust's assets are matters of state law. It is generally recognised that 'state' includes foreign jurisdictions if rights were created under the laws of those foreign jurisdictions. Only after those rights are determined does federal law apply to determine whether they are sufficient to constitute 'property' or 'rights to property' sufficient for the attachment of the federal tax lien.[32]

Under Bahamian law, which is similar to the laws of various other Commonwealth jurisdictions which have asset protections trusts, "it is clear and abundantly well-established ... that a beneficiary of a discretionary trust has no 'entitlement' to any of the trust property. His sole right is to be considered as a potential recipient of benefit by the trustee and he also has a right to have his interest protected by a court of equity".[33]

In a recent case in which several discretionary beneficiaries of a foreign trust sought to challenge the civil forfeiture of trust assets, the US government took the same position: that discretionary beneficiaries do not have a property interest in trust assets (and therefore lack standing to challenge the forfeiture).[34]

The author is involved in current litigation, the essence of which is to determine which state law applies to the determination of property interests in non-US trusts and the threshold in determining whether the tax liability of a US taxpayer/discretionary beneficiary may be asserted against the assets of a non-US trust.

There are relatively few decided cases in this area because most such lawsuits are settled. Especially with offshore asset protection trusts, the costs and uncertainties of dealing with foreign laws often result in creditors accepting low settlements. Even trusts which would not withstand sustained attack in a sophisticated forum work quite well when the creditor, spouse or ex-spouse is unwilling or unable to stay the course. They might not survive a full court challenge, but they can be effective in giving a settlor powerful (often

---

32 See *US v Craft*, 535 US 274, 278 (2002) ("The federal tax lien statute itself 'creates no property rights but merely attaches consequences, federally defined, to rights created under state law'") (quoting *United States v Bess*, 357 US 51, 55 (1958)); *Drye v US*, 528 US 49, 58 (1999) ("We look initially to state law to determine what rights the taxpayer has in the property the Government seeks to reach, then to federal law to determine whether the taxpayer's state-delineated rights qualify as 'property' or 'rights to property' within the compass of the federal tax lien legislation").

33 *Tantular v HM Attorney General* [2014] JRC 128, ¶ 26. See also *id* ¶ 20 ("'[A] right to require trustees to consider whether they will pay you something does not enable you to claim anything. If the trustees do decide to pay you something, you do not get it by reason of having the right to have your case considered: you get it only because the trustees have decided to give it to you'") (quoting *Gartside v Inland Revenue Commissioners* [1968] AC 553 at 607); *id* ¶ 26 ("An ordinary discretionary beneficiary has no any interest, legal or equitable, in the assets of the trust .... It is only on the making of a distribution to the discretionary beneficiary that the beneficiary obtains any interest in property, and then only to the extent of the distribution") (quoting *Hunt v Muollo* 2003 2 NZLR 322 ¶ 11) (further citations omitted).

34 See *United States v All Assets Held In Account Number 80020796*, No Civ A.13-1832 (DDC), Dkt No 163-1, Government's Mem Supp Motion to Strike Claims at 8 (in which the government argued: "Unless and until the trustee exercises its discretion in favor of one or more potential beneficiaries, the beneficial interest in the trust assets is undetermined, and potential beneficiaries have only an expectation that they may, at the trustee's sole discretion, eventually be assigned an interest in the trust's income or capital").

unbeatable) leverage in negotiations. Some advocates and marketers of these trusts are quite open in stating that obtaining negotiating leverage is their real purpose. Judges, particularly those in courts of general jurisdictions without specialised experience or expertise with trusts, are generally reluctant to force the settlor's hand by considering foreign law and making rulings which affect foreign assets, although that reluctance is waning.

In trust disputes relating to matrimonial disputes, the bifurcated jurisdiction of most state court systems creates particular difficulties, usually for the non-moneyed spouse seeking to upset an asset protection trust created by the moneyed spouse, or to at least force the moneyed spouse to access the trust to satisfy an award for alimony/maintenance and/or equitable distribution. Matrimonial judges are most likely not experienced with trusts, particularly offshore trusts, and are therefore reluctant to make orders with which they are unfamiliar. The judges in the Surrogate's Court – however named – who are familiar with trusts have no or very limited jurisdiction in matrimonial cases and their practical experiences in these matters is too often not brought to bear. Getting these issues to the right court in a timely way may be critical. In any event, both judges in the Surrogate's Court and those trying a matrimonial case may be extremely reluctant to get involved in a trust the governing law of which is a foreign country.

Lawyers and other advisers who prepare and advise on trusts should be sure that they and their clients are mindful of the trends discussed above and the message from *FTC v Affordable Media*:[35] "An old adage warns that a fool and his money are easily parted ... [T]he same is not true of a district court judge and his common sense."

The assistance of Alyssa Goldrich, a former colleague and associate at Gallet Dreyer & Berkey LLP, in preparing this chapter is gratefully acknowledge and appreciated.

---

35   179 F 3d 1228, 1231 (9th Cir 1999).

The trustee as fiduciary: some practical considerations

David Faust
Gallet Dreyer & Berkey LLP

This chapter explores the meaning of 'fiduciary' in the context of trusts and some of the practical consequences that follow from the general rule that trustees are fiduciaries.[1]

1. Background

Trusts are creations by contract, constructive trusts being the exception that proves the rule. *Inter vivos* trusts – those created during a settlor/grantor's life – are created by a trust agreement, deed of settlement or deed of trust; different words for essentially the same thing. Testamentary trusts – those created by will – require the designated trustee to accept the trust, thereby agreeing to its terms. In most jurisdictions, there is a body of statutes that underlies trust agreements and defines what they can, what they must and what they may not contain. There is also typically a body of case law in each jurisdiction that interprets and defines the rights and responsibilities of the various parties to trust agreements. In these respects, trust agreements are no different from commercial contracts.

It is basic that all contracts should be tailored to fit the parties' particular needs, wants, facts and circumstances. These are matters that the parties to standard contracts can discuss and negotiate before committing themselves by signing. With trusts, key people – in particular, the beneficiaries – are rarely, if ever, included in the process of the trust's creation. They might not even know that a trust is being created for their benefit. This puts a special burden on the drafter of the trust document. He or she must anticipate, consider and draft according to the needs of beneficiaries who have not been consulted, while simultaneously ensuring the needs and wants of the client who has commissioned – and is paying for – the effort. This affects every decision that

---

1   The introduction to the previous edition of this chapter included a note that the US Department of Labour was then considering a new rule that would impose a heightened fiduciary standard on certain investment advisers. Since that last edition, the Department of Law proposed the new rule and the rule was approved. However, the implementation of the rule was repeatedly delayed and eventually the rule was vacated by the Fifth Circuit Court of Appeals (*Chamber of Commerce of United States of Am v United States Dept of Labor*, 885 F3d 360, 369, 63 Employee Benefits Cas 1957, 2018 WL 1325019 [5th Cir 2018], judgment entered sub nom. *Chamber of Commerce of Am v United States Dept. of Labor*, 17-10238, 2018 WL 3301737 [5th Cir 21 June 2018]).

the drafter must make, from initial and basic decisions regarding the trust's form and jurisdiction (and, for that matter, whether a trust is even advised in the first place) to more complex decisions regarding the identity, rights and responsibilities of the trustee, the grantor, the beneficiary(ies) and possibly a protector.

Third-party beneficiaries – that is, people who are not parties to an agreement, but who are entitled to benefits thereunder – are not unique to trusts. However, the difference between trusts and other contract arrangements lies in the notion that the trustee – who is always a party to the trust agreement – has responsibilities beyond those of a regular contracting party. The trustee is a 'fiduciary'. In jurisdictions where a protector is used, he or she may also be a fiduciary, but that is not always the case.

'Fiduciary' is a word often used, but rarely defined with the precision useful to a practitioner. *Black's Law Dictionary* defines 'fiduciary duty' as "a duty to act with the highest degree of honesty and loyalty toward another person and in the best interests of the other person".[2] Section 1-2.7 of the New York Estates, Powers and Trust Law defines 'fiduciary' to include a trustee; Section 103(21) of the New York Surrogates Court Procedure Act makes clear that fiduciaries include trustees of both lifetime and testamentary trusts.

As defined in the US Internal Revenue Code: "The term 'fiduciary' means a guardian, trustee, executor, administrator, receiver, conservator, or any person acting in any fiduciary capacity for any person."[3]

Treasury Regulation 301.7701-6(b) provides that:

> *(1) In general. – Fiduciary is a term that applies to persons who occupy positions of peculiar confidence toward others, such as trustees, executors, and administrators. A fiduciary is a person who holds in trust an estate to which another has a beneficial interest, or receives and controls income of another, as in the case of receivers. A committee or guardian of the property of an incompetent person is a fiduciary.*
>
> *(2) Fiduciary distinguished from agent. – There may be a fiduciary relationship between an agent and a principal, but the word agent does not denote a fiduciary. An agent having entire charge of property, with authority to effect and execute leases with tenants entirely on his own responsibility and without consulting his principal, merely turning over the net profits from the property periodically to his principal by virtue of authority conferred upon him by a power of attorney, is not a fiduciary within the meaning of the Internal Revenue Code.*

These definitions define who a fiduciary is, but they are of no practical help in defining how a fiduciary should act.

---

2   *Black's Law Dictionary* (10th ed 2014).
3   26 USC § 7701(a)(6).

A trustee has rights as well as obligations under the trust agreement (including, but not limited to, rights to fees, indemnity, possibly not to be terminated without cause and to designate among charitable beneficiaries), all as circumscribed – like other contract rights and obligations – by statutes and case law. Yet a trustee must act with a higher duty of fairness and fidelity than a non-fiduciary contract party. As Judge Cardozo famously stated: "A trustee is held to something stricter than the morals of the market place. Not honesty alone, but the punctilio of an honor the most sensitive, is then the standard of behavior."[4] The eloquence of Cardozo has become a standard reference when describing the duty of a fiduciary. More recently, with specific reference to a trustee, the New York Appellate Division observed that "[a]s a fiduciary, a trustee bears the unwavering duty of complete loyalty to the beneficiaries of the trust no matter how broad the settlor's directions allow the trustee free rein to deal with the trust; the trustee is liable if he or she commits a breach of trust in bad faith, intentionally, or with reckless indifference to the interests of the beneficiaries".[5] However, such eloquence offers little practical guidance to a trustee or lawyer involved in the day-to-day practicalities of trust administration.

The US Court of Appeals for the Eighth Circuit explored the nature of fiduciary obligations in the context of fees charged by an investment adviser.[6] Section 35(b) of the Investment Company Act of 1940 (the '40 act') imposes on investment advisers of registered investment companies "a fiduciary duty with respect to the receipt of compensation for services".[7]

Under current law, broker-dealers are not 'fiduciaries' – a distinction to be explored in another forum. *Gartenberg v Merrill Lynch Asset Mgmt Inc*[8] established six criteria for testing whether investment adviser fees substantively meet this fiduciary standard (the nature and quality of the work; the profitability to the adviser; other benefits to the adviser from advising the fund; economics of scale; comparables; and the independence, conscientiousness and diligence of unaffiliated directors). The Supreme Court in *Jones v Harris Associates*[9] rejected the *Gartenberg* approach to testing investment advisers' fees, holding instead that "[a] fiduciary must make full disclosure and play no tricks but is not subject to a cap on compensation";[10] although the *Jones* court did acknowledge that a fee may be so large as to be *prime facie* evidence of a breach of fiduciary duty.[11]

4   *Meinhard v Solomon*, 249 NY 458 at 464 (1928).
5   *Boles v Lanham*, 865 NYS 2d 360 (2nd Dept 2008).
6   *Gallus v Ameriprise Financial, Inc*, 561 F 3d 816 (8th Cir, 8 April 2009, vacated and remanded by the Supreme Court (559 US 1046 (2010)) for further consideration in light of *Jones v Harris*, 527 F 3d 627 (7th Cir (2008), also vacated and remanded by the Supreme Court 559 US 335 (2010)).
7   15 USC § 80a-35(b), emphasis added.
8   694 F 2d 923 (2nd Cir, 1982).
9   559 US 335 (2010).
10   *Id* at 632.
11   *Id*.

The *Gallus* court held that the fiduciary duty imposed by Section 36(b) of the 40 act includes both the duty to be fair and candid in fee negotiations (the procedural '*Jones* test') and the duty to charge a fee tested by comparison to fees charged by other advisers, fees charged by the adviser to other clients and/or the value of the services rendered or to be rendered (the substantive '*Gartenberg* test'). Although arising under a specific provision of the 40 act, the principles of the *Gallus* decision might equally be applied in testing the fees of trustees who are defined as fiduciaries by different statutes as well as by common law.

The US Supreme Court essentially adopted the *Gartenberg* test, in a unanimous opinion.[12] While the Supreme Court decision is limited on its face to fees of investment advisers under the 40 act, the Supreme Court explicitly referred to the law of trusts (distinguishing between fees negotiated by the trustee and the settlor when a trust is created and fees sought afterwards). Although the Supreme Court's *Gallus* decision was written in the context of a specific provision of the 40 act, it purports to borrow from the trust law concept of 'fiduciary', but curiously defines the applicable standard as "an arm's length bargain":

> *In Pepper v. Litton, 308 U. S. 295 (1939), we discussed the meaning of the concept of fiduciary duty in a context that is analogous to that presented here, and we also looked to trust law. At issue in Pepper was whether a bankruptcy court could disallow a dominant or controlling shareholder's claim for compensation against a bankrupt corporation. Dominant or controlling shareholders, we held, are fiduciar[ies]" whose "powers are powers [held] in trust. Id., at 306. We then explained: "Their dealings with the corporation are subjected to rigorous scrutiny and where any of their contracts or engagements with the corporation is challenged the burden is on the director or stockholder not only to prove the good faith of the transaction but also to show its inherent fairness from the viewpoint of the corporation and those interested therein. . . . The essence of the test is whether or not under all the circumstances the transaction carries the earmarks of an arm's length bargain. If it does not, equity will set it aside." Id., at 306–307 (emphasis added; footnote omitted); see also Geddes v. Anaconda Copper Mining Co., 254 U. S. 590, 599 (1921) (standard of fiduciary duty for interested directors).*
>
> *We believe that this formulation expresses the meaning of the phrase "fiduciary duty"" in §36(b), 84 Stat. 1429. Id at 346.*

Is the *Gallus* definition of a fiduciary's responsibilities limited to the 40 act? The reasoning seems to have broader implications, referring to both trust and bankruptcy law. If the substantive standard is 'arm's length', how does this square with the *Meinhard* standard? How does the concept of 'arm's length' apply to a trustee's duty to the beneficiaries of a discretionary trust?

Are all powers of a trustee or protector 'fiduciary'? An interesting case that

---

12   559 US 335 (2010).

dealt with, among other things, whether the protector's powers at issue were 'fiduciary' was decided in 2008 in Jersey and is explored by Alon Kaplan, Yigal Harkavy and the author in an article entitled "What is a 'fraud on a power' in the context of trusts".[13] See also the discussion of the B Trusts below, in which the Royal Court of Jersey determined that the protector's powers before it were to be exercised "in good faith in the interests of the beneficiaries as a whole" – that is, they were fiduciary in nature.

In contract law, there is a concept of a 'third-party beneficiary'. Courts will decide whether a contract was entered into for the benefit of someone other than the contracting parties and whether any such third party has enforceable rights under the contract. Consider the following example: S contracts with C for C to build a house. C is told that while S is paying for the house and will own it, it will be occupied by G&P, C's elderly and infirm parents. G&P are not signatories to the contract. The contract obliges C to design and build the house to reflect occupancy by G&P. The house is improperly designed and/or improperly built for elderly and infirm occupants. Can G&P bring a claim for breach of contract against C?

While this is a relatively unusual issue in typical contract cases, the principle of the third-party beneficiary is at the heart of trust law. A settlor or grantor enters into a trust agreement whereby legal title to property is transferred to the trustee for the benefit of named or designated beneficiaries who may include the settlor, but almost always include others. The beneficiaries are not parties to the creation of the trust, yet the trust is set up for them. Thus, in the typical trust, they have rights which they did not negotiate or pay for, and the trustee has obligations to beneficiaries that he or she may not know or have any prior relationship with. The issue of who the trustee is primarily obligated to as a fiduciary – the settlor (who funded the trust, whose wishes and instructions set the ground rules for the trust that the trustee is bound to follow, and who defines the beneficiaries who 'own' the economic interests of the trust) or the beneficiaries – is an area in which neither statutes nor case law offers a high degree of clarity, although the interests of the beneficiaries appear to be paramount. As put by Justice Schack in *Becher v Feller*:[14]

> *Chief Judge Wachtler, citing Meinhard, supra and Matter of Rothko's Estate (43 NY2d 305, 319, 372 N.E.2d 291, 401 N.Y.S.2d 449 [1977]), instructed that 'it is elemental that a fiduciary owes a duty of undivided and undiluted loyalty to those who interests the fiduciary is to protect.' (Birnbaum v. Birnbaum, 73 NY2d 461, 466, 539 N.E.2d 574, 541 N.Y.S.2d 746 [1989]). (See In re Estate of Wallens, 9 NY3d 117, 122, 877 N.E.2d 960, 847 N.Y.S.2d 156 [2007]; In re Ryan's Will, 291 NY 376, 407, 52 N.E.2d 909 [1943]). Judge Rosenblatt, for a unanimous*

---

13   *Trust & Trustees*, Vol 15, No 4, June 2009.
14   19 Misc 3d 1138(A), 862 NYS 2d 812 (Sup Ct, NY County, 2008).

> *Court of Appeals (In re Heller, 6 NY3d 649, 655, 849 N.E.2d, 816 N.Y.S.2d 403 [2006]), held:*
>
>> *It is certainly true that the common law in New York contains an absolute prohibition against self-dealing, in that "a fiduciary owes a duty of undivided and undiluted loyalty to those whose interests the fiduciary is to protect." (Birnbaum v. Birnbaum, 73 N.Y.2d 461, 466; 539 N.E.2d 574; 541 N.Y.S.2d 746 [1989]). The trustee is under a duty to the beneficiary to administer the trust solely in the interest of the beneficiary (Restatement [Second] of Trusts § 170[1]).*

2. Trustees' powers: discretion

The issue of the fiduciary nature of trustees' powers is critical because, unlike most parties to a contract, trustees are usually vested with substantial discretion, something not typically found in other kinds of contractual arrangements. A typical party to a well-drawn contract need only turn to the contract to determine his or her rights and responsibilities. Any ambiguity will be resolved by discussion, mediation, arbitration or litigation; not by one party's unilateral discretion.

In trusts, a trustee's discretion typically appears in least two major ways:
- with regard to investing trust assets; and
- with regard to making distributions.

The trustee might also have the discretion to appoint new beneficiaries, appoint additional trustees, change the jurisdiction of the trust, appoint and compensate advisers and a myriad of other matters for which decisions must be made. This is the case whether the trust is testamentary or *inter vivos* and whether it is for asset protection or any of the other purposes for which trusts are used. This chapter will focus on discretion in making investments and distributions.

2.1 Investments

As part of his or her responsibilities, a trustee generally must invest trust assets. Absent trust provisions to the contrary, the trustee must invest as the 'prudent man' or 'prudent woman' would invest the assets. The 'prudent man' is akin to the concept of the 'reasonable man' in tort law.

Section 5 of the Trustee Act of the Bahamas, revised in 1998, includes a 'prudent investor' rule as follows:

> *Section 5(1) Trustees shall make, retain and change investments as a prudent investor would, having regard to the purposes, distribution requirements and other circumstances of the trust and in doing so trustees shall —*
>> *(a) exercise reasonable care and caution and the skill of ordinary persons;*
>> *(b) have regard to the suitability of individual investments, not in isolation,*

but in the context of the trust property as a whole, with a view to obtaining an overall balance of risk and return reasonably suited to the trust; and

(c) have regard to the need for diversification of investment so far as the trustees may consider it to be appropriate to the trust.

(2) Among circumstances to which trustees shall have regard in choosing investments are such of the following as they may consider to be appropriate to the trust or its beneficiaries —

(a) the size of the trust property as a whole and the estimated times and amounts of future distributions of income and capital;

(b) general economic condition;

(c) the possible effect of inflation and deflation;

(d) the expected tax consequences of investment decisions and of distributions;

(e) the expected total return from income and appreciation of capital;

(f) other resources of beneficiaries;

(g) needs of liquidity, regularity of income, and preservation or appreciation of capital;

(h) any special relationship or special value of an asset to the purposes of the trust or to one or more of the beneficiaries; and

(i) intentions or wishes of the settlor or testator, whether or not expressed in the trust instrument.

(3) Trustees shall make reasonable efforts to verify facts relevant to their investment decisions.

(4) Notwithstanding the reference in subsection (1)(a) to the skill of an ordinary person, trustees who have special skills or expertise, or are named or appointed as trustees in reliance upon their representation that they have special skills or expertise, have a duty to the beneficiaries to use such special skills or expertise.

(5) If a trust has two or more beneficiaries, the trustees shall act impartially in investing the trust property, having regard to any differing interests of the beneficiaries.

(6) This section shall apply if and so far only as a contrary intention is not expressed in the trust instrument and shall have effect subject to the terms of that instrument.

Section 11-2.3 of the New York Estates, Powers and Trust Law, the Prudent Investor Act, reads as follows:

(a) Prudent Investor Rule.

A trustee has a duty to invest and manage property held in a fiduciary capacity in accordance with the prudent investor standard defined by this section, except as otherwise provided by the express terms and provisions of a governing instrument within the limitations set forth by section 11-1.7 of this chapter. This section shall apply to any investment made or held on or after January first, nineteen hundred ninety-five by a trustee.

(b) Prudent Investor Standard.

(1) The prudent investor rule requires a standard of conduct, not outcome or performance. Compliance with the prudent investor rule is determined in light of facts and circumstances prevailing at the time of the decision or action of a trustee. A trustee is not liable to a beneficiary to the extent that the trustee acted in substantial compliance with the prudent investor standard or in reasonable reliance on the express terms and provisions of the governing instrument.

(2) A trustee shall exercise reasonable care, skill and caution to make and implement investment and management decisions as a prudent investor would for the entire portfolio, taking into account the purposes and terms and provisions of the governing instrument.

(3) The prudent investor standard requires a trustee:

    (A) to pursue an overall investment strategy to enable the trustee to make appropriate present and future distributions to or for the benefit of the beneficiaries under the governing instrument, in accordance with risk and return objectives reasonably suited to the entire portfolio;

    (B) to consider, to the extent relevant to the decision or action, the size of the portfolio, the nature and estimated duration of the fiduciary relationship, the liquidity and distribution requirements of the governing instrument, general economic conditions, the possible effect of inflation or deflation, the expected tax consequences of investment decisions or strategies and of distributions of income and principal, the role that each investment or course of action plays within the overall portfolio, the expected total return of the portfolio (including both income and appreciation of capital), and the needs of beneficiaries (to the extent reasonably known to the trustee) for present and future distributions authorized or required by the governing instrument;

    (C) to diversify assets unless the trustee reasonably determines that it is in the interests of the beneficiaries not to diversify, taking into account the purposes and terms and provisions of the governing instrument; and

    (D) within a reasonable time after the creation of the fiduciary relationship, to determine whether to retain or dispose of initial assets.

(4) The prudent investor standard authorizes a trustee:

    (A) to invest in any type of investment consistent with the requirements of this paragraph, since no particular investment is inherently prudent or imprudent for purposes of the prudent investor standard;

    (B) to consider related trusts, the income and resources of beneficiaries to the extent reasonably known to the trustee, and also an asset's special relationship or value to some or all of the beneficiaries if consistent with the trustee's duty of impartiality;

    (C) to delegate investment and management functions if consistent with the duty to exercise skill, including special investment skills; and

(D) to incur costs only to the extent they are appropriate and reasonable in relation to the purposes of the governing instrument, the assets held by the trustee and the skills of the trustee.

Diversification of assets by class and by issuer is considered basic to prudent investment. Yet even statutes as precise in defining the prudent investor criteria as the Bahamas Trustee Act provide for an exception if the trust agreement so provides.[15]

Some alternatives include the following:

- Legal list: This is a list of securities, usually issued by state insurance commissioners, identifying highly rated and supposedly safe investments for insurance company reserves. This could be a fallback if the trust agreement is silent. It generally is limited to highly rated, liquid debt and stocks.[16]

- Full discretion: This provides full and absolute discretion, although it could be an invitation to abuse.

- Limited discretion: If a trust contains typical indemnification language, a trustee is fairly well insulated from mistakes made in good faith, even if investment discretion is somewhat limited. However, if and to the extent that discretion is limited, any losses on investments will invite second-guessing and litigation. The drafter who seeks to restrict the discretion of a trustee must be mindful that he or she can do so good a job that the settlor will be unable to find a knowledgeable trustee willing to take on the responsibility.

Special provisions may be appropriate if the trust is funded with real estate or an interest in a privately held corporation or other business, art or other assets that the settlor would like to have held for the beneficiaries of the trust, as compared to a portfolio of liquid assets. In that case, the settlor should specifically and clearly allow the retention of such assets even though that would result in otherwise impermissible concentration of assets or illiquid investments. In such case the settlor may also 'suggest' or designate an adviser or manager for such assets.

(a) Conflicting investment considerations

A basic investment decision is whether to invest to maximise current income or to conserve capital. This conflict is particularly acute if the income beneficiaries are different from the remainderman. Income beneficiaries will want to maximise income, even at the risk to capital. Concerns about, for example, the

---

15   See 5(6) of the Bahamas Trustee Act Section and compare with Section 11-2.3(b)(3)(C) of the New York Estates, Powers and Trust Law.
16   See, for example, Article 14 of the New York Insurance Law.

effect of inflation on the value of trust assets will not concern income beneficiaries, but will be critical to the remainderman. Preservation of inflation-adjusted capital is critical to the remainderman even if such preservation adversely affects current income. Section 5(5) of the Bahamas Trustee Act directs trustees to "act impartially in investing the trust property, having regard to any differing interests of the beneficiaries". How exactly to do so remains elusive. Compare with Section 11-2.3(b)(3)(B) of the New York Estates, Powers and Trust Law, which refers to the same issue, but does not explicitly refer to "any differing interests of the beneficiaries".

Tax considerations are beyond the scope of this chapter; however, they cannot be beyond the scope of a trustee's considerations. See Section 5(2)(d) of the Bahamas Trustee Act and Section 11-2.3 (a)(3) (B) of the New York Estates, Powers and Trust Law, quoted above, which requires a trustee to consider "the expected tax consequences of investment decisions or strategies and of distributions of income and principal". For example, investing in non-dividend paying securities which may reasonably be expected to increase in value will defer taxes and will hopefully result in taxes at long-term capital gains rates, which are lower than ordinary income rates. This might increase the value of the trust corpus that reverts to the remainderman. It will not please income beneficiaries.

Even how a trustee allocates 'net revenue' between ordinary income and capital gains may have elements of discretion and tax consequences – examples include special or liquidating dividends, original issue discount on certain types of debt and the myriad other financial constructs that the wizards of the financial world have created.

Unitrusts are one possible answer to the investment dilemma. They provide for fixed amounts or percentages of trust assets to be distributed without regard to the amount of income, principal or interest. Such distribution can be defined as a fixed amount of money, a fixed percentage of assets or "the greater of $X or Y% of assets" at year end/quarter end. Aside from possible tax consequences, a unitrust method of distribution mitigates the conflict between income beneficiaries and the remainderman in investing for high income or preservation/increase in capital.

An investment protector may help, advise or direct the trustee; but this arrangement simply transfers discretion from one person to another in the absence of limiting provisions in the trust agreement.

2.2 Distributions

Discretionary powers over distributions may present a trustee with even more difficulty than discretionary powers over investments.

(a)   Conflicts

The threshold decision of whether to make a discretionary distribution presents a conflict of interest to many trustees. A trustee's fees are generally determined by agreement. They may be covered in the trust agreement or, in the case of institutional trustees, in a separate fee agreement. In the absence of such an agreement, fees may be set by statutes, which also may cap fees.[17] To the extent that a trustee's fees are calculated based on the value of the trust estate, the trustee has an incentive not to make distributions. Rather, he or she is incentivised to keep the trust estate as large as possible and to let retained earnings increase the trust estate – and related fees.

If a trustee can make discretionary distributions to or for the benefit of himself or herself – which is not unusual in credit shelter trusts, insurance trusts or trusts by, for example, a grandparent to a child for the benefit of grandchildren – for any purpose, then there is an obvious conflict of interest; there is also a risk that the trust assets could be includable in the trustee's estate for estate tax purposes.

Section 10-10.1 of the New York Estates, Powers and Trust Law provides that a trustee-beneficiary cannot make distributions to himself or herself unless:

- the trustee-beneficiary is the grantor of a revocable trust (a type of trust often used to avoid probate);
- distributions are made by reference to an 'ascertainable standard', a term defined by reference to federal tax law; or
- the trust agreement specially allows such self-dealing.

'Ascertainable standard' is defined by reference to US Internal Revenue Regulation 20.2041-1 (c)(2) (which is written in the context of when a power of appointment is/is not includable in the holder's estate for estate tax purposes). This tax concept has been incorporated into the trust laws of states such as New York and Delaware with respect to distributions to a settlor-beneficiary (Delaware) or trustee-beneficiary (New York). The definition of 'ascertainable standard' in the relevant tax regulation is as follows:

> A power to consume, invade, or appropriate income or corpus, or both, for the benefit of the decedent which is limited by an ascertainable standard relating to the health, education, support, or maintenance of the decedent is, by reason of section 2041(b)(1)(A), not a general power of appointment. A power is limited by such a standard if the extent of the holder's duty to exercise and not to exercise the power is reasonably measurable in terms of his needs for health, education, or support (or any combination of them). As used in this subparagraph, the words "support" and "maintenance" are synonymous and their meaning is not limited to the bare necessities of life. A power to use property for the comfort, welfare, or happiness of the holder of the power is not limited by the requisite standard.

---

17   See Section 2309 of the New York Surrogate's Court Procedure Act.

If the trust agreement allows distributions by a trustee to himself or herself without reference to an 'ascertainable standard' as defined under federal tax law, then a beneficiary-trustee who makes distributions to himself or herself may be okay under Section 10-10.1 of the New York Estates, Powers and Trust Law, but the entire trust could be included in his or her estate for estate tax purposes whether or not such power is used.

A trustee is also subject to a conflict of interest and surcharge (ie, a reduction in, or total denial of, the trustee's commissions) if he or she uses trust assets to pay his or her obligations, whether or not he or she, or the person for whose benefit the payment is made, is a beneficiary. This can be an issue, for example, in the case of a trust created by a grandparent for the benefit of grandchildren, where the settlor's child (the parent of the beneficiary) is the trustee. The New York Court of Appeals, New York's highest court, had occasion to address the fiduciary responsibilities of a trustee in this situation, most recently in *Matter of Wallens*.[18] The unanimous court held that:

> To determine whether a trustee's distribution of trust assets was proper, the settlor's intent controls (see Matter of Chase Manhattan Bank, 6 NY3d 456, 460 [2006]). '[T]he trust instrument is to be construed as written and the settlor's intention determined solely from the unambiguous language of the instrument itself' (id., quoting Mercury Bay Boating Club, 76 N.Y.2d at 267).
>
> It is also well settled that 'a fiduciary owes a duty of undivided and undiluted loyalty to those whose interests the fiduciary is to protect' (Birnbaum v Birnbaum, 73 N.Y.2d 461, 466 [1989], citing Meinhard v Salmon, 249 N.Y. 458, 463-464 [1928] [other citation omitted]). As Chief Judge Cardozo famously stated, '[a] trustee is held to something stricter than the morals of the market place. Not honesty alone, but the punctilio of an honor the most sensitive, is then the standard of behavior' (Meinhard v. Solomon, 249 N.Y. 458 at 464). 'This is a sensitive and 'inflexible' rule of fidelity, barring not only blatant self-dealing, but also requiring avoidance of situations in which a fiduciary's personal interest possibly conflicts with the interest of those owed a fiduciary duty' (id. [internal citations omitted]). We have recognized that a 'trustee is under a duty to the beneficiary to administer the trust solely in the interest of the beneficiary' (Matter of Heller, 6 N.Y.3d 649, 655 [2006], quoting Restatement [Second] of Trusts § 170 [1]; see also Mercury Bay Boating Club v San Diego Yacht Club, 76 N.Y.2d 256, 270 ["(T)he trustee must administer the trust for the benefit of the beneficiaries and cannot compete with the beneficiaries for the benefits of the trust corpus"])." 9 N.Y.3d at 122

In *Wallens*, the conflict arose out of a trustee using trust assets to pay for expenses of the beneficiary, his daughter, which were explicitly included in the purpose for which trust funds could be expended, but which he had a direct and personal obligation to pay:

---

18   9 NY 3d 117, 877 NE 2d 960 (2007).

In this case, we agree with the Appellate Division that the education and medical expenditures at issue fall within the class of expenditures authorized by the trust since the terms of the trust explicitly permit trust funds to be used for Maggie's 'support, education, maintenance and general welfare.' But even when the trust instrument vests the trustee with broad discretion to make decisions regarding the distribution of trust funds, a trustee is still required to act reasonably and in good faith in attempting to carry out the terms [***963] of the trust (see Matter of Bruches, 67 AD2d 456, 415 NYS2d 664 [2nd Dept 1979]; In re Albert's Estate, 118 NYS2d 864 [Sur Ct, New York County 1950]). Although father sought and obtained court approval to access the trust for Maggie's college expenses, he did not secure judicial approval to use trust assets to pay his obligation regarding her secondary school tuition and certain medical expenses. Thus, we remit the matter to Surrogate's Court for a hearing to determine whether the expenditures were authorized in good faith and in furtherance of the beneficiary's interests. ***9 N.Y.3d at 123.

The New York Court of Appeals remanded the case to the Surrogate's Court, which has jurisdiction over trusts in New York, to "conduct a hearing as to whether the father carried out his fiduciary duty as a co-trustee to act, in good faith, in his daughter's interest". There is no available decision from the Surrogate's Court indicating how this matter was determined on remand, indicating that the parties most likely settled this family dispute.

A trustee's fiduciary responsibilities may well be put to the test regarding distributions among beneficiaries of the same 'class' with whom the trustee has no relationship other than as trustee. Interestingly, Section 5(5) of the Trustee Act of the Bahamas admonishes trustees to act impartially in investing trust assets having regard to differing interests of the beneficiaries. Presumably, impartially should also be a guide in making distributions. Could one imagine a statute or case law supporting partiality?

A common problem: a couple with young children seeks estate planning. The single most difficult issue is: who will be the children's guardian if both parents die while the children are minors? The next decision is: who will be the trustee for the children's inheritance? The same person? Perhaps different people – one for the children, the other for the money? Each answer has its own problems: if it is the same person, there is an obvious conflict. If there are different people, how do they interface? Should the trustee have full discretion regarding distributions if he or she is also the guardian? Is this too difficult a test of the 'fiduciary' standards that a trustee must meet? Yet if discretion is too limited, who would want the roles and responsibilities?

Smart or well-advised testators realise that simply asking a brother or sister to raise nieces and nephews presents many practical problems – especially since the designated guardians may not be not as financially secure as the parents. The guardian will have the additional expenses inherent in raising the children and also may have to give up his or her own income to act as their guardian full time. Will the guardian need a bigger house or car? Should the guardian own it? Should the trust buy it and lease it to the guardian? If yes, will the transaction be at arm's length or on more favourable terms? Should the guardian pay rent for his or her personal use of the car outside the scope of his or her responsibilities as guardian? How should these decisions be evaluated? Should the guardian be required to raise the children to meet the standard of living to which the children were accustomed or to the standard of living to which the guardian's family is accustomed? Clothing, food, holidays, camp and extra-curricular activities all cost money. Will the guardian be too aggressive in spending trust funds or too reluctant or embarrassed? These are very difficult issues with no right or wrong answer, but they highlight how giving the trustee full discretion over these matters may not be fair to anyone: the trustee, the guardian (if different) or the beneficiaries.

In a typical trust for the benefit of children, the simplest mechanism is to treat all children equally and make distributions accordingly. The settler or testator may feel that a different result is appropriate. Putting aside 'special needs' challenges, which are beyond the scope of this chapter, what if the needs of the beneficiaries are different? Some possible scenarios: one child works in the family business, the other does not; one becomes a doctor, the other pursues a career in the military; one gets an MBA, the other becomes an art historian. What if one child gets involved with drugs or other 'undesirable' activities? How is a trustee to exercise discretion in such situations? What help is it to the trustee to be reminded that he or she is a 'fiduciary'?

A distribution protector may provide a human, personal perspective to an institutional trustee and a measure of protection to the settlor, but is not a full answer. Installing a distribution protector diffuses, but does not clarify, the trustee's responsibility.

As imaginative as trust drafters can be, their ingenuity can pale before the creativity of a plaintiff's lawyer whose client is a beneficiary, or wannabe beneficiary, who sues to contest a trust or for money from a trustee who has not done the settlor's bidding, as the beneficiary interprets it.

How long, and in what detail, can a settlor 'rule from the grave'? In UK law-based trusts, a mechanism to 'guide' (if not rule) from the grave is the letter of wishes. It is a (supposedly) non-binding letter from the settlor to the trustee indicating how discretion is to be exercised. Trustees may appreciate this letter because it gives the trustee helpful guidance without being legally binding. After all, it is a letter of wishes, not a letter of instructions. That said, case law is very limited and inconsistent as to whether such letters are discoverable or in fact binding upon the trustee. Precatory language in a trust document may also be used to indicate a settlor's intent, such as: "My trustee is requested to consider, but not be bound by, my wish that... This expression of my wish does not, and shall not be construed to, limit my trustee's discretion in such matter."

2.3   Other tests of a fiduciary

The testing of fiduciary obligations can arise in a wide variety of ways, not all of which directly involve the investment, disbursement or distribution of trust funds. Examples may be found in the history of the 'B' Trusts in Jersey, Channel Islands. The author was counsel to the *de facto* settlor, initial protector and a member of the class of beneficiaries of these trusts. The background, briefly stated, is as follows.

The settlor, a US citizen, went to Mr B, a director of a trust company in the (Channel Islands) in Jersey, to create asset protection trusts. B created the B Trusts. It is important to reflect on the fact that, like many settlors, the settlor went to a person, not an organisation. While the legal relationship was with the entity, as trustee, the relationship was based on the personal trust that existed with B. For two years, the settlor's only contact at the trust company was with B. When B fled from the scene, the trust company was left to deal with a situation in which it had full legal responsibility as trustee, but no real personal relationship with the people involved, and the settlor and his family were left to deal with people they did not know.

In September 2006 an indictment of the settlor in the United States on a variety of charges became public. The trust company immediately filed a suspicious activities report with the Jersey Financial Crimes Bureau. B ceased all communications with the settlor and the trust company effectively froze the trusts' accounts, without being directed to do so by any Jersey authority and before any request for a freeze by the United States. The Jersey Court did not freeze the trusts until May 2007; it did so then at the request of the attorney general of Jersey, who acted at the request of the United States, many months after the trust company effectively froze the trusts by its precipitous actions in September of the prior year.

A review of the trust documents, prepared by the trust company, indicated that in the trust with the bulk of the trusts' assets, there was no provision to remove the trust company as trustee, even for cause, and the settlor's family were not listed as beneficiaries. Is failure to include a provision for removal of trustees or to properly identify the beneficiaries itself a breach of fiduciary duty by a trustee who prepares the trust documents?

The trust company acted in September 2006, without seeking legal advice as to whether the trust assets were 'proceeds of a crime' under Jersey law. When it did seek such advice, months later, the advice it got was ambiguous to say the least. Was acting as it did – without seeking legal advice, much less a decision under Jersey law from a Jersey court as to whether the trust was funded with the proceeds of a crime under Jersey law – itself a violation of fiduciary duties? Was it acting in the best interests of the beneficiaries of the B Trusts or in its own interest?

An explanation of the trust company's actions after the settlor was indicted might be found in the affidavit of a director of the trust company (other than B). It attested that the trust company was concerned that it might become a target of the United States, and that it was "at risk of becoming a target of criminal investigation or prosecution in the United States" adversely affecting "[T]he ability of [the trust company] to service U.S. based clients", as well as "a risk that any [trust company] director might be arrested on arrival at a U.S. airport" and even be extradited. Is this consistent with a sincere sensitivity to a trustee's fiduciary obligations? Or is it more indicative of a self-protection bordering on the paranoid, and "beneficiaries be damned"?

Given the trust company's actions, the settlor, the trustees and the protector sought to remove the trust company as trustee. The trust company vigorously resisted the validity of appointment of the successor protector and the two new trustees, at the cost of hundreds of thousands of pounds in legal fees to its lawyers, lawyers for the settlor and lawyers for the successor protector and the two new designated trustees. The trust company alleged that these actions were a fraud on the powers of the protector under the relevant agreements and under applicable Jersey law. The Royal Court rejected these allegations in paragraph 108 of its 28 January 2008 decision:

> For these reasons [After an extensive review of the facts and the law] we find that there is no fraud on a power either by [the settlor] in appointing Ghirlandina as protector on 6th September 2006 or by Ghirlandina in appointing Larona and Roenne as additional trustees on 8th September 2006. Their respective intentions when exercising these powers were consistent with the purposes for which the powers were conferred, namely to act in good faith in the interests of the beneficiaries as a whole. (Emphasis added)

Subsequently, the trust company precipitously resigned as trustee of the B Trusts, still refusing to vest the assets of the trusts in new trustees, who had responsibility in light of their appointments but no authority over the trusts' assets. This left administration of the trusts in limbo and also put the viscount of Jersey, who had supervisory responsibility over the trusts, in a most uncomfortable position. Was this consistent with the fiduciary responsibilities of a Jersey trustee?[19]

3.   Conclusion

The adage "the devil is in the detail" is never more apt then when applied to the notion that a trustee is a fiduciary. Cardozo's famous eloquence and the principles restated in high court decisions such as *Wallens* may provide a background, but cannot substitute for the good-faith, fact-based judgement of a trustee possessed of that other elusive characteristic: integrity.

The author gratefully acknowledges the invaluable assistance of Adam J Berkey at Gallet Dreyer & Berkey LLP in preparing this chapter.

---

19   For a more detailed discussion of this case, see Kaplan, Faust and Harkavy, "What is a "fraud" on a power in the context of trusts", *Trusts & Trustees*, Vol 15, No 4, June 2009.

Fiduciary responsibility: the trustee role and its risks

Susan R Schoenfeld
Wealth Legacy Advisors LLC

Trust relationships create many different roles and responsibilities. In general, there are three categories of parties in every trust. The grantor, sometimes referred to as the settlor, is the one who establishes the trust and contributes assets into the trust. The beneficiary is the person, or group of persons, for whose benefit the trust is created. The trustee holds title to the assets in a fiduciary capacity and is charged with administering the trust according to its terms for the benefit of the beneficiary. Recent developments have added supplemental roles such as trust protector, trust investment adviser and the like.

This chapter focuses on the roles, responsibilities and risks of the trustee position.

A trust creates "a fiduciary relationship with respect to property, subjecting the person by whom the title to property is held to equitable duties to deal with the property for the benefit of another person, which arises as a result of a manifestation of an intention to create it".[1]

R Oerton's *Underhill's Law Relating to Trusts & Trustees* (London: Butterworths, 1970) defines a 'trust' as:

> *an equitable obligation binding a person (who is called a trustee) to deal with property over which he has control (which is called the trust property), for the benefit of persons (who are called beneficiary or cestui que trust), of whom he may himself be one, and any one of whom may enforce the obligation. Any act or neglect on the part of a trustee which is not authorised or excused by the terms of the trust instrument, or by law, is called a breach of trust.*[2]

1. Duties of the trustee

The word 'fiduciary' can be used to describe the responsibilities of the trustee towards the beneficiary. There are a number of trustee responsibilities.

1.1 Duty to administer trust according to its terms

When trustees accept their appointment as such, they are duty-bound to carry

---

1   Scott and Fratcher, *The Law of Trusts* (Boston: Little, Brown and Company, 1987).
2   *Duhaime's Law Dictionary*, www.duhaime.org/LegalDictionary/T/Trust.aspx.

out the trust and administer the trust estate in accordance with the terms of the governing instrument and applicable law. Where there is more than one trustee, each co-trustee is responsible for all functions in the administration of the entire trust and each must use reasonable care to prevent co-trustees from breaching the trust.

Although the trustee is responsible for trust administration, delegation of many – but not all – functions in appropriate cases is permissible and is discussed later in this chapter.

The designated trustee should thoroughly review all language in the governing instrument and look for any unusual trust terms and special provisions. Societal issues today have sparked creative trust drafting techniques, and trustees may find themselves with unexpected and unbargained-for duties and potential liability for the performance or non-performance of those duties.

For example, trust settlors are increasingly concerned about withholding distributions in the event of substance abuse on the part of beneficiaries. Some trustees, particularly corporate trustees, are uncomfortable administering a drug test before making a discretionary distribution. The trustee should understand local laws which may require or even prohibit compliance with the prescribed precondition, and perhaps suggest an individual co-trustee who is a family member or friend of the family, who might be more comfortable directing an appropriate course of action in such a situation.

Similarly, certain jurisdictions have special rules with respect to special needs trusts – sometimes referred to as 'supplemental needs' trusts – which hold and manage property intended for the benefit of a beneficiary who may lack the legal capacity to handle his or her own financial affairs. These trusts are generally intended to provide for the beneficiary's lifestyle only over and above the government entitlements to which the beneficiary is otherwise qualified to receive, and great care must be taken not to endanger the beneficiary's rights to continuing government entitlements inadvertently.

1.2 Duty of skill and care

In general, a trustee must exercise the degree of care, skill and caution that a reasonably prudent person would exercise in dealing with his or her own property, and that a knowledgeable trustee would use to accomplish the purposes of the trust. The standard for the minimum degree of skill and attention required is not diminished by any particular trustee's lack of knowledge or experience.

If, on the other hand, the trustee possesses some special skill, and especially if the trustee has been specifically appointed because of that special skill, then that trustee will be held to that higher expectation of skill level.[3] This is

---

3   See Restatement of Trusts (Second) Section 184 and Restatement of Trusts (Third) Section 227.

particularly true for corporate fiduciaries, such as trust companies or other professional fiduciaries, which generally market themselves as skilled in investments, taxation and trust administration.

1.3 Duty to identify, secure and safeguard trust assets

The trustee has a duty to take custody of and keep control over the trust property in accordance with the terms of the trust agreement, which includes not only taking physical possession of the property, but also having it titled in the name of the trust.[4]

This process involves collecting any land, tangible personal property (including collectibles) and documents associated with intangibles, such as stock certificates, and enforcing all rights or claims of the trust against third parties. The trustee must also exercise reasonable care in safeguarding the assets collected, properly insure the trust assets as appropriate and arrange for proper maintenance, security, repairs and other steps necessary to protect the value of the trust assets.

The trustee must also keep trust assets separate from the trustee's own assets and earmark them as specifically associated with the trust.

If the trustee fails to properly perform these steps, the trustee will be absolutely liable (ie, even without fault or negligence) for any loss the property might sustain.

1.4 Duty to account

The trustee must maintain clear and accurate accounts with respect to the trust estate and make regular accountings to the beneficiaries. The accounting should reflect all receipts, including all gains and losses from investments, and disbursements. In addition, depending on local law requirements, the trustee may periodically have to make an accounting to the court with jurisdiction over the trust. If the trustee fails to keep clear and accurate accounts, and such failure results in costs to the trust, the trustee may be held personally liable for those costs. The courts may also reduce or even deny trustee commissions when accounts are incomplete or inaccurate.

For US trusts governed by the law of a state that has adopted the Uniform Trust Code, the trustee must "keep the qualified beneficiaries … reasonably informed about the administration of the trust and of the material facts necessary for them to protect their interests". The trustee must not only provide copies of the trust instrument to the beneficiaries entitled to receive them and provide periodic reports, but also notify qualified beneficiaries of basic functions of the trusteeship itself, including a copy of the trustee's acceptance, contact information and any change in compensation. Some of these

---

4   See *Scott on Trusts*, Section 175 (1987).

responsibilities may be waived by the grantor or beneficiary of the trust, but others are mandatory and non-waivable. Depending on family dynamics, a waiver of beneficiary notice may be appropriate in some cases, where local law permits and the family deems it appropriate.

1.5   Duty to invest and to make property productive

Among a trustee's most important duties is the proper management, investment and protection of the trust assets. "The Trustee is under a duty to the beneficiaries to use reasonable care and skill to make the trust property productive in a manner that is consistent with the fiduciary duties of caution and impartiality."[5]

The Uniform Prudent Investor Act in the United States, approved by the National Conference of Commissioners on Uniform State Law in 1994, and adopted in part in 46 US states, incorporates modern portfolio theory to mandate a prudent investor standard of care for fiduciary investment decisions. Modern portfolio theory assumes that rational investors will use diversification to optimise their portfolios.

Prior to the Uniform Prudent Investor Act, trustees in the United States were limited to statutory lists of permissible investments and were held to a 'prudent man' standard – that is, the trustee was required to make such investments and only such investments as a prudent person would make of his or her own property, having in view the preservation of the estate and the amount and regularity of the income to be derived. The primary focus was the preservation of property, and each investment was individually subject to scrutiny for productivity and safety. It was also not entirely clear whether trustees were permitted to seek professional investment advice, although most trustees did so.

Under the Uniform Prudent Investor Act, many of these concerns were addressed. It makes clear that the entire investment portfolio should be considered when determining the prudence of any individual investment. Section 2(b) of the act states: "A trustee's investment and management decisions respecting individual assets must be evaluated not in isolation but in the context of the trust portfolio as a whole and as part of an overall investment strategy for total return having risk and return objectives reasonably suited to the trust."

Losses in an individual investment are not a breach of the fiduciary's standard of care, so long as that investment was consistent with the overall portfolio objectives. Prudence is determined by the investment process, not by the performance results. No longer is each investment reviewed on its own merits essentially in isolation from all other investments, as was the standard for the prudent man or prudent person rule that preceded it.[6]

---

5   Restatement of Trusts (Third) Section 181.

The trustee should take into account many factors in choosing investments, including:

- the nature and estimated duration of the fiduciary relationship;
- the size of the portfolio;
- liquidity and distribution needs of both the beneficiaries and the trust itself;
- general economic conditions;
- the possible impact of inflation and deflation;
- expected tax consequences;
- the role each investment plays within the overall context of the portfolio; and
- the expected total return.

The prudent trustee should make a point of documenting that such factors have been taken into account, as this will go far to protect the trustee later in litigation should the investments not perform as anticipated.

No category of investment is deemed inherently imprudent in itself. Instead, suitability to the trust's purposes and beneficiaries' needs is the determinant. Fiduciaries are permitted and encouraged to develop greater flexibility in the management of the overall portfolio, but speculation and outright risk taking are not sanctioned. Nevertheless, options, hedge funds, commodities and the like may all have a place in a diversified portfolio: "An investment that might be imprudent standing alone can become prudent if undertaken in sensible relation to other trust assets, or to other non-trust assets."[7]

Diversification is an important tenet of prudent fiduciary investing. "Diversification reduces risk ... [because] stock price movements are not uniform. They are imperfectly correlated. This means that if one holds a well-diversified portfolio, the gains in one investment will cancel out the losses in another."[8]

The Uniform Prudent Investor Act requires diversification as part of the fiduciary's prudent investor standard of care. Section 3 states: "A trustee shall diversify the investments of the trust unless the trustee reasonably determines that, because of special circumstances, the purposes of the trust are better served without diversifying."

---

6   This 'prudence' standard in the United States is traditionally traced back to *Harvard College v Amory*, 26 Mass 446 (1830), where it was held (at 461) that trustees should "observe how men of prudence, discretion and intelligence manage their own affairs, not in regard to speculation, but in regard to the permanent disposition of their funds, considering the probable income, as well as the probable safety of the capital to be invested".
See also Restatement of the Law of Trusts (Second), Section 227 (1959).

7   "Portfolio standard" comment to Section 2(b) of the Uniform Prudent Investor Act.

8   Jonathan R Macey, *An Introduction to Modern Financial Theory* 20 (American College of Trust and Estate Counsel Foundation, 1991).

Trustees should have such an overall investment strategy for the trust portfolio as a whole, not on an individual security basis, as was the case before the Uniform Prudent Investor Act, and should be able to document how each asset category fits into the overall strategy. Such investment strategies should be reviewed periodically and communicated to the beneficiaries, as appropriate.

Managing investment risk is not the same as eliminating investment risk. The risk/return analysis of investments in a trust's portfolio might consider many different types of risk, including not just market risk, but also company-specific risk, industry-specific risk, interest rate, liquidity, currency and geopolitical risk, to name a few. In investing and managing trust assets, the trustee should consider these risks along with general economic conditions, inflation, expected tax consequences, the beneficiaries' other available resources and liquidity needs, and whether a particular asset has any special relationship or special value to the trust purposes (Uniform Prudent Investor Act, Section 2(c)). The comments note that: "tolerance for risk varies greatly with the ... purposes of the trust and the relevant circumstances of the beneficiaries. A trust whose main purpose is to support an elderly widow of modest means will have a lower risk tolerance than a trust to accumulate for a young scion of great wealth."

In an interesting 2014 case involving beneficiaries who sued the trustee of a trust established by former US President John Adams almost 200 years ago, the Massachusetts Supreme Judicial Court ruled against the trustee for failure to diversify the trust investments and failure to act on professional investment advice given to the trustee.[9] The Woodward School for Girls, the income beneficiary since 1953, filed suit against the city of Quincy, as trustee, charging that Quincy had breached its fiduciary duties to keep adequate records, invest the trust's assets properly, exercise reasonable prudence in the sales of real estate and incur only reasonable expenses related to trust management. The court removed the city as trustee and awarded the beneficiary substantial damages to compensate it for unrealised returns starting decades earlier, due to the city's failure to properly invest the money. The decision was approved on appeal, though the amount of damages awarded was recalculated.

1.6   Duty of loyalty to beneficiaries

The trustee is under a duty of absolute loyalty to the beneficiaries, whose interests it is charged with protecting. This duty is at the heart of the fiduciary relationship.

All expenditures should be solely in the interest of the beneficiaries and the trustee must not use the trust as a source of funds for personal activities, interests or investments, or any other transactions that might create a conflict

---

9   *The Woodward School for Girls, Inc v City of Quincy*, 469 Mass.151 – Mass: Supreme Judicial Court 2014.

of interest, especially avoiding any self-dealing. A conflict might arise from a family relationship between the trustee and the beneficiaries, or a business relationship between the trustee and the investment assets owned by the trust. In the United States, the Uniform Trust Code enacted by many states creates a rebuttable presumption of conflict for any transaction between trustees and related parties involving the investment or management of trust assets.

The trustee should avoid even the appearance of self-dealing and should not accept compensation, such as a bonus or commission, or even favourable business terms, from a third party for an act performed in the administration of the trust.

Trustees have been sued for charging excessive fees. Noted artist Robert Rauschenberg's estate created a $600 million trust and his three trustees sought fees of $60 million.[10] The remainder beneficiary, Rauschenberg's charitable foundation, sued the trustees for siphoning funds from the charity's mission, despite an alleged substantial increase in the value of the trust's assets during the period of their stewardship. The court ultimately reduced the trustees' fees from the $60 million requested to approximately $25 million, citing the trustees' unusual skill and experience, exemplary work and loyalty to the estate in support of the substantial fees it did award to the trustees.

In extreme cases, the fiduciary's lack of loyalty can even lead to criminal penalties. Brooke Astor was a New York City philanthropist and socialite who was the beneficiary of a $60 million marital trust established by her late husband. She also established a $30 million charitable remainder trust. Her only son, Anthony D Marshall, was convicted in criminal court of grand larceny and other charges related to the looting of his mother's assets while she suffered from Alzheimer's disease. This case has become prominent in recent discussions of the crime of elder abuse. Marshall received a sentence of one to three years in prison, but was medically paroled and subsequently died the following year.[11]

The trustee's duty of loyalty applies impartially to all beneficiaries. If the trust has multiple beneficiaries, the trustee must act impartially when investing, managing and distributing trust property, giving due regard to all of the beneficiaries' respective interests.

A significant tension arises with this duty of impartiality when the current income beneficiaries pressure the trustee to invest for current income, but the remaindermen prefer investment for long-term growth without diminution by current income distribution. Similarly, the current income beneficiaries might pressure the trustee to exercise its discretion to increase the rate of current distributions, and the trustee must balance the income beneficiaries' needs

---

10   *In Re The Estate of Rauschenberg*, Circuit Court of Florida, 20th Judicial Circuit (Lee County), File 08-CP-2479 (15 August 2014).

11   Joseph A Rosenberg, "Regrettably Unfair: Brooke Astor and the Other Elderly in New York", 30 *Pace Law Review* 1004 (2010). Available at digitalcommons.pace.edu/plr/vol30/iss3/7.

against the interests of the remaindermen, who may be of a younger generation or perhaps in a different branch of the family. This tension is discussed in more detail in section 1.7 of this chapter. If the remainderman is a charitable entity, additional oversight may be required by a local governmental agency charged with protecting the charity's interests, depending on jurisdiction.

1.7   Trust distributions

An essential, and non-delegable, aspect of the trustee's administration of a trust according to its terms is the duty to make distributions to beneficiaries. All mandatory distributions required by the trust instrument must be made in a timely fashion, and the trustee must exercise its discretion in a disciplined manner to determine whether to make allowable but non-mandatory discretionary distributions according to the standard specified in the instrument.

If the trustee, or a family member or other related party of the trustee, is also a permissible distributee of the trust, care must be taken to avoid real or perceived conflicts in distribution determinations. In a case involving Jay Pritzker, settled confidentially out of court, family members claimed that $500 million had been allegedly improperly distributed to offshore trusts for the benefit of the immediate family of Jay's son Thomas who, after his father's death, took over leadership of the family empire, which includes the Hyatt hotel chain. Another $500 million for Thomas and his two cousins in equity stakes in deals financed with family money brought transfers to him of over $1 billion, according to investigations by the *Chicago Tribune*. The private negotiated lawsuit settlement resulted in the breakup of the family empire among the various family branches – an outcome that Pritzker had purportedly not wanted.[12]

The most challenging discretionary distribution decisions often involve the pressure of satisfying the needs of often competing beneficiaries' interests. One of the difficulties with the Uniform Prudent Investor Act in the United States was that trustees who followed it often found themselves investing in asset categories that yielded little or no return for the current income beneficiaries. Particularly in declining interest and dividend markets, many fiduciaries were in a difficult position: if they followed the Uniform Prudent Investor Act, the current beneficiaries would be disadvantaged because insufficient income was being produced for distribution; if they invested for current returns to satisfy the current beneficiaries, they would have to adopt an asset allocation that would otherwise not meet the investment standards of the Uniform Prudent Investor Act and might well disadvantage the long-term growth expected by the remaindermen.

---

12   "Inside the Pritzker family feud", *Chicago Tribune*, 12 June 2005; available at articles.chicagotribune.com/2005-06-12/news/0506120282_1_penny-pritzker-jay-pritzker-family-businesses.

The US Uniform Principal and Income Act provides a mechanism to address this tension. The fiduciary is permitted to 'adjust' between principal and income – that is, to treat some portion of principal as if it were income available for distribution or vice versa – if:

- a fiduciary invests pursuant to the tenets of the prudent investor rule;
- the trust describes the amounts to be distributed to the current beneficiaries by reference to the 'trust's income'; and
- the fiduciary finds itself unable to meet its requirement to treat all beneficiaries equitably.

In this way, the trustee can invest in a prudent manner and still satisfy the income beneficiary's desire for current distributions.

The Uniform Principal and Income Act sets out nine specific factors that a trustee must consider in the exercise of this power (at Section 104(b)):

- the nature, purpose and expected duration of the trust;
- the intent of the settlor;
- the identity and circumstances of the beneficiaries;
- the needs for liquidity, regularity of income and preservation and appreciation of capital;
- the assets held in the trust; the extent to which they consist of financial assets, interests in closely held enterprises, tangible and intangible personal property, or real property; the extent to which an asset is used by a beneficiary; and whether an asset was purchased by the trustee or received from the grantor;
- the net amount allocated to income under the other sections of the act and the increase or decrease in the value of the principal assets, which the trustee may estimate as to assets for which market values are not readily available;
- whether and to what extent the terms of the trust give the trustee the power to invade principal or accumulate income, or prohibit the trustee from invading principal or accumulating income, and the extent to which the trustee has exercised a power from time to time to invade principal or accumulate income;
- the actual and anticipated effect of economic conditions on principal and income and effects of inflation and deflation; and
- the anticipated tax consequences of an adjustment.

The existence of nine mandatory factors (the act provides that the trustee 'shall' consider) can make this process a minefield for the unwary trustee, though some US states have modified the 'shall' standard to provide instead that a trustee 'may', but is not required to, consider certain of these factors. Even in jurisdictions where the Uniform Principal and Income Act either does not exist or has not been adopted, or where the Uniform Principal and Income Act has been adopted but does not require mandatory consideration of these factors, it is nevertheless a helpful framework to follow and demonstrates that the trustee has considered all issues which might impact on the situation.

This power to adjust is not intended as a substitute for an invasion power. In fact, one of the factors that trustees are required to take into account is whether there is such a power of invasion. If there is, then there is an open question about whether it is even appropriate to exercise the power to adjust, and many US fiduciaries will not undertake the exercise of the power to adjust if they can satisfy their fiduciary duties by an invasion power instead.

If the distribution standard is defined according to income, the trustee may make adjustments between income and principal if the trustee determines that doing so will enable the trustee to make appropriate present and future distributions taking into account the prudent investor standard. By giving the fiduciary the power to adjust between income and principal, the US fiduciary now has the ability to invest for total return, adopting a prudent investment allocation under the Uniform Prudent Investor Act, without the need to skew the investment portfolio to satisfy the current beneficiary's need for current income. This power to adjust is therefore inextricably tied to the prudent investor standard. Some US states' versions, in fact, went so far as to include the power to adjust within their prudent investor statute.

In July 2018, the Uniform Law Commission in the United States approved a major revision of the Uniform Principal and Income Act, retitling the act as the Uniform Fiduciary Income and Principal Act (UFIPA). There are a number of significant provisions; one of the most significant is the expanded power to adjust if the fiduciary determines that the exercise of the power to adjust will assist the fiduciary to administer the trust impartially. Another significant change is that UFIPA now allows conversions to unitrust – an annual distribution of a stated percentage of the value of the trust assets each year. These changes will permit even older trusts to invest on a total return basis, while managing expectations of current income beneficiaries.[13] At the time of writing, one US state has already enacted UFIPA (Utah), and it has been introduced in the legislature of another (Tennessee).

2.   Exoneration clauses and indemnification clauses

Given the risks inherent in serving as trustee, with the obligations listed above, how can a trustee protect himself or herself? In the case of outright fraud or wilful misconduct, the trustee will likely be held strictly liable and no attempted

---

13   The Uniform Fiduciary Income and Principal Act drafted by the National Conference of Commissioners on Uniform State Laws and by it approved and recommended for enactment in all the states at its Annual Conference Meeting in its One-Hundred-And-Twenty-Seventh Year Louisville, Kentucky, 20–26 July 2018.

protection will immunise the trustee. In claims for less egregious conduct brought by trust beneficiaries and others, typical solutions include exoneration ('hold harmless') clauses, indemnification clauses and insurance.

The trust instrument itself may provide some protection to the trustee by providing indemnification out of the trust estate against claims of negligence, and often will include a provision limiting the trustee's personal liability to gross negligence or wilful misconduct.

As is mentioned in the Hong Kong chapter, a trustee exemption clause may not relieve trustees of liability for breach of trust caused by the trustee's fraud, wilful misconduct or gross negligence.

Similarly, exoneration clauses in English trusts are valid to prevent the trustees from being liable for all but their own fraud and wilful misconduct, as discussed in greater detail in that chapter. The Law Commission recommends that trustees disclose the extent and effect of any exoneration clause to the trust settlor before the trust is established.

In the United States, even an exculpatory clause or indemnification clause in the governing instrument may not be enough to help a trustee who fails sufficiently to diversify the trust's investment portfolio, depending on all the facts and circumstances. Even where the grantor's intent is directly stated in the governing instrument and the trustee is absolutely directed to hold an investment forever, there is some authority that such a direction must be disregarded.

This situation is particularly common in cases where a single holding created the family's wealth and there is some sentimental attachment among the trust beneficiaries to retaining that concentrated holding. Special care must be taken in these cases objectively to review the holding on a regular and consistent basis to determine whether it should continue to be held at all and, if so, whether the continuing concentration is warranted. If the beneficiaries insist on retaining a concentrated position in the trust despite the trustee's cautionary warning, the trustee would do well to request and retain written documentation of that insistence on a recurring basis.

For example, in two cases substantial surcharges were imposed for continuing to retain concentrated holdings in Eastman Kodak stock, both of which were decided under the prior prudent person standard that did not impose a mandatory diversification rule: *Matter of Janes*[14] ($4 million judgment) and *Matter of Dumont*.[15] In *Janes*, the trustees continued to hold the Kodak stock, roughly 75% of the total trust assets, for over seven years, during which time the value declined from $139 per share to $47 per share. The court surcharged the trustee for failure to diversify.

---

14   90 NY 2d 41 (1997).
15   813 NYS 2d 689 (28 Apri 2006, denied motion for leave to appeal to the Court of Appeals), 809 NYS 2d 360 (App Div, 4th Department 3 February 2006, reversing Surrogate's Court), 781 NYS 2d 625 (Surrogate's Court of Monroe County 2004).

Asset retention clauses in the governing instrument do not always provide the protection to the fiduciary intended by the grantor or the draftsperson. If the beneficiary requests (or insists) that the trustee retain a concentrated position, the trustee might consider requesting written approval and release from the beneficiary, and such decisions not to diversify a concentrated position should be reviewed periodically. It is the pattern of communication with beneficiaries that has protected trustees in many cases.

In *Dumont*, the testamentary trust was funded with a large concentration of Kodak stock, and the trustee could not show that it ever reviewed the continued suitability of retaining that position over many years or discussed the concentrated position with the family. The trustee relied on a clearly worded retention clause in the instrument, but the court rejected that reliance: "A retention clause does not exculpate [the fiduciary] from poor judgment and laziness but instead ... almost requires a greater level of diligence and work."

Indemnification clauses – where the trustee is entitled to reimbursement directly from the trust estate or from the beneficiaries for any loss if the trustee acted within the scope of his or her appointment and exercised the proper reasonable care in administering the trust assets absent negligence or other misconduct – are another mechanism to provide comfort to trustees. Before relying on such an indemnification, however, the trustee would be well advised to confirm that the trust assets will be sufficient to sustain such an indemnification.

In *Americans for the Arts v Ruth Lilly Charitable Remainder Annuity Trust*[16] the Indiana Court of Appeals upheld the grant of a motion for summary judgment brought by the bank trustee of two charitable remainder annuity trusts invested initially solely in one stock because there was a very specific and non-boilerplate retention clause in the governing instrument that permitted the trustee to hold onto that stock, the trust beneficiaries participated actively in the planning process establishing that instrument, and the trustees were in periodic contact with the beneficiaries about the concentrated position.

As the chapter on New Zealand law discusses, New Zealand trust instruments commonly use indemnity provisions. Such clauses are effective only when the trustee has acted reasonably after considering all the facts and circumstances, and the court determines that the trustee has not overreached.

Another approach might be to designate a third party who could give direction to the trustee regarding the retention or sale of the concentrated position or other asset in a jurisdiction that allows the trustee to rely on such directions. Absent wilful misconduct, the trustee will not be held liable for relying on investment instructions from a direction adviser in certain jurisdictions. This arrangement is becoming increasingly common in a number of states in the United States.

---

16   855 NE 2d 592 (Ct App Ind 2006).

Likewise, New Zealand law allows for an advisory trustee – a party who has no fiduciary obligations, but who may advise the trustee on any trust administration matter. A trustee is provided with protection for having followed the advice of the advisory trustee.

If trustee liability insurance is available and the trust instrument or local law permits the insurance premiums to be paid from the trust assets, it can be a solution when soliciting a potential trustee's agreement to accept appointment over the trust, particularly when there are concentrated asset holdings or other factors that might otherwise give the trustee pause:

> *In addition to indemnification that may be available from the trust, the best approach for Individuals serving in the role of trustee, is to also purchase trustee professional liability insurance. This is because trustees are held to a high fiduciary standard and as a result have exposure to professional liability as they oversee management of trust assets. Trustees should work with their insurance broker to have the policy tailored to their specific responsibilities. The trustees would purchase professional liability insurance or commonly known as errors and omissions insurance. The policy provides coverage for defined professional services.* [17]

3.   Trustee succession clauses

Perpetual trusts are becoming increasingly common as ever more jurisdictions repeal the common law rule against perpetuities. Accordingly, greater attention than ever before needs to be paid to trustee succession clauses. Older trust instruments generally do not contain provisions permitting the trustee to resign, permitting the beneficiaries to remove an acting trustee or containing a procedure to effectuate a change, often necessitating expensive court proceedings.

Some drafters intentionally resist provisions authorising beneficiaries to remove an uncooperative trustee, on the theory that the trustee should not be fired for making an unpopular distribution decision. There is equal resistance to provisions authorising corporate trustees to resign from difficult situations, because those challenging scenarios are just why the family named an impartial trustee to serve in the first place. Ultimately, though, forcing the trustee and beneficiaries to continue in an unproductive and uncommunicative relationship serves no one.

Practitioners who are drafting (or are being asked to serve as trustee under) a new trust instrument should consider including resignation provisions in the governing document, as well as provisions allowing the beneficiaries to remove the trustee. The critical corollary is that there must also be a process in the

---

17   Linda Bourn, executive managing director, family enterprise risk practice, Crystal Private Client, A Division of Alliant.

instrument to designate a successor trustee to serve in the event of the trustee resignation, removal or other inability to serve. Some instruments authorise the resigning trustee to name its own successor or the current income beneficiaries may name the successor trustee. Some boilerplate clauses even authorise the drafting law firm to designate a successor trustee in the event of a vacancy in named successors, especially where there is a longstanding client relationship.

4. Delegation

As discussed above, the trustee may delegate many administrative functions, including the investment function, but is ultimately responsible for assembling the team and supervising all of them. The trustee may employ a blend of internal staff and outsourced advisers, and must establish appropriate criteria to decide on the quality of the team members and continually monitor the team for effectiveness, efficiency and attention to the mandate of the trust according to its terms and applicable laws. The trustee cannot avoid liability for negligent act of the advisers and agents he or she hires, and must supervise, monitor and oversee their performance. Costs incurred in hiring such advisers and agents must be reasonable and not otherwise burdensome to the trust.

Typical functions that the trustee may choose to outsource include the record-keeping and reporting functions for income, expenses and distributions of the trust for the benefit of the beneficiaries. This also includes tax preparation and filings and other tax advice from time to time, as well as periodic legal advice on matters related to trust administration.

The trustee might need to hire specialists knowledgeable about particular asset holdings of the trust, such as collectibles, real estate or oil and gas interests, and will need to obtain specialty insurance for those unique assets.

Notwithstanding the relaxation of the prohibition of the common law rules against delegation of trustee functions, the trustee may not delegate its discretion to invade principal. This element of judgement and discretion is non-delegable, and is at the core of why the grantor named the trustee to serve in the first place.

As discussed above, in the United States, the Uniform Prudent Investor Act reversed the previous standard forbidding trustees from delegating investment management decisions. Section 9 provides: "A trustee may delegate investment and management functions that a prudent trustee of comparable skills could properly delegate under the circumstances." If a trustee does delegate all, or even some portion of, the investment function, local statutes may have specific requirements to notify beneficiaries.

The Uniform Prudent Investor Act and most state statutes require that the trustee establish the scope and terms of the delegation and exercise reasonable care, skill and caution in the delegation. The trustee must also periodically review the performance of the delegee, as the trustee has a "continuing responsibility for oversight of the suitability of investments already made as well as the trustee's decisions respecting new investments" (comment to Section 2 of the Uniform Prudent Investor Act).

Regardless of which type of functions the trustees may decide to delegate, they must monitor and supervise the conduct of their agents in accordance with their ultimate obligation to safeguard the beneficiaries' interests, which cannot be delegated. If the trustee merely accepts outside advice without diligently evaluating its suitability for the particular trust's beneficiaries, the trustee could be liable for breach of trust and any losses attributable to this lapse in judgement.

5. Decanting

In 2015, the Uniform Trust Decanting Act (UTDA) was approved by the Uniform Law Commission in the US. Decanting describes the distribution of assets from an original trust into a new trust, like wine is decanted from an original bottle into a new receptacle. In general, the UTDA permits decanting of an irrevocable trust in which the terms of the trust grant the trustee or another fiduciary the discretionary power to make principal distributions. It does not impose any duty on the trustee to exercise the decanting power, but if the trustee does exercise that power, such power must be exercised in accordance with the trustee's fiduciary duties. As a fiduciary power, the decanting power may be exercised without consent or approval of the beneficiaries or the court.[18] At the time of writing, eight US states have enacted the UTDA: Illinois (2019), Alabama (2018), California (2018), North Carolina (2017), Washington (2017), Virginia (2017), New Mexico (2016) and Colorado (2016); and one additional state has introduced it (Massachusetts).

6. Compliance with tax laws and other regulatory requirements

The trustee is responsible for filing all tax returns for the trust itself and for providing required tax information reports to beneficiaries who may receive taxable income from the trust in a particular year. US federal income tax laws for trusts are complex, as are US income tax laws which govern taxability by the individual states, and trustees must seek appropriate tax advisers to make informed tax elections and be mindful of filing deadlines and other requirements. Trusts with multinational beneficiaries have more complex filing requirements and will require a higher level of skill and care, including facility deciphering international tax treaties.

In addition, the trustee must be mindful of any necessary gift, estate and generation-skipping transfer tax filing responsibilities.

Depending on the nature of the trust investments, the trustee should also understand its obligations under the applicable securities laws.

---

18   Uniform Trust Decanting Act drafted by the National Conference of Commissioners on Uniform State Laws and by it approved and recommended for enactment in all the states at its Annual Conference Meeting in its One-Hundred-And-Twenty-Fourth Year Williamsburg, Virginia, 10–16 July 2015.

7.   Minimising risk

In order to minimise the risk of fiduciary litigation, the nominated trustee should adopt certain best practices before even accepting the appointment. First, the trustee should understand all terms and requirements under the governing trust instrument and under all applicable laws, including trust laws, tax laws and securities laws. The trustee should also gain a full appreciation of the nature and extent of all the assets that will be funded into the trust, both to assess liability and to determine whether any special skills will be needed with respect to those assets.

The trustee must also carefully evaluate whether he or she will have any conflict of interest with respect to any aspect of the trust administration, especially if the trustee is also employed by – or related to – the trust's grantor or beneficiaries in another capacity. In the case of a trust instrument still being drafted, it is helpful for the settlor to acknowledge and waive the conflict of interest directly in the governing instrument. Even with such waiver, a conflicted trustee should be particularly transparent and communicative in order to avoid the appearance of impropriety.

In determining whether to accept the appointment, the nominated trustee would be wise also to consider the family's history of litigation, if any, and potential for future litigation. Such factors might include unequal treatment of different family members, especially if children from a parent's first marriage receive different percentages from those from the second or third marriage. Another litigation risk factor might be a trust amendment or restatement shortly before the grantor's disability or death resulting in a dramatic change in beneficiary expectations.

Once the trustee has accepted the appointment, he or she must provide all required notices to the beneficiaries in a timely manner; hire and supervise investment, legal and tax advisers; invest prudently; and exercise prudent discretion over distributions to beneficiaries.

8.   Conclusion

Fiduciary liability of trustees encompasses every aspect of trust administration. While the responsibility ultimately emanates from the governing instrument itself, additional duties and liability may be found in statutes, court cases, regulatory authority, tax rules, investment restrictions and numerous other sources. Of paramount importance throughout the process is regular and consistent communication with the trust beneficiaries. Trustees must seek advice from qualified professionals before, during and after the period of trust administration in order to fulfil their various obligations.

Waqf as a form of trust

Mohammad Abu Obied

Judge of the High *Sharia* Court of Appeal, Jerusalem

Most of the common and legal systems concerning *Waqf* are informed by the general Islamic concept of *Waqf*. Therefore, the general principles can serve as a guideline for dealing with *Waqf*, taking into account the modifications from one legal system to another. The general principles reflect the various definitions of *Waqf* set out by judicial scholars. This chapter discusses the application of *Waqf* and its terms, with the main focus on the Hanafi School.

Historically, things have been assigned as *Waqf* since the beginning of Islam. The first *Waqf* was the building of the *Kaaba* in Makkah, which the *Qur'an* mentions was the first house of worship built for the people. The Bible likewise mentions assigning *Waqf* for the sake of Allah. The *Qur'an* states that the mother of Mariam (the mother of Jesus) vowed to bring up her child for the service and worship of *Bait al-Maqdis* – a form of *Waqf*. If children were made *Waqf* for the houses of Allah, this is good reason to believe that other items were also made *Waqf*. Islam broadened the concept of *Waqf*.

Many examples of *Waqf* can be found in the early periods of Islam. Uthman (the third *Khalipha*) made the well of Roma *Waqf*. Imam Bukhari, in his Sahih, narrates the incident of the *Waqf* made by Umer (the second *Khalipha*). He made the land which he acquired from the battle of Khaibar *Waqf* and stipulated that it could not be sold, gifted or inherited. The income derived therefrom would be spent on travellers, guests, soldiers, the poor and needy, and the family members of Umer. Hafsa was the first trustee and thereafter Ibn Umer. After their demise, the eldest from the family of Umer became the trustees. The trustees could eat from the land an ordinary amount of produce, but were not allowed to hoard and stock it.

Islam has given great support to such organisations and investment schemes. The prophet said: "When a person passes away, his actions from him are terminated, except in three cases. He gave something in charity which is continuing, or knowledge which is benefited from, or son who makes dua (prayers) for him."

1. The meaning of Waqf

Waqf – endowment (in Arabic, 'وقف', pronounced 'Wahqf') – translates as 'forbidding' or 'freezing'. The meaning of '*Waqf* endowment' is very close to that of '*habs*' (literally 'locking up'). As regards the exact legal definition of the *Waqf* endowment, scholars differ in their views, depending on their jurisprudential affiliation. However, the basic meaning is the same for all. The Hanafi define it as "estopping any person from owning the property, with the benefit generally being dedicated to help the poor or for some other charitable purpose". The Hanbali define it as "bequesting the property and dedicating the fruit". *Waqf* is also used to name the body that manages the endowment.

These definitions imply that if the *Waqf* is made correctly, the right of ownership of the subject matter of the *Waqf* is withdrawn from the person making the *Waqf* (the *Waqif*). He or she loses his or her right over it and deposits it in Allah's trust; and neither that person nor his or her heirs nor anybody else can sell it, buy it, give it as a gift, inherit it or carry out any transaction or disposition of title on it. Neither can anybody claim ownership of it. Once the offer of the *Waqf* is made, it is irreversible and cannot be broken, either by the *Waqif* or by anybody else. Its fruits and benefits must be enjoyed by the named beneficiaries set by the *Waqif* in accordance with the terms and conditions of the *Waqf*.

This means that the *Waqif* is not responsible for the expenditure, maintenance or care of the subject matter, unless he or she volunteers. Therefore, the *Waqif* is not obliged to repair the property. Instead, all of these expenses are taken care of by the *Waqf* and whoever is responsible for it (the *Mutawalli*, or trustee), in conformity with the terms and conditions devised for each *Waqf* or the general rules of endowments.

Waqf can be divided into two types: family *Waqf* and charitable (public) *Waqf*. A precondition for establishing a family *Waqf* is an expressed intention to convert to a charitable *Waqf* at some stage (eg, "the fruit of the *Waqf* shall be to my inheritance and their inheritance and then for a charitable purpose"). In the absence of such express condition, a *Waqf* cannot be concluded or established.

2. Establishing *Waqf*

A *Waqf* is established by express and clear statement of the owner concerning the subject matter – for example: "I hereby declare that this land or property is *Waqf* for the benefit of the named beneficiaries and then after for the sake of God."

At the time the *Waqif* completes his or her announcement, the *Waqf* is established and the property ceases to be considered his or her own, even if the declaration was not registered formally.

It is not necessary to utter the formal declaration of *Waqf* in Arabic. If, for example, a person says, "I have *Waqf*ed this book for the students," it will be considered valid. In fact, *Waqf* is also established by conduct. Therefore, if a person spreads a mat in a mosque with an intention of *Waqf* or constructs a building with the appearance of a mosque with the intention of giving it away as a mosque, the *Waqf* will be established.

The *Waqif* needs no acceptance to validate his or her announcement, even on the part of the beneficiaries, in the case of public *Waqfs*, such as a mosque, a *madressah* (school), any public utility or *Waqf* for the poor or for *Sadqat* (charity). *Waqf* does not require anyone to make a formal acceptance. The *Waqf* is established immediately upon its declaration as such. In fact, even private *awqaf*, such as those created for one's own children, require no acceptance.

A private *Waqf* will be valid when the property which has been *Waqf*ed is given away, at the disposal of beneficiaries of the first category or their representatives or guardians. If a person *Waqf*s something upon his or her minor children and looks after it on their behalf with the intention that it will become their property, the *Waqf* is in order.

It is well known among scholars that a witness who hears an announcement declaring a *Waqf* will have standing to bring an action in court for the registration of the *Waqf*, even if the *Waqif* refuses to do so. Moreover, the *Waqif* has no power to withdraw from his or her announcement. The manner in which a *Waqif* is eligible to initiate *Waqf* in accordance with the general rules concerning the *Waqif*, the subject matter and the statement initiating the *Waqf* will be dealt with later in this chapter.

The announcement must be direct and clear, with no condition as to its validity; otherwise, the *Waqf* will not be established. If a person *Waqf*s a property, he or she should make it a perpetual *Waqf* from the day he or she declares the *Waqf*. Therefore, if he or she says, "This property is *Waqf* after my death," the *Waqf* will not be valid, because it will not cover the period from the time of declaration until his or her death. Also, if he says, "This property will remain *Waqf* for 10 years and will not be *Waqf* thereafter," or "It will be *Waqf* for 10 years and thereafter it will not be *Waqf* for five years and will become *Waqf* again after the expiry of that period," such a *Waqf* will not be valid.

Registration of the *Waqf* in court is not a precondition for its validity; it is a mere formality in order to preclude others from denying the existence of the *Waqf*. *Waqf* can also be proved by hearsay evidence and courts are obliged to accept this evidence as an exceptional rule of evidence. In Islamic law, a party to a completed contract has the right to withdraw from the contract within a maximum three-day period. However, this privilege is not available to the *Waqif*; his or her direct pronunciation is binding, since it was made of his or her own free will. Even in cases of mistaken intention, the courts will validate the *Waqf* and not void it.

3. Conditions on the *Waqif*

The person who makes a *Waqf* (the *Waqif*) should be *Baligh* (adult, mature) and sane, and should do so of his or her own free will. Also, he or she should have the right, according to *Sharia*, of disposal and discretion over his or her property. Based on this, a feeble-minded person who squanders his or her wealth and is therefore debarred cannot make a valid *Waqf*. Also a person who is a declared bankrupt or insolvent cannot make a valid *Waqf*, since, as mentioned above, the purpose of *Waqf* is perpetual endowment for the sake of God and, under Islam, debts to people take priority over God's rights. The *Waqif* must not be on his or her deathbed; but if he or she makes a *Waqf* in such circumstances, the *Waqf* will be valid if it is one-third or less of his or her legacy.

4. Conditions on the subject matter (the asset)

Any asset which is capable of being bequeathed in perpetuity can be subject to *Waqf*; however, immovable assets are preferable. Muslim societies have made *Waqf* of land, buildings, camels, cows, sheep, books, jewellery, swords, agriculture, industrial tools and similar.

The asset must be known and available at the time of initiating the *Waqf*. It must be in the full ownership of the *Waqif* and must not be subject to mortgage or foreclosure. A property transferred to the *Waqif* by a voidable agreement can be *Waqf*ed. The asset must be known and fixed, although shares in joint property can be *Waqf*ed.

5. Beneficiaries

Any person or group can be a beneficiary. The *Waqif* can also be a beneficiary of the *Waqf*, provided that it stipulates that the poor and the needy are to become beneficiaries at some stage. The underlying idea is that the poor are a permanent group and will never disappear, and that therefore it will always be possible to find beneficiaries from this group. The *Waqif* has complete discretion to decide on the beneficiaries and their share of the *Waqf*. Their shares relate not to a fixed part of the *Waqf*, but to its benefits. The beneficiaries have no title to the *Waqf* property or asset; their interest is in the fruit of the *Waqf* and no more. This benefit is personal and does not form part of their legacy, unless their successors are also eligible as beneficiaries.

Beneficiaries can be named persons or a defined group. If the *Waqif* has decided that the beneficiaries are named persons, then they must be in existence at the time of creating the *Waqf*. Otherwise, the *Waqf* will go directly to a defined group that is everlasting, such as the poor or the needy.

If a person creates a *Waqf* for himself or herself – for example, if he or she *Waqf*s a shop for himself or herself so that its income may be spent on the construction of his or her tomb after death – the *Waqf* is in order, but this condition is not valid. But if he or she creates a *Waqf* for the poor and later on himself or herself becomes poor, the *Waqif* can benefit from the accruals of that *Waqf*.

If property is made *Waqf* for an unborn child, it is *Ishkal* (problematic) for that *Waqf* to be valid and caution should be exercised in this case. However, if *Waqf* is created for a group of people who exist at the time of its creation and also for persons who will be born later, even if they may be in the womb when the *Waqf* is made, it will be in order. For example, if a person *Waqf*s a property for his or her children and after them for his or her grandchildren, and for every succeeding generation to benefit therefrom, the *Waqf* is in order.

6.   General terms

At the time the *Waqf* is declared, all powers are given to the *Waqif*. The *Waqif* can:

- set conditions and terms managing the *Waqf*;
- define the group of beneficiaries;
- decide whether the *Waqf* is private or public;
- choose the organs of the *Waqf*;
- appoint the *Mutawalli* (trustee);
- divide the benefits; and
- set any terms he or she chooses, provided that these do not contradict the spirit and general rules of *Waqf*.

If a term does indeed contradict the spirit or the general rules of *Waqf*, then such term is void, but the *Waqf* itself remains valid. There are also certain conditions that can be valid if the *Waqif* appoints himself or herself as *Mutawalli*, but will cease to be so if he or she appoints another as *Mutawalli*. The *Waqif* can include a term that he or she can sell the *Waqf* and buy another property, or exchange the property for another property, at which point the new property will automatically become *Waqf*; in these circumstances no new announcement of *Waqf* is needed. The *Waqif* can also empower the trustee to carry out the same actions; however, this empowerment is no longer valid on the death of the *Waqif*, unless he or she made an express declaration of continuity.

The *Qadi* (judge) may assume the powers of the *Waqif* if circumstances arise where this becomes necessary to protect the interests of the *Waqf*.

7.   The *Mutawalli* (trustee)

The trustee is the managing figure in the *Waqf*. He or she is responsible for taking care of the *Waqf*, managing it and protecting it from any abuse or mismanagement. He or she is also responsible for collecting the fruits of the *Waqf* and dividing them in accordance with the *Waqif*'s conditions. If the *Waqif* did not appoint the trustee at the time of initiating the *Waqf*, then the *Waqif* will become the trustee and can delegate his or her authority to *Qayim*.

The *Mutawalli* can be one person or many and the function can also be carried out by a board. The *Mutawalli* must be *Baligh* (adult, mature) and sane, trustworthy and capable of dealing with all of his or her responsibilities.

The *Waqif* can specify a mechanism to choose the *Mutawalli*. If a *Waqif* appoints a *Mutawalli* (trustee) of the property *Waqf*ed by him or her, the trustee should act according to his or her instructions. But if the *Waqif* does not appoint a trustee and, say, has *Waqf*ed the property for a particular group, such as his or her children, the discretion rests with them; and if they are not *Baligh*, the discretion rests with their guardian. The permission of the *Qadi* is not needed for the appropriation of any benefit from the *Waqf*. However, for any such steps taken to safeguard the interest of the *Waqf* or the interest of future generations, such as repairing or hiring it for the benefit of a future generation, then permission from the *Qadi* is required.

If a person *Waqf*s a property – for example, for the poor or for charitable purposes – and does not appoint the trustee for the *Waqf*, the discretion with regard to that *Waqf* rests with the *Qadi*.

If a person *Waqf*s a property for a particular group, such as his or her descendants, so that every generation should benefit from it successively, and to achieve that purpose the trustee of the *Waqf* leases it out, and then he or she dies, the lease will not become void. But if the *Waqf* has no trustee and one generation for whom the property has been *Waqf*ed leases it out and they die during the currency of the lease, and the next generation does not endorse the lease, the lease becomes void; and if the lessee has paid rent for the entire period, he or she is entitled to a refund of the rent for the period from the time of death until the end of the period of lease.

If the *Waqf*ed property is ruined, its position as *Waqf* is not affected, except when the *Waqf* is of a special nature and that special feature ceases to exist. For example, if a person endows a garden and the garden is ruined, the *Waqf* becomes void and the garden reverts to the heirs of the person.

If one part of a property has been *Waqf*ed and another part has not, and the property is undivided, the *Qadi* or trustee of the *Waqf* or the beneficiaries can divide the property and separate the *Waqf* in consultation with the experts.

The *Mutawalli* can assign his or her powers to a third party and can pay it from the fees he or she receives from the *Waqf*. If the *Waqif* has assigned all of his or her powers to the *Mutawalli*, then the *Mutawalli* can assign those powers to a third party if such assignment is made with the consent of a *Qadi*.

The *Mutawalli* can be paid a salary for managing the *Waqf*. The salary may be fixed by the *Waqif* if the *Mutawalli* was appointed by him or her. If the fixed salary appears to exceed the effort needed to manage the *Waqf*, the extra is considered as shares on the *Waqf* benefit and the figure cannot be reduced. If, however, the fixed salary set by the *Mutawalli* is less than the effort needed to manage the *Waqf*, a *Qadi* can increase it to the appropriate level. Meanwhile, if the *Mutawalli* was appointed by a *Qadi*, then the salary shall not exceed a level which is appropriate to the job. On the death of a *Mutawalli*, payment of his or her salary will cease and the extra part will not pass to his or her inheritance, unless the *Waqif* made express provision for this in the *Waqf* document. The *Qadi* has no powers to dismiss the *Mutawalli* who was appointed by the *Waqif*, except in case of fraud or serious misconduct.

The *Mutawalli's* office has all the powers over the *Waqf* that any owner has over his or her property, except the power to sell the *Waqf* or any act of disposal that leads to the destruction of the property that is the subject of the *Waqf*. He or she must comply in any action with any terms set by the *Waqif*, provided that those conditions are eligible. He or she must also invest the *Waqf* and pay its expenses, even if the *Waqif* made no specific mention of this in his or her conditions, because this is in the interests of the *Waqf*.

On the other hand, the *Mutawalli* will not be allowed to exchange the subject matter of the *Waqf* and cannot change the shares of the beneficiaries, unless he or she is expressly allowed to do so. Neither is the *Mutawalli* allowed to rent or lease the *Waqf* for his or her own interest, even if he or she pays appropriate rent. He or she may not add buildings to the *Waqf* without the prior consent of the beneficiaries if doing so will affect their shares. The *Mutawalli* cannot mortgage the *Waqf* to create a debt for the *Waqf* or for the beneficiaries, knowing that a mortgage may end with the sale of the *Waqf*. However, the *Mutawalli* is allowed to borrow for the benefit of the *Waqf*, provided that this is sanctioned by the *Waqif* or the judge. In the event of litigation, the *Mutawalli* cannot admit liability in the name of the *Waqf* and any judgment against the *Waqf* should be proved by the general rules of evidence and not by the *Mutawalli's* admission.

The *Mutawalli* is not accountable and will have no personal responsibility for losses or damages if he or she has acted in good faith and without negligence. The burden of proof rests with those who claim the contrary, and the *Mutawalli* has immunity from being held personally responsible for his or her actions where he or she has acted reasonably and without recklessness. However, he or she can be held personally responsible if he or she has acted maliciously or in direct contradiction of the terms set by the *Waqif*. He or she can also be held responsible if he or she has acted recklessly or neglected his or her duties.

Where the *Mutawalli* has neglected to store the property of the *Waqf* in appropriate storage facilities and such property is ruined or stolen, he or she will be personally responsible.

If the *Mutawalli* has refused to divide the property of the *Waqf* without good reason, despite demands by the beneficiaries to do so, and the property is then ruined without any negligence on his or her part, he or she will be held responsible because he or she will be deemed to have prevented the beneficiaries from exercising their rights, even if he or she did so without any malicious intention.

If the *Mutawalli* uses the property of the *Waqf* for his or her own benefit, he or she will be held personally responsible. Moreover, if he or she sells the property of the *Waqf* in order to purchase other property and is allowed to do so, and then spends the money or does not manage it with due care, then he or she will be held responsible.

8. **The rules of the *Qadi***
    The *Waqif* is free to set terms and conditions when announcing the *Waqf*, provided that these conditions do not contradict the spirit of the *Waqf*. However, the *Qadi* can ignore some conditions that may be lawful and not contrary to the spirit of the *Waqf*, if convinced that the interest of the *Waqf* is compelling. Thus, the *Qadi* can:
    - order the exchange of the property of the *Waqf* for another property;
    - order the spending of the fruits of the *Waqf* on the construction and maintenance of the *Waqf* prior to dividing it in favour of the beneficiaries;
    - lease it for a period of more than one year, even if the *Waqif* has limited the maximum to one year's rent;
    - dismiss the *Waqif* from the position of *Mutawalli* if the latter has acted against the interests of the *Waqf*; and
    - add another *Mutawalli*, even if the *Waqif* has stated in his or her conditions that this is not allowed.

    The *Qadi* can also grant permission to lease the property of the *Waqf* for a long period of time (such a lease being called *Hikir*), provided that three conditions are met:
    - There is no available fund in the *Waqf* budget to maintain the *Waqf*;
    - There is no offer for the property to be rented with pre-rent payment; and
    - The property cannot be exchanged for other property.

    In these circumstances the *Waqf* can be leased for a long period and the fees should not be less than the market price. If the leaseholder constructs buildings or plants trees, then the lease cannot come to an end if the leaseholder pays the set fees, provided that those fees are equivalent to the market value.

9. **Court jurisdiction**
    Section 52 of the King's Order-in-Council in Palestine, 1922 states that the Muslim religious courts have exclusive jurisdiction over matters involving the creation of a *Waqf* and the internal administration of a *Waqf* created for the benefit of Muslims. Section 52 refers to the Law of *Sharia* Procedures, 1333 Hijri, 1915. Thus, the Muslim religious courts have jurisdiction over all matters concerning the internal administration of the *Waqf*, define the identity of the

Mutawalli and have powers over the appointment and dismissal of the *Mutawalli*. The religious courts also have the power to vary and limit the terms and conditions of the document of initiation of the *Waqf* if the court find that certain terms contravene the law or *Sharia* principles or the spirit of the *Waqif*, and has reasonable reasons to do so in the best interests of the *Waqf*. The powers of the courts are very broad and the discretion of the *Qadi* is considered as long as it complies with the interests of the *Waqf*.

The Muslim religious courts in Israel apply the Hanafi methods when dealing with *Waqf* cases. As this rule of the Hanafi is separate in many sources of the Hanafi school of Islamic law, it has been difficult for the *Qadi* and the parties to refer to the right principle in relevant cases. Today, the *Qadis* use the Book of *Waqf* of Qadri Pasha. Pasha was a Hanafi scholar from the late 19th century, who collected all the Hanafi principles concerning *Waqf* in the *Qanoon Al Adel Wa Al Insaaf Lilqadaa A'la Mushkilat Al Awqaf*, which comprises 646 sections. This book is the guideline for every *Qadi* when dealing with *Waqf* issues and is well known as a reference source among the public. If the *Waqif* stipulated no terms or conditions in the *Waqf* initiation document, then the rules set out in this book will apply.

Sections 99 and 100 of the book state that any condition that prejudices the interest of the *Waqf* or the interests of the beneficiaries will not be considered; while Section 100 states that any term or condition that contravenes Islamic law is void.

As discussed, there are two types of *Waqf*: a family *Waqf* and charitable (public) *Waqf*. The *Waqif* often singles out certain group of relatives from being beneficiaries of his or her wealth via using the *Waqf*. By establishing family *Waqf*, the *Waqif* can overcome and bypass the fixed Islamic law rules of inheritance, name the beneficiaries and specify the proportion of the *Waqf* for each. By contrast, the fixed rules set out in Islamic inheritance law cannot be deviated from.

10. Conclusion

The permanent nature of the *Waqf* has resulted in the accumulation of *Waqf* property all over the Muslim world. The size and objectives of *Waqf* play an important role in the socio-political life of Muslim societies and communities. Vast swathes of property have come into the hands of the *Mutawallis*; in some countries, this accounts for a significant percentage of all land. And because the revenues of the *Waqf* are often spent on mosques – including the salaries of *imams* (preachers and prayer leaders), teachers and the financing of Islamic studies – religious leaders and teachers have been able to adopt social and political positions independent of the ruling class.

This has resulted in a negative stance towards *awqaf*. In some countries – such as Syria, Egypt, Turkey, Tunisia and Algeria – the *Waqf* has been added to the public property of the government and distributed through land reforms and other means, while the relevant governments have assumed responsibility for spending on mosques and some religious schools. In Israel, the Muslim *Waqf* was added to state property and became public property under the absentee property law, which regards any property to be without ownership if its owner is absent from the state at the time set by law. The absentee property law also stipulates that the absence of either the beneficiaries or the trustee (or both) converts the property to absentee property and conveys it into the hands of the state, regardless of the *Waqif's* conditions (ie, it becomes normal land with no *Waqf* limitation on it).

Settlor control and influence using settlor-reserved powers and private trust companies

Paul Matthams
Stonehage Fleming

1. Introduction

For many individuals contemplating a trust to hold their family wealth or other assets, the idea of giving up legal ownership and control of assets to trustees is a difficult one to accept, notwithstanding the onerous duties and obligations which the law imposes on trustees. This chapter considers the extent to which powers may be retained by the settlor himself or herself or given to parties other than the trustees, together with other ways in which control, direct or indirect, may be exercised by a settlor once his or her trust has been established. We will look at the different types of powers that may be retained; at provisions to deal with such powers in the event of the settlor's death or incapacity; at protections that might be provided to trustees in circumstances where powers are retained by or reserved to settlors or third parties; and at particular pitfalls to be avoided by the drafter of the trust deed.

Even without directly held settlor powers, it has long been considered perfectly acceptable for a settlor to exercise an indirect influence over certain trustee decisions – for example, by the use of a third-party protector, normally a person known and trusted by the settlor, to whom is given the power to veto exercises of certain trustee powers, such as the power to add or remove beneficiaries or change the governing law of a trust. A protector can be, and frequently is, given more active powers: not just powers of veto, but powers held by the protector himself or herself, independently of the trustees, such as powers to add or remove trustees.

For the settlor who wants some influence over the trust assets without the reservation of specific powers or the granting of powers to a protector, another option in common use for many years has been to establish a private trust company to act as the trustee of one or more family trusts. In such a case, powers that would otherwise have been reserved by the settlor or made subject to the consent of a protector will instead be retained by the trustee. However, the trustee will be a corporate entity, whose board of directors could include the settlor or one or more other individuals whom the settlor trusts to know and understand his or her wishes. I return to private trust companies later in this chapter.

2.   Reservation of powers by the settlor

The ultimate settlor-reserved power is the power to revoke the trust. The settlor has made a gift of property to the trustee, but subsequently decides to 'undo' the gift and call back the property or other property representing it. In earlier centuries, the revocable trust could be of particular use in circumstances where a chattel or family heirloom was to be deposited with someone for safekeeping while the settlor departed on a long and dangerous journey and the chattel or heirloom could be returned following a safe return. In more modern times, a power of revocation may be appropriate – perhaps for a trust to achieve US grantor trust status, or where it may be important to show for tax or other purposes that there has not in fact been an irrevocable disposal of the property by the settlor.

If a power of revocation is to be inserted in the trust deed, the drafter must make clear what is to happen to the assets if that power is exercised. If there is a complete revocation of the trust and the trust deed is silent as to what happens in that event, a resulting trust is likely to arise as a matter of general law.[1] If there is to be a partial revocation of the trust, assuming this to be permitted by the express power, care will need to be taken to clarify the particular assets in respect of which the revocation is to apply, in addition to the destination of those assets following the exercise of the power.

The power of revocation is an extremely significant and valuable power in the hands of the settlor. A settlor holding such a power may be vulnerable to an attack by creditors seeking (as was done successfully in the *TMSF* case)[2] an order from the court that the power to revoke be delegated or transferred to court-appointed receivers for judgment creditors.

In *TMSF* the Privy Council noted various US authorities in which both courts and legislatures have been prepared to treat the assets of a revocable trust as subject to the claims of the settlor's creditors, both during the settlor's lifetime and after the settlor's death.[3] The Privy Council confirmed that the power of revocation cannot be regarded as in any sense a fiduciary power and considered the powers of revocation in the trusts under consideration as "tantamount to ownership".[4]

However, a settlor may wish to retain powers in respect of the assets which are not quite as extreme as the power to revoke the trust, but which may still give significant control over trust assets and the exercise of trustee powers, and such powers may be expressly reserved to the settlor in the trust deed. In most established trust jurisdictions, it has always been possible to draft trusts with

---

1   See Trusts (Jersey) Law 1984, Article 40(3): "Subject to the terms of the trust, if it is revoked the trustee shall hold the trust property in trust for the settlor absolutely."
2   *Tasarruf Mevduati Sigorta Fonu v Merrill Lynch Bank and Trust Company (Cayman) Limited* [2012] 1 WLR 1721, a decision of the Privy Council on appeal from the Court of Appeal of the Cayman Islands.
3   See also the United States Third Restatement of Trusts (2003) Section 25(2).
4   [2012] 1 WLR 1721 at para 62

certain powers reserved to the settlor; but in many jurisdictions, including the author's home jurisdiction of Jersey, a decision was taken some years ago to confirm the validity of expressed settlor-reserved powers by the addition of specific wording in the trust statute.[5]

There are various points to make about the Jersey provision. First, it confirms the pre-existing law on the topic; it does not make new law. Second, it does not contain an exhaustive list of powers, the inclusion of all or any of which will not affect the trust's validity. A power which does not appear in the list may still be included without necessarily affecting the validity of the trust. In addition to being able to exercise specific reserved powers, the provision permits the inclusion of a power vested in the settlor to give directions for the making of advancements, appointments and the like. These powers must be contained in the trust deed itself. The legislation confirms the validity of powers expressly contained in the trust's terms, but does not itself create or vest any of these powers in a settlor. Furthermore, the provision applies not just to powers reserved by a settlor to himself or herself, but also to powers granted by a settlor to someone else. For example, a settlor could create a revocable trust, but give the power of revocation to a third party.

As far as the trustee is concerned, while the Jersey legislation provides protection to a trustee who is obliged to act in a certain way following the exercise of a power by the settlor, it is advisable to ensure that an exoneration is also contained in the trust deed.

---

5   See Article 9A of the Trusts (Jersey) Law 1984,:

9A Powers reserved by settlor

(1) The reservation or grant by a settlor of a trust of –

  (a) any beneficial interest in the trust property; or

  (b) any of the powers mentioned in paragraph (2),

shall not affect the validity of the trust nor delay the trust taking effect and in construing the terms of the trust, if the trust is not expressed to be a will or testament or to come into effect upon the death of the settlor, it shall be presumed that the trust shall take immediate effect, except as otherwise expressed.

(2) The powers are –

  (a) to revoke, vary or amend the terms of a trust or any trusts or powers arising wholly or partly under it;

  (b) to advance, appoint, pay or apply income or capital of the trust property or to give directions for the making of such advancement, appointment, payment or application;

  (c) to act as, or give directions as to the appointment or removal of –

    (i) an officer of any corporation, or

    (ii) an officer of a limited liability partnership, separate limited partnership or any other partnership having separate legal personality,

  in which the trust holds an interest whether or not such interest in the corporation or partnership is wholly, partly, directly or indirectly held by the trust;

  (d) to give directions to the trustee in connection with the purchase, retention, sale, management, lending, pledging or charging of the trust property or the exercise of any powers or rights arising from such property;

  (e) to appoint or remove any trustee, enforcer or beneficiary, or any other person who holds a power, discretion or right in connection with the trust or in relation to trust property;

  (f) to appoint or remove an investment manager or investment adviser;

  (g) to change the proper law of the trust;

  (h) to restrict the exercise of any powers or discretions of a trustee by requiring that they shall only be exercisable with the consent of the settlor or any other person specified in the terms of the trust.

(3) Where a power mentioned in paragraph (2) has been reserved or granted by the settlor, a trustee who acts in accordance with the exercise of the power is not acting in breach of trust.

2.1 Can a settlor reserve too many powers?

On its face, the legislation permits the settlor to retain all of the listed powers and, as already indicated, it is clear from the wording that the list is not exhaustive. Accordingly, the question can be asked as to whether it is possible to reserve so many powers that you do not have a valid trust at all. For example, supposing you inserted a clause in your trust deed that said: "All of the powers vested in trustees in this trust deed may only be exercised with the prior written consent of the settlor."

While a settlor may have considerable freedom to decide the terms of the trust, there are limits to such freedom. First, applicable trusts legislation may provide that certain statutory provisions may be "subject to the terms of the trust", but other provisions may not be overridden by the wording in the trust deed. For example, Article 21(2) of the Trusts (Jersey) Law 1984 Law states: "subject to this Law a trustee shall carry out and administer the trust in accordance with its terms." So one looks to the terms of the trust, but keeps in mind the fact that the provisions of the law will take precedence. We can then look at specific provisions of the law. By Article 16(1), "subject to the terms of the trust, a trust must have at least one trustee". The trust deed may therefore specify the requirement for a higher minimum number of trustees.

By Article 21(3):

Subject to the terms of the trust, a trustee shall –

(a) So far as is reasonable preserve the value of the trust property;

(b) So far as is reasonable enhance the value of the trust property.

The law permits a trust deed to override these statutory provisions and this is frequently done.

However, by Article 21(1):

A trustee shall in the execution of his or her duties and in the exercise of his or her powers and discretions –

(a) ...

(b) observe the utmost good faith.

A settlor would, it is suggested, be unable to insert a provision in a trust relieving the trustee of the duty to act in good faith. What about the duties to act with diligence and prudence? To quote the oft-cited dictum of the then Lord Justice Millett in *Armitage v Nurse*:

> *I accept that there is an irreducible core of obligations owed by the trustees to the beneficiaries and enforceable by them which is fundamental to the concept of a trust. If the beneficiaries have no rights enforceable against the trustees there are no trusts. But I do not accept the further submission that these core obligations include the duties of skill and care, prudence and diligence. The duty of the trustee to perform the trusts honestly and in good faith for the benefit of the beneficiaries is the minimum necessary to give substance to the trusts, but in my opinion it is sufficient...*[6]

Furthermore, there is no reason why a trust deed cannot reflect a provision in the governing statute – for example, the removal (in part) of the trustee's duty of care in relation to the supervision and monitoring obligations of shares of an underlying company under the Virgin Islands Special Trusts Act.[7]

Justice David Hayton wrote over 20 years ago of the "irreducible core content of trusteeship of property that sets limits to the free will of the settlor".[8] The idea of holders of fiduciary powers having a duty to account to beneficiaries, who have a corresponding right to have the court enforce those obligations to account, is essential to the trust concept. Both powers reserved by a settlor or powers granted by a settlor to a third-party protector, unless those powers may be exercised in the power holder's own interest,[9] will usually be considered to be held as a fiduciary. The protector will owe duties that could be enforced by the beneficiaries if necessary. In the cited article Hayton considers that trustees could not be protected by a settlor reserving to himself or herself an overriding power to release those trustees from any liability. If the interests of the beneficiaries were capable of enforcement only at the whim of the settlor, what in essence would exist would be a bare trust or nominee arrangement for the settlor, and not a trust for the stated beneficiaries.

2.2 Tax and other risks

As far as tax is concerned, the jurisdiction in which the settlor resides may try to levy tax on the basis that the settlor has control over the trust assets. That argument cannot easily run if the only retained powers are in connection with the appointment of investment advisers or a change in the governing law. On the other hand, the retention of a power of appointment over the trust assets places significant control in the settlor's hands, and if the settlor is a beneficiary could be used to his or her own benefit.

A court may try to force a settlor to exercise a power in a certain way. For example, a divorce court may order that a part of the trust fund established by the settlor be paid to the settlor's ex-spouse who may not be a beneficiary of the trust at the time. If the settlor has the power to add beneficiaries and is subject to the jurisdiction of the divorce court, the court may order the settlor to exercise his or her power in a way that would not be of the settlor's choosing – for example, to appoint assets in favour of the ex-spouse or to create a trust for the ex-spouse.

2.3 Transfer of power or power of veto

We have already seen how powers which would otherwise have been given to

---

6   [1998] Ch 241; a case on trustee exemption clauses.
7   Virgin Islands Special Trusts Act 2003.
8   David Hayton, "The Irreducible Core Content of Trusteeship" in AJ Oakley (ed), *Trends in Contemporary Trust Law* (Clarendon Press, Oxford, 1996).
9   For example, a settlor's power of revocation (see above).

the trustees may be vested in a protector. We have also seen how some powers may remain vested in the trustees, but the exercise of those powers may be subject to the consent of the protector.

Similar considerations will apply in relation to powers held by a settlor. The drafter of the trust deed should consider with the settlor whether the relevant powers should be held by the settlor instead of by the trustees, or whether the powers should remain with the trustees, but should be exercisable by them only with the settlor's consent. Of course, there is no reason why certain powers may not be reserved by the settlor and not vested in the trustees at all, while others may be vested in the trustees but made subject to settlor consent.

However, in the hands of the settlor, a power in the latter category is no more than a power of veto. If the settlor wishes a particular change to be made, he or she may suggest a decision to the trustees, but cannot force the decision on them. For example, if the settlor holds a power of veto over the appointment of investment managers and he or she wishes the trustee to appoint someone whom the trustees consider to be totally unsuitable, the trustees may refuse to make the appointment and there is little that the settlor can do short of seeking the court's assistance and claiming that the trustees are not exercising their powers properly.

Needless to say, it is fundamental to the drafting of the settlor-reserved powers that it is clear how each power is to be exercised, and that this is understood both by the settlor and by the trustees.

2.4 Documentation

It will normally be appropriate for the exercise of powers reserved by a settlor to require the use of a deed or other formal legal written instrument. There are various reasons for this. It is always important in trust law to be clear which power is being exercised, and to ensure that the power is being exercised correctly and in accordance with any formalities laid down in the document in which the power is granted. If a trust instrument requires a document in writing, nothing else will suffice. If a trust instrument requires prior written consent, prior oral consent which is subsequently reduced to writing will not suffice; nor will a post-event ratification, unless the court is prepared to assist.[10]

The discipline of preparing a formal deed or similar document is helpful because the drafter is forced to check the original trust deed to establish which power or powers are to be exercised and how they are to be exercised. The drafter may have to consider the issue of revocability (discussed later) and timing. It may be possible for the power to be exercised with effect from a future date.

---

10   For example, to cure a formal defect in the exercise of a power; see the Jersey case of *Re Shinorvic* [2012] 1 JLR 325.

Even with the giving of consents pursuant to veto-holding powers, a document in writing should always be required, even if the formality of a deed or similar document is not strictly necessary. Such consent should always be signed and dated, to show both when it was given and that it was actually given by the holder of the power. These are matters of evidence, but later arguments about the interpretation of emails, informal letters and so on could be easily avoided by the simple expedient of requiring that a power be exercised by a document containing certain prescribed formalities.

2.5   Death and incapacity

Unless the settlor is a company or foundation (or other vehicle) of unlimited duration, death is a certainty and incapacity is always a possibility. The drafter of settlor reserved powers must cater for both and there are three ways of doing this:

- The power can be allowed to lapse;
- The power may become vested in the trustees; or
- The power may become vested in someone else.

The first option will not usually be a particularly attractive one, but may be appropriate in the case of the settlor who wishes to exercise control during his or her lifetime, but is happy to let matters take their course thereafter. The vesting of powers in the trustees on the death or incapacity of the settlor will be appropriate where the settlor is content to let matters take their course and is content to let the trustees exercise powers which in many trusts they would ordinarily hold anyway.

The third option is to vest the powers in someone else. There are a number of options here. First, provision can be made for a settlor to have the power to appoint successor holders of the relevant powers or indeed for the power holders themselves to appoint their successors. Care needs to be taken with the drafting.

Any clause authorising a settlor to nominate holders of successor powers should contain provisions confirming how that power itself is to be exercised, but should also contain default provisions to cover the possibility that the individual may die or lose capacity without having exercised the power of nomination. While another individual could be named in the trust instrument as the holder of successive settlor powers, that individual may not be alive or of full capacity when needed. It may therefore be preferable to require the trustees for the time being of the trust to nominate a successor holder of the relevant powers and for their own powers to be limited to the preservation of the trust assets pending such appointment. It is important for the drafter of the original trust instrument to discuss with the settlor which of the various options to incorporate in the trust deed.

It is also important for the drafter to ensure that the wording is adequate to vest the necessary powers in the successor holder of those powers. In the case of protector provisions, it is often the case that the first (original) protector is named in the trust deed and for the protector to be defined as "the original protector or other person appointed to act as the protector from time to time". The importance of this wording is that the protector is an office and the powers attached to that office will pass automatically from holder to holder. It is different with settlor-reserved powers. The powers do not sit with anyone who is "the settlor from time to time". The wording will therefore need to be effective to vest the relevant powers in the person appointed to hold them on his or her appointment coming into effect. That person would not be the settlor, of course; that would be the person holding the powers formerly vested in the settlor.

2.6 Revocability

The trust deed should make it clear whether the particular reserved power is to be capable of exercise revocably or irrevocably, and should always cater for the fact that the person drafting the later document to exercise the power may not specify which is to apply. There should always be a default provision, such as "unless expressed to be revocable the exercise of this power shall be irrevocable".

2.7 Are the powers fiduciary?

As indicated above, both powers reserved by a settlor and powers granted by a settlor to a third-party protector will usually be considered to be held as a fiduciary, unless those powers may be exercised in the power holder's own interest. If the trust deed is silent, a court is likely to consider that such powers are fiduciary in nature unless there are particular circumstances suggesting the contrary. The powers are normally included for the protection of the interests of the beneficiaries; and when exercising those powers, the settlor must have regard to the interests of the beneficiaries.

It is advisable to make the position clear in the drafting – for example:

Settlor reserved powers

The powers of the Settlor contained in Schedule [ ] are fiduciary in nature.

Nevertheless, where overriding powers are reserved to the settlor – for example, powers of appointment, advancement and resettlement – and the settlor is a beneficiary, the settlor is in essence changing his or her mind about the original provision made in the trust deed. It is therefore quite reasonable to treat these as wholly beneficial powers, and to put the matter beyond doubt specific provisions can be included, such as:

The powers contained in Schedule [ ] (the 'Overriding Powers') are personal to the Settlor and may not be exercised by any person on his behalf.

The Overriding Powers are not fiduciary and may be exercised in the Settlor's own interests without regard to the interests of any other beneficiaries.

The first paragraph above is important, as the powers may well be assets of value in the hands of the settlor and if, for example, the settlor became bankrupt, a trustee in bankruptcy might try to exercise them on his or her behalf. This clause makes it clear that such powers will not vest automatically in any other person. If the person wishes to be able to delegate all or any of his or her powers, specific provision should be made in the trust deed. It is perfectly possible to provide that certain powers are fiduciary in nature and others are not.

As a holder of fiduciary powers, a settlor may face claims for breaches of the duties attached to those powers. A settlor may therefore seek an exoneration clause confirming that the settlor will not be liable in respect of the exercise of those powers in the absence of fraud, wilful misconduct or gross negligence. A specific provision can also be inserted providing protection to the settlor who acts in accordance with appropriate legal advice. The wording will need to cover the position that the powers may be passed to a subsequent holder who is not the settlor.

3.   Private trust companies

The use of private trust companies by wealthy families has increased dramatically in recent years. Many clients are now prepared to establish structures which are more complicated than the traditional discretionary trust with an independently owned regulated trust company acting as trustee, and the use of a private trust company usually enables a settlor to achieve a degree of influence over the management and administration of a trust.

However, there are other uses for such companies, including to act as trustees of trusts established to engage in bespoke activities or to hold trust funds in riskier investments than those which an institutional trustee may be prepared to accept. Furthermore, a private trust company gives a settlor who creates a number of trusts, perhaps for different purposes or different family members, the ability to consolidate the trusteeships in a single trustee entity.

The settlor may wish to establish a number of trusts for different purposes – perhaps wealth preservation for the family as to a part of an individual's assets, and charitable and philanthropic giving as to another part – or for different groups of beneficiaries, such as second families following a divorce and remarriage, or trusts from which certain family members are excluded. The settlor may wish to undertake activities through a series of companies holding different classes of assets: quoted investments, unquoted investments, real estate holdings, boats and aircraft and so on. In these circumstances, a private trust company may be considered to be a useful option to ensure that unified oversight can be provided, with certain board members having particular expertise or interest in relation to certain parts of a settlor's business activities. However, a private trust company is still a trustee with the onerous duties and obligations that come with the office, including duties of due diligence, prudence and good faith, and the settlor needs to understand this.

3.1 Definition

A private trust company is usually a company that exists to provide trustee services in respect of a specific trust or trusts, and which does not solicit from or provide trust company business services to the public.

It is not always the case that the trustee services are provided only to trusts established by one individual. For example, a private trust company could act as the trustee of a number of trusts established by different promoters of a single business. Where the trustee services are provided in a jurisdiction where such services are regulated, there is likely to be a specific regulatory regime for private trust companies, so the company and the activities undertaken by it will need to comply with the relevant regulatory requirements.[11] These may include capitalisation provisions, approved director requirements and, in some jurisdictions, oversight by a regulated business if the private trust company is not to be regulated itself. The jurisdiction may also contains restrictions as to the terms of the trust in respect of which a private trust company act as the trustee.[12]

3.2 Ownership

Private trust companies are normally established as companies limited by shares or as guarantee companies. If the company is limited by shares, the issue arises as to who should own the shares. A frequently used option, where such an entity is permitted, has been to use a non-charitable purpose trust, usually with a regulated trust company business as the trustee. In jurisdictions where the non-charitable purpose trust legislation requires the appointment of an enforcer (whose role is to ensure that the trustees use the trust assets for the stated purposes), there is usually no reason why the settlor should not appoint a family member or adviser as the enforcer of the private trust company and vest in that person powers including those to change the directors of the private trust company. Another option is for the trustee company to be owned by an entity that can hold shares, but does not have an owner of its own, such as a foundation.

If a company limited by guarantee is used, consideration should be given to who will be the guarantor of the company's liabilities. One possibility is for

---

11   For example, Paragraph 4 of Part 1 of the schedule to the Financial Services (Trust Company Business (Exemptions)) (Jersey) Order 2000.

12   For example, the rules in the British Virgin Islands concerning 'unremunerated' and 'related' trust business.

family members to act as guarantors. However, that could still give rise to family members being treated as the owners of the private trust company; and just as family members can themselves own the shares of a private trust company established as a company limited by shares, it would normally be considered more appropriate to hold that ownership interest through another entity such as a non-charitable purpose trust or a foundation.

3.3 Governance issues

As already indicated, an advantage of the private trust company is that it enables the settlor to select the directors of the company. These could include family members or advisers. Care should be taken with family members if there are tax issues that could make it inadvisable certainly for the settlor to be a director and possibly also for close family members to be on the board. In some jurisdictions the regulatory regime may require certain approved persons to act as directors, or may require administration or other services to be provided by a regulated entity in the jurisdiction where the company is established.

It is important to remember that normal corporate governance rules will still apply. The board members of the trust company are directors, and are subject to the articles of association of the company concerned and to the duties and obligations imposed by company law. Decisions taken by the board of the private trust company must be properly authorised, board meetings must be quorate with interests declared and so on. It is normally advisable for the director of a regulated trust company business or other suitably qualified person to be on the board of the private trust company, in order to ensure that proper attention is paid to these matters. A power purportedly exercised by a private trust company pursuant to a resolution of an inquorate board will not be a validly exercised trustee power.

It is also important to remember that even with a private trust company, other methods of direct or indirect settlor influence or even control, such as the use of a protector or settlor-reserved powers, remain available. Sometimes a family committee can be formed with appointment powers, such as the power to appoint protectors who themselves hold the power to appoint the board members of the private trust company, or of the council of a foundation which may own the private trust company.

In complex cases one may therefore have a structure of three tiers, comprising a trust with a private trust company trustee owned by a foundation and below the trust a series of investment holding companies or, in jurisdictions where this is permitted, a single company with separate 'cells'. The different companies or cells could hold different classes of assets, investments, property, yachts and aircraft, and so on.

The settlor or members of the settlor's family or advisers can participate at various levels within the structure:

- as a director of the underlying companies;
- as a director of the private trust company;
- as a protector or member of a protectorship committee or director of a protectorship company of the discretionary trust;
- as a member of the foundation council; or
- as the guardian of the foundation.

3.4 Location of the private trust company

The private trust company acts as a trustee and should therefore be located in a jurisdiction which recognises and enforces trusts, and understands the roles and responsibilities of trustees. It is fundamental to the law of trusts that the assets which a trustee holds are not owned beneficially by it and are therefore not available to its creditors, save in respect of matters where it has incurred liabilities in its capacity as the trustee of a particular trust. The private trust company should not be located in a jurisdiction whose courts would not recognise this. Many, but not all, established trust jurisdictions contain limited recourse wording in their trust statutes, the effect of which may be to limit a trustee's liabilities to the trust property.[13] Private trust companies will almost invariably have limited capital of their own, unless they operate in a regulated trust business environment which requires a corporate trustee to hold significant capital of its own.

The directors of a private trust company should also pay attention to relevant rules on insolvent trading, given the possibility that in the trust company's capacity as trustee, it may incur liabilities which exceed the assets of the relevant trust.

Subject to these points, it is not normally the case that the private trust company must be located in the jurisdiction of the governing law of the trust or indeed, if different, the jurisdiction from which the trust is administered; although as ever, relevant local laws will apply. It is also likely to be possible to locate the entity that owns the private trust company in another jurisdiction. Mention has already been made of the importance of the relevant regulatory regime and where entities in a complex structure are located in a number of different jurisdictions, the regime in each jurisdiction will need to be considered.

In addition, the requirements of the Common Reporting Standard and economic substance regimes and other global transparency issues may have an impact both on the structure used and on the jurisdiction or jurisdictions where the entities in the structure are located.

---

13   For example, Article 32 of the Trusts (Jersey) Law 1984.

4.   Summary

In this chapter, we have looked principally at two particular methods by which a settlor may retain, directly or indirectly, elements of influence or control over a trust that he or she has established. For some settlors, the ability to reserve specific powers to themselves (or grant them to third parties), rather than confer them on their trustees, provides considerable security of mind. As we have seen, appropriate powers may be incorporated in trust deeds without jeopardising or undermining the integrity or validity of the structure itself. However, depending on the particular powers reserved, such provisions may cause a closer link – or at least the appearance of a closer link – to be retained between the settlor and the assets transferred to the trustees than might be the case in other circumstances. If tax mitigation or asset protection motives govern the creation of the structure, the trust may be perfectly valid, but may not provide the anticipated benefits.

Where a different solution is required, the private trust company offers an important refinement to the traditional discretionary trust structure for wealthy clients, which is particularly useful where a settlor seeks influence beyond that afforded by a memorandum of wishes or use of a protector, but without reserving specific powers. As shown, the private trust company can still be used in conjunction with other methods of settlor influence.

5.   Conclusion

As ever, when considering with a settlor the best form of trust to receive the settlor's assets, great care must be taken to establish the settlor's clear wishes, the relevant and applicable laws and taxes, the regulatory regimes and the degree of complexity of structure that is appropriate.

It is also fair to say that the drafting and exercise of the various types of powers contained in trust deeds remain some of the most technically difficult aspects of trust law. Accordingly, great care must be taken and legal advice obtained when drafting such clauses to avoid the expensive remedy of rectification by the court at a later date.

The UK tax treatment of offshore trusts

Maggie Gonzalez
Buzzacott LLP

1. Introduction

1.1 Trust taxation in the United Kingdom

The offshore trust has proved a popular tool for financial planning in the United Kingdom – not only to minimise the incidence of UK tax on income, gains and assets, but also to provide financial security for the settlor's family. Over the last 40 years, the United Kingdom has developed extensive anti-avoidance legislation targeted at offshore trusts to ensure that UK income tax and capital gains tax cannot be avoided using offshore trusts. Such trusts, however, can still afford tax-planning benefits, particularly for those domiciled outside the United Kingdom.

1.2 Offshore trusts

The term 'offshore trust', although not legal or statutory, is universally used to denote a trust that is resident outside the United Kingdom, usually but not necessarily in a low-tax jurisdiction. In this chapter, the terms 'offshore trust' and 'non-resident trust' are used interchangeably.

1.3 Domicile

An individual's domicile status is important for UK tax purposes, particularly in relation to offshore trusts. This is the case for both settlors and beneficiaries, even after becoming deemed domiciled in the United Kingdom.

1.4 Deemed domicile

From 6 April 2017 an individual who has been resident in the United Kingdom for 15 of the previous 20 tax years is deemed to be domiciled in the United Kingdom for all tax purposes. For inheritance tax, at least one of the previous three years or the current year must also be a year of residence, allowing those with a foreign domicile who leave the United Kingdom to lose their deemed domiciled status in their fourth year of non-residence.

Deemed domicile also applies to a non-domiciled individual with a UK domicile of origin who was born in the United Kingdom, if he or she becomes UK resident, known as a 'formerly domiciled resident'.

Prior to 6 April 2017, deemed domicile applied only for inheritance tax purposes, taking effect for those resident in the United Kingdom for at least 17 of the last 20 years.

Deemed domicile for inheritance tax is also attributed to an individual who has given up his or her UK domicile within the previous three years.

1.5 The remittance basis

Individuals who are resident but not domiciled in the United Kingdom will be liable to UK tax on all UK-source income arising and capital gains realised, but in respect of foreign income (known as relevant foreign income) and gains may elect annually to be liable to UK tax only to the extent that it is remitted to the United Kingdom.

From 5 April 2008, long-term UK resident taxpayers aged 18 or over are subject to the remittance basis charge on the making of such a claim. A long-term UK resident taxpayer is an individual who has been resident in the United Kingdom for at least seven out of the nine years preceding the year of claim. The rates of remittance basis charge (for 2019?2020) are as follows:

Years of residence	Remittance basis charge
7 of the preceding 9	£30,000
12 of the preceding 14	£60,000

Where an individual's unremitted foreign income and gains for a year are less than £2,000, no claim is required and the remittance basis will apply automatically. In addition, a claim is not required if an individual has no UK income or gains and remits no relevant foreign income or gains, provided that he or she is not long-term UK resident or is under 18 years of age at the end of the year.

From 6 April 2017 an individual who is deemed to be domiciled in the United Kingdom is no longer able to choose to be taxed on the remittance basis.

Under the remittance basis, foreign income and gains are treated as remitted to the United Kingdom and taxable on an individual if they are brought to, or received or used in, the United Kingdom by or for the benefit of a relevant person. The definition of a 'relevant person' is very wide and includes not only the individual, but also:

- his or her spouse (including co-habitees);
- minor children and grandchildren (and those of his or her spouse);
- closely held companies in which a relevant person is a participator;
- trustees of a settlement of which a relevant person is a beneficiary; and
- a body connected with such a settlement.

A remittance can occur not only through the direct transfer of the income to a UK bank account, but also by bringing an asset acquired with foreign income to the United Kingdom, or using foreign income to pay interest or to repay the capital of a loan offshore relating to UK property or services.

1.6 Residence of trusts

Strictly speaking, a trust does not have a residence, since it is not a separate legal person in its own right. However, it is a convenient legal fiction to which even the legislation resorts, and one needed for the purposes of this chapter.

It is the residence status of the trustees, and not that of the settlor or beneficiaries, that determines whether a trust is an onshore trust or an offshore trust. The residence and domicile status of the settlor and beneficiaries plays a key role, however, in determining how the trust income and gains are taxed.

Historically, there was no single definition of 'residence' that applied to trustees across all taxes. However, since 6 April 2007 the definitions for income tax and capital gains tax have followed the existing income tax definition, which is enacted as Section 475 of the Income Tax Act 2007.

(a) Income tax

From 6 April 2007, for income tax purposes, trustees are treated as if they were a single person, distinct from the persons who are the trustees of the settlement from time to time. To determine the residence of that person, the general rule for residence of individuals (or of companies for a corporate trustee) must be applied to each trustee in turn. One of three situations will apply:

Residence status of trustees	Residence status of trust
All UK resident	UK resident
All non-UK resident	Non-UK resident (ie, offshore)
Mixed	Depends on status of settlor

A trustee is deemed to be UK resident, for the purpose of this test, where he or she acts as a trustee in the course of a business carried on in the United Kingdom through a UK branch, agency or permanent establishment, even though he or she is not personally UK resident.

Where some of the trustees are resident and some non-resident, the question is determined by Sections 475 and 476 of the Income Tax Act 2007, by reference to the residence and domicile status of the settlor. If the settlor is resident or domiciled (including deemed domiciled from 6 April 2017) in the

United Kingdom at one or more key times, then the presence of even one UK resident trustee will make the trust as a whole UK resident (the non-resident trustees are deemed to be resident regardless of whether they are in the majority, and regardless of where the trust is actually administered). The key times referred to are the point of creation of the trust and any time thereafter when funds are provided directly or indirectly by the settlor. For this rule, the meaning of 'settlor' is extended to include not only the original creator of the trust, but also "any person who has provided funds directly or indirectly for the purposes of the settlement".

Although an individual is either resident or not resident in the United Kingdom for the whole of a tax year, the statutory residence test, brought in from 6 April 2013, provides for split-year treatment on departure from the United Kingdom or arrival in the United Kingdom under certain conditions. Split-year treatment does not divide the year into resident and non-resident periods, but instead taxes the individual as if he or she were non-resident in the 'overseas' part of the year, subject to a few exceptions. Although split-year treatment cannot apply to a trust, an individual acting as a trustee will not be regarded as UK resident during a split year, when determining the residence status of the trust, if he or she is only a trustee in the overseas part of the year.

An individual trustee coming to the United Kingdom should resign as a trustee before arrival to ensure that the trust does not become accidentally UK resident and subject to significant UK tax liabilities. Assistance may be provided by the United Kingdom's double tax treaty network where a trust is also resident in another jurisdiction under domestic law, with treaty residence likely to be determined on the basis of the place of effective management of the trust. Not all treaties provide a tie-breaker for trusts (eg, see the UK-US treaty), in which case the treaty residence of a trust is left for the competent authorities of the two territories to determine.

(b)   ***Capital gains tax***
From 6 April 2007, residence for capital gains tax is the same as for income tax and is enacted as Section 69 of the Taxation of Chargeable Gains Act 1992.

(c)   ***Inheritance tax***
The residence of a trust is largely irrelevant for the purposes of inheritance tax. However, it may be important for reporting and liability purposes.

1.7   Protectors
The office of protector is not recognised by trust or tax law, but care must be taken to ensure that the protector is not, by virtue of his or her actions or powers, deemed to be either a trustee or a factor influencing the management of the trust.

If a UK resident protector has powers which effectively make him or her an additional trustee or is effectively making trust decisions, there is a danger that Her Majesty's Revenue & Customs (HMRC) will argue that the trust is UK resident.

2.   Income tax

2.1   Trusts in general

A trust cannot be liable to tax because it is not a separate legal person. Liability to income tax on trust income can therefore fall on the trustees, the beneficiaries or the settlor. In fact, in most cases, it is the trustees and/or the beneficiaries who are liable to tax on the trust income. The settlor is not normally liable (except as a beneficiary), but there are certain anti-avoidance provisions that deem trust income to be income of the settlor for tax purposes.

2.2   The offshore interest-in-possession trust

In an interest-in-possession trust, it is the beneficiary who is primarily liable to income tax on the trust income, not the trustees. To that extent, the residence status of the trustees is irrelevant. Although the trust is treated as a mere conduit, the trustees remain liable to account for tax at the appropriate rate on UK-source income of the trust and are responsible for filing a self-assessment trust tax return with HMRC. In computing the amount of income assessable to tax, they may deduct the expenses properly deductible for that source of income. For the treatment of trust expenses, see section 2.2(d).

Some of the income received from the United Kingdom will have had tax withheld at source; where this is not the case, the trustees must pay tax at the appropriate rate. The appropriate rate (for 2019–2020) is as follows:

Dividend income	7.5% (the dividend ordinary rate)
All other income	20% (the basic rate)

The UK resident and domiciled beneficiary will be liable to UK income tax on the trust's worldwide income as it arises, whether or not it is actually paid to him or her. The income does not lose its character by passing through the trust – that is, rental income from land will be assessable as such, on the beneficiary. A beneficiary who is resident but not domiciled in the United Kingdom may elect annually to be liable only on UK-source income and foreign income remitted to the United Kingdom.

(a) **Treatment of interest, dividends and rental income**

UK-source interest received by the trustees will have been subject to tax of 20% withheld at source. In some cases, the trustees, as non-resident persons, may apply to have the interest paid gross.

The UK resident beneficiary is liable to tax on the gross amount of the interest (ie, on the net interest received, plus the tax withheld), but may claim the tax withheld as a credit against his or her liability to tax on the interest. Foreign-source interest will be taxable as foreign savings income and the beneficiary may claim any foreign tax withheld as a credit, limited to the UK tax liability on the interest.

Non-resident trustees in receipt of UK dividends are treated as having paid tax at the dividend ordinary rate, so satisfying their liability to UK tax. A UK resident beneficiary is liable to tax on the amount of the dividend, without the benefit of any tax credit attributed to the trustees.

Foreign dividends are generally taxable at the same rates as UK dividends. Credit may be claimed for any foreign withholding tax up to the limit of the UK tax liability on the dividend.

Rental income from a UK property will have borne tax at a rate of 20%, which will have been deducted from the rents by the tenants or the managing agents of the property before receipt by the trustees. It is possible for non-resident landlords, including trustees, to apply to have the rents paid gross (without deduction of tax), provided that:

- they have had no previous liability to UK tax;
- they do not expect to be liable to UK tax; or
- their UK tax affairs are up to date.

The trustees must also undertake to comply with all their UK tax obligations in the future. Although it is the beneficiary who is ultimately taxable on the income, it is the trustees who are regarded as carrying on the 'property business' (ie, the letting business) and are liable to account to HMRC for the liability arising from that activity. In this respect, there is no difference between the trustees of an interest-in-possession trust and those of a discretionary trust.

Tax paid or suffered by the trustees may be claimed as a credit by the beneficiary. Again, the rental income received or arising to the beneficiary must be grossed up to include this tax when computing the beneficiary's liability to income tax.

(b) **UK resident but non-domiciled beneficiaries**

Beneficiaries who are resident but not domiciled in the United Kingdom and taxed on the remittance basis are liable to UK tax on the UK-source income to which they are entitled, as described in the previous section. Their foreign income is taxable only when remitted to the United Kingdom.

(c) Non-resident beneficiaries

A non-resident beneficiary of an offshore interest-in-possession trust will potentially be liable to UK income tax in respect of UK-source income only.

(d) Trust expenses

Provided that the trust deed allows them to do so, the trustees may deduct expenses of managing the trust from the trust income before it passes to the beneficiary. Because different types of income may be involved, the order of set-off may directly affect the beneficiary's liability to tax and is therefore prescribed by Section 503 of the Income Tax Act 2007.

Only expenses that are properly chargeable against income as opposed to capital (overriding in this respect any contrary provision in the trust deed) may be deductible. The expenses are first offset against UK dividends and similar income, followed by the equivalent foreign income, then savings income and finally against other income.

For non-resident beneficiaries, management expenses are allocated between UK-source and foreign-source income in the proportion one bears to the other. Trust management expenses may not be deducted by the trustees against the income on which they are assessable to tax, but only against the income payable to the beneficiary.

2.3 The offshore discretionary trust

(a) The liability of trustees

In a discretionary trust, no beneficiary has an absolute entitlement to income, so the primary liability for income tax falls on the trustees. If the trustees are non-resident, their only liability to UK tax will be in respect of UK-source income. If they have UK resident beneficiaries, the whole of their UK income will be charged; otherwise, only UK property and trading income will be subject to UK tax. The first £1,000 (for 2019?2020) of income is charged at the basic rate or dividend ordinary rate, depending on the nature of the income. The remaining income is charged at the dividend trust rate or the trust rate. For 2019?2020, the former is 38.1% and the latter 45%. Income is chargeable at either of these rates to the extent to which it is to be accumulated or is payable at the discretion of the trustees.

'Distribution income', chargeable at the dividend trust rate, consists of dividends and other distributions from UK corporations and is treated as the highest part of the trustees' total income. Distribution income in the hands of non-resident discretionary trustees is treated as carrying a notional 7.5% tax credit, which is not repayable. They are therefore liable to pay 30.6% tax on this income (the 38.1% dividend trust rate, less the 7.5% credit).

All other income of the trust is chargeable at 45%.

Trustees of an offshore discretionary trust may apply for UK-source deposit interest to be paid gross, if they declare to the deposit taker that they have no reasonable grounds to believe that any of the beneficiaries is an individual resident in the United Kingdom or a UK resident company.

(b)   Trust management expenses

In contrast to the rule with an interest-in-possession trust, trust management expenses are deductible from the income on which the trustees are liable to tax at the trust rate (45%) or the dividend trust rate (38.1%). Income against which the expenses are applied is then taxed not at either of these two rates, but at the rate at which it would be taxed if not received by discretionary trustees. When deducting those expenses, they must be grossed up at the relevant rate of tax (ie, at the basic rate of 20% or the dividend ordinary rate of 7.5%). That rate is the rate applying to the income against which they are offset. The order of set-off is as given in section 2.2(d) above.

(c)   Payments to UK resident beneficiaries

A UK resident beneficiary receiving a payment of income from non-resident trustees is in law treated as receiving income from a foreign source, however great the proportion of UK-source income in the income out of which the payment is made. The income assessable is the amount actually paid and no credit is available, either for UK income tax or for any foreign tax suffered on the income. The reason for this is that the UK and foreign tax (where applicable) has been paid and is the liability of the trustees, not of the beneficiary. Nor can the beneficiary invoke Section 111 of the Taxation (International and Other Provisions) Act 2010, which allows beneficiaries to 'look through' income received under deduction of foreign tax from a discretionary trust and claim the corresponding foreign tax credit, as this is also effectively limited to beneficiaries of UK resident discretionary trusts.

A measure of relief is available against the harshness of the law under Extra-Statutory Concession (ESC) B18. This concession allows UK resident beneficiaries receiving income payments from an offshore discretionary trust to claim a credit for UK tax actually paid by the trustees on the income out of which the payment is made if the beneficiary would have been liable to UK tax on the income had he or she received it directly. Credit may be claimed only for tax actually paid; any amounts that the trustees could not have offset under Section 496 of the Income Tax Act 2007 from tax due on their payment had they been UK resident are not available to the beneficiary. Chief among these is the notional 7.5% tax credit on UK dividends (see section 2.3(a)). A non-repayable foreign tax credit may also be claimed for non-UK tax suffered by the trustees on foreign income, limited to the relevant UK double tax treaty rate.

This concessionary treatment is made available only where the trustees:

- have made full UK tax returns, giving details of income and payments to beneficiaries in every relevant year;
- have made full settlement of all UK tax liabilities (including penalties, interest and surcharges); and
- have kept tax certificates for inspection.

Beneficiaries must claim credits under this concession no later than five years and 10 months after the end of the year in which the payment from the trustees is received.

(d) *Limitation of UK tax on non-residents*
Non-residents in receipt of UK-source investment income enjoy a cap on their total liability. In effect, their liability on interest and dividends is limited to tax deducted at source. This cap does not apply to non-resident trustees of a discretionary trust where there is a beneficiary (companies as well as individuals) resident in the United Kingdom, to whom the trustees may pay all or part of the trust income.

(e) *Payments to UK resident but non-domiciled beneficiaries*
Where the beneficiary is resident in the United Kingdom, but is a non-domiciliary to whom the remittance basis applies, the beneficiary's liability extends only to so much of the payment as is matched to UK-source income or to overseas income that is subsequently remitted.

(f) *Payments to non-resident beneficiaries*
Payments of income by offshore discretionary trustees to beneficiaries who are not resident in the United Kingdom are entirely free of UK income tax in the beneficiary's hands. The trust will still, of course, have suffered UK tax on any UK-source income received, as described in section 2.3(a). A non-resident beneficiary receiving a payment out of income of the trustees which, had it been received directly, would have been chargeable to UK tax may claim a credit for the UK tax paid by the trustees under ESC B18, as described in section 2.3(c)

2.4 Attributing income to the settlor

(a) *Introduction*
As a matter of trust law, once the settlor has established a trust, his or her function is completed. However, there is a complex series of anti-avoidance provisions in tax law deeming the income of a trust to be income of the settlor. These provisions can be divided into two categories. The first applies generally to all trusts, wherever resident, and is contained in Part 5, Chapter 5 of the Income Tax (Trading and Other Income) Act 2005; the second (Part 13, Chapter

2 of the Income Tax Act 2007) is not limited to trusts, but counters the transfer of assets abroad to avoid UK tax and may thus be directly relevant to offshore trusts.

(b)   Retention of interest by settlor

Under Section 624 of the Income Tax (Trading and Other Income) Act 2005, income arising under a settlement is treated as the settlor's during his or her lifetime where the settlor has retained an interest in the trust property.

A settlor is deemed to have retained an interest where the trust property or any property derived from the trust property could become payable to, or for the benefit of, the settlor or his or her spouse in any circumstances whatsoever.

To avoid this provision, the trust deed must be worded with great care to remove any possibility that trust property may accidentally revert to the settlor or his or her spouse.

Future spouses, widows and widowers, and separated spouses in circumstances where the separation is likely to be permanent, are excluded. There are also exceptions for trusts under which property reverts to the settlor only by way of:

- the bankruptcy of a beneficiary;
- the death of both parties to a marriage settlement and any children of the marriage;
- an assignment of or charge on the property made or given by a beneficiary; or
- the death of a child of the settlor who had become beneficially entitled to some or all of the trust property or derived property at the age of 25 or less.

In addition, a settlor is not regarded as having an interest as long as there is a person living and under the age of 25 during whose life the settlor or spouse is excluded, except on the happening of the events outlined in the first and third bullets above.

Where the settlor of a discretionary trust has retained an interest under this provision, the trustees remain liable to income tax at the trust rate or dividend trust rate, depending on the nature of the income.

The settlor is taxed as if all the income of the trust were his or hers, with all the allowances, reliefs and tax credits to which he or she would have been entitled had he or she actually received the income. This includes credit under a double tax agreement for foreign taxes paid by the trustees. For the purposes of calculating how much, if any, of the income is taxable at the higher rates, the deemed income is treated as the highest part of the settlor's taxable income.

The settlor has the right to recover any tax paid by him or her under these provisions from the trustees. However, where the application of these provisions results in the settlor's receiving an income tax repayment greater than he or she would have received had the income not been treated as his or hers, the settlor must repay the excess to the trustees or any other person to whom the income is payable under the trust. Failure by the settlor to exercise this right to recovery (except where a genuine but unsuccessful effort has been made) could result in the settlor being deemed to have provided funds to the trust. Where the trust is non-resident, this could cause significant capital gains tax liabilities (see section 4.6). Further, if the settlor is UK resident at the time, this could affect the residence status of the trust for income tax purposes (see section 1.6(a)).

(c)   *Payments to unmarried minor children*

Where the settlor and the settlor's spouse are completely excluded from benefit, but payments are made, during the lifetime of the settlor from the trust to or for the benefit of any of the settlor's unmarried minor (ie, aged under 18) children, the payments are treated as paid to the settlor under Section 629 of the Income Tax (Trading and Other Income) Act 2005.

In a discretionary trust, income may be accumulated. This may also be the case in an interest-in-possession trust, since trust law (unless specifically disapplied) allows trustees to retain income of a minor during his or her minority, whether or not with an interest in possession, at their discretion. Where income is accumulated in this way, it is not treated under these provisions as the settlor's income, but becomes part of the trust capital. However, if part of the capital is then paid to, or for the benefit of, the minor unmarried child at some future date while the minority continues, there is then a charge under these provisions, to the extent that there is any income that has arisen to the trust from its inception that has not already been treated as:

- the settlor's;
- paid to, or for the benefit of, a beneficiary other than an unmarried minor child of the settlor;
- income of an unmarried minor child and taxed in the hands of that child in any of the years 1995 to 1996, 1996 to 1997 or 1997 to 1998; or
- defrayed in meeting trust expenses.

In assessing the settlor to tax under these provisions, the same rules apply as for Section 624 of the Income Tax (Trading and Other Income) Act 2005 (ie, the settlor is entitled to the same allowances and reliefs as if he or she had actually received the income etc – see section 2.4(b)). In the case of an offshore discretionary trust, the settlor is unable to claim a tax credit for the tax paid by the trustees. However, an extra-statutory concession, parallel to B18 for beneficiaries receiving payments from offshore discretionary trusts (see section 2.3(c)), gives a measure of relief to UK resident settlors in such a situation. They may invoke the concession to claim credit for UK tax paid by the trustees to the extent that the payment treated as made to them derives from income received by the trustees in the six years ending on 5 April of the year in which the payment is made. Thus, for example, if the payment is made in the year 2019–2020, credit may be claimed in respect of income received no earlier than 6 April 2014. For the purposes of the concession, the payment is treated as made pro rata out of the trustees' various sources of income on a last-in, first-out basis. No credit is available for foreign tax paid by the trustees or in respect of income from foreign sources. The same conditions, requiring the trustees' compliance with their reporting and payment liabilities, are imposed.

(d)   Capital payments to the settlor

Trust income may be treated as the settlor's income where the settlor or the settlor's spouse directly or indirectly receives a capital sum from the trust or a connected company. A 'capital sum' is widely defined in Section 634 of the Income Tax (Trading and Other Income) Act 2005 to include "any sum paid otherwise than as income" for less than full consideration in money or money's worth, and specifically, a loan or repayment of a loan, even where made for full consideration. Discharging a debt owed by the settlor or the settlor's spouse is also included. However, payments made only as a result of one of the excepted occasions for retention of interest (eg, bankruptcy of a beneficiary – see section 2.4(b)) are excluded. Payments that the trustees make to a third party at the settlor's direction, or to a person to whom the settlor has assigned his or her right to receive them, are also treated as paid to the settlor.

The charge also applies where the capital sum is paid not by the trustees, but by a company connected with the trust; but in this case, the trustees must make or have made an 'associated payment' to the company within a period of five years before or after the payment to the settlor.

A company relates to the trust if it is a closely held company and the trustees are participators. An 'associated payment' is any capital sum paid by the trustees to the company or any other sum paid or asset transferred for less than full consideration in money or money's worth. In practice, this would usually take the form of a loan from the trustees to the company.

The charge is made to the extent that there is available undistributed income in the trust. This is the aggregate income of the current and previous years which has not:

- already been considered for a previous charge under these rules;
- been treated as the settlor's income; or
- been distributed.

Where the capital sum is greater than the available undistributed income, the balance is carried over to the following year and charged to tax then up to the income available in that year, and so on for a maximum of 10 years.

The settlor is treated as receiving a gross sum on which tax at 45% has been paid, leaving a net sum equal to the payment charged to tax. Again, the settlor is entitled to claim the full allowances and reliefs to which he or she would have been entitled had an equivalent sum of income actually been received by him or her.

(e) Non-resident and non-domiciled settlors

If the settlor is not resident or not domiciled in the United Kingdom and subject to UK tax on the remittance basis, the charge is restricted to UK-source income. However, if the attributed income or payment is actually remitted to the United Kingdom while the settlor is resident and the settlor would be taxable on that amount if he or she were actually entitled to the income, it is taken into account, even if the income arose in a year in which the settlor is not within the charge to UK tax (eg, because of non-residence).

Unremitted foreign trust income at 5 April 2017 retained within the trust may be remitted by the trustees after 5 April 2017 without resulting in a charge on the settlor.

(f) Exception for protected foreign source income

With effect from 6 April 2017, 'protected foreign source income' is not attributed to a settlor domiciled outside the United Kingdom under Section 624, 629 or 634 of the Income Tax (Trading and Other Income) Act 2005. Income of a non-resident trust arising after 5 April 2017 is protected foreign source income for a tax year, provided that:

- the income would be relevant foreign income if it were a UK resident individual's income;
- the trust was settled when the settlor was domiciled outside the United Kingdom and, if after 5 April 2017, not deemed domiciled in the United Kingdom;
- at no time during the tax year is the settlor domiciled in the United Kingdom or a formerly domiciled resident; and
- no property or income is added directly or indirectly to the trust by the settlor or by trustees of another trust of which the settlor is a beneficiary or settlor after 5 April 2017, at a time when the settlor is domiciled or deemed domiciled in the United Kingdom.

The addition of value to trust property is treated as the direct addition of property to the trust. When considering whether a trust has been tainted, property may be added to a trust without being treated as an addition if it is:

- a transaction entered into at arm's length, other than a loan;
- an amount provided without any intention to confer gratuitous benefit, otherwise than as a loan;

- the principal of a loan to the trustees made on arm's-length terms;
- payment of interest to the trustees under a loan on arm's-length terms;
- repayment to the trustees of the principal of a loan made by them on arm's-length terms;
- property or income provided in pursuance of a liability incurred by anyone before 6 April 2017; or
- amounts provided to meet the trust's tax and administration expenses, to the extent that they exceed its income, or if greater, exceed the expenses that may be paid out of income.

Where a loan is made to the trustees by the settlor or a connected trust, interest of at least the HMRC 'official rate' must be paid at least annually for the loan not to be treated as an addition. For existing loans at 6 April 2017, where the settlor was deemed domiciled, transitional provisions allowed the trustees to avoid an addition by:

- repaying the loan, including any interest due, before 6 April 2018; or
- changing the terms of the loan to bear interest at the official rate from 6 April 2017 and paying the interest due up to 5 April 2018 by that date.

Where, after 5 April 2018, a benefit is provided from the trust to a beneficiary, protected foreign source income may be treated as the settlor's if the settlor is UK resident and the recipient is:

- the settlor; or
- a close member of the family of the settlor who is:
  - non-resident; or
  - subject to UK tax on the remittance basis and does not remit the benefit.

The charge arises to the extent that there is available protected income and benefits received are not already taken into account under this or the transfer of assets abroad provisions. Where untaxed benefits exceed the available protected income, the benefits are carried forward to the following year and charged to tax in that year up to the available protected income in that year and so on.

A 'close family member' is:

- the settlor's spouse;
- the settlor's minor child; or
- the minor child of the settlor's spouse.

In this context, the definition of 'spouses' includes co-habiting partners.

(g)   Onward gifts

Further anti-avoidance provisions took effect from 6 April 2018, which seek to treat gifts received by the settlor or a close member of his or her family as if that person had received a distribution from an offshore trust where a non-resident or a UK resident claiming to be taxed on the remittance basis, who is a close family member, has acted as a conduit for the distribution. Where the provisions apply, protected income matched to the gift is treated as that of the recipient. If the donee is not taxable because he or she is non-resident or taxed on the remittance basis and does not remit the gift, the income is attributed to the UK resident settlor.

The detailed conditions required for an onward gift are set out in section 2.5(f), as they apply for income subject to the transfer of assets abroad provisions.

2.5   Transfer of assets abroad

(a)   Extent of the provisions

The most important anti-avoidance provisions aimed at countering income tax avoidance in offshore trusts are found in Part 13, Chapter 2 of the Income Tax Act 2007. These provisions require an avoidance motive and potentially apply to any UK resident settlor or beneficiary of an offshore trust. These provisions come into play only where the income would otherwise escape UK tax.

(b)   Attribution of income to the settlor

Sections 714 to 730 of the Income Tax Act 2007 are aimed at transfers of assets abroad with the view of avoiding UK income tax. The main charging rules are found in Sections 720 and 727. In essence, they require such an individual, as a result of the transfer and/or any associated operations, whether immediately or in the future, either:

- to have the power to enjoy any income of a non-resident person or non-domiciled individual; or
- to receive or be entitled to any capital sum in any way connected to the transfer or any associated operation.

'Associated operations' is very widely defined, even to the extent that it required a court to hold that death is not an associated operation. 'Assets' include property or rights of any kind, and 'transfer' includes the creation of rights. The foreign person to whom the income becomes payable can be an individual, company or trust. The associated operations need not follow the transfer; they can precede it.

It is possible to sum up all the conditions as follows:

- a transfer of assets;

- by an individual (the transferor) or his or her spouse (who is now) resident in the United Kingdom;
- as a direct or indirect result of which income becomes payable to a non-resident or non-domiciled person (the foreign person); and
- either the transferor or his spouse has or will have the power to enjoy any of the income of the foreign person; or
- he or she has received or will receive a capital sum connected with the transfer.

Where the charge arises because the individual has received a capital sum, it is clear from the legislation that the amount chargeable is the income that has become payable to the foreign person as a result of the transfer and any associated operations. Where, however, the charge is on the basis of the power to enjoy (ie, under Section 720), it is not clear from the legislation whether it is the whole of the income of the foreign person in respect of which the individual is chargeable or only in respect of the extent to which the income stems from the transfer and any associated operations. Following *Vestey*, HMRC limits the assessment to the income connected with the transfer.

The transfer of assets need not be made from the United Kingdom to another jurisdiction. The transfer can equally take place from one foreign jurisdiction to another.

The power to enjoy income can be an individual's in one of five ways:
- where the income inures to the benefit of the individual;
- where the receipt or accrual of the income serves to increase the value of any assets held by or on behalf of the individual (eg, the receipt of income by a company in which the individual is a shareholder);
- where the individual receives or becomes entitled to receive a benefit directly or indirectly arising out of that income;
- where the individual may become entitled to the beneficial enjoyment of the income as a result of the exercise or successive exercise of powers by any person; and
- where the individual can directly or indirectly control the application of the income.

A beneficiary with the power to appoint trustees has been held not to be able to control the application of the income of his or her discretionary trust.

A 'capital sum' is defined virtually identically to Section 634 of the Income Tax (Trading and Other Income) Act 2005 (capital sums paid to settlors – see section 2.4(d) above) – that is, as:
- any sum paid or payable by way of loan or repayment of a loan; or
- any other sum paid or payable otherwise than as income and for a consideration that is less than full in money or money's worth.

Further, where a third-party receives, or is entitled to receive, any sum at the direction of an individual, or because the right to receive it has been assigned to him or her by the individual, that individual is treated as receiving it or as entitled to receive it.

However, where a loan has been wholly repaid before the beginning of a particular year, an individual can no longer be in receipt of the capital sum represented by that loan in that or any subsequent year.

In HMRC's view, an individual will also be caught by these provisions if he or she procures the transfer.

Where both Sections 624 of the Income Tax (Trading and Other Income) Act 2005 and 720 of the Income Tax Act 2007 could apply, Section 624 will take priority.

(c) *Non-domiciled transferors*
The charge under Sections 720 and 727 on the transferor applies where the transferor would have been liable to income tax on the income had he or she actually received it in the United Kingdom. However, in the case of a non-domiciled transferor to whom the remittance basis applies, the charge under these sections is restricted to UK-source income, if the foreign income is not remitted to the United Kingdom. For income arising within an offshore trust after 5 April 2017, the remittance basis will rarely be relevant for the transferor.

Unremitted foreign income retained within an offshore trust at 5 April 2017 may be remitted to the United Kingdom by the trustees without resulting in a charge on the settlor but this does not extend to the income of an underlying company.

(d) *Exception for protected foreign source income*
'Protected foreign source income' is not treated as the settlor's income under either Section 720 or 727 from 6 April 2017, where the settlor is not UK domiciled and not a formerly domiciled resident. The definition of protected foreign source income for the purpose of Section 720 is found in Section 721A. Income of a non-resident trust or a non-resident company in which the trustees are participators, arising after 5 April 2017 is protected foreign source income for a tax year, provided that:

- the income would be relevant foreign income if it were the individual's income;
- the trust was settled when the settlor was domiciled outside the United Kingdom and if after 5 April 2017 not deemed domiciled in the United Kingdom;
- at no time during the tax year is the settlor domiciled in the United Kingdom or a formerly domiciled resident;
- no property or income is added directly or indirectly to the trust by the

settlor or by trustees of another trust of which the settlor is a beneficiary or settlor after 5 April 2017, at a time when the settlor is domiciled or deemed domiciled in the United Kingdom; and

- where the income arises in a company or a chain of companies, the individual's power to enjoy the income results from the trustees being participators.

The definition of protected foreign source income for Section 727 is the same as for Section 720 for income at trust level. Where the income arises in a company or chain of companies, the trustees must be participators as a result of a relevant transaction and the income must have become the company's income as a result of that transaction.

The detailed definition of an addition of value and transitional provisions for existing loans at 5 April 2017 are the same as for protected foreign source income under the settlor-interested trust income tax provisions (see section 2.4(f)).

(e)   ***The charge on beneficiaries (non-transferors)***

Section 731 of the Income Tax Act 2007 charges individuals resident in the United Kingdom who receive a benefit stemming directly or indirectly from a transfer of assets, but are not themselves taxable under Section 720 or 727. This will include benefits received by a UK resident, non-domiciled settlor matched to protected income after 5 April 2017. The following circumstances must apply:

- There is a transfer of assets, as a direct or indirect result of which, alone or in conjunction with associated operations, income (relevant income) becomes payable to a person resident or domiciled outside the United Kingdom (the foreign person); and
- A UK resident individual, who is not taxable under Section 720 or 727, as a result of the same transfer receives a benefit provided out of the assets available for that purpose, as a direct or indirect result of the transfer or of any associated operations.

The charge is on the benefit received, to the extent that there is available relevant income arising in the same year (or available relevant income brought forward from previous years) to the foreign person which can directly or indirectly be used to provide the benefit. If the value of the benefit is greater than the amount of available relevant income, the balance is carried forward and is charged on the UK individual in the next following year in which there is available relevant income. Income is not available if it has already been paid away to some person other than the beneficiary chargeable under Section 731.

A benefit need not be a monetary benefit to be caught under this provision.

The free use, or use under beneficial terms, of trust property would constitute a benefit potentially taxable under Section 731, as would a loan at below-market rates of interest. However, the creation of a life interest for a beneficiary, or the receipt by a beneficiary of the sale proceeds of his or her life interest, is not a benefit (presumably because it cannot be said that the life interest is provided out of the assets transferred). A statutory valuation rule was brought in from 6 April 2017, covering both income tax and capital gains tax (see section 4.7(h) for details). Under the statutory rule, any consideration provided in exchange for the benefit will reduce the taxable amount only if paid in the relevant year.

Where a benefit is provided to a member of the settlor's close family, from 6 April 2017, but is outside the Section 731 charge because the beneficiary is non-resident or is taxed on the remittance basis and does not remit the benefit, income is attributed to the UK resident settlor, to the extent that the benefit is matched to available protected income.

(f) Onward gifts

From 6 April 2018, provisions were introduced to treat gifts received by UK residents, which could be traced back to benefits received by a non-resident or a UK resident taxed on the remittance basis from an offshore trust structure, as if he or she had received a benefit from the trust. The recipient of a gift after 5 April 2018 may be subject to a charge under Section 731, where:

- an individual receives a benefit (the original beneficiary);
- it is matched to relevant income that is protected income;
- at the time of receipt, there is an intention to pass on the benefit to a UK resident;
- the gift is made within three years of or at any time before receiving the benefit in anticipation of the receipt;
- the gift is of or derives from the benefit or is of other property where the benefit was provided to facilitate the gift; and
- when the benefit is provided, the original beneficiary is non-resident or taxed on the remittance basis and does not remit it.

Where the conditions in the fourth and fifth bullets above are met, there is a presumption that the third is also met, unless the contrary is shown. If the recipient of the gift is a non-resident or taxed on the remittance basis and does not remit the gift, he or she can also be treated as making a further onward gift if he or she makes a gift to a UK resident.

If the recipient of the gift is a close family member of the UK resident settlor, the gift is attributed to the UK resident settlor if it is not taxed on the recipient as a non-resident or remittance basis user.

(g) *UK resident but non-domiciled beneficiaries*

As with Sections 720 and 727, a non-domiciled beneficiary to whom the remittance basis applies (used here in the sense of the person receiving a benefit liable under Section 731, not in the strict trust sense) cannot be assessed under Section 731 on any non-UK source benefit not received in the United Kingdom. The rules on constructive remittances are specifically extended to include the determination of when a benefit is received in the United Kingdom for this purpose.

(h) *The interaction of the transferor and non-transferor charges*

Since Section 731 applies in the same circumstances as Section 720 to tax the recipient of a benefit (which need not take the form of income), there are situations where both the settlor and a beneficiary may be chargeable on the same income. Generally, the transferor will be taxed under Section 720, in priority to the non-transferor beneficiary, where both would be chargeable in the same year and it is clear that the income is the same. However, where the transferor is taxed on the remittance basis, a beneficiary taxed on the arising basis or remitting the benefit received may be taxed instead. HMRC is required under Section 743 of the Income Tax Act 2007 to make a just and reasonable apportionment where more than one person may be taxed on the same income.

(i) *Payments out of a discretionary trust*

Where a capital payment to which Section 731 applies is made to an individual out of trust property, that individual is not entitled to any tax credit for UK tax at source on the income making up that capital. This contrasts to the situation under Section 720, where any UK tax paid by the trustees on an income distribution that falls within Section 720 may be claimed as a credit by the individual liable. A non-UK-domiciled recipient of such a payment to whom the remittance basis applied would thus not be taxable on non-UK source income under Section 731 if the payment were not remitted to the United Kingdom.

Where the income of the person abroad has suffered foreign tax, a transferor may benefit from foreign tax credit relief to offset his or her UK tax liability on that income as if the income were his or hers directly. Such relief is not available to a non-transferor.

(j) *Exceptions*

There are three defences under statute against a charge under Section 720, 727 or 731 of the Income Tax Act 2007, collectively known as the 'motive defence'. The individual on whom the charge would otherwise fall must show that:

- avoiding liability to taxation was not the purpose or one of the purposes of the transfer of assets or any associated operations;

- the transfer and any associated operations were *bona fide* commercial transactions, and were not designed to avoid liability to taxation; or
- the EU defence applies (see section 2.5(k) below).

It is not enough that tax avoidance may not be the main purpose of any of the transactions; it must not be even a subsidiary purpose. Although the legislation would appear to be aimed at individuals seeking to avoid liability to income tax, case law has established that 'taxation' is not limited to income tax, but extends to any UK tax.

Thus, a non-domiciled individual who sets up an offshore trust with the purpose of avoiding UK inheritance tax (the trust property will be exempt – see section 3.1(f)) before coming to the United Kingdom will potentially be within Section 720 if he or she is a beneficiary of the trust at any time after becoming UK resident.

In HMRC's opinion, the commercial defence cannot apply where there is a significant element of tax avoidance; and it interprets a *'bona fide* commercial purpose' as one concerned with a trade or business only, and not with making or managing investments.

These tests were further tightened for transfers and associated operations made on or after 5 December 2005. The first limb of the test requires one to take account of all circumstances, including the intentions of advisers, in determining whether there was a tax avoidance purpose. The second requires that, taking account of all circumstances, it would not be reasonable to conclude that the transactions were designed more than incidentally for the purpose of avoiding tax.

(k)   The EU defence

The European Commission issued proceedings against the UK government in 2011 for infringement of the fundamental freedoms of establishment and movement of capital in respect of the transfer of assets abroad legislation. This resulted in a new defence against a charge under Section 720, 727 or 731 of the Income Tax Act 2007 for genuine transactions effected after 5 April 2012. The relevant transaction may be either the original transfer or an associated operation. To be genuine a transaction must be:

- a genuinely commercial transaction, made on arm's-length terms; or
- made for personal reasons, wholly for the benefit of others and with the transferor having received no consideration for the transfer.

A charge under the transfer of assets abroad provisions would, in contravention of a relevant treaty provision, constitute an unjustified and disproportionate restriction on a freedom protected under that relevant treaty provision.

In addition to the statutory EU defence, *Fisher v HMRC* established an EU case law defence which will disapply the transfer of assets abroad provisions by interpreting the motive defence in such a way as to construe the definition of 'avoidance' in a narrow sense, where the individual is exercising a treaty freedom.

3. Inheritance tax

3.1 Introduction

(a) General

Inheritance tax applies to transfers of property made on death and to any lifetime gifts not specifically exempted that were made within seven years of death. For most lifetime gifts into trust since 22 March 2006, there is also a charge to inheritance tax when the gift is made, regardless of whether the donor lives for a further seven years.

Liability to inheritance tax depends on domicile (in the strict UK sense). For individuals domiciled in the United Kingdom, including those deemed domiciled in the United Kingdom for inheritance tax purposes, inheritance tax has no territorial limits; it applies to assets wherever situated. For non-domiciled individuals, inheritance tax applies where the assets transferred are situated in the United Kingdom.

Despite its name, inheritance tax is charged on the transferor, on the entire value of the amount transferred (the deceased's entire estate, in the case of death), subject to specific exemptions. The domicile or residence status of the transferee is largely irrelevant.

The basis of the charge to inheritance tax is the value transferred (measured by the loss to the transferor's estate, not by the increase in value of the transferee's estate) by a non-exempt transfer. The rate of tax depends on previous cumulative transfers. A seven-year cumulation period applies to gifts and inheritances.

(b) Relevant property

The concept of relevant property is the key to understanding the inheritance tax charges that arise on settled property, since only relevant property is charged to tax. Relevant property is settled property in which there is no qualifying interest in possession, other than:
- property held for charitable purposes;
- property held on accumulation and maintenance trusts;
- property held on trusts for bereaved minors;
- property held on age 18 to 25 trusts;
- property held on trusts for the disabled;

- property held on certain protective trusts;
- property held on certain employee trusts;
- excluded property;
- property held on approved maintenance funds for historic buildings;
- property held by certain pension schemes; and
- property held on certain trade compensation funds.

For occasions of charge after 5 April 2009, a work of art situated in the United Kingdom for public display, cleaning or restoration and for no other purposes is not regarded as relevant property if the person beneficially entitled to it is domiciled outside the United Kingdom or if it is comprised in an excluded property trust.

(c)   *Qualifying interests in possession*
A person who is beneficially entitled to a qualifying interest in possession in trust property is treated for inheritance tax purposes as if he or she were beneficially entitled to that property. A qualifying interest in possession is an interest in possession existing at 22 March 2006 or a new interest arising on or after 22 March 2006 if it qualifies as:
- an immediate post-death interest;
- a transitional serial interest; or
- a disabled person's interest.

Immediate post-death interests: An immediate post-death interest is an interest in possession in settled property arising on or after 22 March 2006 where:
- the settlement arose under a will or intestacy;
- the interest arose on the death of the testator or on intestacy;
- the property is not also held on trust for bereaved minors and is not a disabled person's interest; and
- from the date the interest arose, the property has never been held on trust for bereaved minors or as a disabled person's interest.

Transitional serial interests: A transitional serial interest is an interest in possession in settled property where an interest in possession, which arose before 22 March 2006, came to an end before 6 October 2008 and was immediately replaced by a new interest in possession in the settled property, provided that the trust does not qualify as one for bereaved minors or disabled persons.
   In addition, a transitional serial interest may be created on the death of the life tenant after 5 October 2008 where:
- the surviving spouse succeeds to the life interest, provided that the trust does not qualify as one for bereaved minors or disabled persons; or

- the settled property consisted of or included rights under a contract of life insurance entered into before 22 March 2006, provided that the trust does not qualify as one for bereaved minors or disabled persons.

Where the property consists of a contract of life insurance held before 22 March 2006, successive transitional serial interests may arise.

Disabled person's interests: A disabled person's interest is:
- an interest in possession in settled property for a disabled person; or
- a deemed interest in possession in settled property held on a disabled person's trust.

(d)   *Types of transfer*
It is important to distinguish between three different types of transfer: the chargeable transfer, the exempt transfer and the potentially exempt transfer. The concept of a gift with reservation should also be mentioned.

Chargeable transfers: A chargeable transfer is a transfer of value that is not an exempt transfer. A transfer of value is any disposition made by a person which diminishes the value of his or her estate. A disposition need not be an act of commission; a deliberate omission by a person to exercise a right can be a disposition if it diminishes the estate of that person and increases the estate of another person or the value of a trust, not forming part of any individual's estate. Inheritance tax is charged on the value transferred by a chargeable transfer.

Exempt transfers: An exempt transfer is a transfer of value that is specifically exempt under the Inheritance Tax Act 1984. Exempt transfers include:
- transfers to spouses (but see below);
- aggregate lifetime transfers of value of no more than £3,000 in any one year;
- transfers representing normal expenditure out of income;
- lifetime gifts of up to £5,000 in consideration of marriage;
- gifts to charities;
- gifts to certain political parties;
- gifts to national heritage bodies;
- gifts of assets of scientific, cultural or historic interest to non-profit bodies; and
- lifetime dispositions for the maintenance of the family.

Transfers to spouses are completely exempt, whether on death or during life, provided that the spouse is domiciled or deemed domiciled in the United Kingdom. Where the transferor spouse is domiciled in the United Kingdom, but the transferee spouse is not, total lifetime transfers up to the value of the nil rate band (£325,000 for 2019–2020) are exempt. However, if the transferor spouse is non-domiciled, this restriction does not apply. From 6 April 2013 a non-domiciled spouse may elect to be deemed UK-domiciled for inheritance tax in relation to transfers of value made after 5 April 2013.

Although not exempt as such, most transfers of business property and agricultural property (as defined) are to all intents and purposes exempt, as they qualify for a 100% reduction in value.

Potentially exempt transfers: Most lifetime transfers fall into the category of potentially exempt transfers. A potentially exempt transfer is a transfer of value that is made by an individual and would otherwise be a chargeable transfer, but is one of the following:

- an outright gift to another individual;
- a gift to an interest-in-possession trust prior to 22 March 2006;
- a gift to an accumulation and maintenance trust prior to 22 March 2006;
- a gift to a disabled trust; or
- a gift into a bereaved minor's trust on the ending of an immediate post-death interest.

No charge to inheritance tax arises when a potentially exempt transfer is made; it is assumed to be an exempt transfer and indeed becomes an exempt transfer if the transferor survives for seven years after making the gift. Where the transferor dies before seven years have elapsed, the potentially exempt transfer becomes a chargeable transfer treated as made at the time it was actually made but charged to tax at the death rates (see section 5.2(b)), subject to any tapering relief.

(e) **Gifts with reservation**

A gift with reservation is an incomplete gift in the sense that either:

- there is no good-faith assumption of possession and enjoyment of the property by the donee; or
- the property is not enjoyed to the entire, or virtually the entire, exclusion of the donor.

A gift made before 18 March 1986 (when the concept was first introduced) cannot be treated as a gift with reservation.

In the first case above, the test is applied at the time of the gift. In the second case above, there is a gift with reservation if the donor is not excluded or virtually excluded at any time between the making of the gift and the donor's death (but looking back no more than seven years from the date of death). A typical example of a gift with reservation within the second case would be one in which a widowed parent transferred ownership of her house to her children, but retained the right to remain living in the house for the rest of her life.

Where there is a gift with reservation, the normal rules apply at the time the gift is made (ie, the gift may be a chargeable transfer, an exempt transfer or a potentially exempt transfer), but when the donor dies, the property that was the subject of the gift is treated as still forming part of the deceased donor's estate (unless more than seven years have elapsed since the retained benefit was surrendered, in the case of gifts falling within the second bullet above).

A gift of property to a trust in which the settlor has the sole interest in possession from 22 March 2006 or a gift by the settlor to a discretionary trust in which the settlor (but not his or her spouse) is or can be a beneficiary is a gift with reservation, and remains part of the settlor's estate, even though it is also a chargeable transfer, on which there is an immediate charge to inheritance tax.

From 6 April 2005, where the settlor of a trust retains an interest in trust property previously owned, without falling foul of the gifts with reservation rules, a 'pre-owned assets' income tax charge may arise. The charge seeks to tax the benefit of the asset on an annual basis, subject to several exemptions and a de minimis limit.

(f) Excluded property

An important inheritance tax concept for offshore trusts is that of 'excluded property'. Where property transferred by a chargeable transfer is excluded property, its value is left out of account in determining the charge to tax. There are three main classes of excluded property:

- property situated outside the United Kingdom, to which an individual domiciled outside the United Kingdom is beneficially entitled;
- UK government securities exempt from tax, if in the beneficial ownership of persons neither domiciled nor resident in the United Kingdom; and
- trust property situated outside the United Kingdom, where the trust was created by a person domiciled outside the United Kingdom (an excluded property trust).

From the point of view of offshore trusts, it is property falling within the third bullet above that is clearly of most interest. Two conditions must be satisfied for trust property to be excluded property:

- The settlor must be non-domiciled when the trust is created; and
- The property must be situated outside the United Kingdom at the time of the transfer.

Two different times are involved. The condition relating to the settlor need be satisfied only when the trust is created. The foreign property remains excluded property even if the settlor later becomes domiciled in the United Kingdom. However, even where the settlor remains non-domiciled, the property will not be excluded property if it subsequently becomes situated in the United Kingdom and is still situated there at the time of the transfer giving rise to the potential inheritance tax charge. In neither case does it matter whether the trust is resident (onshore) or non-resident (offshore).

A word of warning, however: as mentioned below, the meaning of 'settlor' extends for inheritance tax purposes to persons adding property to the trust after it has been created. Clearly, then, property added by a person other than the original settlor, if that person is UK domiciled, will not be excluded property even if it is situated abroad and the original settlor was non-domiciled when the trust was created.

For occasions of charge on or after 17 July 2013, liabilities incurred to finance the acquisition or maintenance of excluded property (directly or indirectly) may not be deducted in establishing the taxable value of relevant property, even if secured on the relevant property.

From 6 April 2017, where the settlor becomes deemed domiciled as a formerly domiciled resident, any excluded property trusts settled while non-domiciled lose their excluded property status and become relevant property trusts. Should the settlor later become non-UK resident again and cease to be deemed domiciled, any such trusts will revert to excluded property, provided that the settlor has retained his or her non-UK domicile.

(g) *Non-excluded overseas property*

From 6 April 2017, Schedule A1 of the Inheritance Tax Act 1984 removes excluded property status from UK residential property interests. To the extent that the value of an interest in a foreign close company or partnership is attributable to UK residential property, the interest is not excluded property.

In addition, loans used to finance the purchase, maintenance or enhancement of the value of UK residential property are not excluded property.

On disposal of an interest in a company or partnership containing a UK residential property or repayment of a relevant loan while the UK residential property is retained, the proceeds will remain non-excluded property for a further two years.

As a result, the common practice of holding such property through a non-resident company no longer provides a shelter from inheritance tax for non-UK-domiciled individuals and excluded property trusts.

3.2 Property entering the trust

There is a potential inheritance tax charge on the settlor when he or she transfers property to the trust, whether at the time of its creation or subsequently, unless:

- the settlor is a foreign domiciliary at the time of gift and the property is excluded property;
- the gift is to a disabled trust; or
- the gift was made before 22 March 2006 to an interest-in-possession trust or accumulation and maintenance trust and the settlor survives seven years.

For the purposes of inheritance tax, the term 'settlor' has an extended definition. It includes not only the direct or indirect creator of the trust, but also any person who has provided funds directly or indirectly for the trust. It also includes a person who has made an arrangement with another person for that other person to create the trust.

3.3 The periodic (10-year) charge

Relevant property held in a trust is subject to a periodic charge to tax at every 10-year anniversary. Relevant property includes accumulated income, but excludes undistributed and unaccumulated income.

The value of the relevant property immediately before the 10-year anniversary is charged at 30% of the effective rate, currently 20%. This is further reduced if the property was not relevant property for the whole 10 years, by 1/40th for each successive quarter year during which it was not relevant property. The maximum charge, based on rates for 2019–2020, is 6%.

For charges falling after 5 April 2014, unaccumulated income which arose on relevant property within the settlement more than five years before the 10-year anniversary is treated as relevant property, provided that no person was entitled to an interest in possession in the property from which the income arose. No reduction in the rate applied to accumulated income is made for quarters during which it was not relevant property.

The effective rate is the tax chargeable as a percentage of the value of the property on an assumed transfer of:
- the value of the taxable trust property immediately before the 10-year anniversary; plus
- the value, at the time it commenced, of relevant property comprised in any other trusts created by the settlor on the same day as the trust in question; plus
- (for charges after 5 April 2015) the value, at the time it became trust property, of property added to any other trusts on the same day as any of the property in the trust in question if it does not also fall within the second bullet above.

For charges falling before 19 November 2015, the value at the time it became trust property of any trust property that has never been relevant property is also included in the calculation. This meant that up until 18 November 2015, excluded property trusts holding a small amount of relevant property at a 10-year anniversary would always have an inheritance tax charge if the trust had ever held property in excess of the nil rate band.

The assumed transfer is calculated as if made by a transferor who has made chargeable transfers in the previous seven years equal to the sum of:

- the total of previous chargeable transfers made by the settlor in the seven years ending on the day the trust was created, disregarding transfers made on or before 27 March 1974; plus
- the amounts on which exit charges have been imposed in the 10 years preceding the current anniversary.

If property has been added to the trust since it was created, the charge is recalculated for each addition, using the seven years immediately preceding the date of addition instead of the seven years preceding the creation of the trust for the settlor's previous transfers. Whichever of the computations yields the greater amount of tax prevails.

3.4 Property leaving the trust

(a) General
A potential charge to inheritance tax arises when property leaves the trust.

Property can leave a trust where:

- the trust itself is dissolved;
- a beneficiary becomes absolutely entitled to it; or
- the trustees exercise powers under the trust deed to transfer it to another trust.

(b) Qualifying interest-in-possession trusts
When a qualifying interest in possession comes to an end, whether or not there is a disposal by the holder of that interest, there is deemed to be a transfer of value, equal to the value of the underlying property. Any money or money's worth received in return for the disposal reduces the value transferred for inheritance tax purposes. There is no charge to tax under this provision if the holder of the interest becomes, on the same occasion, beneficially entitled to the property itself (ie, it passes out of the trust to him or her absolutely) or to another qualifying interest in possession in the same property.

There is also no charge to tax when a qualifying interest in possession terminates during the settlor's life and the underlying property then reverts to the settlor. Nor is there a charge if, on the termination of a qualifying interest in possession, the beneficial interest in the underlying property passes to the settlor's spouse (or if the settlor has died no more than two years previously, to the settlor's widow or widower).

A transfer before 22 March 2006 by the trustees of a qualifying interest in possession from one individual to another is a potentially exempt transfer, as is the creation of a transitional serial interest (see section 3.1(c)).

(c)   *Discretionary trusts and non-qualifying interest-in-possession trusts*
An exit charge before the first 10-year anniversary is calculated as for the 10-year anniversary charge, except that the assumed chargeable transfer includes the relevant property at its value when it first entered the settlement or most recently became relevant property, rather than immediately before the time of the charge. Once the first 10-year anniversary has passed, exit charges are calculated using the effective rate at the last 10-year anniversary, recomputed for changes in the tax rates and the nil rate band. There are various exemptions from the exit charge. These include the following:

- The transfer takes place no later than three months after the trust is created or the latest periodic charge; and
- The amount transferred is income chargeable to income tax in the hands of the transferee (or would be chargeable if the transferee were UK resident).

An exit charge can also arise where no property leaves the trust, if the trustees make a disposition that diminishes the value of trust property.

Where tax is payable on an exit charge, it is normally the liability of the transferee. If the trustees pay the tax, the value of the transfer must be grossed up for the tax, as with other lifetime transfers on which the transferor pays the tax.

3.5   Reversionary interests
Normally, a reversionary interest is excluded property (ie, exempt), except where:

- it has at some stage been acquired for consideration in money or money's worth;
- it is one to which the settlor or the settlor's spouse is or has been beneficially entitled; or
- it is one expectant on certain leases for life.

Where trust property is situated abroad (whether in an onshore or an offshore trust), and the settlor was non-domiciled when the trust was created, a reversionary interest in that property is not excluded property, in contrast to an existing interest, unless the person beneficially entitled to the reversionary interest is also a non-domiciliary.

3.6   Property moving between settlements

For the purposes of the provisions on trusts without a qualifying interest in possession, when trust property passes from one trust to another and no person becomes beneficially entitled to the property in the interim, the property is regarded as remaining in the first trust. Where the property was excluded property in the first trust because it is foreign property and the settlor was not domiciled in the United Kingdom when the trust was created, it will remain excluded property, no matter where situated, only if the settlor of the second trust was also non-domiciled when the second trust was created.

3.7   Accumulation and maintenance trusts

An accumulation and maintenance trust is a discretionary trust (ie, a trust in which no interest in possession subsists) created before 22 March 2006, under which:

- one or more persons (the beneficiaries) will, on attaining a specified age (which can be no greater than 25), become beneficially entitled to the trust property or to an interest in possession (eg, a life interest) in the trust property;
- the income of the trust is accumulated, to the extent it is not applied for the maintenance, education or benefit of the beneficiaries; and
- all the persons who are or have been beneficiaries are or were either:
    - grandchildren of a common grandparent; or
    - children, widows or widowers of such grandchildren, who were themselves beneficiaries but died before becoming beneficially entitled to or to an interest in possession in, the trust property.

After 5 April 2008 a trust will continue to qualify as an accumulation and maintenance trust only if the beneficiaries become beneficially entitled to the trust property at the age of 18. Where a trust ceases to qualify as an accumulation and maintenance trust on 6 April 2008 due to this restriction, there is no exit charge.

The inheritance tax privileges previously enjoyed by accumulation and maintenance trusts are as follows:

- A gift into an accumulation and maintenance trust is a potentially taxable event, not an immediately chargeable event;
- The accumulation and maintenance trust is exempt from the periodic charge;
- There is no exit charge when a beneficiary becomes beneficially entitled to the trust property, or to an interest in possession in the trust property, on reaching the specified age or on the death of a beneficiary before reaching that age; and
- Where exit charges do apply, a special scale of rates is used.

3.8 Trusts for bereaved minors

From 22 March 2006, a trust for bereaved minors is a trust where settled property (including property settled before 22 March 2006) is held on:

- statutory trusts for a bereaved minor on intestacy;
- the will trust of a deceased parent of a bereaved minor; or
- trust under the criminal injuries compensation scheme for a bereaved minor.

The minor must become absolutely entitled at 18 and no one else can benefit from the income before the fund vests. A bereaved minor is an individual under 18 with at least one deceased parent. An inheritance tax charge will arise where settled property ceases to be held on a trust for bereaved minors, except as a result of:

- the minor reaching 18 and receiving the fund absolutely;
- the minor receiving the fund absolutely before reaching 18;
- the death of the minor; or
- funds being paid for the advancement of the minor.

Where exit charges do apply, a special scale of rates is used. There are no periodic charges.

3.9 Age 18 to 25 trusts

An age 18 to 25 trust is a trust which would qualify as a trust for a bereaved minor except that funds do not vest until the age of 25. While the beneficiary is under 18, it is taxed in the same way as a trust for a bereaved minor. When funds vest between the age of 18 and 25, an exit charge will arise based on the period from the date the beneficiary reaches the age of 18 or, if later, the date on which the trust first becomes an age 18 to 25 trust. For an exit charge arising on any other occasion, a special scale of rates is used. There are no periodic charges.

Under transitional provisions, an accumulation and maintenance trust may be varied and become an 18 to 25 trust between 22 March 2006 and 5 April 2008, provided that funds will vest at the age of 25.

3.10 Disabled trusts

A disabled trust is a discretionary trust settled before 8 April 2013 under which at least half of the trust property must be applied during the life of a disabled person for his or her benefit. For trusts settled after 7 April 2013, all of the income must be applied for the benefit of a disabled person, apart from a *de minimis* annual limit of the lower of £3,000 and 3% of the maximum value of the trust property during the year.

A disabled trust may also be settled after 21 March 2006 by an individual, for his or her own benefit, in circumstances in which he or she is expected to become a disabled person.

Although this type of trust is a discretionary trust, the disabled person is treated for inheritance tax purposes as if he or she were beneficially entitled to a qualifying interest in possession in the trust property. It follows that none of the discretionary trust provisions applies to such a trust. There is therefore no 10-year charge and no exit charge, except for those normally applying to qualifying interest-in-possession trusts. A gift to a disabled trust is a potentially exempt transfer.

3.11   Information powers

Any person who is liable for tax on a chargeable transfer either as transferor or as trustee must deliver an account to HMRC within six months of the end of the month in which the transfer took place (or if later, within three months of the end of the month in which that person becomes liable to tax).

In addition, any person (other than a barrister acting in the exercise of his or her profession) who, in the course of business, has been involved in the creation of a trust and knows or has reason to believe that the settlor was domiciled in the United Kingdom, but that the trustees are or will become non-resident, must file a return within three months of the creation of the trust. The return must specify the names and addresses of the settlor and the trustees. This obligation does not apply to testamentary trusts, or where a return in relation to the trust has already been made or an account delivered by another person.

For this purpose only, trustees are regarded as non-resident where the general administration of the trust is ordinarily carried on outside the United Kingdom and the trustees or a majority of them are non-resident.

HMRC also has power to require any information it thinks necessary for the purposes of the Inheritance Tax Act 1984. This power can be exercised only with the consent of the First-tier Tribunal. There is protection for legally privileged documents.

There are penalties for failure to comply with the above provisions.

4.   Capital gains tax

4.1   Introduction

Capital gains tax is a tax on the gain arising on a disposal or deemed disposal of an asset and is governed by the Taxation of Chargeable Gains Act 1992. Where the disposal is made by individuals or trustees, the gain is calculated as the difference between:

- the net disposal proceeds; and
- the cost of acquisition and the cost of any enhancement reflected in the state of the asset at the time of disposal.

Where the asset was held at 31 March 1982, the market value at 31 March 1982 is treated as the acquisition cost. A disposal includes not only a sale, but also a transfer for no consideration (eg, a gift), as well as the loss or destruction of an asset. It is thus possible for a lifetime gift to be liable to both capital gains tax and inheritance tax. Where this is the case, an election may be made for the gain to be held over, but not where the transferee is non-resident or trustee of a settlor-interested trust.

Not all capital gains are liable to capital gains tax; gains that are liable or potentially liable are known as 'chargeable gains'. No gains accruing before 6 April 1965 (when capital gains tax was introduced) are liable to tax.

Where the capital gains computation results in a loss, those losses must be offset against gains in the same year. If there is an excess of losses over gains, the excess may be carried forward to future years without limit. The current year's losses are offset in preference to losses brought forward. Losses may not be carried back, except those of the year of death (which may be carried back for up to three years).

Trustees are eligible for an annual exemption for the first £6,000 in 2019–2020 of net gains as reduced by losses. If the settlor has made other trusts, the amount is divided by the total number of trusts, but by no more than 10. Certain disabled trusts qualify for an annual exemption of £12,000 in 2019–2020, with the same rule where there is more than one trust. Only so much of any losses brought forward as are needed to reduce net gains to the amount of the annual exemption need be offset. There are restrictions on the set-off of certain losses (most importantly, those arising from transactions with connected persons).

Death is not an occasion of charge for capital gains tax. In fact, there is a tax-free uplift of the deceased's property, as his or her personal representatives are deemed to acquire the deceased's assets at their market value.

4.2 Capital gains tax and non-residents

A person who is not resident in the United Kingdom at any time in a tax year is not liable to capital gains tax in respect of any chargeable gains accruing to him or her in that year, except where the assets are situated in the United Kingdom and connected with a UK permanent establishment. From 6 April 2015, non-residents are also liable for capital gains tax on gains on UK residential property. The capital gains tax charge is made on the appreciation since 5 April 2015. From 6 April 2019, non-residents disposing of all other UK land or assets deriving at least 75% of their value from UK land become subject to capital gains tax on the appreciation since 5 April 2019.

Capital gains realised by closely held non-resident companies are attributed to participators who are UK residents or non-UK resident trustees with at least a 25% (10% for years up to 5 April 2012) interest in the company, unless the disposal was of a trading asset used in the company's trade. When measuring a participator's interest in a company, for the purpose of the 25% test, the interests of connected persons to whom gains could be apportioned are aggregated. Since 6 April 2012, a motive defence has been available to prevent such attribution where the disposal, acquisition and holding of the asset by the company did not form a scheme or arrangement with a main purpose of avoiding capital gains tax or corporation tax.

Persons cannot, however, escape capital gains tax liability by emigrating (ie, ceasing to be resident) from the United Kingdom and then resuming residence within five years of departure. A resumption of residence within that five-year period will cause some chargeable gains accruing to that person during the years of absence to become liable to capital gains tax in the year of return. This provision does not apply unless the person was resident in at least four out of the seven years immediately preceding the year of departure.

It will be immediately obvious that non-resident trustees could realise gains completely free of UK capital gains tax, except to the extent they were carrying on a business in the United Kingdom or holding UK property interests. To counter this opportunity for avoidance, there is a large and complex set of capital gains tax anti-avoidance provisions relating to offshore trusts. These provisions were significantly strengthened in 1981, 1991, 1998, 2008 and again in 2017 and 2018.

Because of the importance and complexity of these provisions, the following text concentrates on them and the basic capital gains tax provisions relevant to trusts are explained only where necessary to the understanding of the anti-avoidance provisions.

4.3 Person becoming absolutely entitled

When a person becomes absolutely entitled to any trust property, there is a deemed disposal and immediate reacquisition of that property by the trustees at its market value. This means that any increase in value of the property while held in trust is deemed to be realised by the trustees and the beneficiary takes over the property at an acquisition cost equal to its market value. This rule is still of relevance to an offshore trust because there are circumstances in which gains made by the trustees are treated as made by the settlor.

Where the trustees incur a loss on the deemed disposal, they must first set it against gains on other property subject to the deemed disposal or against other gains made by them in the same year. To the extent that losses remain unrelieved, they pass to the beneficiary, but may be used only against chargeable gains accruing on the subsequent disposal of the same property.

4.4 Termination of a qualifying interest in possession by reason of death

Where the holder of a qualifying interest in possession (see section 3.1(c)) dies and the interest in possession thereby terminates, the trustees are deemed to make a disposal and reacquisition at market value of all the property in which the interest subsisted and which remains in the trust, but no chargeable gain accrues to them. This means, in effect, that the trustees benefit from a tax-free uplift in the acquisition cost. The same rule applies whenever a person entitled to a qualifying interest in possession dies, even if the interest itself does not come to an end.

There is also no chargeable disposal (ie, no charge to tax on the trustees) if the death of the person entitled to an interest in possession is also the occasion on which some other person becomes absolutely entitled. However, if the property reverts to the settlor, the trustee is instead treated as making a disposal at no gain and no loss. This rule thus overrides that described in section 4.3 above.

4.5   Transfer of assets into an offshore trust

When a settlor settles assets on a trust, he or she makes a disposal. The disposal is treated as made for a consideration equal to the market value of the assets concerned. The settlor is regarded as having disposed of the entire property, whether or not the trust is revocable, whether or not he or she retains an interest as a beneficiary of the trust and whether or not the settlor is also a trustee (even the sole trustee) of the trust.

If the assets are standing at a loss, the settlor may apply the loss only against gains accruing to him or her in other transactions with the trustees.

Clearly, if the settlor is not resident in the United Kingdom when the assets are settled, there is no capital gains tax liability on the settlor (unless the assets settled are UK property interests or trading assets). However, the anti-avoidance provisions against temporary non-residents must be borne in mind.

Where the settlor is resident but not domiciled in the United Kingdom, gains on settling non-UK assets may be protected from charge through a claim to be taxed on the remittance basis. A tax liability on these gains may later arise for the settlor if the assets, or funds traced back to those assets, are remitted to the United Kingdom by the trustees or any other relevant person in relation to the settlor, at a time when the settlor is UK resident.

4.6   Realisation of gains and their attribution to the settlor

(a)   *Introduction*

Prima facie, gains realised by the trustees of an offshore trust (except those associated with a trade carried on in the United Kingdom or on UK property) are exempt from capital gains tax, since the trustees are not UK resident. In order to counter this obvious opportunity for avoidance, there is a series of provisions attributing offshore trust gains to the settlor. These provisions apply where the settlor or an associated person has retained an interest in the trust and therefore parallel the income tax provisions of Part 5, Chapter 5 of the Income Tax (Trading and Other Income) Act 2005.

These provisions ('the Section 86 charge') apply only if each of the following six conditions is satisfied in any year:

- The trust is a qualifying trust;
- The trust is an offshore trust during any part of the year;
- The settlor is domiciled (including deemed domiciled from 6 April 2017) and resident in the United Kingdom for some part of the year;
- The settlor has an interest in the trust at any time during the year;
- There is a disposal during the year of trust property originating from the settlor, in respect of which the trustees would be liable to capital gains tax if they were resident in the United Kingdom; and
- The settlor is alive at the end of the year.

There can therefore be no Section 86 charge on a settlor who is not domiciled in the United Kingdom (and not deemed domiciled for capital gains tax purposes), even if he or she is UK resident. After 5 April 2017, if the settlor is deemed domiciled, the charge will also not apply if the trust meets the conditions for protection. Further, even if the settlor is UK domiciled or deemed domiciled, the Section 86 charge applies only if he or she is also resident. Where from 6 April 2013 the year is a split year under the statutory residence test, all the trust gains are treated as arising in the UK part of the year.

(b) *Qualifying trusts*

Qualifying trusts are those trusts potentially caught by the legislation (where the other conditions listed in section 4.6(a) apply). A qualifying trust is:

- any trust created after 18 March 1991 (in the year in which it is created and in subsequent years); or
- a trust created before 19 March 1991 (in 1999 to 2000 and subsequent years) that is not already a qualifying trust (ie, it is tainted), unless it was or was converted into a protected trust before 6 April 1999.

(c) *Trusts in which the settlor has an interest*

General rule: Essentially, the settlor has an interest where he or she and members of his or her immediate family ('the defined persons') benefit or may possibly benefit from any property or income originating from the settlor.

The 'defined persons' are:

- the settlor;
- the settlor's spouse;
- any child of the settlor or of the settlor's spouse;

- the spouse of any such child;
- (from 17 March 1998 only) any grandchild of the settlor or of the settlor's spouse;
- the spouse of any such grandchild;
- a company controlled by any of the preceding persons; and
- a company associated with any such company.

A person will 'benefit or may possibly benefit' where:
- there is property originating from the settlor which is, or may at any time be, included in the trust property and which is, or will or may become, applicable for the benefit of, or payable to, that person in any circumstances whatever;
- there is income originating from the settlor which arises, or may arise, under the trust and which is, or may become, applicable for the benefit of, or payable to, that person in any circumstances whatever; or
- that person already enjoys a benefit directly or indirectly from any such property or income.

Property 'originates' from the settlor where it has been directly or indirectly provided by him or her, or is property representing such property. Where property is of mixed origin, it must be apportioned on a just basis among the originators. Income 'originates' from the settlor where it is income arising from property originating from the settlor or it is income directly or indirectly provided by him. Property or income provided by closely held companies is deemed to be provided by the person(s) controlling them in proportion to their shareholdings. However, where there is more than one person who taken alone has control of the company, each such person is deemed to contribute an equal share. Holders of less than 5% are deemed to provide nothing.

Exceptions: There are circumstances in which a settlor's interest arising from property or income provided by him or her (as defined above) is ignored. This happens where the property or income originating from the settlor can become applicable for his or her benefit only on the occasion of:
- the bankruptcy of some person who is or may become beneficially entitled to the property or income;
- any assignment of or charge on the property or income given by such a bankrupt;
- in the case of marriage settlements, the death of both spouses and of any children of the marriage; or
- the death under the age of 25 (or some earlier vesting age) of a person who would have become beneficially entitled to the property on attaining that age.

The settlor's interest is also ignored throughout a period during which there is living an individual under 25 during whose life none of the property or income can become applicable for the benefit of a defined person, except on the bankruptcy of that individual or an assignment or charge given by the individual.

Where the settlor's interest in the trust arises through the existence of a single defined person who is benefiting or may possibly benefit from the trust, and that single person either dies or ceases to be married to the settlor, child or grandchild as appropriate during the year, there is no Section 86 charge on the settlor for that year.

Similarly, if there is more than one person through whom the settlor's interest arises, and they both or all die during the year, there is no Section 86 charge on the settlor in that year. Strangely, there is no exception in the situation where both or all of the persons fall out of the defined person category by ceasing to be married.

Finally, if the settlor dies during the year, there is no Section 86 charge in that year.

Protected trusts: A trust is a protected trust at any time in a year if, at that time, the beneficiaries are confined to persons falling within any of the following descriptions:

- children of a settlor or of a spouse of a settlor who are under the age of 18 or who were under 18 at the end of the previous year;
- unborn children of the settlor, or of a current or future spouse of the settlor;
- future spouses of any children or future children of a settlor, or of a spouse or future spouse of a settlor;
- future spouses of a settlor; and
- persons who are not defined persons (see above in relation to any settlor).

'Spouse' does not include widows or widowers or former spouses, but includes separated spouses, unless the separation is permanent.

'Beneficiary' has a special definition for this rule. Broadly speaking, a person is a beneficiary if there are any circumstances whatever in which he or she may benefit from property or income originating from a settlor, or where he or she already enjoys a benefit directly or indirectly from such property or income.

A child includes a stepchild.

Essentially, a trust is a protected trust if the beneficiaries are limited to children (including a spouse's children from a previous relationship) under the age of 18, children's spouses, future spouses and persons outside the immediate family.

Even where a trust meets these conditions – that is, it is a protected trust as at 6 April 1999 – it will still be a qualifying trust (and not be excluded from these provisions) if any of the following five conditions is satisfied:

- Property is added to the trust at any time after 18 March 1991 (except under an arm's-length transaction or in satisfaction of a liability incurred on or before 18 March 1991); if the trust's administration expenses and tax liability exceed its income in any year, property to make up the excess may be added without ill effect;
- The trust emigrates at any time after 18 March 1991 or, being dual resident, becomes treated for treaty purposes as resident outside the United Kingdom;
- The trust conditions are varied after 18 March 1991 to admit for the first time a defined person to the list of beneficiaries or potential beneficiaries;
- A defined person enjoys a benefit from the trust for the first time after 18 March 1991 and that person is not one who, looking at the terms of the trust as they were immediately before 19 March 1991, would have been capable of enjoying a benefit from the trust after that time; or
- The trust ceases to be a protected trust at any time after 5 April 1999.

If any of the conditions in the first four bullets above is satisfied before 6 April 1999, the trust becomes a qualifying trust from the year in which that condition is first satisfied (ie, the old tainting rules, which are to all intents and purposes identical to those in the first four bullets above, except in relation to grandchildren, still apply in relation to events before 6 April 1999).

There is one further point to note here. HMRC has stated that it will not regard a trust created before 19 March 1991, where the beneficiaries as at 6 April 1999 include both children under 18 and grandchildren (and their spouses) of whatever age as the only members of the settlor's immediate family who can benefit from the trust, as causing the trust to fall outside the definition of a protected trust.

Grandchildren's trusts: Before 17 March 1998, an offshore trust for the benefit of the settlor's grandchildren (including their spouses) – a grandchildren's trust – was excluded from the Section 86 charge, since grandchildren were not among the class of defined persons by reference to whom the settlor was deemed to have retained an interest in the trust.

However, grandchildren, grandchildren of spouses and the spouses of such grandchildren are included as defined persons, with effect for disposals from 17 March 1998. The Section 86 charge was thereby extended to cover all grandchildren's trusts created after 16 March 1998. Where the trust was created before 17 March 1998, any gains made by it do not come within the Section 86 charge unless made in the year during which certain conditions become satisfied. These conditions parallel the conditions causing a protected trust to lose its protected status (see above). They are as follows:

- Property is added to the trust at any time after 16 March 1998 (except under an arm's-length transaction or in satisfaction of a liability incurred on or before 17 March 1998);
- The trust emigrates at any time after 16 March 1998 or, being dual resident, becomes treated for treaty purposes as resident outside the United Kingdom;
- The trust conditions are varied after 16 March 1998 to admit for the first time any grandchild of a settlor or of the spouse of a settlor, or the spouse of any such grandchild, a company controlled by any of the preceding persons or a company associated with any such company to the list of beneficiaries or potential beneficiaries; or
- Any person within the third bullet above enjoys a benefit from the trust at any time after 16 March 1998, and that person is not one who, looking at the terms of the trust as they were immediately before 17 March 1998, would have been capable of enjoying a benefit from the trust after that time.

Protections for deemed domiciled settlors: From 6 April 2017, Section 86 does not apply for a particular year if the conditions for protection are met, as follows:

- The tax year is 2017 to 2018 or later;
- At the time the settlement was created, the settlor was not domiciled in the United Kingdom and, if after 5 April 2017, not deemed domiciled;
- There is no time in the year when the settlor is domiciled in the United Kingdom or a formerly domiciled resident; and
- No property or income is provided directly or indirectly for the purposes of the settlement by the settlor or by the trustees of another settlement of which the settlor is the settlor or a beneficiary after 5 April 2017, at a time when the settlor is domiciled in the United Kingdom or deemed domiciled.

Although the policy intent appeared to be to block the attribution of all gains to a non-domiciled settlor, offshore income gains (essentially capital gains realised on certain offshore fund investments that are subject to income tax) continue to be subject to a charge under Section 86 as income, unless the settlor is taxed on the remittance basis in the year the gain is realised.

The detailed definition of an addition of value and transitional provisions for existing loans at 6 April 2017 are the same as for the income tax provisions, described in sections 2.4(f) and 2.5(d).

(d)   *Computing the charge*

General rules: The final necessary condition for there to be a Section 86 charge on the settlor is that the trust makes a disposal of assets during the year and that the trustees would, if they were resident in the United Kingdom, be chargeable to capital gains tax as a result. In computing the charge on the settlor, four special rules must be borne in mind:

- The annual exemption available to UK resident trustees is left out of account;
- The settlor charge on UK resident settlor-interested trusts (applying to years up to 5 April 2008) is overridden;
- Where the trustees are participators in a non-resident closely held company and their interest in the company originates from the settlor, gains made by that company are attributed to the trust, subject to the availability of the motive defence; and
- Capital losses made by the trustees on other disposals of property originating from the settlor in the year, and unrelieved losses from such disposals brought forward from previous years in which all the conditions for the Section 86 charge were satisfied, may be offset against gains within Section 86. Thus, where a trust was at one time UK resident, unrelieved losses incurred in that period are not available for set-off against Section 86 gains.

No account is taken of disposals made before 19 March 1991 (when the Section 86 charge was introduced). Gains on the disposal of UK residential property, after 5 April 2015, and on the disposal of UK land and assets deriving their value from UK land, after 5 April 2019, which are subject to capital gains tax or corporation tax on non-residents, are not attributed to the settlor.

In computing the Section 86 charge, the trustees are entitled to make all the normal elections and claims to relief to which UK residents would be entitled, subject to the computational rules above. Once the gains have been attributed to the settlor, he or she can set his or her personal capital losses against the attributed gains.

Once the net gains liable to Section 86 have been computed, they are attributed to the UK-domiciled or deemed domiciled and resident settlor and form the top slice of the settlor's gains for this purpose.

As to treaty relief, the position is not clear. HMRC maintains that the gain attributed to the settlor under Section 86 is not the same as the gain made by the trustees, but merely an amount equivalent to that gain. Accordingly, its view is that treaty articles exempting particular gains from UK tax cannot be invoked by the settlor as an exemption from the Section 86 charge. This view has not yet been challenged in the courts. HMRC does, however, concede that the settlor may claim double tax relief in respect of foreign tax suffered on the trust gains. Where there is no treaty, unilateral relief will be allowed.

Dual-resident trusts: As explained above, the Section 86 charge applies equally to dual-resident trusts deemed to be resident abroad under the terms of a double tax treaty. In the case of such dual-resident trusts, there is a further computational rule, which effectively acts as a relief by treating the property originating from the settlor as protected assets under the treaty.

Settlor's right to recovery: A settlor who becomes liable to a Section 86 charge and actually pays capital gains tax as a result has the right to recover the tax paid from the trustees; HMRC is obliged to provide the settlor with a certificate of tax paid if the trustees require the settlor to provide such a certificate.

Of course, in practice, the offshore trustees may view a provision of UK law as not binding on them and it would be advisable for settlors to incorporate such a right in the trust deed. Such a right is not regarded as creating an interest in the trust for income tax or capital gains tax purposes, or as a reservation of benefit for inheritance tax purposes. However, a settlor who waives or fails to enforce the right to reimbursement is regarded as providing property to the trust for the Section 86 rules themselves. A failure by the settlor to enforce the similar right to recover income tax paid under Part 5, Chapter 5 of the Income Tax (Trading and Other Income) Act 2005 under the settlor-interest provisions has a similar effect there. This rule is not applied where the settlor has made a genuine but unsuccessful attempt to enforce the right to recovery.

4.7   The Section 87 charge on beneficiaries

(a)   Introduction

The third occasion on which capital gains tax may become payable in connection with an offshore trust is when a capital payment is made, or a benefit out of capital is provided, to a UK resident beneficiary. Provided that the necessary conditions are satisfied, gains made by the trustees are attributed to such a beneficiary.

The Section 87 charge does not apply prior to 6 April 2008 to persons who are resident in the United Kingdom but are not UK domiciled, no matter how long they may have been resident.

From 6 April 2008, extensive changes to the rules for the taxation of non-UK-domiciled individuals were introduced. As part of these changes, a Section 87 charge may arise on capital payments received by non-UK-domiciled beneficiaries.

(b)   *Definitions*

The meaning of 'trust' and 'settlor' for the Section 87 charge needs to be understood. A 'trust' (in the legislation, a 'settlement') has the wide definition that applies for the income tax charge under Part 5, Chapter 5 of the Income Tax (Trading and Other Income) Act 2005. Similarly, a 'settlor' is any person who has made a settlement as defined there and the definition is extended to include persons who have made a settlement indirectly by a reciprocal arrangement.

(c)   ***The basic rule***

General: For the Section 87 charge to apply in any year up to 5 April 2008, the following conditions must be satisfied:

- There must be a beneficiary who is both UK domiciled and resident in the United Kingdom at some time in the year;
- The trust must be an offshore trust throughout the year;
- The trust must have trust gains in that year (or unmatched gains from an earlier year); and
- The beneficiary must receive a capital payment in that year or have received a capital payment in previous years.

From 6 April 2008, the beneficiary need not be UK domiciled. Where from 6 April 2013 the year is a split year under the statutory residence test, the amount chargeable under Section 87, up to 5 April 2018, is calculated by time apportioning the full amount between the UK part and the overseas part of the year. From 6 April 2018, the full amount is treated as falling in the UK part of the year.

Beneficiary: A 'beneficiary' is not only a person qualifying as such under the terms of the trust, but also any person who would not otherwise be a beneficiary, but has received or is treated as having received a capital payment after 18 March 1991 from the trust. However, neither the trustees of the trust in question nor the trustees of any other trust can be considered as beneficiaries under this rule.

Trust gains: 'Trust gains' are gains made by the trustees in any year in respect of which they would have been chargeable to capital gains tax if they were resident, plus such gains made in previous years and not already attributed to beneficiaries or subject to the Section 86 charge on the settlor ('unattributed gains'). Trust gains include gains realised by a closely held non-resident company that are apportioned to the offshore trustees as direct or indirect participators.

Trust gains will not include gains realised on UK land and on assets deriving their value from UK land, which are subject to capital gains tax or corporation tax on non-residents.

Capital payments: A 'capital payment' is a payment that:
- in the case of a recipient who is resident in the United Kingdom, is not chargeable to income tax; or
- in the case of a non-resident beneficiary, is received otherwise than as income.

A payment received as part of an arm's-length transaction is not a capital payment if received after 18 March 1991. A payment includes:
- the transfer of an asset;
- the conferral of any other benefit; and
- any occasion on which trust property becomes held by the trustees as nominees or held for a person who is absolutely entitled to that property against the trustees, or would be so entitled if not a minor or under some other disability.

A beneficiary is treated as receiving a payment from the trustees where:
- he or she receives it from them directly or indirectly;
- it is directly or indirectly applied by the trustees in paying any of the beneficiary's debts or is otherwise paid or applied for the beneficiary's benefit; or
- it is received by a third party at the beneficiary's direction.

(d) Payments made by and to companies
There are provisions which prevent a closely held company being interposed between the trustees and the beneficiary in order to avoid the Section 87 charge.

A payment made by such a company controlled by the trustees, either alone or together with a settlor or a person connected with a settlor after 18 March 1991, is treated as made by the trustees.

In addition, a payment made to such a company which is non-resident and controlled by at least one person who is resident in the United Kingdom is treated as made by the trustees to that person(s) and if more than one in equal shares.

Where there are two or more persons who together control the company and each of them is UK resident, the capital payment is apportioned among all the participators (whatever their residence status) on a just and reasonable basis (likely to be in proportion to their holdings). A person who is treated as receiving less than 5% of the capital payment on this basis is exempt from the Section 87 charge on these grounds, as is any person not resident in the United Kingdom.

(e) **Transitional provisions**

For the Section 87 charge to have applied in respect of gains arising prior to 17 March 1998, it was necessary for the settlor or one of the settlors to have been domiciled and either resident or ordinarily resident in the United Kingdom, either in the year in question or when the trust was created (or property provided, as the case may be).

(f) **Transfers between trusts**

There are provisions dealing with the transfer of property from one trust to another, except where the transfer is made for full consideration. Broadly speaking, the rules transfer unattributed trust gains from the transferor trust to the transferee trust, so that the Section 87 charge is not avoided. They exist alongside the equivalent specific rules for computing the supplementary charge on beneficiaries on a transfer of property from one trust to another (see section 4.8(b)). These rules will apply whether the transferee trust is onshore or offshore.

If part only of the transferor trust's property is transferred, its unattributed gains are apportioned by reference to the relative values of the property transferred and the property remaining, and only those gains apportioned to the property transferred are themselves then considered transferred under the above rules.

(g) **Transfers linked with trustee borrowing**

From 20 March 2000, if at the time of a 'transfer of value' there is outstanding trust borrowing, the proceeds of which have not been applied for normal trust purposes, the trustees are deemed to have disposed of and immediately reacquired chargeable assets up to the value of the amount transferred (or, if lower, the amount of trustee borrowing). The gains arising under the deemed disposal are charged on the settlor if the trust is subject to the Section 86 charge or under Section 87 if UK resident beneficiaries receive capital payments.

Trustees make a 'transfer of value' in this context where they:

- lend money or any asset to any person;
- transfer an asset to any person for less than market value; or
- issue a security to any person for less than market value.

Borrowings are applied for 'normal trust purposes' where the trustees make a payment in respect of 'ordinary trust assets' and the following conditions apply:

- The transaction is on arm's-length terms;
- The assets forms part of the trust property immediately after the 'transfer of value'; and
- The payment is an allowable deduction in calculating a gain on disposal of the asset.

'Ordinary trust assets' are:

- shares and securities;
- tangible property, whether moveable or immovable, or a lease of such property;
- property used in a trade, profession or vocation carried on by the trustees or a beneficiary with an interest in possession in the settled property; and
- any rights or interests in assets in the first three bullets.

From 8 April 2003, Section 87 gains accrued at the end of the tax year in which the transfer of value is made are aggregated to form a 'Schedule 4C pool', to be attributed to UK resident beneficiaries receiving capital payments from any relevant settlement. A relevant settlement is the transferor settlement and any transferee settlements which include property representing directly or indirectly the proceeds of the transfer of value. Transitional provisions applied to bring equivalent gains arising from 20 March 2000 into the Schedule 4C pool at 8 April 2003.

(h)   *Computing the Section 87 charge*

General: Where the capital payment takes the form of a loan or other non-outright payment of money, its value is the benefit conferred. The making of a loan gives rise to a charge at the time of the loan, which will be on a negligible benefit if the loan is repayable on demand. There is then an ongoing benefit for the duration of the loan if it does not carry interest of at least the official rate. From 6 April 2017, it is not sufficient that the loan carries interest at the official rate; the interest must actually be paid for a beneficiary to escape a benefit charge.

The benefit from the use of a trust asset, other than land, from 6 April 2017, is calculated as the official rate of interest applied to the trustees' capital cost of the asset. The benefit from the use of trust land is its rental value, based on the landlord bearing the cost of repairs, insurance and other costs required to maintain the property in a state to command that rent. To the extent that the beneficiary bears any of the landlord's costs, they will directly reduce the value of the benefit for the year in which they are paid. As for loans, rent and trustees' expenses must actually be paid by the beneficiary after 5 April 2017 if the benefit is to be reduced or eliminated.

Trust gains are computed by assuming that the trustees are resident in the United Kingdom, allowing for deduction of losses arising in that year and unrelieved losses brought forward. The settlor charge (under Sections 77 to 79 of the Taxation of Chargeable Gains Act 1992) which applied to gains arising from 6 April 1991 to 5 April 2008 on settlor-interested trusts is, in general, overridden. Gains that have already been subject to the Section 86 charge on the settlor are excluded from trust gains liable to Section 87. No annual exemption is available to the trustees.

Dual-resident trusts: The Section 87 charge also applies where the trust is a dual-resident trust (ie, resident both in the United Kingdom and elsewhere) treated for the purposes of a double tax treaty with the jurisdiction in which it is also resident as resident there and not in the United Kingdom.

In such cases, the trust gains liable under Section 87 are the smaller of:

- the trust gains computed on the assumption that the double tax treaty did not apply; and
- the trust gains computed on the assumption that they are limited to gains on protected assets and the treaty does not apply.

Matching gains with payments, in general: The trust gains attributed to a beneficiary cannot exceed the capital payments or benefits received by that beneficiary; the legislation therefore calls for matching of gains with payments. Where trust gains (including unattributed gains from previous years) exceed capital payments, trust gains are attributed to the extent of capital payments and the balance is carried forward as unattributed gains for attribution in future. Where capital payments (including unmatched payments from previous years) exceed trust gains, they are matched to the extent of the gains and the balance is carried forward as unmatched payments for matching against future trust gains.

Gains are attributed to all beneficiaries who have received capital payments. Where there is more than one such beneficiary, the gains are attributed in the proportion in which the beneficiaries have received capital payments. Capital payments are left out of account to the extent that they have given rise to attributed gains in previous years.

Once trust gains are attributed to a beneficiary, he or she may not offset personal capital losses against those gains. However, there is no provision, as there is for the Section 86 charge, that those gains form the top slice of the beneficiary's income and gains. Indeed, HMRC is prepared to accept that Section 87 gains are to be considered the lowest slice of the beneficiary's total gains, so that the annual exemption may be applied so as to reduce or extinguish them.

Matching gains with payments before 6 April 2008: In the years up to 5 April 2008, there could be no capital gains tax charge on a beneficiary who was not domiciled in the United Kingdom at some point in the year, or on general principles on a beneficiary who was neither resident nor ordinarily resident. It follows that the capital gains tax charge on UK resident and domiciled beneficiaries could be reduced by first making capital payments to the maximum extent to non-liable beneficiaries.

Matching was on a first-in, first-out basis, taking the first capital payment of any year first and matching it with the earliest unattributed trust gain.

Matching gains with payments after 5 April 2008: From 6 April 2008, chargeable gains accrue to non-UK domiciled beneficiaries who receive capital payments. However, it is necessary for both the capital payment and the matched gain to be made after 5 April 2008. Thus, if gains accrue to a non-domiciled beneficiary on the receipt of a capital payment after 5 April 2008, he or she will not be liable to capital gains tax if the payment is matched with gains arising before 6 April 2008. Equally, excess capital payments made to a non-domiciled beneficiary prior to 6 April 2008 cannot later become chargeable, although they can be matched to gains arising from that date. Indeed, such was the fear that trustees would make substantial payments to non-domiciled beneficiaries between the date that the changes were announced and their coming into effect that further provisions act to leave capital payments made between 12 March and 6 April 2008 out of account for matching purposes, so long as the beneficiary remains non-domiciled. This introduces the danger of an unexpected capital gains tax charge for individuals who become UK-domiciled, having previously received capital payments between 12 March and 6 April 2008.

Matching is on a last-in, first-out basis, taking each tax year at a time. Capital payments of any year are matched pro rata with the unattributed trust gains for the year of payment and then earlier years in sequence until either all gains or all capital payments are fully matched.

Matching gains with payments after 5 April 2018: From 6 April 2018, capital payments to non-residents are disregarded unless made in the year the trust ceases to exist. These include unmatched capital payments to non-residents brought forward at 6 April 2018. In the final year of the trust, gains are attributed to non-resident beneficiaries receiving capital payments, where:

- two or more beneficiaries receive capital payments;
- at least one is a UK resident; and
- at least one is a non-resident.

A capital payment to a non-resident who is a close family member (see section 2.4(f)) of a UK resident settlor is attributed to the settlor, as are capital payments to UK resident close family members.

Where after 5 April 2018 a UK resident beneficiary receives a capital payment or a capital payment is attributed to the settlor, at a time when there are no unmatched gains, the unmatched capital payment is disregarded if the relevant individual subsequently becomes non-resident.

Limitations: No regard is to be taken of the following:

- any capital payment received before 10 March 1981;
- any capital payment received between 10 March 1981 and 6 April 1984, insofar as it represents a chargeable gain which accrued to the trustees before 6 April 1981;
- any capital payment received before 6 April 1991, where Section 87 applies for a tax year due to the operation of the rules for dual-resident settlements; or
- any capital payment received before 17 March 1998, or any gains or losses accruing before that date to the trustees of a settlement to which Section 87 applies at any time after 5 April 2008, if:
  - the settlement was created before 17 March 1998;
  - the settlor was non-UK domiciled and neither resident nor ordinarily resident in the United Kingdom when the settlement was created; and
  - the settlor is non-UK domiciled and neither resident nor ordinarily resident in the United Kingdom in the tax year in question (after 5 April 2008).

The remittance basis as it applies to Section 87: Where chargeable gains are attributed to a non-UK domiciled beneficiary after 5 April 2008, to whom the remittance basis applies, a capital payment will be taxable only on remittance to the United Kingdom. Where the payment is matched to a gain made by the trustees on the disposal of UK assets, the gain is nevertheless treated as foreign source and thus not charged on the arising basis.

Rebasing election: Trustees may opt to make an election to rebase assets held directly, or owned by companies in which the trust is a participator, on 6 April 2008. As a result of the election, on a subsequent disposal, gains on assets held at 6 April 2008 are apportioned between the pre-6 April 2008 gain and the post-5 April 2008 gain, by reference to their market values at 6 April 2008. The pre-6 April 2008 element is not taxable if matched with a capital payment made to a non-domiciled beneficiary, whether or not the remittance basis applies. The gains are apportioned by comparing the trustees' total net gains for the tax year calculated using original acquisition costs with those calculated using 6 April 2008 values for assets held at that date and not on an asset-by-asset basis.

The election is irrevocable and must be made by 31 January following the first tax year after 5 April 2008 in which one of the following events occurs:

- A capital payment is made to a UK resident beneficiary; or
- The trustees transfer all or part of the trust assets to another settlement to which Section 87 applies or will apply.

Capital payments to companies: Where after 5 April 2008 a capital payment to a non-UK resident closely held company is not treated as received by some other person (see section 4.7(d)), no account is taken of that payment.

Migrant trusts: Where a trust that has been UK resident for one or more years becomes non-resident so that the conditions for Section 87 are satisfied, capital payments received by beneficiaries while the trust was resident are ignored for Section 87 purposes, unless made in anticipation of a disposal when offshore.

In the reverse situation, where a trust that has been non-resident becomes resident, any unattributed gains from previous years are not washed out, but are attributed to beneficiaries receiving capital payments in the first year in which the trust is resident and so on until all the gains have been attributed.

Interaction with income tax provisions: Where a capital payment would give rise to both a Section 87 capital gains tax charge on the beneficiary and an income tax charge under Section 731 of the Income Tax Act 2007 on that beneficiary (transfer of assets abroad: charge where benefit received), the income tax charge takes precedence. However, an actual capital gains tax charge in one year takes precedence over a potential income tax charge in a subsequent year (the Section 731 charge is imposed only if there is relevant income).

Double tax relief: No mention is made in the legislation or in statements of practice and so on of whether a beneficiary charged under Section 87 is entitled to claim double tax relief on any foreign tax paid on a trust gain attributed to him or her. Credit for foreign tax borne on capital gains as provided by Section 277 of the Taxation of Chargeable Gains Act 1992 requires not that the foreign tax and the UK tax be charged on the same person, but that the foreign tax be computed by reference to the same gain as the UK tax.

It is therefore believed that the exclusion of Section 87 gains from treaty exemption would be difficult to sustain. Given that HMRC concedes that double tax credits for foreign tax paid on Section 86 gains are available, arguably the same should apply to Section 87 gains. However, HMRC takes the view that the beneficiary is taxed under Section 87 on the capital payment received and not the gains on which the trustees have suffered foreign tax, and so denies the relief. A deduction may be taken for the foreign tax paid on the gains when calculating the gains under UK rules.

Onward gifts: Provisions were introduced from 6 April 2018 to counter the use of a non-resident or remittance basis user to act as a conduit to pass capital payments to UK residents without a tax charge. The recipient of a gift after 5 April 2018 may be subject to a charge under Section 87 where:

- a capital payment is received by a beneficiary (the original beneficiary);

- at the time of receipt, there is an intention to pass on the capital payment to a UK resident;
- the gift is made within three years of or at any time before receiving the capital payment in anticipation of the receipt;
- the gift is of or derives from the capital payment or is of other property where the capital payment was made to facilitate the gift;
- the donee is UK resident at the time of the gift; or
- when the capital payment is received, the original beneficiary is non-resident or taxed on the remittance basis and does not remit it.

Where the conditions in the third and fourth bullets above are met, there is a presumption that the second is also met, unless the contrary is shown. Although the provisions apply only where the onward gift is made after 5 April 2018, the capital payment may have been received earlier.

The matching of gains to capital payments is made on the basis that capital payments to non-residents are not disregarded if there is an onward gift, to attribute trust gains and/or unmatched capital payments to the donee. Where the donee is a member of the settlor's close family, attribution is to the settlor if UK resident.

4.8   The supplementary charge on beneficiaries

(a)   *The general rule*
A further charge was imposed on beneficiaries of offshore trusts in 1991. This is a charge that applies whenever a capital payment is matched with a trust gain arising more than one year previously. By simply not making capital payments, offshore trustees can indefinitely defer the tax otherwise due by UK resident beneficiaries on trust gains.

This supplementary charge is made where a capital payment is matched with a trust gain arising before the immediately preceding year of assessment. It consists of an increase in the tax payable of 10% per annum over the period beginning on 1 December in the year following that in which the gain is realised and ending on 30 November in the year following that in which the capital payment is made. However, the maximum number of years for which the increase can be charged is six. The maximum effective rate of capital gains tax payable by a beneficiary (for 2019–2020) under Section 87 is therefore 32% (ie, 20% + 60% of 20%).

From 6 April 2008, matching is on a last-in, first-out basis. Where a single capital payment is matched with trust gains from several years, it is split into as many subsidiary payments as there are years concerned and the supplementary charge is computed accordingly, with the tax in respect of the capital payment being apportioned in the most beneficial manner for the beneficiary.

(b) Transfers between trusts

Provisions dealing with the computation of the supplementary charge when property is transferred from one trust to another exist alongside the general rules for the Section 87 charge on transfers between trusts.

Where all of the trust property is transferred from one trust to another, and at the end of the year in which the transfer takes place the transferor trust has unattributed gains, the transferee trust is treated as realising the equivalent amount of gains in the same years as they were realised by the transferor trust, and that amount is deducted from the transferor trust's gains for each such year. It does not matter for this purpose whether the transferee trust was in fact subject to Section 87 in any of those years or whether the transferee trust even existed in any year in which the transferred gains were realised.

Where part only of the trust property is transferred, the unattributed gains are apportioned by reference to the relative values of the property transferred and the remaining property; the gains apportioned to the property transferred are themselves then transferred as described above.

Unmatched capital payments are not transferred – only unattributed gains.

Where the transferee trust has its own unattributed gains or unmatched payments, matching for years before the year of transfer is done by reference to the trust's own gains only (ie, by reference to the situation that prevailed before the transfer). Thereafter, matching takes place with the combined gains.

4.9 Temporarily non-resident settlors and beneficiaries

Persons returning to the United Kingdom after less than five years of residence abroad are charged to capital gains tax on gains accruing to them while non-resident. There are special provisions regulating how this rule interacts with the Section 86 and Section 87 charges.

Where a settlor (as defined for Section 86) returns to the United Kingdom after less than five years of non-residence and gains (or losses) have accrued to him or her in the years of absence, the settlor is deemed to realise those gains in the year of return, thereby becoming liable to capital gains tax on those gains. Where those gains include gains attributed to an individual under Section 86 as settlor of an offshore trust, only so much of those gains as have not already been attributed to beneficiaries under Section 87 are chargeable. This adjusted amount then charged on the settlor is treated as deducted from the unattributed gains brought forward for the purposes of Section 87 for the year of return.

Where a capital payment to a non-resident beneficiary after 5 April 2018 is disregarded for the purposes of Section 87, it will be treated as received in the year of return if the beneficiary was temporarily non-resident. Similarly, an unmatched capital payment disregarded for the purposes of Section 87 on migration of the beneficiary, or settlor if attributed to the settlor, is treated as received in the year of return if the individual was temporarily non-resident.

4.10 Emigrating trusts

(a) The general rule

The fourth major occasion on which a capital gains tax charge can arise in connection with offshore trusts is on the emigration of a previously UK resident trust. Emigration (the cessation of UK-residence) can take place either by:

- the appointment of new non-resident trustees; or
- the physical emigration of previously UK resident trustees, in the situation where:
  - all trustees become non-resident where previously they were all UK resident; or
  - all trustees become non-resident where previously there were some UK resident trustees and the settlor was UK domiciled at the time of key events (see section 1.6(a)); or
  - at least one trustee becomes non-resident where previously they were all UK resident and the settlor were non-UK domiciled at the time of key events (see section 1.6(a)).

When a trust emigrates, the trustees are deemed to dispose of and immediately reacquire the trust property for its market value immediately before the trust emigrates, so there is effectively an exit charge.

(b) Excepted assets

The charge applies to all the trust assets, with two exceptions:

- assets used in a trade, profession or vocation carried on by the trustees in the United Kingdom through a permanent establishment (such assets remain within the UK capital gains tax charge); and
- assets the taxing rights on the disposal of which have been surrendered by the United Kingdom in its double tax treaty with the jurisdiction to which the trust emigrates.

Trustees holding UK land on emigration, on which they remain liable for capital gains tax as non-residents, may elect to postpone the charge on its deemed disposal until the subsequent disposal of the land.

(c) Death of a trustee

There are relieving provisions where the trust emigrates as a result of the death of a trustee, provided that within six months of the death the trust is repatriated to the United Kingdom. In such a case the exit charge applies only to:

- such assets as are disposed of while the trust is an offshore trust; or
- assets forming trust property immediately after repatriation, the gain on

the disposal of which would be exempt from UK capital gains tax under the terms of a double tax treaty.

There are also corresponding provisions dealing with the reverse situation where an offshore trust is repatriated as a result of a trustee's death and is then re-exported within six months. Where this is the case, the exit charge on re-exportation is limited to those assets that were acquired:

- by the trustees while the trust was UK resident; or
- in a transaction subject to holdover relief on the transfer of business assets or on transfers immediately chargeable to inheritance tax.

(d) Dual-resident trusts

The exit charge also applies where the trustees, while remaining UK resident, also become resident in another jurisdiction and become treated for the purposes of the United Kingdom's double tax treaty with that jurisdiction as resident there and not in the United Kingdom, and there are trust assets ('protected assets') that are protected from UK capital gains tax on disposal under the terms of the treaty.

(e) Liability of past trustees

As insurance against non-payment of the exit charge by the newly non-resident trustees, HMRC has the power to pursue its claim for the outstanding tax from persons who were trustees at any time in the 12 months immediately preceding the trust's emigration. This power may be exercised only if the tax remains unpaid for more than six months after it becomes due and must be exercised no later than three years after the amount of tax payable has been finally determined. Ex-trustees who can show that at the time they gave up their office there was no proposal for the trust to emigrate are excepted.

A trustee who becomes liable to pay the tax as a result of these provisions, and actually does so, has the right to recover the tax paid from the offshore trustees (although enforcement of that right in a foreign court may be problematic). Where the ex-trustee successfully enforces the right to recovery, this does not constitute a capital payment under Section 87; nor are there income tax or inheritance tax consequences.

4.11 Disposal of an interest in an offshore trust

The fifth and final occasion on which a capital gains tax charge may arise in connection with an offshore trust is on the disposal of an interest in the trust or in a trust that has ever been an offshore trust. The disposal of an interest in a trust is normally exempt, unless:

- the trust is non-resident at the time of disposal; or
- the trust was at any previous time non-resident or dual resident, but

regarded as non-resident for treaty purposes and the disposal occurred after 5 March 1998.

The exception under the second bullet above is extended where any property comprised in the trust derives directly or indirectly from an offshore or dual-resident trust as specified. No charge arises where the disposal is a deemed disposal of an interest on becoming absolutely entitled to the underlying property.

The disponor's gain is calculated by reference to the actual disposal proceeds or market value (if the disposal is not at arm's length). Reliefs may be available to prevent double taxation where the trust has emigrated before the disposal is made.

4.12 Reporting obligations

Naturally, given the many occasions on which a charge to capital gains tax may arise, the law imposes several reporting obligations on the trustees, settlors and beneficiaries of offshore trusts. The less connection any of these persons has had with the United Kingdom, the more likely it is that, in the absence of professional advice, these obligations will be overlooked. The obligations, in brief, are as follows:

- Within 12 months of a transfer of property to an offshore trust created before 17 March 1998, in circumstances such that the trust may become tainted, the transferor must report details of the property transferred, the date of transfer and the consideration (if any), and identify the trust.
- Within three months of creating an offshore trust or a dual-resident trust regarded for treaty purposes as resident solely in the other jurisdiction (where this occurs after 2 May 1994), the settlor must report his or her own address and the names and addresses of the trustees and the date of creation. This obligation does not extend to non-domiciled settlors or to settlors who, while being domiciled in the United Kingdom, are neither resident nor ordinarily resident (but see the following point).
- Within 12 months of becoming both domiciled and resident in the United Kingdom, a settlor of an offshore trust, or of a dual-resident trust regarded for treaty purposes as resident solely in the other jurisdiction, who was not so resident or domiciled when the trust was created (provided that the trust was created after 18 March 1991), must report his or her name and address, the date of creation and the names and addresses of the trustees.
- The trustees of a UK resident trust that emigrates or is dual resident and comes for treaty purposes to be regarded as resident solely in the other jurisdiction must, within 12 months of that event, file a return specifying the day of creation of the trust, the name and address of each

person who was a settlor immediately before the event, and the name and address of each trustee immediately before the event.

The above obligations are waived to the extent that any of the information required has already been delivered to HMRC by any other person or becomes the subject of an obligation of any other person, during the return period.

HMRC also has the power to require any person to provide it with particulars that it considers necessary for the purposes of the Section 87 charge. At least 28 days must be allowed for the person on whom the notice is served to respond. The information that HMRC may legitimately require is extensive, and it has the power to require solicitors and banks to provide names and addresses of persons for whom they have acted, with certain safeguards.

4.13   UK Trust Register

Regulations came into force on 26 June 2017, establishing a UK register of beneficial ownership of relevant trusts. All UK resident express trusts already registered for self-assessment or liable for income tax, capital gains tax, inheritance tax, stamp duty land tax or stamp duty reserve tax in 2016–2017 or later years became liable to register with HMRC. Offshore trusts with a UK tax liability on UK-source income or assets also became liable to register. Information about the trust to be included on the register includes:

- the name of the trust;
- the date it was settled;
- contact address and telephone number;
- country of residence;
- a description and value of the trust assets when first settled;
- the identity of the settlor, trustees and beneficiaries, together with other persons, such as protectors, who exercise control over the trust; and
- the name of the agent, if any, acting on behalf of the trustees in relation to the trust register.

Identity information must include the person's:

- name;
- date of birth:
- national insurance number or UK tax reference (or, if none, residential address); and
- if non-resident, passport or ID number, country of issue and expiry date.

Each year the trustees are required to update the registered details for any changes if they have a UK tax liability.

5. Tax rates

5.1 Income tax

For the year 2019–2020 (the year ending 5 April 2020), the rates of income tax for individuals are as follows.

Taxable income	Rate of income tax	
	All income excluding dividends	Dividends
First £5,000	0 (starting rate for savings)	0 (starting rate for savings)
First £37,500	20% (the basic rate)	7.5% (dividend ordinary rate)
Next £112,500	40% (the higher rate)	32.5% (dividend upper rate)
Balance over £150,000	45% (the additional rate)	38.1% (dividend additional rate)

The starting rate for savings is available only where non-savings income is less than the maximum for that rate.

Rates of income tax for trusts are as follows.

Table 2. Trust income tax rates for 2019-2020

Taxable income	Rate of income tax	
	All income excluding dividends	Dividends
First £1,000	20% (starting rate)	7.5% (starting rate)
Over £1,000	45% (trust rate)	38.1% (dividend trust rate)

5.2 Inheritance tax

(a) *Rates applying to lifetime transfers*

Value of chargeable transfer in 2019–2020	Rate of tax
First £325,000	0
Balance over £325,000	20%

Chargeable transfers within the previous seven years must be aggregated. If the transferor pays the tax, the value of the transfer is grossed up to include the tax.

(b) *Rates applying to transfers on death*

Value of chargeable transfer in 2019–2020	Rate of tax
First £325,000	0
Balance over £325,000	40%

If a chargeable transfer takes place within three years of the transferor's death, the value of the transfer is included in the estate at death and the tax payable is recomputed using full death rates. Any tax paid at the time of the transfer (at lifetime rates) is credited against the resulting liability. If the chargeable transfer takes place more than three, but less than seven years before death, the same procedure is followed, but the tax payable at death rates is reduced as follows.

Number of years before death	Percentage of full death-rate charge applicable
Over 3 but not more than 4	80%
Over 4 but not more than 5	60%
Over 5 but not more than 6	40%
Over 6 but not more than 7	20%

5.3 Capital gains tax

A uniform rate of tax of 20% applies to gains realised by trustees. The tax is charged on the aggregate of gains over losses for the year. Gains realised by individuals are taxed at either 10% or 20%. The 10% rate applies to the extent that chargeable gains, when added to taxable income and treated as the top slice for this purpose, fall within the basic rate band (see section 5.1). To the extent that they do not, the rate is 20%.

Gains realised on disposals of residential property, whether situated overseas or in the United Kingdom, and carried interests are subject to capital gains tax rates of 28% for trustees and 18% and 28% for individuals.

6. The future of offshore trusts

Over the years, there have been many and varied attacks made on offshore trusts by successive governments of both the left and the right. The result has been to create an extensive body of complex legislation intended to eliminate any tax advantages which might be available to UK residents structuring their finances through offshore trusts. This legislation has been built piecemeal, so that the interaction of several competing anti-avoidance provisions will often lead to uncertainties in the treatment of a particular transaction. Despite this, the offshore trust remains an important tool in UK tax and financial planning, particularly for those domiciled outside the United Kingdom.

Following the tax changes that came into effect on 6 April 2017, the availability of the remittance basis of taxation for long-term UK residents has been curtailed. The solution for those individuals is to make use of offshore trusts, which are now of even more importance in structuring their affairs.

The role of trust and company service providers in the fight against money laundering and terrorist financing

Yehuda Shaffer
Independent consultant

In June 2019, 30 years after it was founded, the Financial Action Task Force (FATF) published a guidance paper entitled "Risk-Based Approach for Trust and Company Service Providers",[1] to combat money laundering (ML) and terrorist financing (TF). This late response was not because the FATF had been unaware of the potential abuse of corporate vehicles and arrangements such as trusts in laundering the proceeds of crime and concealing funds and property relating to TF; but was rather due to the complexity of the topic and the challenge of providing practitioners with a practical tool to assess and mitigate these risks.

The new FATF guidance emphasises that it is the responsibility of senior management of trust and company service providers (TCSPs) to promote a culture of compliance as a core business value, and to ensure that TCSPs are committed to managing their ML/TF risks when establishing and maintaining business relationships. The guidance outlines the obligations of TCSPs regarding the identification and verification of beneficial ownership information, and the importance of supervision of beneficial ownership requirements and nominee arrangements. It underscores how a proper supervisory framework can help to ascertain whether accurate and up-to-date beneficial ownership information on legal persons and legal arrangements is maintained by TCSPs and is made available in a timely manner to competent authorities as required.

In the past, this FATF document may not have attracted much attention. Today, however – in light of evolving international standards, as well as additional initiatives aimed at reducing the global abuse of tax havens, the creation of beneficial ownership registers and additional steps taken in some

---

[1] www.fatf-gafi.org/publications/fatfrecommendations/documents/rba-trust-company-service-providers.html.

jurisdictions to confiscate the proceeds of crime, including unexplained wealth[2] – all practitioners involved in establishing or managing trusts might find themselves referring to this document quite often. This chapter outlines the background to these initiatives and sets out some suggestions that should assist practitioners in mitigating the potential risk of abuse of trusts.

1.   Background

Ever since the establishment of the FATF by the G7 in 1989, it has focused on the financial war against serious and organised crime. Given the weaknesses of criminal law and the failure both to deter criminals and to reduce crime through traditional punitive measures such as imprisonment, the FATF emphasised the financial aspects of crime, suggesting a regime of international standards set forth in 40 recommendations to be implemented in each country through domestic legislation. These standards include a series of measures aimed at combating ML on three levels. The first level comprises preventative measures to be taken by financial institutions (and other designated businesses, such as lawyers, notaries, accountants and TCSPs)[3] to ensure the transparency of legal entities and arrangements and to identify the ultimate beneficial owners of property, together with additional measures such as client identification and 'know your customer' procedures, record-keeping requirements, suspicious transaction reporting and training requirements with regard to all of these duties. The second level comprises recommendations intended to punish not only the criminals who commit predicate offences, but also those who help them to launder their proceeds, by introducing criminal ML offences and enhancing international and domestic cooperation between agencies to facilitate effective prosecution of these crimes. The third level comprises recommendations to assist in identifying, locating, confiscating and forfeiting criminal proceeds, in addition to punishment, or to assist in civil actions, thus promoting the idea that such proceeds should be returned to the public for the common good.

The potential misuse of corporate vehicles is a major policy concern of the FATF. Several reports on the topic have been issued, all of which have implications for trusts.[4] These reports, and the policy recommendations based on them, have placed the issue firmly on the international agenda and have

---

2   See, for example, *National Crime Agency v Hajiyeva* (Rev 1) [2018] EWHC 2534 (Admin) (3 October 2018), www.bailii.org/ew/cases/EWHC/Admin/2018/2534.html.

3   Defined by FATF as 'designated non-financial businesses and professions' (DNFBPs).

4   See, for example, the United Nations Office on Drugs and Crime (UNODC) (at that time, the UNODCCP) 1998 report entitled "Financial Havens, Banking Secrecy and Money Laundering, Protecting the EU Financial System from the Exploitation of Financial Centers and Offshore Facilities by Organised Crime"; the 2000 EUROSHORE report entitled "Protecting the EU financial system from the exploitation of financial centres and offshore facilities by organised crime"; the 2001 OECD report entitled "Behind the Corporate Veil: Using Corporate Entities for Illicit Purposes"; the 2002 report commissioned by the International Trade and Investment Organisation and written by Stikeman Elliot entitled "Towards a Level Playing Field Regulating Corporate Vehicles in Cross-Border Transactions"; the 2005 FATF report entitled "The Misuse of Corporate Vehicles, Including Trust and Company Service Providers"; and the 2010 FATF report entitled "Money Laundering Using Trust and Company Service Providers".

contributed to the formulation of international standards on the transparency of legal entities and arrangements.

The old FATF recommendations[5] on customer due diligence required financial institutions to establish the identities of the beneficial owners of legal persons and arrangements. They further[6] obliged countries to ensure that adequate, accurate and up-to-date information on beneficial ownership and control of legal persons and legal arrangements was available and could be obtained or accessed by competent authorities in a timely fashion. Today, over 200 jurisdictions around the world have committed to the FATF Recommendations through a global network of FSRBs[7] and FATF membership. Assessments undertaken in these jurisdictions confirm that compliance levels on this issue are generally very low, which has generated considerable concern and debate among the G20 leaders. The updated version of the FATF standards now includes 40 recommendations and 11 immediate outcomes which measure the actual implementation of the recommendations and their effectiveness in preventing and punishing crime. All recommendations are now to be assessed through a risk-based approach and accordingly all jurisdictions must conduct ML/TF national risk assessments.[8]

Especially noteworthy in the context of this chapter is the introduction of tax offences as predicate offences to ML and Immediate Outcome 5, which examines the extent to which misuse of legal persons and arrangements for ML or TF purposes is prevented, and the extent to which information on their beneficial ownership is freely available to competent authorities.

In recent years, the FATF has assessed different jurisdictions to determine whether measures are in place to prevent the use of legal persons and arrangements for criminal purposes (including effective, proportionate and dissuasive sanctions); whether the ownership of legal persons and arrangements is sufficiently transparent; and whether accurate and up-to-date basic and beneficial ownership information is available on a timely basis. It also examines the extent to which basic information is publicly available and the extent to which beneficial ownership information is available to competent authorities.[9]

---

5   Old FATF Recommendtions 5 and 12.

6   Old FATF Recommendtions 33 and 34.

7   FATF-style regional bodies such as Moneyval in Europe, the Asia/Pacific Group on Money Laundering in Asia-Pacific and the Caribbean Financial Action Task Force (CFATF) in the Caribbean region.

8   See, for example, the UK national risk assessment for ML and TF 2017, which acknowledged that the misuse of trusts is a global problem and that trusts remain vulnerable to abuse. Foreign trusts were identified as posing a much higher risk than UK trusts. TF through legal persons or arrangements is rare and deemed a low risk. The 2017 national risk assessment concluded that TCSPs pose a medium risk of ML and a low risk of TF. However, the United Kingdom recognised that TCSP risks are heightened when combined with other financial, legal and accountancy services, often with the involvement of UK-based professional enablers; https://assets.publishing.service.gov.uk/government/uploads/system/uploads/attachment_data/file/655198/National_risk_assessment_of_money_laundering_and_terrorist_financing_2017_pdf_web.pdf.

9   See, for example, the Isle of man Moneyval Mutual evaluation report, www.fatf-gafi.org/media/fatf/documents/reports/mer-fsrb/Mutual-Evalutaion-Isle-of-Man.pdf; and the Cayman Islands CFATF mutual evaluation report (p142) criticising the lack of a process for obtaining basic and beneficial ownership information on legal arrangements within the jurisdiction, www.fatf-gafi.org/media/fatf/documents/reports/mer-fsrb/CFATF-Cayman-Islands-Mutual-Evaluation.pdf.

The FATF is now calling on its assessors to consider the level of international cooperation that competent authorities can provide in attempting to identify beneficial ownership information for legal persons and arrangements. Special consideration in this context is to be given to examining questions such as the following:

- To what extent is information on the creation and types of legal persons and arrangements in the country publicly available?
- How well do the competent authorities identify, assess and understand vulnerabilities and the extent to which legal persons created in the country can be or are being misused for ML/TF purposes?
- What measures has the country implemented to prevent the misuse of legal persons and arrangements for ML/TF purposes?
- To what extent can competent authorities obtain adequate, accurate and up-to-date basic and beneficial ownership information on all types of legal persons established in the country, in a timely manner?
- To what extent can relevant competent authorities obtain adequate, accurate and up-to-date beneficial ownership information on legal arrangements in a timely manner? To what extent are effective, proportionate and dissuasive sanctions applied against persons that do not comply with the information requirements?[10]

In the FATF's recent mutual evaluation report of the United Kingdom,[11] it recognised the jurisdiction as a global leader in promoting corporate transparency, which has gone beyond the FATF Recommendations both in promoting the use of public registers of beneficial ownership in a variety of forums and in establishing a public register of beneficial ownership information and a register of trusts with tax consequences in the United Kingdom.[12]

As illustrated by other recent mutual evaluation reports (eg, relating to the Isle of Man and the Cayman Islands), the FATF is examining in particular contextual information on:

- the types, forms and basic features of legal persons and arrangements in each jurisdiction;
- the experiences of law enforcement and other relevant competent authorities;
- ML and TF typologies;
- examples of the misuse of legal persons and arrangements and the sources of basic and beneficial ownership information; and

---

10 See FATF, new methodology for assessing the 40 recommendations – Immediate Outcome 5.
11 www.fatf-gafi.org/media/fatf/documents/reports/mer4/MER-United-Kingdom-2018.pdf, p145.
12 See also Her Majesty's Revenue and Customs Guidance on trust registration, www.gov.uk/guidance/ register-your-clients-trust. The United Kingdom has until 10 January 2020 to incorporate the Fifth Anti-Money Laundering Directive into domestic law and must then implement the trust registration requirements by 10 March 2020. The UK government has already confirmed that this will happen irrespective of Brexit.

- the role played by 'gatekeepers' such as TCSPs, accountants and legal professionals in the formation and administration of legal persons and arrangements such as trusts.

Examples include measures taken to enhance the transparency of legal persons (including dealing with bearer shares and share warrants, and nominee shareholders and directors) and arrangements, and to ensure that accurate and up-to-date basic and beneficial ownership information on legal persons (and changes made) is maintained.

So what is the extent of information that trustees disclose to financial institutions and designated non-financial businesses and professions (DNFBPs)?

According to the FATF methodology, the 'beneficiaries' of a trust are the persons who are entitled to the benefit of any trust arrangement. A beneficiary can be a natural or legal person or arrangement. All trusts (other than charitable or statutory permitted non-charitable trusts) must have ascertainable beneficiaries. While trusts must always have some ultimately ascertainable beneficiary, trusts may have no defined existing beneficiaries, but only objects of a power until some person becomes entitled as beneficiary to income or capital on the expiry of a defined period, known as the 'accumulation period'. This period is normally coextensive with the trust perpetuity period which is usually referred to in the trust deed as the 'trust period'.[13]

2. Obligations for TCSPs: new FATF document

Today, the FATF is promoting the adoption of a risk-based approach in relation to both obliged entities (eg, TCSPs) when conducting their business and supervisors. The key elements of a risk-based approach include the following:

- Risk identification and assessment: identifying the ML/TF risks facing a firm, given its customers, services and countries of operation, and in light of publicly available information regarding ML/TF risks and typologies;
- Risk management and mitigation: identifying and applying measures to effectively and efficiently mitigate and manage ML/TF risks;
- Ongoing monitoring: putting in place policies, procedures and information systems to monitor changes to ML/TF risks; and
- Documentation: documenting risk assessments, strategies, policies and procedures to monitor, manage and mitigate ML/TF risks.

As the FATF explains, the risk-based approach is not a 'zero failure' approach; there may be occasions where a TCSP has taken reasonable and proportionate ML/TF measures to identify and mitigate risks, but is still used for

---

13   New FATF recommendations – definition of beneficiary.

ML or TF purposes in isolated instances. Although there are limits to any risk-based approach, ML/TF is a real and serious problem that TCSPs must address so that they do not encourage or facilitate it, unwittingly or otherwise.

3.   OECD tax initiatives

A parallel initiative to the FATF is the Organisation for Economic Co-operation and Development's (OECD) focus on international tax systems,[14] putting them at the forefront of the international policy agenda. This has also been endorsed by the G20, which is prioritising calling time on tax havens and recognising that an international tax framework developed 100 years ago is no longer fit for purpose.

The Common Reporting Standard (CRS), developed in response to the G20's request and approved by the OECD Council on 15 July 2014, calls on jurisdictions to obtain information from their financial institutions and automatically exchange that information with other jurisdictions on an annual basis. It sets out the financial account information to be exchanged, the financial institutions required to report, the different types of accounts and taxpayers covered, as well as common due diligence procedures to be followed by financial institutions.

The CRS specifies the financial account information to be exchanged, the financial institutions that need to report and the different types of accounts and taxpayers covered. To capture a wide range of information, it requires the reporting of account balances, interest, dividends and sale and redemption proceeds from financial assets by deposit-taking banks, custodial institutions, certain investment entities and certain insurance companies. Also under obligation are what the OECD calls 'non-financial entities' (NFEs) – essentially, any entity that is not a financial institution. NFEs are split into passive NFEs and active NFEs, with additional procedures required in relation to passive NFEs (reflecting the greater tax evasion risks they pose). The general rule is that a passive NFE is an NFE that is not an active NFE. The definition of 'active NFE' essentially excludes entities that primarily receive passive income or primarily hold amounts of assets that produce passive income (eg, dividends, interest, rent), and includes entities that are publicly traded (or related to a publicly traded entity), government entities, international organisations, central banks and holding NFEs of non-financial groups. An exception applies to investment entities that are not participating jurisdiction financial institutions, which are always treated as passive NFEs.

In a detailed new manual published in 2018 by the OECD,[15] a separate

---

14   www.oecd.org/tax/automatic-exchange/common-reporting-standard/.
15   Standard for Automatic Exchange of Financial Account Information in Tax Matters: Implementation Handbook, 2nd edition, www.oecd.org/tax/exchange-of-tax-information/implementation-handbook-standard-for-automatic-exchange-of-financial-information-in-tax-matters.pdf.

chapter is dedicated to trusts under the CRS, with several examples of trust-related situations illustrated. The CRS will generally apply to trusts where:

- a trust is a reporting financial institution; or
- a trust is an NFE that maintains a financial account with a reporting financial institution.

For example, in the case of a trust that is considered a passive NFE, reporting financial institutions are obliged to report discretionary beneficiaries only in the year in which they receive a distribution from the trust, and only if such financial institutions have appropriate safeguards and procedures in place to identify whether a distribution is made by trust account holders in a given year.

The standard may well require reporting to the tax authorities by financial institutions that may not have previously been obliged to do so, such as fund industry players, TCSPs and insurance companies. A trust is considered to be resident for reporting purposes in the participating jurisdiction where one or more of its trustees are resident, unless all information required to be reported in relation to the trust is reported in another participating jurisdiction because it is treated as resident for tax purposes there. In the case of trusts (and entities equivalent to trusts), the term 'controlling persons' is explicitly defined in the standard to mean settlors, trustees, protectors (if any), beneficiaries and classes of beneficiaries and any other natural persons exercising ultimate effective control over the trust. If the settlor, trustee, protector or beneficiary is an entity, the reporting financial institution must identify the controlling persons of such entity in accordance with the FATF recommendations discussed above.

Changes reflected in the 2018 second edition of the handbook provide additional, more up-to-date guidance on certain areas. For example, it is confirmed that, with respect to new accounts, the definition of 'controlling persons' is intended to correspond to the term 'beneficial owner" as described in Recommendation 10 in the FATF 2012 Recommendations.

With respect to trusts that are passive NFEs, a jurisdiction may allow reporting financial institutions to align the scope of the beneficiaries of a trust treated as controlling persons of the trust with the scope of the beneficiaries of a trust treated as reportable persons of a trust that is a financial institution. In such case the reporting financial institutions need only report discretionary beneficiaries in the year in which they receive a distribution from the trust. Jurisdictions that allow their financial institutions to make use of this option must ensure that such financial institutions have appropriate safeguards and procedures in place to identify whether a distribution is made by trust account holders in a given year.

Under the CRS rules, a trust is considered to be resident in a CRS participating jurisdiction where one or more of its trustees are resident, unless all information required to be reported in relation to the trust is reported to another participating jurisdiction's tax authorities because it is treated as resident for tax purposes there.

In the case of trusts (and entities equivalent to trusts), the term 'controlling persons' is explicitly defined in the CRS to mean settlors, trustees, protectors (if any), beneficiaries or classes of beneficiaries and any other natural persons exercising ultimate effective control over the trust. If the settlor, trustee, protector or beneficiary is an entity, the reporting financial institution must identify the controlling persons of such entity in accordance with the FATF recommendations.

The CRS will generally apply to trusts in two circumstances:

- where a trust is a reporting financial institution; and
- where a trust is an NFE that maintains a financial account with a reporting financial institution.

The most likely scenario in which a trust will be a financial institution is if it falls within the definition of an 'investment entity'. This is the case where a trust has gross income primarily attributable to investing, reinvesting or trading in financial assets and is managed by another entity that is a financial institution. This would also include trusts that are collective investment vehicles or other similar investment vehicles established with an investment strategy of investing, reinvesting or trading in financial assets.

In applying the CRS to a trust, reporting financial institutions review their financial accounts to identify their reportable accounts by applying the due diligence rules and then report the relevant information where the trust is considered to be resident for tax purposes in a particular participating jurisdiction; and the trust reports all the information required to be reported with respect to reportable accounts maintained by the trust that will relieve it from reporting in the jurisdictions of residence of the other co-trustees. In order to obtain such relief, each trustee should be able to demonstrate that all necessary reporting by the trust is actually taking place.

Where a trust is itself considered to be a financial institution, it must apply the due diligence rules in the CRS in order to determine the identity and residence of its account holders. Where an equity interest (eg, the interest held by a settlor, beneficiary or any other natural person exercising ultimate effective control over the trust) is held by an entity, the equity interest holder will instead be the controlling persons of that entity. As such, the trust will be required to look through a settlor, trustee, protector or beneficiary that is an entity to locate the relevant controlling person. This look-through obligation should correspond to the obligation to identify the beneficial owner of a trust under domestic ML/know your customer procedures.

If a non-financial passive trust holds an account with a reporting financial institution, the reporting financial institution may be required to report the trust for CRS purposes. In instances where the trust is an active NFE, the trust itself may have a reportable account with the financial institution, which must be determined considering the relevant due diligence procedures.

Where the beneficiaries are not individually named, but are identified as a class, the CRS does not require that all possible members of the class be treated as reportable persons. Rather, when a member of a class of beneficiaries receives a distribution from the trust or intends to exercise vested rights in the trust property, this will be a change of circumstances, prompting additional due diligence and reporting as necessary. This reflects a similar obligation under the FATF standards.

A settlor is to be reported under the CRS rules regardless of whether it is a revocable or irrevocable trust. Likewise, both mandatory and discretionary beneficiaries are included within the definition of 'controlling persons'. Unlike the case of an equity interest in a trust that is a reporting financial institution, discretionary beneficiaries will be reported regardless of whether a distribution is received in a given year. However, when implementing the CRS, a jurisdiction may allow reporting financial institutions to align the scope of the beneficiaries of a trust reported as controlling persons of the trust with the scope of the beneficiaries of a trust treated as reportable persons of a trust that is a financial institution.

Where a passive NFE (eg, in the form of a trust) maintains a financial account with a reporting financial institution, that reporting financial institution must look through the chain of ownership and control to identify controlling persons – that is, natural persons who are reportable persons.

The reports under CRS are to be sent multilaterally to all relevant jurisdictions (in which relevant actors are resident). Both the OECD CRS and the US Foreign Account Tax Compliance Act initiatives potentially impose obligations on all trusts, whether or not they have any US connections, US assets or US income. STEP has therefore issued a guidance note for trusts.[16]

4.   The potential misuse of trusts

ML is typically described as a three-stage process.[17] In the initial stage – placement – the launderer introduces the illegal profits into the financial system. This might be done by breaking up large amounts of cash into less conspicuous smaller sums which are then deposited directly into a bank account; or by purchasing a series of monetary instruments which are then collected and deposited into accounts of financial institutions (not necessarily banks). After the funds have entered the financial system, the second stage –

---

16   STEP Guidance Note: CRS and Trusts John Riches TEP, Chair, STEP Public Policy Committee, 8 March 2017, www.step.org/sites/default/files/Policy/Guidance_note_CRS_and_trusts.pdf.
17   www.fatf-gafi.org/faq/moneylaundering/#d.en.11223.

layering – takes place. In this phase, the launderer engages in a series of conversions or movements of the funds to distance them from their source. The funds might be channelled through the purchase and sale of investment instruments; or the launderer might simply wire the funds through a series of accounts at various banks across the globe, especially in those jurisdictions that do not cooperate with law enforcement ML investigations. In the third stage – integration – the funds re-enter the legitimate economy. The launderer might choose to invest the funds in real estate, luxury assets or business ventures.

Trusts can be misused by criminals to conceal the proceeds of crime at all three stages of the money-laundering process:[18] as a means of the initial placement of 'dirty' cash, in the layering stage when transferring wealth between jurisdictions or when integrating the laundered proceeds back into the legitimate financial world. The secretive nature and flexibility of trusts explain their appeal to money launderers. Some trusts are designed to hide any information relating to the settler who places the assets in the trust and of the beneficiary who holds the interest in the trust assets, to the point where the trust deed – if one exists and can be traced – will be misleading. Others give the trustee discretion to administer the trust as he or she sees fit. Trusts are often set up in conjunction with front companies, further confusing audit trails and hiding the identities of the parties. While a trust need not necessarily be set up by a solicitor or require the involvement of a financial adviser or accountant, as with criminal misuse of financial products, there is cumulative international evidence of growing connections between criminals and such professionals, who set up trusts as a means to launder money, which has caused the FATF to take action.

There are three main types of potential abuse of trust structures in the ML/TF context: concealment, protection and 'sham' trusts.

4.1 Concealment

This is the potential use of trusts and related company vehicles and bank accounts to conceal assets which are the proceeds of crime from police, customs, prosecutors and courts. One possible way to do this is through the abuse of a discretionary trust to hide the true beneficiaries, who remain unknown to financial institutions and DNFBPs.

The potential risk of such abuse of trust structures in general, and of discretionary trusts in particular, is recognised in most jurisdictions. This risk is exacerbated by the lack of transparency regarding trust documents such as letters of wishes, which in some cases may include vital information as to the identity of ultimate beneficiaries of an asset.

---

18   United Kingdom Threat Assessment of Serious and Organised Crime 2003, www.ncis.gov.uk/ukta/2003/threat06.asp.

This point can be illustrated in a Court of Appeal decision[19] which was an action for the recovery of assets held by a Jersey trust which it was claimed were the traceable proceeds of bribes, secret commissions and other fraudulent payments received by Maluf family members in Sao Paulo, Brazil. Three letters of wishes were issued by the settlor there, which the court found was not unusual in itself; nevertheless, the third letter of wishes, instructing a beneficiary change from the children back to the settlor – absent any other explanation and considered along with a bank transfer made – was found by the court on its face to be unusual and cogent evidence establishing Maluf as a party to the fraud and the beneficial ownership of the bank account there.

4.2   Protection

This involves the use of trusts to try to secure their assets so that, even if discovered, they shall be beyond the reach of domestic or foreign law enforcement's effort of confiscation. One example of this is the use of a 'flee clause' – a provision which is sometimes included in trust deeds that provides for the automatic replacement of the existing trustees by new trustees, or the automatic change of the management and administration of a trust to a different jurisdiction, in certain eventualities (eg, a breakdown of law and order in the place where the trust is administered). Most jurisdictions do not include specific examples of events (eg, the bringing of criminal charges or restraint orders) that might not trigger flee clauses, and such clauses are not commonly in use. That said, where flee clauses are abused to avoid the legal consequences of foreign law enforcement efforts, the general powers of the law will generally be used to find them void for public policy reasons. Furthermore, if a trustee acts on a flee clause, in most jurisdictions that will constitute powerful evidence of an 'arrangement' to facilitate the possession or control of criminal property, and will therefore result in potential liability for a substantive money-laundering offence. Nevertheless, the potential abuse of such clauses can hamper international cooperation with overseas jurisdictions where such clauses are triggered for disreputable reasons.

Another example is the abuse of a discretionary trust where, through the trust documents (eg, letters of wishes), the settlor *de facto* enjoys the use of the trust assets (eg, for as long as he or she lives). This was the case in *Tantular*,[20] in which the settlor established a Jersey trust (who was convicted of banking offences and sentenced to nine years' imprisonment in Indonesia), of which the beneficiaries were listed as the settlor, his wife, his three children and his wife's younger sister. In a letter of wishes the settlor expressed the hope that during his lifetime, the trustee would consider him – the settlor – as the principal

---

19   *Federal Republic of Brazil v Durant International Corporation* [2013]JCA071, 11 April 2013.
20   *Tan Chi Fang v HM AG (In the Matter of the Realisable Property of Robert Tantular)*, June 2014.

beneficiary. When charged with fraud and money-laundering offences, the Jersey Royal Court refused to grant a temporary seizure order (called a *saisie judiciaire* in Jersey), and held that the settlor – although a beneficiary of a discretionary trust – was not to be considered 'beneficially entitled' for the purposes of confiscation, and that the court could not grant a *saisie judiciaire* over the assets of a discretionary trust merely on the grounds that the offender (or suspected offender) was a beneficiary of such a trust, thus ignoring the letter of wishes which *de facto* named the settlor the principal beneficiary during his lifetime.

4.3   Sham trusts

A third type of potential risk is an arrangement whereby the trustees recognise that the assets remain *de facto* the settlor's in all but name. No reputable trustee or trust managing company would be part of such an arrangement, which would be illegal. However, although the scenario in the case discussed above was different, the information regarding the true *de facto* beneficial owner was revealed only after an examination of all relevant trust documentation, including the letter of wishes. Under most legal regimes, this will not regularly be available to financial institutions when performing due diligence.

Given the rise of serious and organised crime, heightened focus has been placed on ML at both the national and international levels. In 2001 the OECD issued a report which demonstrated that trusts are an instrument that may be exploited by money launderers. Although they are usually used for perfectly legal operations, the benefits they afford – such as privacy – may lead criminals to try to misuse them.

ML laws and regulations inherently conflict with the traditional obligations of trustees – that is, the duty of confidentiality and the duty to account. Some domestic laws have abrogated the duty of confidentiality owed by professionals to their clients and customers. In some cases, provisions afford immunity against actions for breach of confidence. Although confidentiality is essential in a trust context, the scope of this immunity remains unclear. The rules on tip-offs – which prohibit the disclosure of information which is likely to prejudice a police investigation in relation to ML – are particularly challenging in this regard. Beneficiaries, exercising their right to information, could possibly make trustees 'tip off'. Many issues remain unclear and recent case law[21] has demonstrated that trustees may be faced with the dilemma of violating either their fiduciary obligations under trust law or their new duties under ML legislation.

---

21   *The Governor and Company of the Bank of Scotland v A Limited* (2000) All ER (D) 864.

5. The FATF recommendations and their impact on trusts

As mentioned above, in 2003 the FATF took a big step forward and applied its recommendations not only to financial institutions, but also to DNFBPs, which are now required under the new Recommendation 22 to comply with several of the requirements set out in the 40 recommendations. The FATF defines these as lawyers, notaries, other independent legal professionals and accountants when they prepare for or carry out transactions for a client in relation to the following activities:

- the purchase and sale of real estate;
- the management of client money,[22] securities or other assets;
- the management of bank, savings or securities accounts;
- the organisation of contributions for the creation, operation or management of companies;
- the creation, operation or management of legal persons or arrangements; and
- the purchase and sale of business entities.

TCSPs will be considered DNFBPs when they prepare for and carry out transactions for a client in relation to the following activities:

- acting as a formation agent of legal persons;
- acting as (or arranging for another person to act as) a director or secretary of a company or a partner of a partnership, or assuming a similar position in relation to other legal persons;
- providing a registered office, business address or accommodation, correspondence or administrative address for a company, a partnership or any other legal person or arrangement;
- acting as (or arranging for another person to act as) a trustee of an express trust;[23] and
- acting as (or arranging for another person to act as) a nominee shareholder for another person.[24]

5.1 Customer due diligence

The main principles of customer due diligence have not changed in the new 2013 FATF standards (now in Recommendation 10), and are as follows:

---

22 'Management of client money' is narrower than simply handling the client's money and includes situations where, for example, solicitors may be managing money or other assets on behalf of clients. It seems logical that the simple operation of a solicitor's client account is not intended to be caught within the scope of the recommendation. Other related activity – such as payment on account of costs to a solicitor, payment of a solicitor's bill, legal advice, participation in litigation, will writing and publicly funded work – should not usually fall under the scope of the FATF recommendations.

23 Under the FATF recommendations, an 'express trust' is a trust that is clearly created by the settlor, usually in the form of a document (eg, a written deed of trust). It may be contrasted with trusts which come into being through the operation of law and which do not result from the clear intent or decision of a settlor to create a trust or similar legal arrangements (eg, a constructive trust).

24 Recommendation 22 of the New FATF 2013 Recommendations.

- identifying the customer and verifying the customer's identity;
- identifying the beneficial owner and taking reasonable measures to verify the identity of the beneficial owner (ie, the natural person who ultimately owns or controls the customer);
- understanding and, as appropriate, obtaining information on the purpose and intended nature of the business relationship; and
- conducting ongoing due diligence on the business relationship.

The changes to Recommendation 10 mostly concern clarification and guidance. Especially significant is the clarification of the requirement to identify and verify the beneficial ownership of customers that are legal persons (companies) or legal arrangements (trusts) – a very difficult requirement to implement under the previous regulations.

In particular, there is now more guidance on the three steps that financial institutions should take to identify the beneficial owner of customers that are legal persons – who they should seek to identify and, where that is not possible, what alternative persons they should identify.

Two recommendations require countries to ensure that competent authorities have timely access to beneficial ownership information on legal persons (eg, companies) (Recommendation 24) and legal arrangements (eg, trusts) (Recommendation 25). These are closely linked to the customer due diligence requirements for financial institutions to collect information on the beneficial ownership of their customers. The fundamental principles have not changed: authorities should be able, where necessary, to identify the beneficial owners of any company or trust in the jurisdiction.

As the old version of the FATF standards was rather vague, the requirements were interpreted inconsistently and the overall level of compliance was very low. In the context of the G20 call to the FATF to reinforce the transparency requirements, the objective was to reassert the fundamental principle of the recommendations while providing greater clarity and specificity as regards the practical steps that countries should take. This issue was one of the most difficult aspects of the revision to negotiate within the FATF, both because of differences in legal systems (common law/civil law) and because some obligations apply to companies and non-professional trustees – entities which previously had been subject to no ML/TF requirements.

5.2   Specific measures for legal persons and legal arrangements

In the new recommendations (10.8), for customers that are legal persons or legal arrangements, financial institutions are now required to understand the nature of the customer's business and its ownership and control structure. They are also (10.9) required to identify the customer and verify its identity through the following information:

- name, legal form and proof of existence;
- the powers that regulate and bind the legal person or arrangement;
- the names of the relevant persons with a senior management position in the legal person or arrangement; and
- the address of the registered office and, if different, a principal place of business.

For trusts, the recommendations (10.11) specifically require financial institutions to identify and take reasonable measures to verify the identity of beneficial owners, including the settlor, the trustee(s), the protector (if any), the beneficiaries or class of beneficiaries, and any other natural person exercising ultimate effective control over the trust (including through a chain of control/ownership).

Typically, all trusts (other than charitable or statutory permitted non-charitable trusts) must have beneficiaries, who may include the settlor; and a maximum duration, known as the perpetuity period, which is often 100 years. While trusts must always have some ultimately ascertainable beneficiary, they may have no defined existing beneficiaries, but only objects of a power until some person becomes entitled as beneficiary to income or capital on the expiry of a defined period, known as the accumulation period. This period is normally co-extensive with the trust perpetuity period, which is usually referred to in the trust deed as the 'trust period'.

One important issue is this context is beneficial ownership. Under the FATF recommendations, countries must take measures to prevent the unlawful use of legal arrangements in relation to ML/TF by ensuring that their commercial, trust and other laws require adequate transparency concerning the beneficial ownership and control of trusts and other legal arrangements. Examples of mechanisms[25] that countries can use to this end include a system of central registration (or upfront disclosure system) through which a national registry records details on trusts (ie, settlors,[26] trustees, beneficiaries and protectors) and other legal arrangements registered in that country. The relevant information could be either publicly available or available only to competent authorities. Changes in ownership and control information would need to be kept up to date. Other examples include:

- requiring trust service providers to obtain, verify and retain records of the details of the trust or other similar legal arrangements; and
- relying on the investigative and other powers of law enforcement,

---

25 These examples are summaries of mechanisms set out in the OECD report entitled "Behind the Corporate Veil. Using Corporate Entities for Illicit Purposes", 2001.
26 For the purpose of the FATF recommendations, 'settlors' are persons or companies that transfer ownership of their assets to trustees by means of a trust deed. Where the trustees have some discretion as to the investment and distribution of the trust's assets, the deed may be accompanied by a non-legally binding letter setting out what the settlor wishes to be done with the assets.

regulatory, supervisory or other competent authorities in a jurisdiction to obtain or have access to the information.

As the FATF has explained, these suggested mechanisms are largely complementary and countries may find it desirable and beneficial to use a combination of them. Above all, it is crucial that competent authorities can obtain or access in a timely fashion adequate, accurate and current information on the beneficial ownership and control of legal arrangements, and in particular the settlor, the trustee and the beneficiaries of express trusts.

5.3   Customer due diligence

Financial institutions and DNFPBs need not repeatedly perform identification and verification every time that a customer conducts a transaction. The general rule is that customers should be subject to the full range of customer due diligence measures. However, there are circumstances in which it would be reasonable for a country to allow its financial institutions to apply the extent of these measures on a risk-sensitive basis.[27] For customers that are legal persons or legal arrangements, financial institutions and DNFBPs should be required to take reasonable measures to:

- understand the ownership and control structure of the customer; and
- identify the natural persons who ultimately own or control the customer, including those persons who exercise ultimate effective control over a legal person or arrangement.

Examples of the types of measures that would be normally needed to satisfactorily perform this function for trusts include identifying the settlor, the trustee or the person exercising effective control over the trust, and the beneficiaries.

DNFBPs must perform enhanced due diligence for higher-risk categories of customers, business relationships and transactions. Examples of higher-risk categories (which are derived from the Basel customer due diligence paper)[28] may include non-resident customers, private banking, legal persons or arrangements such as trusts that are personal asset holding vehicles, and companies that have nominee shareholders or shares in bearer form.

As there are so many different types of trusts, a risk-based approach is needed to determine what information should be obtained in each case to satisfy these requirements. Different approaches may therefore be taken when

---

27   Examples of the types of customer information that could be obtained and the identification data that could be used to verify that information are set out in a paper entitled "General Guide to Account Opening and Customer Identification", issued by the Basel Committee's Working Group on Cross-Border Banking.

28   *Supra* note 27.

dealing with a long-established family settlement as opposed to an offshore discretionary trust or a trust established by a non-profit active in areas of conflict.

When acting for trusts, a lawyer must establish the identity of his or her client and refer to the document establishing the trust (and, if appropriate, documents dealing with the appointment of the current trustees). Identities should be established using procedures as prescribed in national legislation or guidelines. For example, the extent to which all trustees and all living settlors should be established might be determined only after assessing the ML risk, depending on the nature, purpose and original source of the funding for the trust. When acting for trustees who are based in offshore jurisdictions with strict bank secrecy and confidentiality rules, or in jurisdictions that are especially vulnerable to ML risk, more comprehensive enquiries may be warranted in order to obtain details of the settlor (eg, full name and business or home address). When acting for the settlor in establishing the trust, it will be necessary to establish his or her identity. It is also normal practice for a firm of solicitors to check the identity of beneficiaries before making any distribution of funds.

In conducting customer due diligence of a trust, financial institutions must also obtain copies of (or at least review carefully) all relevant trust documentation, such as the trust deed, letters of wishes and trust minutes. As illustrated above, in certain cases information contained in this documentation (eg, letters of wishes) may be essential to determine who exercises effective control over the trust or to understand the nature and purpose of the business relationship.

5.4 Reporting suspicious transactions

If a financial institution suspects or has reasonable grounds to suspect that funds are the proceeds of a criminal activity or are related to TF, it should be required, directly by law or regulation, to report promptly its suspicions to the financial intelligence unit.[29] The requirement to report in case of suspicion is a subjective test (ie, the person suspects that a transaction involves criminal activity). By contrast, the requirement to report where there are 'reasonable grounds to suspect' is an objective test, which can be satisfied if the circumstances surrounding the transaction would lead a reasonable person to suspect that the transaction involved a criminal activity. Countries may choose between either alternative.

The FATF recommendations call for national legislation to impose reporting requirements on DNFBPs, similar to those that exist for financial institutions, with some exceptions. First, dealers in precious metals and stones need only

---

29   FATF Recommendation 20 for financial institutions and 23 for DNFBPs.

report transactions (or attempted transactions) with a value of more than $/€15,000.[30] Second, countries may allow lawyers, notaries, other independent legal professionals and accountants acting as independent legal professionals to send their suspicious transaction reports to self-regulatory organisations, and need not always send them to the financial intelligence unit. These reporting obligations have not been fully implemented in all FATF countries (eg, the United States, Israel and Canada); and even jurisdictions which have formally adopted them, such as the United Kingdom, have been criticised for ineffective implementation.[31]

5.5 Professional privilege or legal professional secrecy

Lawyers, notaries, other independent legal professionals[32] and accountants acting as independent legal professionals need not report suspicious transactions if the relevant information was obtained in circumstances where it is subject to legal professional privilege or legal professional secrecy. In deciding whether a certain activity falls within the scope of the FATF recommendations, lawyers should take a cautious approach. While, for example, litigation or advice on seeking asylum or other classic criminal law work for a client might fall outside the scope of the recommendations, making arrangements for the investment or management of any funds received by the same client – even by way of settlement or acting on a house purchase – will fall within the boundaries of the FATF recommendations.

It is for each jurisdiction to determine the matters that fall under legal professional privilege or legal professional secrecy. This will normally cover information that lawyers, notaries and other independent legal professionals receive from or obtain through a client in the course of ascertaining that client's legal position, or in defending or representing the client in or concerning judicial, administrative, arbitration or mediation proceedings. In jurisdictions where accountants are subject to the same obligations of secrecy or privilege, they need not report suspicious transactions.

5.6 Terrorist financing

After the 9/11 attacks in the United States, international consensus was reached on the need to enhance global cooperation against TF.[33] Consequently, the

---

30 The designated threshold includes situations where the transaction is carried out in a single operation or in several operations that appear to be linked (cases of 'smurfing'/'structuring').

31 See UK Mutual Evaluation Report, supra footnote 11: "While the full range of financial institutions (FIs) and designated non-financial businesses and professions (DNFBPs) are required to report SARs, there remains an underreporting of suspicious transactions by higher risk sectors such as trust and company service providers (TCSPs), lawyers, and accountants."

32 This refers to sole practitioners, partners and employed professionals within professional firms. It is not meant to refer to 'internal' professionals who are employees of other types of businesses or to professionals working for government agencies who may already be subject to measures to combat money laundering.

33 UN Council Resolution 1373.

FATF[34] adopted the existing 40 ML recommendations as an effective tool against TF and further decided on eight special recommendations regarding TF.[35] In 2003 the Egmont Group of Financial Intelligence Units amended its statement of purpose to include TF.[36] Traditionally, the politicisation of this issue has prevented the international community from reaching agreement, even with regard to the definition of 'terror'. A common definition of 'terror' was ultimately agreed[37] in the International Convention for the Suppression of the Financing of Terrorism. This definition encompasses all violent terrorist activity without exception, even where there are 'legitimate' potential motives (eg, freedom fighters). As a result, the ML regime – and specifically the information reported by the financial sector – is now used to combat TF.

In a October 2015 report following terrorist attacks in Europe, the FATF[38] acknowledged that while the number and types of terrorist groups and related threats have changed over time, the basic need for terrorists to raise, move and use funds has remained the same. However, as the size, scope and structure of terrorist organizations have evolved, so too have their methods of raising and managing funds. The FATF found that terrorist organisations use funds not only for operational needs, but also for propaganda, recruitment and training, and the techniques used to manage these funds include the allocation of specialised financial roles. Highlighting the emerging TF risks, the FATF explored the threats and vulnerabilities posed by:

- foreign terrorist fighters;
- fundraising through social media;
- new payment products and services; and
- the exploitation of natural resources.

(a) Money laundering and terror financing

There is a strong link between ML and TF, although there are also several relevant differences between ML and TF. In contrast to traditional organised crime:

- the objectives of terror groups are usually not acquisitive;
- their funding often takes the form of 'clean' donations and contributions;
- there is often a lack of clarity regarding the purpose of funds; and
- terror groups, unlike criminals, seek to operate outside the formal financial and banking systems.

---

34 FATF Special recommendations on financing of terror; http://www.fatf-gafi.org.
35 Which became nine special recommendations when SR 9 regarding cross-border cash was added in 2004. All are incorporated in the 2013 FATF 40 recommendations.
36 The Egmont Group of Financial Intelligence Units, Statement of Purpose of Guernsey, 23 June 2004, www.egmontgroup.org/.
37 Article 2 of the International Convention for the Suppression of the Financing of Terrorism, 9 December 1999.
38 www.fatf-gafi.org/media/fatf/documents/reports/Emerging-Terrorist-Financing-Risks.pdf.

That said, there are also similarities between criminal and terror groups. Terror organisations use crime to raise funds and achieve their objectives; they share the characteristics of ongoing criminal enterprises and their objectives are considered criminal. Furthermore, both involve international activity and use international financial tools. Thus, as for any other criminal organisation, a successful terror group is one that can build and maintain an effective financial infrastructure.[39] It is thus only logical that the regulations and institutions put in place to combat organised crime and ML should also be utilised to fight terror and its financing.

(b) Characteristics of terror financing

A common misunderstanding concerns the ability of financial institutions or law enforcement agencies to track down the relatively small amounts of money needed by individual terrorists to execute terror attacks. As discussed, terror organisations need large sums of money to maintain their organisational infrastructure. Such is the case, for instance, with Middle East terror group Hamas, which maintains a 'social welfare' (Da'awa) network as the basis for its terror activity. Hamas utilises this network to facilitate terror attacks and build grassroots support among the Palestinian population. Frequently, Hamas Da'awa operatives ferry suicide bombers and explosives to the point of departure for their missions. Numerous Hamas members with terrorist track records are officials of Hamas charity committees.[40]

Another point to consider is the cost of spectacular terror events. The costs of executing the 9/11 attacks were estimated at $400,000; but how much would a terror attack involving weapons of mass destruction cost?[41] Efforts should thus focus not on detecting the financial trails of individual terrorists, but on detecting the financial infrastructure of terror groups and their criminal enterprises.

(c) Why and how terror groups launder money

Terror organisations use all known money-laundering techniques[42] in order to disguise both the source and the purpose of their funds, and to distance

---

39   FATF, Guidance for Financial Institutions in Detecting Terrorist Financing, www.fatf-gafi.org.

40   Levitt Matthew, *Charitable Organizations and Terrorist Financing: A War on Terror Status-Check march 19, 2004*, the Washington Institute for Near East Policy.

41   Allison, Graham, *Nuclear Terrorism: The Ultimate Preventable Catastrophe* (New York, NY: Henry Holt & Company 2004).

42   See, for example, the Isle of Man Moneyval Mutual Evaluation Report for criticism regarding the understanding of foreign TF risks not yet being sufficiently comprehensive, as high-risk situations (eg, transactions to high-risk jurisdictions) are not monitored at a national level; www.fatf-gafi.org/media/fatf/documents/reports/mer-fsrb/Mutual-Evalutaion-Isle-of-Man.pdf. Also see the Cayman Islands CFATF mutual evaluation report (p88) for a description of a suspicions report relating to TF involving a trust company domiciled in another jurisdiction and affiliated with a local law firm involving an individual allegedly linked to terrorism and possibly TF, and two other suspicious activity reports related to civil litigation linked to a previous major terrorist attack; www.fatf-gafi.org/media/fatf/documents/reports/mer-fsrb/CFATF-Cayman-Islands-Mutual-Evaluation.pdf.

themselves from their financiers.[43] The FATF ML recommendations thus have special relevance with regard to trusts and their potential abuse by terror organisations and organised crime, focusing on three relevant vulnerabilities of the international financial system: wire transfers, alternative remittance systems and the abuse of non-profit organisations. The FATF called for the imposition of ML requirements on alternative remittance systems, the strengthening of customer identification measures in international and domestic wire transfers, and the introduction of measures to ensure that entities – in particular, non-profit organisations – cannot be misused to finance terrorism.

Terror organisations use wire transfers to move funds intended for their activities. The financial support structures revealed after the 9/11 attacks in the United States and attacks in Europe confirmed the essential role of wire transfers in providing both terrorists and those promoting radical ideologies with the necessary financial means to plan and execute attacks.[44] Wire transfers do not involve the actual movement of currency; they are rather a rapid and secure method of transferring value from one location to another.

The ongoing development of worldwide networks such as SWIFT[45] has enhanced the reliability and efficiency of inter-bank payment systems and – complemented by services such as telephone and internet banking – has heightened the potential for abuse by terrorist financiers and money launderers. The increased speed and volume of wire transfers – along with the lack of international standards on how key information relating to such transactions should be recorded, how such records should be maintained and how relevant information should be transmitted – are hindering investigative authorities in tracing individual transactions. Another characteristic of their activity is to structure the flow of funds through several different financial institutions, so that the wire transfers appear to come from seemingly unrelated sources.

In many cases terror groups transfer funds through non-bank financial institutions or alternative remittance services, or by informal money or value transfer systems, on the premise that avoiding mainstream financial institutions should help the transfers to remain undetected by financial monitoring systems or investigatory authorities. In many cases transfers take place through non-bank financial institutions such as money remitters and bureaux de change, which perform wire transfer functions either directly with counterpart businesses in their own country or abroad or through conventional financial institutions.

---

43 See, for example, the Panama Papers, alleging that law firm Mossack Fonseca – which is based in Panama, but has offices around the world – has worked with at least 33 individuals or companies listed on the US Treasury Department's Office of Foreign Assets Control list; www.icij.org/investigations/panama-papers/20160404-sanctioned-blacklisted-offshore-clients/.
44 See interpretive note to the FATF special recommendations, supra note 3.
45 Society for Worldwide Interbank Financial Telecommunications, a network that facilitates the exchange of payments and other financial transactions worldwide.

Non-profit organisations have also been identified as vulnerable to possible abuse by terror financiers. The FATF thus considers it best practice for non-profit organisations that handle funds to maintain registered bank accounts, keep their funds in them and use formal or registered financial channels to transfer funds, especially overseas. It has also emphasised the need to verify adequately the activities of non-profit organisations. In several instances, programmes of non-profit organisations were not being implemented as reported; the funds were actually being diverted to terrorist organisations. Non-profit organisations should be in a position to verify that funds are being spent as advertised and planned.

6.   Conclusion

The evolution of ML and TF standards, such as the FATF's 40 recommendations and the OECD's CRS initiative, has had a significant impact on trusts and their management. These standards not only encompass a much wider range of activities of DNFBPs, including trusts, but also shine a spotlight on the measures that jurisdictions are implementing to prevent legal persons and arrangements from being used for criminal purposes, including tax evasion; to make legal persons and arrangements sufficiently transparent; and to ensure that accurate, up-to-date basic and beneficial ownership information is available on a timely basis.

These developments require practitioners to familiarise themselves not only with domestic rules and laws, but also with all relevant risk factors, as well as details of international standards. Trusts will no doubt remain an important tool used for various legitimate purposes; nevertheless, it is expected that their establishment and management will become more challenging, to ensure that they are not abused for tax evasion, ML or TF purposes.

As the relevant rules and regulations become more complex, it is essential that TCSPs conduct ML/TF risk assessments and prioritise their compliance efforts through a risk-based approach.

Trusts and divorce

Ziva Robertson
McDermott Will & Emery

1.   Introduction

Since the early 2000s, the legal profession has witnessed a significant shift in the approach of the family courts in various jurisdictions to the division of assets upon divorce. Following the decision in *White v White*,[1] it is now widely accepted that the Family Division of the English court would apply the yardstick of equality as the appropriate starting point in high-value financial provision cases, where there are surplus matrimonial assets after the needs of the spouses and any children of the family have been met. The presumption of equality may be displaced in cases where one of the spouses had inherited or accumulated wealth prior to the marriage or had made a stellar contribution to the wealth of the family. In its approach to the division of assets, the Family Division has shown increasing willingness to:

- characterise trust assets as 'nuptial', or matrimonial, assets;
- vary trusts to make provisions for the spouses and children of the family; or
- divide the matrimonial property on the basis that trust assets are a resource available to one spouse or the other.

Such orders are not confined to English trusts and extend to the assets of foreign (including offshore) trusts. While each case in the Family Division is fact specific and decided on its own merits, recent reported cases have significantly developed this area of the law in a way which impacts on foreign law trusts as well as domestic ones. At the same time, there have been important developments in the offshore world as regards the enforcement or recognition of foreign non-money judgments. This chapter reviews these developments and their significance to trustees, beneficiaries and other fiduciaries.

2.   Financial provision: an overview of the position in England and Wales

Family Division judges have a wide-ranging discretion, derived mainly from

---

1   [2001] 1 All ER 1, HL.

Sections 23 to 25 of the Matrimonial Causes Act 1973, to make orders for financial provisions on divorce.[2] Such orders may cover:

- the payment of maintenance to (or for) the spouses or children;
- the payment of a lump sum by one spouse to, or for the benefit of, the other spouse or the children;
- the transfer of property to, or for the benefit of, either of the spouses or a child of the family;
- a direction to one party to settle a specified property on the other party or on the children;
- the variation of any pre-nuptial or post-nuptial settlement made (either by the parties themselves or by close third parties such as other family members) on either of the spouses or children of the family;
- the sale of any property in which the parties are interested; and
- a pension-sharing order.

In exercising its discretion, the court's first consideration is the welfare of the children of the family. Historically, the court then turned to make provision for the 'reasonable requirements' of the applicant (being the financially weaker party). Where the matrimonial resources significantly exceeded those needs, the financially stronger party – the breadwinner – often emerged with the balance, which constituted the larger share of the matrimonial assets and/or income. The 2000 case of *White v White*[3] fundamentally changed that approach. In that case, the House of Lords held that the correct analysis should be one which results in a fair outcome for the parties and, while the presumption of equality was developed only in subsequent cases, the court in *White* suggested that future decisions should be measured against "the yardstick of equality". The court was particularly careful to stress that there should not be a presumption that the contribution of the breadwinner to the welfare of the family is more worthy or significant than the contribution of the homemaker; and that, as a general guide, "equality should only be departed from if there is a good reason for doing so" (per Lord Nicholls).

Subsequent cases have confirmed that the 'yardstick of equality' should be the appropriate test in short marriages as well as long ones, where the couple's wealth was acquired during the marriage.[4] In *Miller v Miller* and *McFarlane v McFarlane*,[5] the House of Lords sought to clarify the position further by

---

2   The provisions of Part 2 of the Matrimonial Causes Act 1973 apply with equal force to civil partnerships and married same-sex couples by virtue of Section 72 of and Schedule 5 to the Civil Partnership Act 2004. No statutory protections are currently offered to unmarried couples.

3   *Op cit* (note 1).

4   Although where one party's contribution to the family's finances has been greater than the other's during a short marriage, the court will seek to put the parties back to their pre-marriage position: *Foster v Foster* [2003] EWCA Civ 565.

5   The appeals in these two cases were heard together and reported at [2006] UKHL 241.

suggesting a three-strand test based on needs, compensation and sharing. Following this authority, the court should consider in the first instance the needs of the parties and the children of the family. If surplus funds remain after the needs of the parties and the children have been met, the court will turn to consider the yardstick of equality, which requires that the spouses share the matrimonial assets in a way that achieves fairness to both.

The concept of 'compensation' is also intended to achieve a fair result, by recognising that the homemaker may have forgone an opportunity to develop a career or seek remunerative employment and should be compensated for that sacrifice upon the breakdown of the marriage. There is no hard-and-fast rule as to whether 'sharing' should come before 'compensation' or vice versa.

A slightly different approach may be applied to cases involving pre-marital or inherited property, or where one of the spouses has made an exceptional (or 'stellar') contribution to the family's financial welfare.

2.1 Property acquired prior to the marriage or through an inheritance

In high-value cases, where the resources significantly exceed the needs of the parties and the children of the family, the court may disregard 'non-matrimonial' assets such as inheritance or wealth acquired prior to the marriage. In *White*, the court recognised that in such cases the claim of the spouse who contributed the assets would be stronger than the claim of the other spouse.[6] Similarly, the court may, at its discretion, disregard an inheritance received by one of the parties either before or during the marriage, in circumstances where the parties did not have recourse to the inherited assets during the marriage. In *H v H*,[7] the husband had received two sets of inheritances: one from each of his grandmother and his great aunt, both of which he had kept separate from the family assets and did not have recourse to during the marriage; and a separate (and smaller) one from his father, which he had applied towards the purchase of the matrimonial property. The wife had also inherited assets on the death of her father, which were gradually liquidated and invested with the help of the husband. The court held that the parties' inheritances from their respective parents would be taken into account, having been treated as matrimonial assets. However, the husband's inheritance from his grandmother and great aunt, which had not been treated in that way, was left out of account, since it was not necessary to have recourse to it in order to achieve a fair result.[8]

---

6   Although in cases where the non-matrimonial assets were required to meet the needs of the parties, the fact that they were contributed by one party rather than the other would not carry much weight.

7   [2007] EWHC 459 Fam.

8   A similar result was achieved *in Y v Y* [2012] EWHC 2063 Fam and *S v S* [2006] EWHC 2339 Fam, where the wealth acquired by the husband post-separation was excluded.

2.2   Pre-nuptial agreements

Where one of the spouses brings considerable wealth to the marriage, he or she may increasingly be advised to enter into a pre-nuptial agreement in a jurisdiction which permits and recognises the validity of such agreements, although for the agreement to have full effect the parties would need to have a close connection with that jurisdiction and preferably conduct any divorce proceedings there.

Pre-nuptial agreements are not binding under English law, and they have historically been thought to be contrary to public policy[9] and a fetter on the court's discretion. However, recent developments would tend to suggest that the judicial mood is changing and the courts are increasingly willing to give significant weight to such agreements. In *S v S*,[10] Mr Justice Wilson warned that where other jurisdictions have increasingly recognised that it may be appropriate, in certain circumstances, to hold the parties to the terms of a pre-nuptial agreement, the English courts should be cautious about "too categorically asserting the contrary". In *K v K*,[11] a case involving a short marriage of some 14 months, the court upheld the pre-nuptial agreement which had been signed by both parties with the benefit of legal advice.

Perhaps the clearest indication of the court's shift towards recognition of pre-nuptial agreements is to be found in *Radmacher v Granatino*,[12] in which the Supreme Court[13] upheld the decision of the Court of Appeal to hold the parties to the terms of their pre-nuptial agreement. In that case, the husband was a French national and the wife, whom he married in 1998, was German. The wife came from a wealthy background and at her instigation the parties had signed a pre-nuptial agreement valid under German law. The husband left his career in banking and embarked on research studies at Oxford University. In 2006 the parties separated and divorce proceedings were commenced in the United Kingdom. Although the pre-nuptial agreement had stated that neither party would seek maintenance from the other in the event of divorce, on the application of the husband the High Court disregarded that provision and awarded him £5.6 million, to provide him with an annual income for life and enable him to purchase a home where his daughters could visit. The wife appealed and the Court of Appeal allowed the appeal, principally on the ground that the judge had not afforded sufficient weight to the pre-nuptial agreement. Summarising the position in the lead judgment, Lord Justice Thorpe said: "In future cases broadly in line with the present case on the facts, the judge should give due weight to the marital property regime into which the parties freely

---

9   *Hyman v Hyman* [1929] AC 601.
10   [1997] 2 FLR 100.
11   [2003] 1 FLR 120.
12   [2010] UKSC 42.
13   Formerly the House of Lords.

entered. This is not to apply foreign law, nor is it to give effect to a contract foreign to English tradition. It is, in my judgment, a legitimate exercise of the very wide discretion that is conferred on the judges to achieve fairness between the parties to the ancillary relief proceedings."

The Supreme Court upheld the decision of the Court of Appeal by a majority of eight to one. Lord Philips, delivering the lead judgment, observed that the modern practice of separation agreements and nuptial agreement called for a new approach by the court. He identified the following issues for the court to consider:

- Parties must enter into a pre-nuptial agreement voluntarily, without undue pressure, and should be informed of its implications. Factors such as material lack of disclosure, information and advice will be a relevant consideration for the court in deciding whether to uphold the validity of the agreement.
- Did the foreign elements of the case enhance the weight that should be accorded to the agreement? In the present case, the fact that the agreement was valid under German law was relevant to the question of whether the parties intended it to be effective.
- Are there any other circumstances that would make it fair or just to depart from the agreement? A nuptial agreement cannot be allowed to prejudice the reasonable requirements of any children of the family, but the parties' autonomy and their reasonable desire to make provision for the division of their existing property on divorce should be given appropriate weight. In the right case a pre-nuptial agreement can have decisive or compelling weight.

There have been several authorities in respect of nuptial agreements since *Radmacher*. In *Z v Z (Financial Remedy: Marriage Contract)*,[14] a week or so before the marriage, the parties, who were both French, entered into a French marriage contract which affected (among other things) the rights of the parties on divorce and provided that each party would retain such assets as they saved into their own name during the marriage. The parties had pre-marital assets of about £1 million and the husband, a banker, saved a further £14 million in his sole name and transferred funds into other bank accounts to meet the parties' expenses during the marriage. Following the marriage, the parties moved to live in England, where the wife ultimately issued divorce proceedings. The court upheld the efficacy of the marital contract and rejected the wife's claims for 'sharing' in the assets beyond the resources required to meet her needs. However, the court did vary the agreement to provide the wife with approximately 40% of the matrimonial assets to meet that need. It is likely that

---

14   [2012] 1 FLR 1100.

the French court would have awarded the wife a significantly lesser amount pursuant to the agreement.

In contrast, in *Ipekci v McConnell*[15] the court refused to give effect to a pre-nuptial agreement governed by New York law. The case involved the breakdown of a 12-year marriage that produced two children. When the husband and wife met, he was a concierge in a New York hotel and she was one of the heirs to the Avon company fortune. A pre-nuptial agreement was prepared by the wife's lawyers and two weeks before the marriage the husband received 'independent' legal advice from a London solicitor who had acted for the wife in her divorce from her first husband. The agreement stipulated that the husband, who had no assets of his own, would get a share of any increase in the value of properties brought into the marriage by the wife, but nothing else. At the time of the divorce, the properties had not appreciated in value and the husband stood to leave the marriage with nothing at all. The judge noted that the agreement suffered from defective execution which, even under New York law, would render it unenforceable; but he also considered that pre-nuptial agreements should be enforced if they are fair to both parties. He found the present agreement to be unfair because:

- the husband had not been given advice by a New York qualified lawyer who would explain to him the meaning and effect of the agreement;
- the English lawyer appointed to him was not an independent adviser, having acted for the wife previously;
- if the agreement was unenforceable in New York, it should not be enforced in the United Kingdom; and
- the agreement did not meet the financial needs of the husband.

The judge did not give the agreement any weight, and in making an order for financial provision against the wife, he found that, as a matter of fact, she was entitled to significant assets out of various family trusts, as well as the assets directed owned by her, and he took those assets into account.

Legislation proposed by the Law Commission in 2014, intended to regularise and bring certainty to this area of the law, has not yet been enacted.

2.3 Stellar contributions

The approach of the Family Division has also developed in material ways – and is continuing to evolve – in relation to stellar (or special) contributions by one of the spouses to the financial welfare of the family. Following *White*, the court was initially reluctant to revert to the assessment of relative contributions where the breadwinner's financial contribution was markedly greater than the homemaker's. Thus, while the husband who built up a significant fortune in

---

15   [2019] EWFC 19.

Cowan v Cowan[16] was awarded 62% of the matrimonial assets on the grounds of his special contribution to the family's financial welfare, that decision was subsequently criticised by the Court of Appeal in *Lambert v Lambert*,[17] which overturned an award of 63% to the husband and reduced it to 50%. However, more recent decisions have reflected a shift in the court's approach and an increasing willingness to award a larger share to a spouse whose 'spark of genius'[18] has resulted in a stellar financial contribution to the family wealth.

Such was the case in *Charman v Charman*.[19] In that case, the husband had made a large fortune in the insurance field, some of which he had settled onto a Jersey trust. When the husband became a tax exile in Bermuda, the wife refused to join him there and the marriage came to an end. The husband failed in his argument that the wife's 'abandonment' of him should weigh against her in the financial division of the assets and the court refused to disregard the Jersey trust in calculating the matrimonial assets. Nevertheless, the court recognised that the husband's multimillion-pound empire amounted to a special contribution and awarded him 63% of the value assets, with the wife receiving the remaining 37%. Mr Justice Coleridge suggested in his judgment that perhaps the future lies in setting 'percentage bands' as guidelines, where the presumption of equality would be gradually displaced the greater the fortune in question, in the hope that such guidelines may provide a measure of certainty which is missing at this time. It remains to be seen whether this suggestion is adopted in future cases.

It is interesting to note that the Divorce (Financial Provision) Bill referred to above[20] proposes that all matrimonial property should be divided equally on divorce unless:

- the parties have otherwise agreed;
- either party has destroyed, dissipated or alienated matrimonial property;
- the needs of the children of the family under the age of 21 require an unequal division; or
- unequal division of the matrimonial assets is appropriate having regard to the actual or prospective liability of the parties for any expenses of valuation or transfer of property in connection with the divorce.

If this bill is passed into law in its current form, the stellar contribution of one party would not justify unequal division of assets upon divorce.

---

16   [2001] EWCA Civ 679.
17   [2002] EWCA Civ 1685.
18   An expression used by Madam Justice Bennett to describe the husband's contribution in *Sorrell v Sorrell* [2005] EWHC1717 (Fam).
19   [2006] EWHC 1879 (Fam).
20   *Op cit* (note 14).

3. Variation of settlements: the approach of the English court

How, then, does the court apply the aforementioned principles when a significant part of the couple's wealth is held in trusts or settlements, rather than by the parties personally?

3.1 The statutory powers

The Family Division of the English court has broad and extensive powers to vary trusts upon divorce. Those powers derive from Sections 24(1)(c) and (d) of the Matrimonial Causes Act 1973, which provide as follows:

> On granting a decree of divorce, a decree of nullity of marriage or a decree of judicial separation or at any time thereafter ... the court may make any one or more of the following orders, that is to say...
>
> (c) an order varying for the benefit of the parties to the marriage and of the children of the family or either or any of them any ante-nuptial or post-nuptial settlement (including such a settlement made by will or codicil) made on the parties to the marriage, other than one in the form of a pension arrangement (within the meaning of section 25D below);
>
> (d) an order extinguishing or reducing the interest of either of the parties to the marriage under any such settlement, other than one in the form of a pension arrangement (within the meaning of section 25D below).

Similar powers exist upon the dissolution of a civil partnership under the Civil Partnership Act 2004, Schedule 5, Paragraph 7, which enable the court to make property adjustment orders varying a 'relevant settlement', meaning "a settlement made, during its subsistence or in anticipation of its formation, on the civil partners including one made by will or codicil but not including one in the form of a pension arrangement".[21]

3.2 What is an ante- or post-nuptial settlement?

The English court has applied a broad interpretation to the meaning of the word 'settlement' in the Matrimonial Causes Act 1973 which, in addition to express trusts, includes a variety of mechanisms put in place for the financial provision of the spouses, such as agreements to provide periodic payments to a spouse,[22] life insurance policies,[23] a power of appointment over trust property[24] and tenancy arrangements over trust property.[25]

In approaching the question of what is an ante- or post-nuptial settlement, the court has been concerned less with notions of proprietary rights and more with notions of equality and the desire to do justice between the parties. In this

---

21   Civil Partnership Act 2004, Schedule 5 para 7(3).
22   *Worsley v Worsley* [1869] LR1 P&D 648.
23   *Lort-Williams v Lort-Williams* [1951] 2 All ER 241.
24   *Compton (Marquis of Northampton) v Compton* [1960] 3WLR 476.
25   *N v N* [2006] 1FLR 856.

respect, the approach of the Family Division to trusts and trust law may at times seem to be at variance with the approach of the Chancery Division to similar questions. In order to be classified as 'nuptial', the settlement must make provisions for the husband and wife in their characters as spouses, or for the children of the family. A nuptial settlement is capable of variation whether it was made before or during the marriage; it may even be made after the commencement of divorce proceedings and still be classified as a nuptial settlement if it makes provisions for the spouses or their children.[26] It need not be made by the spouses themselves: a settlement made by a close relative, such as the husband's father, naming his son, the son's wife and their children as beneficiaries, was held by the court to be a nuptial settlement capable of variation.[27] In *Melvill*, Lord Justice Greer was of the view that "you cannot have a settlement after a marriage which has not some relation to marriage if it settles property on one of the parties to the marriage, and still more if it settles property on the children of the marriage".

Although some authorities seem to indicate that it is sufficient if the settlement is made on "both or either of the parties to a marriage",[28] it is suggested that if the settlement pre-dates the marriage and does not make express provisions for spouses (eg, including them in the class of beneficiaries or having an express power to add them), it would be far more difficult to characterise it as a nuptial settlement rather than a settlement created during the marriage or one which makes provisions for both spouses or the children of the family.[29]

However, family law cases being heavily fact-specific, each case will be decided according to its specific circumstances and merits. Once the court considers a settlement to be nuptial in nature, that status is difficult to lose. In *Charalambous v Charalambous*,[30] the Court of Appeal considered whether a trust settled by the husband's mother during the parties' marriage had lost its nuptial character when both of the spouses were excluded as beneficiaries, leaving their children in the beneficial class with themselves as protectors. The Court of Appeal considered that the settlement must have a nuptial character at the time of the order, and was of the view that there may be circumstances in which a settlement previously nuptial in character would lose that character due to the conduct of the parties. However, in *Charalambous* the settlement was said to have retained its character by the spouses' role as joint protectors and their ability to influence distributions and to be added back to the class of beneficiaries. The fact that the husband had actually benefited from the trust

---

26   *Melvill v Melvill* [1930] P159.
27   See, for example, *E v E*, below.
28   *Brooks v Brooks* [1995] 3 All ER 257.
29   For an example of a settlement created prior to marriage but held not to be a nuptial settlement for the purposes of the Matrimonial Causes Act 1973, see *Hargreaves v Hargreaves* [1926] P42.
30   [2004] EWCA Civ 1030.

even after his exclusion also supported that conclusion. This was also the result in *Charman*, where the husband's argument that the settlement was 'dynastic' in nature and intended to benefit not the spouses, but future generations similarly failed.

4. Variation of settlements

While the powers of the English court are wide-ranging and, in principle, extend beyond the territorial jurisdiction of that court, the court will not ordinarily make orders which it did not have the power to enforce or supervise. Thus, orders seeking to vary foreign settlements are usually made in circumstances where the property subject to the settlement is situated in England or Wales, or where the trustees have submitted to the jurisdiction of the English court. The former proposition is illustrated by the 1990 case of *E v E*,[31] where the husband's father purchased a London property which was to serve as the matrimonial home of the husband and the wife. The property was owned by a Panamanian company, the shares of which the father settled onto an offshore trust. The husband, the wife and their children were discretionary beneficiaries of the trust, with the father serving as protector and reserving the power to approve or veto distributions. The father – a strong patriarchal figure and a successful businessman – employed members of the family (including his son, the husband) in the family business and exercised tight financial control over them. When the relationship between the husband and wife broke down and she left with another man, the father expressed his strong disapproval of her conduct and made it clear that he did not wish her to benefit from the trust. The English court, upon hearing the wife's application for financial provision, held the trust to be a post-nuptial settlement and made an order varying its terms. The trustee, who participated in the proceedings and had thus submitted to the jurisdiction of the court, was directed to make an outright distribution of a specified sum to the wife, and the court granted the wife a life interest in part of the fund with the remainder to the children of the family. Notwithstanding that the trust was governed by the law of another jurisdiction and that neither the trustee nor the protector was resident in England, the court proceeded to remove and replace both the trustee and the protector on the grounds that it was in the best interests of the children that it should do so.

Similarly, in *C v C*[32] the court considered an application to vary a Cayman settlement made by the husband two years prior to separation, into which he transferred the shares of an English company. The Cayman trustee did not submit to the jurisdiction and was not represented at the hearing, but it wrote a letter to the court stating that the Cayman court was unlikely to allow the

---

31   [1990] 2 FLR 233.
32   [2003] EWHC 1222 (Fam).

recognition and enforcement of a foreign judgment varying a trust governed by Cayman law. The court considered that it had jurisdiction to vary the settlement, and that it had adequate powers to enforce any such order, especially where the trust assets (or some of them) were situated within the jurisdiction. The wife was insistent that she should be entitled to receive company shares rather than cash, in light of her contribution to the success of the company and the likelihood that the shares would increase in value. Her argument prevailed and the trust was varied to award the wife a shareholding of approximately one-third of the shares previously held by the trust.

More recently, in *Mubarak v Mubarak*,[33] the English court had made a number of orders granting the wife financial provisions in divorce proceedings. The husband flouted the court orders for a number of years and declined to transfer assets to the wife as directed by the court. After seven years of proceedings and £4 million in costs, the wife applied to the court under Section 24(1)(c) of the Matrimonial Causes Act 1973 to vary a settlement governed by Jersey law and grant her an absolute interest in £7.6 million out of the trust fund, in satisfaction of the debt owed to her by the husband. The settlement, known as the IMK Trust, had been made by the husband and wife as settlors in 1980 and it named the husband, the wife, their children and unborn issue as the discretionary beneficiaries. The trust fund included the shares in a Bermudan company, which held the husband's business assets. The husband, who had a power to remove and exclude beneficiaries, had removed and excluded the wife in 1998 so the trustee could not make distributions to her. The adult children of the family, as beneficiaries, were supportive of their mother's application. In view of his history of non-compliance with court orders, the court required that the husband, as a precondition of his further participation in the English proceedings, write a letter to the trustee irrevocably instructing the trustee to comply with, and give effect to, any orders of the English court. The husband ultimately did so; and while the trustee neither participated in the proceedings nor submitted to the jurisdiction of the English court, the court made an order varying the trustee and requiring the trustee to transfer the sum of £7.6 million to the wife.

The trustee, on receiving notice of the outcome, applied to the Royal Court of Jersey for directions on whether to comply with the order of the English court. The Jersey court held that it had no jurisdiction to direct the trustee to exercise powers other than those conferred on it by the trust deed, as such an order would amount to a variation of the trust, which would ordinarily require the consent of all adult beneficiaries with full legal capacity. However, the court could sanction an 'alteration', which is a change in the terms of the trust achieved through an exercise of the powers already contained in the trust deed.

---

33   [2009] 1 FLR 664; [2008] JLR 250.

In the present instance, the Jersey court could not authorise the trustee to comply with the order of the English court, as the reinstatement of the wife as a beneficiary after her exclusion would amount to an impermissible variation. However, the court considered that the support of the adult children and the letter of the husband to the trustee directing it to comply with any order of the English court amounted to the requisite consent to a variation, and the Jersey court therefore sanctioned a variation on behalf of the minor and unborn beneficiaries, thereby achieving the result contemplated by the English court, albeit by a circuitous, rather than direct, route.

The Hague Convention on the Law Applicable to Trusts and their Recognition, incorporated into English law by the Recognition of Trusts Act 1987, would appear to be of no assistance even when the trust is governed by foreign law. In *Charalambous*, the Court of Appeal considered the effect of an exclusive jurisdiction clause in a trust deed and upheld the decision of the High Court that such a clause cannot oust the jurisdiction of the English Family Division to make financial provisions under Section 24 of the Matrimonial Causes Act 1973. This was on the grounds that the power to vary the settlement derives not from the settlement itself, but from domestic legislation; though the court acknowledged that an additional legal action may be necessary in the trustee's own jurisdiction to enforce or give effect to the order. In that case, the court observed that in previous cases the Royal Court of Jersey had been prepared, as a matter of comity, to give effect to English court orders.

5.   Settlement funds as a resource: orders against the parties

As discussed above, and notwithstanding the principles of comity, the English court is reluctant to make orders in circumstances where it would be difficult to oversee enforcement. However, where there is a trust fund and a trustee whom the court believes would make a distribution to one of the parties in a 'rainy day' situation, the court has generally been willing to bring about that rainy day if doing so achieves a fair division of assets between husband and wife. An order for capital transfers which a party cannot comfortably meet without distributions from the trust may put that party in a state of need; and if that party is (or can become) a beneficiary of the trust, then there may be a compelling reason for the trustee to make that distribution, whether or not it would have made it but for the order. In *Brown v Brown*,[34] the majority of the divorcing parties' assets were held in offshore trusts set up with assets contributed by the wife's mother. The wife was a beneficiary of those trusts, but the husband was not. Every request for a distribution made by the wife during the marriage was acceded to by the trustee and the High Court therefore concluded that she was in effective control of the trust fund. She was ordered

---

34   [1989] 1 FLR 291 (CA).

to pay the husband a lump sum of £175,000, but she could only raise £60,000 without a distribution from the trusts. The wife appealed and at first refused to make the payment to the husband; but by the time the appeal was heard, full payment had been made. The Court of Appeal upheld the decision of the High Court that the wife had immediate access to the funds; the court's 'judicious encouragement' of the wife to obtain a distribution yielded the appropriate result.

This approach was again applied and confirmed by the Court of Appeal in *Thomas v Thomas*,[35] where Mr Justice Glidewell issued the following guidelines (at p 678):

   (a) *Where a husband can only raise further capital, or additional income, as the result of a decision made at the discretion of trustees, the Court should not put improper pressure on the trustees to exercise that discretion for the benefit of the wife.*

   (b) *The Court should not, however, be 'misled by appearances'; it should 'look at the reality of the situation'.*

   (c) *If on the balance of probability, the evidence shows that, if trustees exercised their discretion to release more capital or income to a husband, the interests of the trust or of other beneficiaries would not be appreciably damaged, the Court can assume that a genuine request for the exercise of such discretion would probably be met by a favourable response. In that situation if the Court decides that it would be reasonable for a husband to seek to persuade trustees to release more capital or income to him to enable him to make proper financial provision for his children and his former wife, the Court would not in so deciding to be putting improper pressure on the trustee.*

In both *Mubarak* and *Charman*, the court made an order against the husband personally on the basis that the trust fund was a resource available to him. In *Mubarak*, the order varying the trust was made only after the husband failed to discharge the personal orders made against him.

In considering the particular circumstances of the parties, the court may invite representations from the trustee. It did so in *PJC v ADC*,[36] where the court adjourned the proceedings and issued an order inviting the trustees of a trust settled by the husband's father to intervene and attend the hearing and giving permission for them to file a statement. The trustees obliged and assisted the court by confirming that, contrary to the husband's belief, they would be willing to consider a distribution to help him meet his obligations towards the wife if the trust fund were considered to be a resource available to him. The analysis of the Family Division and its approach to the construction of trust and interests thereunder differ in significant respects from the traditional approach

---

35   [1995] 2 FLR 668 (CA).
36   [2009] EWHC 1491 (Fam).

of chancery practitioners, and create potential uncertainty for trustees and beneficiaries alike. The courts' notions of fairness as between the spouses may not accord with those of the trustees; and while the Chancery Division judges are usually reluctant to exercise the fiduciaries' discretion for them, which they will do only in extreme and specific cases, the judges of the Family Division have been much more willing to do so in matrimonial proceedings.

In *Ipekci v McConnell*,[37] the court noted with approval that in the Hong Kong case of *KEWS v NCHC*[38] the chief justice of Hong Kong rejected the concept of 'judicious encouragement' and considered it should be abandoned in cases of this kind. The judge agreed but, as noted above, made a finding of fact that the wife was "solely and beneficially entitled to the trust assets", and that on the balance of probabilities the trustees would make funds available to her if necessary to satisfy an order made against her.

Most commonwealth jurisdictions have legislation designed to vary trusts and settlements, which includes a prerequisite of consent on the part of all the adult beneficiaries with full legal capacity; the courts' variation powers may be exercised only to approve a variation on behalf of beneficiaries lacking capacity, and cannot be exercised to compel a dissenting beneficiary to consent to the variation. Not so in the Family Division, which can vary settlements without hearing representations or receiving consents from the beneficiaries. The dichotomy between the courts' powers under trust law and under matrimonial legislation is stark; yet the latter may have a far-reaching impact on the former. The creation of a 'rainy day' in divorce proceedings, by bringing 'judicious encouragement' to bear on one of the parties, often results in changed circumstances for the beneficiary spouse. Arguably, the trustee of a discretionary trust would have a duty to consider discharging the beneficiary's debt,[39] and failure to consider making a distribution to alleviate the hardship may amount to a breach of fiduciary duty. Thus, the tension between the fairness test in the Family Division and the stricter concept of equitable ownership in the Chancery Division may result in different outcomes and create a degree of uncertainty for fiduciaries and beneficiaries for the foreseeable future.

6.   An alternative strand of attack: sham trusts

An alternative way to bring the trust funds into the marital pot is to mount an attack on the validity of the trust on the grounds of sham. The leading case on sham remains *Snook v London and West Riding Investments*,[40] where Mr Justice Diplock described the concept of sham as "acts done or documents executed by

---

37   *Supra*, fn 15.
38   [2013]2 HKLRD 314, [2013] 16HKCFAR 1 at [53].
39   Though the reduction of a debt may not always amount to a 'benefit': *In Re Esteem Settlement* [2001] JLR 7, and more recently, *DG v WM* [2009] JRC 140.
40   [1967] 2QB 786 (CA).

the parties to the 'sham' which are intended by them to give to third parties or to the court the appearance of creating between the parties legal rights and obligations different from the actual legal rights and obligations (if any) which the parties intend to create".

He added that for the trust to be a sham, all of the parties to the deed must have common intention to mislead. The common intention test has been reaffirmed in subsequent decisions,[41] with the result that where there is a professional or corporate trustee, it would be difficult to establish that the trustee shared the settlor's intention to mislead.

In *Hitch v Stone (Inspector of Taxes)*,[42] Lady Justice Arden proposed a checklist against which the court should consider whether the trust in question was a sham of a genuine settlement. This included the following:

- The court should consider any external evidence, such as external corroborating evidence of the parties' conduct and their explanation of their intentions;
- The court should also consider whether the parties in fact intended to create different rights and obligations from those appearing on the face of the document;
- The fact that an arrangement appears uncommercial or artificial does not render it a sham;
- It is the original intention that matters: the fact that the parties may have subsequently departed from their original intention does not mean that they originally intended to mislead; and
- In order to be a sham, there must be a common intention to mislead or give a false impression.

In the Family Division, the sham doctrine was considered in *A v A*,[43] where the wife mounted an attack on two discretionary trusts settled by the husband's brother and his parents. The husband and the wife had met in 1982 and married in 1984, when the husband's first divorce had become final, but while he was still involved in financial provision proceedings with his first wife. The trusts were settled in November 1984, when those proceedings were still afoot, and the trust funds consisted of shares in three family companies. The second marriage broke down in 2001 and the financial proceedings took a very long time to conclude. The second wife argued that the two trusts were a sham and were settled because the husband wanted to present himself as a minority shareholder in his dispute with his first wife. The second wife maintained that although the beneficial class consisted of the descendants of the husband's

---

41   Notably in *In Re Esteem Settlement* [2003] JLR 188 and in *Shalson v Russo* [2003] EWHC 1637 (Ch).
42   [2001] STC 214.
43   [2007] EWHC 99 (Fam).

parents (the husband himself, his childless brother and his children from the first marriage), the husband was "the *de facto* controller and beneficiary".

Mr Justice Munby considered and applied the authorities and noted that the court must be more cautious in its approach where third-party interests may be affected, although he also commented that "it may be easier to 'pierce the corporate veil' in the context of a small family company than in some larger or more purely commercial context".

Applying the authority in *Shalson v Russo*,[44] the judge held that a trust which is not initially a sham cannot subsequently become a sham: once the trust is properly constituted, it cannot lose its character as trust property save in accordance with the terms of the trust itself. Any other application of the trust property would necessarily be a breach of trust. On the other hand, the court considered that a trust which begins its life as a sham may subsequently lose that character and become a genuine trust – for example, if a subsequent trustee accepts office in good faith and administers the trust on the footing that it is a genuine structure. In the circumstances of that particular case, the judge found that there was no common intention to mislead and the trusts were not a sham.

7. *Prest v Petrodel*: piercing the corporate veil

In *Prest v Petrodel Resources Ltd*[45] the Supreme Court considered whether, in divorce proceedings, properties owned by companies of which the husband was the controlling director could be sold or transferred to his wife as part of the divorce settlement. The wife argued that the companies, which were held in trusts settled by the husband's father and his brother, were the husband's alter ego, and that the corporate veil should be pierced to attribute the companies' assets to the husband (thus making them assets available for division in the divorce proceedings).

The court held that the corporate veil may be pierced only in circumstances where the company is used to evade its controller's legal obligations or in a case of fraud, and then only to the extent that the controller has benefited from his fraud or evasion of obligations. However, in order to achieve fairness between the husband and the wife, in relation to the company which held the former matrimonial home the court held that the transfer of that property to the company, without valuable consideration, created a resulting trust for the husband. This decision has been widely criticised (since most transfers into trust do not involve the payment of consideration), but it demonstrates that the courts will enquire more deeply into corporate structures and the purchase of assets – in particular, where an asset has been transferred to the company for a nominal value or where the individual has provided the company with the moneys to purchase the asset.

---

44   *Op cit* (at note 39).
45   [2013] UKSC 34.

8. Recognition and enforcement of foreign judgments

Obtaining an order which alters the beneficial interests in a settlement is rarely the end of the story when the proper law of the trust is not English law or when the trustee and the assets are in another jurisdiction. In such cases, it is often necessary for a foreign court to give recognition to, and/or enforce, a judgment of the Family Division, failing which the successful applicant would need to issue fresh proceedings in that jurisdiction. Recognition and enforcement of English judgments in other jurisdictions would depend on whether the relevant parties were properly served with the proceedings or alternatively submitted to the jurisdiction of the court. The question is more relevant where the judgment seeks to vary a foreign trust. The trustee may be properly served with English proceedings if he or she is resident or present (even if only temporarily) in the jurisdiction or, in the case of a company, has a registered office there. Alternatively, if the trustee submits to the jurisdiction by returning the relevant acknowledgement of service form without contesting the jurisdiction of the court, he or she is deemed to have submitted (although he or she may raise arguments of *forum non conveniens* – that is, that the English court is not the appropriate forum for the dispute – which are beyond the scope of this chapter).

When a person is properly served in, or submits to, the jurisdiction of the English court in proceedings, that court has jurisdiction over the defendant/respondent. Under common law, the court of another jurisdiction may enforce the order of the English court if it too has jurisdiction over the defendant/respondent and:

- the judgment is final and conclusive;
- the judgment is for a fixed sum of money; and
- the judgment is not liable to be set aside by the second court on the grounds that it was obtained by fraud or is against the rule of natural justice, or on the grounds of public policy.

Historically, judgments which did not fall into the above categories could not be enforced by the courts of another jurisdiction and the successful applicant (or plaintiff) would have to bring fresh proceedings in the country in which the assets were to be found, for example, in order to enforce the judgment. In trust cases, where judgment is often declaratory in nature, enforcement was thus the exception rather than the norm. Recent cases in several jurisdictions have altered that position somewhat and in future the enforcement of trust judgments (including those of the Family Division) may prove easier.

In the Isle of Man case of *Pattni v Ali*[46] the Privy Council held that a decision of the Court of Kenya ordering the transfer of shares in an Isle of Man company

---

46   [2007] 2 AC 85.

should be recognised by the courts of the Isle of Man, despite being an order for specific performance of an agreement reached by the parties rather than a money judgment. The Grand Court of the Cayman Islands applied this decision in *Miller v Gianne*[47] and *Bandone Sdn Bhd v Sol Properties Inc*,[48] where it was held that: "there had been a change to the common law rule against the enforcement and recognition of foreign non-money *in personam* judgments and it had been accompanied by judicial discretion to ensure that it did not jeopardise the integrity of the local judicial system. The court should have regard to general considerations of fairness and ensure that domestic law was not extended to suit foreign litigants, when deciding whether or not to enforce non-money judgments."

The same result was achieved in the Jersey case of *Brunei Investment Agency v Fidelis*.[49] It therefore seems that, as in other areas of legal life, the tide is turning in favour of international and cross-border recognition and cooperation. The discretion retained by the courts of these offshore jurisdictions should give fiduciaries and beneficiaries a measure of comfort: the ability to rely on *res judicata* and avoid the need for further protracted and expensive proceedings will be welcomed, while the ability of the foreign courts to ensure that only appropriate cases are enforced should provide assurance that recognition will be granted only in appropriate cases.

9.   Conclusion

As the matrimonial courts continue to react to the increasing globalisation of wealth and the mobility of families, they will likely continue to develop this area of the law. Political changes, such as the impact of Brexit on domestic legislation, may also play a part in these changes. For the time being, this area of the law remains in flux, and lawyers and their clients would be wise to review and update, from time to time, the structures they have in place to ensure they remain current and fit for purpose, and able to withstand the scrutiny of the family (as well as chancery) courts.

The author would like to acknowledge the assistance of Catrin Hughes in the preparation of this chapter.

---

47   [2007] CILR 18.
48   [2008] CILR 301.
49   [2008] JRC 152.

The trust protector: a mini-revolution in trust law

Alexander A Bove, Jr
Bove & Langa Law Firm

In a process that has taken the better part of two decades, the trust protector has finally become a term of art and a necessary consideration in trust planning. As flexible as we recognise the trust to be, the addition of a protector and the added flexibility it offers has effected a sort of mini-revolution in trust law and practice. This chapter will outline the reason for its attractiveness, while reviewing the responsibilities that attach to the position. It will consider the effect of the many powers that may be granted to the protector, the relationship between the protector and the trustee, and whether the protector should be regarded as a fiduciary. These and other relevant topics will assist readers and practitioners in deciding whether, when and to what extent to use this 'revolutionary' tool in a trust.

1. What is a protector and why has the concept become so popular?

The first trust protector statute appeared in Cook Islands law in 1989, then in US law much later (in 1997).[1] Until that time, there was no statutory law, very few cases and very little written on the subject, unless we consider the similarity of the role of trust adviser to trust protector.

Although a formal definition of 'protector' might be helpful, it would still leave numerous questions unanswered, as we shall see. In this regard, we can find formal definitions of 'protector' in the laws of a number of foreign jurisdictions, the earliest being that of the Cook Islands as noted above, which was followed in both time and substance by a number of other offshore jurisdictions, such as Belize and Nevis.[2] The law of Nevis, for instance, defines the 'protector' as follows: "'Protector' in relation to an international trust means a person who is the holder of a power which when invoked is capable of directing a trustee in matters relating to the trust and in respect of which matters the trustee has a discretion and includes a person who is the holder of a power of appointment or dismissal of trustees."[3]

---

1 Alaska Statutes Section 13.36. 370 (2003); Delaware Code Title 12 Section 3313 (2006); Idaho Code Section 15-7-501 (Michie 1999); South Dakota Codified Laws Sections 55-1B-1, 55-1B-7 (Michie 1997, 2005, 2006); Cook Islands International Trust Amendment Act, Section 3 (1989).

2 Belize Trust Act 1992, Part 3 Section 16; Nevis International Exempt Trust Ordinance 1994 (as amended 1995) Part 2 Section 10.

3 *Ibid* at Section 2(c).

As suggested, this definition is helpful to orient our analysis in the sense that it broadly describes the position as it relates to the trust and the trustee. A closer look at the question, however, would suggest that perhaps the definition could have been condensed to: "a party with powers over the trust, but who is not a trustee." And that is about the essence of it – or rather, the beginning of it.

In fact, a simple powerholder under a trust is not typically regarded as a trust protector. Clearly, if a settlor, under his or her trust, grants his or her spouse the power to allocate trust assets among their descendants, this is a power over the trust and the spouse is not a trustee; but it does not make the spouse a protector, as the spouse's power is a personal power. The modern usage of the term 'protector' refers to a party who is given powers that are specifically intended to facilitate the administration of the trust and the accomplishment of the purposes of the settlor in establishing the trust. Such powers may be narrow or broad. The power could be negative, such as a veto power over some proposed act by the trustee; or positive, such as the power to remove and replace trustees, to add beneficiaries, to amend the trust or even to terminate the trust – and all this without the need to petition a court and seek formal reformation of the trust. Furthermore, a protector's power can be personal (eg, where the protector is also a beneficiary) or it can be a position; and although a protector can have a power that is personal and another that is a position, the same power cannot be both. The potential addition of such a broad choice of powers has opened a new door to flexibility. It is easy to see how generations of practitioners who have been forced to follow tradition and draft trusts with only the accepted forms of flexibility (the removal of trustees or the inclusion of a power of appointment, and even then in limited cases) could get carried away with this new form of super-flexibility. While unlimited flexibility without court involvement may be attractive, it virtually reverses the original concept of a settlor who thoughtfully establishes a trust for specified classes of beneficiaries with specified terms and specified trustees. It is this nascent super-flexibility brought about by the addition of a protector – which seems, or at least promises, to allow us to deal with virtually every conceivable future circumstance (including the rectification of shortcomings in drafting) – that makes the position of protector increasingly attractive.

2. How old is the protector really?

While a number of commentators all too hastily attribute the popularity of the trust protector solely to the offshore asset protection trust in jurisdictions such as the Cook Islands or the Bahamas, this conclusion is less a question of fact than it is a lack of thorough research and thoughtful consideration of the position.[4]

---

4 See Alexander A Bove, Jr, *Trust Protectors – A Practice Manual With Forms* (Juris Publishing, 2014) (www.jurispub.com).

What may come as a surprise to many is the fact that the concept of trust protector, especially in the history of US law, is not new at all; at best, it is only the term that is new, as well as practitioners' recent 'discovery' of what actually is an old concept in trust law. As noted below, trust attorneys have been employing the concept of trust advisers for decades; but unlike the protector, it was more the role of the trust adviser than the name tag that was given formal recognition. It is appropriate to note at this point that, in this context, we are speaking of an adviser who is granted certain specific powers under the trust, such as directing the trustee with respect to investments, as opposed to an adviser who is merely designated as a resource that the trustee is requested to consult (without in any way causing the trustee to be bound by the results of such consultation) before the trustee exercises certain discretionary powers under the trust.[5] Thus, in earlier days it was not at all uncommon, for instance, for a settlor to name an adviser who had the power to direct and control all trust investments, or to remove and replace trustees.

Although the term 'adviser' is still customarily used where a power over only trust investments is granted, if the power extends beyond that, today that party is more likely to be called a 'protector'. So let's consider this revised definition: "A trust protector (which by definition includes a trust 'adviser') is a party who has overriding discretionary powers with respect to the trust but who is not a trustee." An adviser/protector may be given 'positive' powers, such as the ability to modify the trust or compel the trustee to act; or 'negative' powers, such as a veto power over changes in trust investments or over trust distributions. In this regard, the adviser with powers is in every respect the same as the protector we see today. In fact, at least one state has statutorily agreed with that conclusion, stating: "For purposes of this subsection [on trust advisers], the term 'advisor' includes a trust protector..."[6]

Over the years, hundreds of cases in the United States have dealt with trust advisers of one designation or another; and in the courts, if not in the practice of law and trust administration, the position has not been regarded as new or unusual. Many such cases are cited in the popular treatise by Scott[7] in an exhaustive and illuminating analysis of the position of adviser, examining the extent of powers that can be and have been granted to trust advisers. When one reflects on the perceived role of the protector and considers the analysis undertaken by Scott, it quickly becomes apparent that the term 'protector' could be substituted for the term 'adviser' wherever used in Scott's discussion, without exception.

It is difficult to determine exactly when the concept of trust adviser first

---

5   Cook Islands, International Trusts Amendment Act 1989, Part IV, Section 20, Nevis International Exempt Trust Ordinance 1994 Section 9(1); Belize Trusts Act 1992 Section 16(1).
6   Tennessee Code, Section 35-16-108(b) (2011).
7   Austin Scott & William Fratcher, *The Law of Trusts*, 4th edition, Section 185.

appeared, but the earliest US case I found was decided in 1823.[8] Later, between the end of the 19th century and the first half of the 20th century, numerous cases were heard reflecting the increasing use of the trust adviser, primarily with respect to control over trust investments; but the issues were by no means confined to that and nor were they confined to the use of a single adviser. In a 1946 case, for instance, the settlor appointed a committee of advisers (perhaps one of the first anywhere to utilise a committee), which was given the power to remove and replace trustees and to accelerate principal distributions on certain conditions.[9] These are, in fact, very typical of powers given to today's trust protector.

The concept became far more common in the second half of the 20th century, as reflected in a larger number of cases dealing with various aspects of the role. Furthermore, during that period a number of very informative law review and journal articles began to appear;[10] but, oddly, the idea never really attracted serious widespread professional notice until the last two decades or so, when it took the title of protector. Despite the name tag and the date on the tag, however, there should be no question that we are dealing with the very same personage, generally governed by the very same legal principles and concepts.

3.   The protector and the asset protection trust

For better or for worse, the recent surge in popularity of the protector has been fuelled to a great extent by the equally fast-growing popularity of the offshore asset protection trust. While asset protection trusts, as such – like the position of protector – are not new, it is safe to say that their use has grown exponentially over the past 10 to 15 years. Since the typical asset protection trust is one where the settlor gives up control to prevent creditors from exercising such control through a court order, the concept of the protector seems to offer the settlor the opportunity to have it both ways. That is, although the settlor would have no apparent control over the trust, he or she could have indirect (if not direct) control over the protector, who in turn could control the trust. Thus, assuming that the settlor is comfortable with the selection of the protector, the more powers given to the protector the more comfortable the settlor will feel in establishing and funding an irrevocable trust with a foreign trustee in a strange jurisdiction on the other side of the world. Technically – although absolutely not recommended – the protector could be a spouse or child of the settlor, or a close trusted friend or in aggressive cases – but never recommended – even the settlor. Selecting the settlor, a spouse or children as protector generally indicates a lack of understanding of the role, a lack of or disregard for any asset protection

---

8   *Howard v Ducane*, 1 Turn & R 81 (1823).
9   *Jewett v Brown*, 65 NE 2d 307 (MA 1946).
10   See, for example, "Trust Advisors", 78 *Harvard Law Review* 1230 (1965); "Directory Trusts and the Exculpatory Clause", 65 *Columbia Law Review* 138 (1965).

concerns (as noted below), a lack of a good adviser or just a devil-may-care approach. In any event, unsurprisingly, as practitioners and settlors have become more attracted to and intrigued by this 'newly discovered' key to flexibility, the concept is now finding its way into domestic trusts and legislation, as referenced above.

Further to the selection of a protector, where asset protection issues of US settlors are concerned, one of the more serious risks that is taken by practitioners is to allow the settlor to name a domestic protector – for example, a US person – or worse, to allow the settlor himself or herself to serve as protector. Where the protector has extensive powers, this could be fatal for asset protection purposes. A real-life illustration of this is the so-called *Anderson* case,[11] where the US settlors established and funded an offshore asset protection trust, naming themselves (incredibly) as co-trustees and (equally incredibly) as co-protectors of that trust, and retaining considerable powers in each capacity. Charges were brought against them by the US Federal Trade Commission in connection with an allegedly fraudulent scheme, and a US district court judge issued a temporary restraining order on the Andersons. When ordered by the judge to repatriate the offshore trust funds, which, as trustees, the Andersons had the power to do, the Andersons immediately sent notice to the offshore trustee requesting the funds pursuant to the court order. Such a notice typically triggers the anti-duress clause commonly found in asset protection trusts; this notice not only invoked the anti-duress clause, but also caused the Andersons to be automatically removed as trustees. Thus, when the court asked again that the funds be repatriated, the Andersons responded that they were unable to do so, since they had been removed as trustees. Subsequently, the court discovered they were also co-protectors of the trust (thereby having the power to comply with the court's order); and when the Andersons failed to comply with the reiterated court order, they were jailed for contempt of court.

Thus, if asset protection is an objective of the trust, it is generally a bad idea to name a domestic protector and a worse idea to allow the settlor to be the protector, since both are subject to local court orders and possible contempt charges for failing to comply with such orders. An exception to this may lie where the protector (preferably someone other than the settlor) is given only negative (veto) powers. In that event there could be no positive acts of the protector, the performance of which may be ordered by the court. At the same time, however, restricting the protector to negative powers would seriously limit the value of having the protector at all, so it is not a good alternative.

4.   Using a protector in domestic trusts

By 'domestic trusts', I refer to trusts that are established in and subject to the

---

11   *Federal Trade Commission v Affordable Media, LLC*, 179 F 3d 1228 (1999).

laws of the jurisdiction of the settlor's domicile (eg, a UK trust established by a person domiciled in the United Kingdom). Thus, an offshore trust is regarded as one established in a jurisdiction other than that of the domicile of the settlor (eg, a Liechtenstein trust established by a person domiciled in Spain). Further, certain jurisdictions are understood to be included when a practitioner or commentator refers to 'offshore trusts', because of their attraction for asset protection purposes. They are, generally, the Cook Islands, Liechtenstein, Gibraltar, the Isle of Man, the Bahamas and a few others. Therefore, while a trust established in the United Kingdom by a person domiciled in the United States is certainly an offshore trust, it is definitely not intended to be included in the context of the term, as it would offer no asset protection at all unless established in one of the 15 states that recognise self-settled asset protection trusts.[12]

As observed throughout this discussion, it is to some extent inappropriate to credit offshore trusts with the idea of the trust protector, given that the protector is nothing more than a trust adviser with a different name – although admittedly, often given greater powers than the traditional trust adviser. Perhaps it is the latter feature that is the cause of the credit, and justifiably so. The traditional trust adviser is typically given powers over trust investments and nothing more, while the trust protector is often given powers over almost everything except trust investments. Although I do not advocate unlimited powers for the protector, I believe that this extension of powers is what can make the protector invaluable in trusts other than asset protection trusts and for domestic trusts in particular. By this I mean such trusts as life insurance trusts, special needs trusts,[13] purpose trusts,[14] trusts which are to hold family business interests, dynasty trusts, voting trusts and any other type of trust where there may be special administrative concerns, likely changes in circumstances or near-total uncertainty of both, such as with a dynasty trust. In these cases, asset protection by the settlor is generally not the prime issue, so the selection of a protector who is outside the jurisdiction of the courts of the settlor's domicile is not an issue. Asset protection may still be provided for trust assets under the normal spendthrift rules.

This is not necessarily to say that a protector should be used in every trust, since the circumstances of many are reasonably predictable. For instance, in the typical family with a typical estate plan, a protector may not be needed. Where assets are held for a surviving spouse and then distributed outright to children or even grandchildren on the spouse's death, a protector is usually not provided for in the trust and in most instances a protector may not be necessary. But in any of the other trusts noted above, the very objectives, terms and duration of

---

12   www.OSHINS.com|IMAGES|DAPT_RANKINGS.
13   Thomas D Begley, Jr and Angela E Canellos, *Special Needs Trusts* (Aspen Publishers, 2008).
14   Alexander A Bove, Jr, "The Purpose of Purpose Trusts", *Probate & Property*, Volume 18 No 3 (May/June 2004).

the trust make it advisable to consider a protector, or at least a 'springing' protector as discussed in section 14 below. This provides the settlor and the trustee with a mechanism to deal with changes in circumstances, changes in the law or trust disputes, without repeated petitions to the courts.

Where a protector is used in a domestic trust, particular attention should be given to the local tax implications. For example, if the settlor is a US person and a US protector is chosen, advisers must be mindful of the potential income, gift and estate tax ramifications, depending on the choice of protector. (See section 12 for a brief discussion of the tax implications.)

5. What powers should be given to the protector?

As observed above, there is a difficult-to-resist temptation to give the protector as many powers as possible to provide for the ability to contend with any future changes in circumstances, the law or the beneficiaries.[15] It is this perceived benefit, however, that can cause us casually to include powers that do little more than produce conflicts between the protector and the trustee which would result in costly legal disputes, unnecessary tax exposure, the possible deletion of beneficiaries that may have been important to the settlor and even a distortion of – or, worse, a diversion from – the original trust purposes. Such an approach can therefore be dangerous, if not reckless, and just the opposite approach is often better.

That is, having in mind the purposes of the trust and using history as a guide, the settlor and the professional should attempt reasonably to anticipate the powers that would likely assist in carrying out the trust purposes which would be better held in the hands of someone other than the trustee or the beneficiaries. For instance, a very common power given to protectors is the power to remove and replace trustees. To give this power to one or more beneficiaries is not usually conducive to an objective evaluation of whether a trustee should or should not be removed, since many beneficiaries would hasten to remove a trustee who did not accommodate their every wish, or at least accede to what the protector/beneficiaries decided were 'reasonable' requests. Further, there could be serious US tax ramifications where a beneficiary has such a power.[16] Similarly, the power to add or delete beneficiaries would obviously be best if held by a party outside the trust, as would the power to amend the dispositive provisions of a trust (with the caveats observed in the tax discussion below). On the other hand, the power to amend the trust's administrative provisions could be held by either the trustee or a protector.

While there is no standard set of powers to be given to the protector,

---

15   For an extensive list of possible powers, some of them admittedly undesirable, see Antony Duckworth, "Protector – Fish or Fowl?", *Journal of International Trust and Corporate Planning*, Volume 4 No 3, (December 1995).
16   Treasury Regulations Section 20.2041-1 and discussion below.

depending upon the wishes of the settlor and the aggressiveness of the attorney, the following is a list of powers commonly seen in whole or in part in trusts which utilise a protector (note that not infrequently, only a few such powers may be included – most commonly the power to remove and replace trustees, the power to veto distributions, and to direct or advise on investments):[17]

- remove, add, and replace trustees;
- veto or direct trust distributions;
- add or delete beneficiaries;
- change the situs (legal location) and governing law of the trust;
- veto or direct investment decisions;
- consent to the exercise of a power of appointment;
- determine whether an event of duress has occurred;
- amend the trust as to administrative provisions;
- amend the trust as to dispositive provisions;
- approve trustee accounts;
- terminate the trust; and
- mediate disputes between the beneficiaries and the trustee.

While it is apparent that the protector cannot be given a power to further an illegal purpose, it may not always be so apparent when public policy questions arise. For instance, could the protector be given the power to prevent anyone, including a beneficiary, from seeing a copy of the trust? Or to exculpate a trustee for failure to account? Or the power to deny a beneficiary the right to an accounting? Clearly, such powers offend the very premise of a trust and would likely be struck down.[18]

As observed, although it is a great temptation to include extensive protector powers in order to be able to deal with future problems and unforeseeable circumstances, it may become a question of whether what we are really looking for is a 'substituted settlor', giving the protector the collective power completely to redraft the trust at any time and from time to time. Such a result challenges the very concept of the role of the settlor, if not the trust and the trustee as well. One respected author stated, for instance: "The assent of the protector has the effect of making the trustees not responsible for their actions. This turns the figure of the trustee upside down and makes him in substance an agent."[19]

Thus, when deciding on the powers to be given the protector, the most serious consideration should be given to the realistic purposes of the trust and a reasonable selection of classes of beneficiaries, and these should be reflected in the language specifying the protector's powers, with restrictions or stated

---

17   This is by no means an exhaustive list or a recommended schedule of powers. In fact, an uninformed use of some of these powers can lead to undesirable legal and tax ramifications as discussed below.
18   Duckworth, *op cit* (note 17), at 137.
19   Marizio Lupoi, *Trusts, A Comparative Study* (Cambridge University Press, 2000), at 258.

wishes, if necessary, designed to keep the exercise of the powers within the desired goals of the settlor. Otherwise, the settlor could run the risk that his or her assets could effectively end up in someone else's (ie, the protector's) trust.

6. What is the relationship between the protector and the trustee?

To a great extent, the answer to this question (the relationship of the protector with the trustee) depends upon whether the protector is deemed to be a fiduciary, a critical issue and one discussed in greater detail below. This is because if and to the extent that the protector is not a fiduciary – or, to put it more precisely, if the power in question held by the protector is a personal power rather than a fiduciary power – the trustee's position in relation to the protector will be virtually reversed. That is, an individual holding a personal power cannot be forced to exercise it and in fact need not even consider whether to exercise it. And that individual does exercise such a power, he or she may do so on a whim or even for a spiteful or malicious reason, so long as no fraud is committed on the power.[20] Therefore, a trustee, who must in some way consider or react to a personal power, is under no duty to look behind the protector's exercise (or non-exercise), or to review the motives for or reasonableness of its exercise, so long as the terms governing the exercise have been satisfied.[21]

On the other hand, if the protector's powers are fiduciary in whole or in part, which is much more likely the case, then the trustee is in a far more delicate and responsible position, and the delicacy of the position will be increased where the applicable trust provision contains an exculpatory clause (as it often does), such as words to the effect that: "The trustee shall not be held liable for acting or for not acting in following the directions of the protector pursuant to the powers given the protector hereunder." Even a brief reflection on the import of such a provision quickly reveals how troublesome and misleading such language can be in a fiduciary setting.

Would one assume from this statement, for instance, that a trustee can freely follow a protector's direction which appears patently improper with respect to the trust purposes, although technically within the protector's powers? And is a trustee exculpated if he or she proposes an improper act which is carried out only because the act was given the required consent of the protector? In a case illustrating the point (that one fiduciary may be responsible for the actions or inactions of another), an individual co-trustee had veto power over investments, and the corporate co-trustee was held liable for not seeking court instructions where the individual co-trustee repeatedly refused to consent to a

---

20   Geraint Thomas, *Thomas on Powers*, 1st edition (Sweet & Maxwell, 1998); *Pitman v Pitman*, 50 NE 2d 69 (MA 1943).
21   Restatement of The Law (Second) of Property Section 18.2 (1986).

sale of securities as proposed by the corporate trustee, resulting in a loss of nearly all the trust assets.[22] But compare this with:

- a Georgia (US) statute providing that where a trust gives an adviser the authority over trust investments, the trustee shall be exonerated from responsibility for any losses resulting from following the adviser's instructions;[23] and
- a British Virgin Islands statute providing that a trust may contain provisions requiring the trustee to obtain the consent of a person, "and if so provided in the instrument the trustees shall not be liable for any loss caused by their actions if the previous consent was given".[24]

Clearly, the purpose of such legislation is to give recognition to the settlor's choice of adviser and relieve the trustee of having to second guess every investment or other decision made by the adviser. Whether statutes of this sort will exculpate a trustee who carries out a patently improper investment, distribution or other act, however, remains to be seen. The Georgia statute, for instance, makes an exception if the trustee acts with "reckless indifference" to the interests of the beneficiaries.[25]

The concept of a trust adviser to direct trust investments has become so widespread and accepted that a considerable number of US states have adopted a statute similar to that of Georgia exculpating a trustee for following the directions of a trust investment adviser.[26] Interestingly, these statutes generally relate quite specifically to investments; but is there any reason that the same standard of care should not be extended to any power of direction given to an adviser? Would it be reasonable to assume, for example, that an adviser's power to remove and replace trustees or to add and delete beneficiaries would provide the same exculpatory relief for a trustee who simply acceded to these acts, even though highly questionable? If so, the trustee could simply stand by while the adviser (or protector) exercised bad judgement, and neither would have any liability.

In fact, it is not at all so clear that a trustee's duties to the trust may be so easily eliminated. An absolute exculpation, as suggested in some statutory language relating to trustees' liability in following the direction of a protector or adviser,[27] regardless of the circumstances, would be repugnant to the very concept of a trust and would undoubtedly be against public policy. One commentary appropriately stated: "Exculpatory clauses should be held against public policy if they allow the liability to fall somewhere between the trustee

---

22   *In re Cross*, 172 A 212 (NJ 1934), (reversed on other grounds) 176 A 101 (NJ 1935). See also Scott, *op cit* (note 2), Section 185, at 574.
23   Georgia Code, Section 53-12-194(c) (1991).
24   British Virgin Islands, Trustee (Amendment) Act, Section 86(1) (1993).
25   Georgia Code, Section 53-12-194(a) (1991).
26   Scott, *op cit* (note 2), at Section 185, note 20.
27   See, for example, Codified Laws, Chapter 55, Section 55-1B-2 (1997, 2006).

and the holder of the power [ie, the adviser or protector], and leave the beneficiary without any remedy for mismanagement of the estate."[28]

Thus, there has to be some fundamental duty of the trustee to see that the adviser or protector is acting in a reasonable manner that is in the best interests of the beneficiaries and the purposes of the trust.[29]

In view of this, it would appear that – regardless of the extent of the powers of the protector and the extent of exculpatory language relieving the trustee of duty or responsibility for the protector's actions or inactions – the trustee must nevertheless recognise and honour his or her fiduciary obligations and question the protector where called for. If we were to hold otherwise, the very premise of the trust would fail and, to paraphrase Lupoi, quoted earlier, the trustee would not be a trustee at all but rather an agent for the protector,[30] with no responsibility to the beneficiaries.

It is also quite significant to note that the Uniform Trust Code completely agrees with this position. Section 808(b) provides that: "If the terms of a trust confer upon a person [other than the settlor of a revocable trust] power to direct certain actions of the trustee, the trustee shall act in accordance with an exercise of the power unless the attempted exercise is manifestly contrary to the terms of the trust or the trustee knows the attempted exercise would constitute a serious breach of a fiduciary duty that the person holding the power owes to the beneficiaries of the trust."[31]

Thus, unless the protector's powers are personal (and not fiduciary), a trustee who blindly complies with a protector's direction cannot be exculpated, even though the trust language expressly attempts to do so, if the protector's directions clearly conflict with the purpose of the trust, the role of the trustee or the interests of the beneficiaries.

7. Who may serve as protector and is the protector a fiduciary?

The reason these questions are posed together is that in some cases the answer to one may suggest the answer to the other. For example, say that the protector is given the power to add or delete beneficiaries without restriction, and in the first instance, a settlor names his daughter as protector. Pursuant to the power, the daughter proceeds to delete her siblings and their issue from the pool of beneficiaries and to add her spouse and children as beneficiaries. Under these circumstances, it is likely that the settlor would have contemplated that the daughter could, and in fact might well, exercise the power in such a way, and

---

28 "Directory Trusts and the Exculpatory Clause", 65 *Columbia Law Review* 138, 151 (1965).
29 See, for example, "Directory Trusts and the Exculpatory Clause", 65 *Columbia Law Review* 138 (1965); "Liability of a Trustee Where Control Over His Acts or the Trust Property is Vested in Another", 28 *Cornell Law Quarterly* 239 (1943); Cronin, "Effectiveness of Exculpatory Clauses in Directory Trusts", *Trusts & Estates*, November 1959.
30 Lupoi, *op cit* (footnote 21).
31 Uniform Trust Code Section 808(b) (2001).

so the power may be considered a personal power and the daughter's exercise may be appropriate. On the other hand, say that the settlor's attorney was named protector and given the same power. Would it be appropriate for the attorney to delete the settlor's children and grandchildren as beneficiaries and substitute his own? In the latter case, of course, unless expressly stated otherwise, the power would not be construed as a personal one and the attorney would clearly have a duty to consider the intentions of the settlor and the purpose of the trust in a fiduciary capacity. Any exercise of the power that benefited the attorney in such a case, directly or indirectly, would likely be invalid as a breach of fiduciary duty as well as a fraud on the power.[32] On the other hand, in cases where the settlor is the protector,[33] it would have to be concluded that the power is a personal one, since it would be little different, depending on the extent of the power reserved by the settlor, from a power reserved by the settlor to amend or revoke the trust without restriction.[34]

Then there may be cases where the power is personal, but with fiduciary aspects, such as the power in a beneficiary of a discretionary trust to remove and appoint trustees. In such case, absent a specific prohibition in the trust, would it be appropriate for a beneficiary to appoint himself or herself as a trustee? Similarly, could a beneficiary with the power to appoint a protector appoint himself or herself to that position? Clearly, the intent of the settlor is the first issue to consider; but, absent any specific motive or express language, it would seem that a settlor would merely want the beneficiary to use his or her best judgement in filling the trustee or protector position. An excellent illustration of this is the *Circle Trust* case.[35] There the settlor gave the beneficiaries of his trust the power to appoint a protector of the trust by majority vote, and the protector had the power to remove and appoint trustees. There was a dispute among the beneficiaries and a majority voted to appoint a protector, who in turn appointed one of the beneficiaries as trustee. Of course, the disputing beneficiaries (who were in the minority) sought relief from the court on the basis that although the power to appoint may have been personal, there was nevertheless a fiduciary duty to appoint a proper person to fill the position. The court agreed with the petitioners, holding that both the beneficiaries' power to appoint a protector and the protector's power to appoint a trustee were fiduciary powers, and that either appointment would be invalid if it were "tainted by irrationality, bad faith, or impropriety of purpose". Accordingly, it would follow that the protector's appointment of a trustee could be rescinded on those grounds.

It should be clear, then, that as to the question of whether the protector

---

32   Restatement of The Law (Second) of Property, Section 20.2 (1986).
33   *Federal Trade Commission v Affordable Media, LLC*, 179 F 3d 1228 (9th Cir 1999).
34   David Hayton, "English Fiduciary Standards and Trust Law", 32 *Vanderbilt Journal of Transnational Trust Law*, Volume 32 555, at 585 (1999).
35   *In the Matter of The Circle Trust*, 2006 CILR 323 (Grand Court of the Cayman Islands).

should be viewed as a fiduciary, some considerable inference can be drawn from the settlor's choice of protector (as well as successor protectors), in addition to the particular powers granted. As a general rule, if the appointed protector is a beneficiary or a person who would likely be an object of the settlor's bounty, and there is no language or facts to dictate otherwise, then to the extent that the exercise of a particular power could benefit the protector, there is likely to be a presumption that it is a personal power;[36] but, depending on the power itself, its exercise may nevertheless be subject to a fiduciary standard, as discussed above. If the protector is someone in an advisory capacity to the settlor, is an otherwise disinterested party or is someone the settlor would be unlikely, under normal circumstances, to name as a beneficiary, the power will likely be a fiduciary one.[37] If the power is deemed to be a fiduciary power, then it imposes a duty on the person accepting the power to consider whether to exercise it; and such consideration and the resulting decision must be impartial and motivated by what the fiduciary – in this case, the protector – believes to be in the best interests of the beneficiaries; not the settlor, not the trustee and most certainly not the protector. Of course, an obvious way to avoid the question would be to include appropriate language in the trust, simply providing that the protector's powers must be exercised in a fiduciary capacity.

Unfortunately, just the opposite appears to be the common approach. That is, many drafters have come to believe that the inclusion of a statement to the effect that the protector shall not be deemed to be a fiduciary will conclusively settle the question. This is a little like saying, "Regardless of what type of animal walks through these gates, it will be deemed to be a horse." While such a statement is bound to be correct at some point if enough different animals pass through the gates, why would we not want to identify each animal correctly – or in this case, each protector, and each power? And as a general rule, most attorneys would have to admit that despite language denying fiduciary status, the huge majority of protectors are in fact intended and expected to exercise their powers for the furtherance of the trust and not for themselves. In fact, the Uniform Trust Code states the point quite clearly: "A person, other than a beneficiary, who holds a power to direct is presumptively a fiduciary who, as such, is required to act in good faith with regard to the purposes of the trust and the interests of the beneficiaries."[38]

The attempt of some practitioners to have it both ways is undoubtedly to prevent potential protectors from being scared off by the assumption of possible liability, which is the same reason for the language exculpating a trustee for

---

36   *Rawson Trust v Perlman*, Bahamas Supreme Court, 25 April 1990.
37   Uniform Trust Code, Section 808(d) (2001). As of the start of 2016, 30 US states and the District of Columbia have adopted a version of the Uniform Trust Code, with New Jersey scheduled to introduce a version in 2016 (see www.uniformlaws.org/LegislativeFactSheet.aspx?title=Trust%20Code).
38   *Ibid.*

submitting to the powers of the protector. Other than that concern, however, and where the power is not a personal one, it is truly a challenge to understand why a settlor would grant extensive powers to an unrelated individual (or committee) for any purpose, other than to see to the objective and thoughtful carrying out of the settlor's wishes in establishing the trust. What would be the sense of it? If, for instance, a protector is given the power to change the situs and governing law of the trust, would anyone conclude that the power was given so that the protector could arbitrarily and for no apparent reason shift the situs from one jurisdiction to another just for the fun of it? Or would it rather be that while the settlor felt the original jurisdiction seemed a good choice at the inception of the trust, being unable to foresee the future, he or she wanted to allow for a change of jurisdiction if it appeared to be in the best interests of the beneficiaries and the trust?

And what about the power to remove and replace trustees? Could that not be some sort of neutral power that is neither fiduciary nor personal in nature, as many attorneys seem to think? This very issue was raised in a 1994 Bermuda case. In *Von Knieriem v Bermuda Trust Co, Ltd*[39] a protector was given the power to remove and replace the trustee, the Bermuda Trust Company (BTC). BTC as trustee was asked to vote shares it held in favour of keeping the settlor on the board of directors of the subject company. Before complying, BTC understandably wanted additional information and time to consider the request, but the impatient protector decided not to risk receiving a negative response from the trustee and exercised his power to remove BTC as trustee, appointing a successor corporate trustee. BTC, concerned over the possibility of facing a breach of fiduciary duty claim by the beneficiaries, questioned the protector's actions and petitioned the court for instructions before it would turn over the shares. (Note that at the same time, the protector petitioned the court asking that BTC be ordered to transfer the shares to the successor trustee.)

In its consideration of the case, the court focused on the key questions of whether the protector was a fiduciary, or at least whether the power to remove and replace the trustee must be exercised in a fiduciary capacity. In addressing these issues, the court first noted that it would depend on the facts of the particular case and in some respects on the nature of the power. In this case, the court pointed out that the power to remove and replace trustees was viewed to be essential to the integrity of the trust and the interests of the beneficiaries (when would it not be?), quoting (in part) from an English case, stating: "The power of appointing trustees ... imposes on the person who has the power ... the duty of selecting honest and good persons who can be trusted with the difficult ... duties which the trustees have to perform. He is bound to select to the best of his ability the best people he can find for that purpose."[40]

---

39   *Von Knieriem v Bermuda Trust Co Ltd*, 1 BOCM 116 (Bermuda High Court, 1994).
40   *In re Skeats Settlement*, 42 ChD 522, 526 (1889).

Finding, therefore, that the position was a fiduciary one, as was the duty to select a suitable successor trustee, the court concluded that the protector's selection was reasonable and approved the protector's exercise of the power.[41] It is also significant to note that the court in the *Circle Trust* case, discussed above, cited *Von Knieriem* in its opinion.

Another situation arguing convincingly in favour of fiduciary status is where the position of protector is established as an office, as it is with the trustee, rather than as the appointment of an individual, as such. That is, where the trust provides for the office of protector, including the appointment, removal and resignation of a protector, the appointment of one or more successor protectors, the powers and compensation of the protector and so on, it will be extremely difficult, at best, to refute the argument that the powers attach to the office rather than to the individual holding the office. Such a structure would unquestionably require the office holder to act reasonably and not for personal motives, having in mind the obvious purpose behind the creation of the office: to protect the integrity and carry out the purposes of the trust. When one considers the extent of the powers often given the protector over the trust, the trustees and the beneficiaries, evidence that the powers are personal rather than fiduciary would have to be overwhelming and nearly incontestable before a court would refuse to interfere, especially where the effect of the protector's acts or refusal to act could clearly conflict with the purpose of the trust or the purpose of the protector's appointment in the first place.

In the Canadian case of *In re Rogers*, for instance, the relevant instrument provided that the trustee was prohibited from acting on a certain investment (shares of stock in a particular company) without the consent of a named individual (effectively, a protector). No successor protector (called an adviser in the instrument) was provided for and the settlor gave the power to him exclusively. Further, the provision granting the power expressly released the trustees "from all liability for any action that may be taken" at the adviser's request. After the settlor's death, the adviser acquired, for his own account, shares of the same company held by the trust and entered into negotiations with other parties that conflicted with the interests of the trust in that investment. In effect, the adviser wanted to be able to sell his shares, but withhold his consent to a sale of the trust shares by the trustee if it affected his (the adviser's) sale. The trustee petitioned the court to intercede, since it desired to sell the shares held in the trust and distribute the proceeds to the trust beneficiaries (the children of the settlor), but pursuant to the power given to the

---

41   See, for example, James Wadham, *Willoughby's Misplaced Trust*, 2nd edition, at 150 (Gostick Hall Publications, 2002); and Andrew Penney, "Rights and Powers of Trust Protectors: Rahman Revisited", *Journal of International Corporate & Trust Planning*, Volume 4 No 1 (April 1995). It is interesting to note that the protector in *Von Knieriem* was, in fact, acting more for the settlor than for the beneficiaries, since the underlying issue was the upcoming corporate vote to allow the settlor to remain on the board of the company whose shares were held by the trust, and some trust analysts have taken issue with this.

adviser, the trustee was prohibited from negotiating on its own without the adviser's consent. If the power were truly a personal power, the adviser, who was otherwise unconnected to the trust, would have been free to withhold consent, as he did, even though such withholding of consent would have been detrimental to the beneficiaries. In fact, the adviser asserted to the court that his power to give or withhold consent was "conclusive" (ie, personal), and therefore the court had no authority to override it. The court flatly disagreed and, in directing that the trustee could act without the adviser's required consent, stated: "To contend that the so-called control over the management of the estate given him [the adviser] can hamper or limit the power of the Court to advise the trustees and to give directions for the due administration of the estate is to place Beaton [the adviser] in the extraordinary and quite unknown position of a sort of super-trustee who is neither responsible to the trustees or the beneficiaries nor subject to the control or direction of the Court."[42]

Perhaps one of the most debated issues regarding the protector's fiduciary duties is the question of whether the particular power given requires the protector to monitor the trustee or the operation of the trust in order to decide whether to exercise the power. For instance, if the protector is given the power to remove and replace the trustee, does this carry with it the responsibility periodically and overtly to inquire into the trustee's performance, or may the protector remain completely passive until facts come to light that would call for action on the protector's part? I strongly believe that a duty to monitor and inquire accompanies the power given, and that a protector who has a fiduciary duty to the trust cannot sit idly by, where, for example, a trustee is needlessly dissipating trust funds but the protector has not had the occasion to see it, and so the trust suffers a loss because of a sleeping protector. Of course, even where it may be held that there is no duty to monitor, if the protector becomes aware of a situation that could cause or is causing harm to the trust and fails to act, then personal liability for resulting loss must follow.

In the first US case dealing with the duties of a trust protector, the protector, who was declared a fiduciary by the terms of the trust, had the power to remove and replace the trustee. When the trustee dissipated nearly all of the trust funds on needless and excessive expenditures, the successor trustee sued the protector for failing to remove the trustee who wasted the assets. After appeal and remand on a judgment in favour of the protector, the lower court held (and the appeals court affirmed) that because the terms of the trust did not call for monitoring of the trustee by the protector, the protector did not have a duty to monitor. But the court went on to state expressly that once it came to the protector's attention that the trustee had breached its fiduciary duty, the protector would then have a duty to act.[43]

---

42   *In re Rogers*, 63 OLR 180 (Ontario 1928).
43   *McLean v Davis*, 283 SW 3d 386 (Mo Ct App 2009).

Lastly, we should consider the case where, instead of naming one person as protector, we name a corporate protector, or a law firm, or a committee of several individuals, as discussed below. What then? Would anyone argue, for instance, that a corporate protector has no fiduciary duty in exercising or not exercising its powers?

In sum, and at the risk of oversimplification, if the protector is in fact appointed to 'protect', then the protector must be regarded as a fiduciary as to the powers falling into that category and cannot be released from his or her obligations merely by language stating the contrary. If the protector accepts the position knowing the attendant powers, he or she must consider whether to exercise those powers and must act reasonably, having in mind the interests of the trust and the beneficiaries – it is not like deciding whether to read a newspaper or to go to the movies.

8.   Professional protectors

With the advent of the position of protector and in apparent recognition of the numerous issues associated with it, a number of 'professional' protectors have surfaced. It is becoming fairly common for corporate trustees, attorneys and law firms in the various offshore jurisdictions to make themselves available to act as trust protector for an annual fee. The fee is usually a nominal one for stand-by services, with the understanding that it is to cover correspondingly nominal involvement. Where the protector is required to become actively involved, the fees will increase in proportion to the services rendered. In the typical case, the trustee will recommend one or two professional protectors with whom he or she is familiar. In addition, we are now seeing some formally structured organisations which hold themselves out as professional protectors. Typically, these are organisations which are also qualified to act as trustee, but where a trustee is already named, they offer protector services. Of course, it is not necessary that the protector and the trustee be in the same jurisdiction. Such organisations can offer independent and experienced protector services anywhere in the world.[44]

Some advantages of naming a professional protector organisation, as opposed to an individual, include continuity of services (they are not vulnerable to deaths, moves, retirement or disability, as an individual protector would be), and collective knowledge and experience of the individuals who make up the entities. A committee, on the other hand, although attractive to some advisers, offers neither the cohesiveness of a professional organisation nor the flexibility of an individual. In addition, the use of a committee necessitates numerous additional provisions, adding complexity to the trust.

---

44   See, for example, Marxer & Partner, Rechtsanwälte, Liechtenstein (www.marxerpartner.com, tel: +423-235-8181, email: peter.Marxer@marxerpartner.com); Walch & Schurti, Liechtenstein (tel: +423-237-2121, www.walchschurti.net); Codex Treuhand AG, Liechtenstein (tel: +423-388-2000, email: office@codextrust.com); Asiaciti Trust Pacific Limited, Cook Islands (www.asiaciti.com); Alexander Jeeves (www.Jeeves-group.com); and see Alexander A Bove, Jr, "Selecting a Protector", *Trusts & Estates Magazine*, February 2013.

For instance, the maximum and minimum number of participants required to serve on the committee should be clearly specified, along with the number required to carry a vote (eg, a majority or by unanimous consent), as well as provisions to break a deadlock. There should also be provisions as to notice for meetings, whether in person or by other means, and rules on whether and to what extent expenses for attending such meetings may be reimbursed by the trust. And, of course, there should be clear provisions for removal of a committee member and filling vacancies on the committee, as well as rules for carrying a vote while any vacancies remain unfilled. Typically, neither the settlor nor any other interested party should serve on the committee.

In short, having a committee of protectors might be far more expensive and cumbersome than an individual protector or an organisation, due to fees, expenses and time involved in arranging meetings, not to mention potential disputes and lengthy discussions before arriving at a vote.

In any event, it ought to be clear that the engagement of a professional protector can only serve to buttress the position that the protector owes fiduciary duties to the trust and its beneficiaries. It would be difficult, if not preposterous, to argue that the professional protector was being paid a fee for protecting – carrying out duties such as removal and replacement of trustees, amendment of the trust, distributions to beneficiaries, change of situs and the like – but had no fiduciary duty to anyone.

In regard to attorneys or accountants as logical choices for protectors, this may be acceptable from the settlor's standpoint, but in view of the suggested exposure to fiduciary liability, is it a good idea for the attorneys and accountants? As to attorneys, many are surprised to discover (hopefully not too late) that their malpractice policy may not cover them for fiduciary positions such as protector; and in fact, most insurance companies are probably unfamiliar with the position of protector, although most professional liability policies do cover attorneys while serving as a fiduciary. Nevertheless, if the attorney/protector insists that the trust expressly declares him or her not to be a fiduciary, then it is likely that a malpractice policy will not cover the attorney/protector in a lawsuit, because he or she is acting neither as a fiduciary nor as an attorney!

Accordingly, attorneys or accountants who are interested in acting as protectors would be wise to obtain confirmation that such activities are covered by their professional liability policy (and should also be sure to insist on the inclusion of provisions in the trust instrument for reimbursement and indemnification of the protector by the trust, as discussed later), as it would not be at all unusual or unexpected for a disgruntled beneficiary to sue the protector along with the trustee.

For instance, in one of the rare US cases specifically involving a trust protector, *Thornbrook International v Rivercross Foundation*,[45] brought in the

Illinois district court, the settlor/beneficiary of a revocable trust transferred several million dollars to the trustee, with special provisions relating to the investments. The trust also provided for a protector, who entered into a written contract, agreeing, among other things, to ensure the trustee's compliance with the trust provisions. The settlor/beneficiary subsequently notified the trustee of its decision to revoke the trust and requested distribution of funds. The trustee failed to make full payment, and the settlor/beneficiary sued both the trustee and the protector, among others. The case settled.

9. Can the protector's fiduciary duty be legislated away or drafted away?

As we have noted more than once, many drafters attempt simply to draft away the protector's fiduciary responsibility by stating in the document that the protector is not a fiduciary. As we have also noted, unless the power is a personal power, just wishing (and drafting) will not make it so. It would be little different from providing that the trustee shall have no fiduciary duty in administering the trust. But what if the governing jurisdiction itself passes legislation that expressly exculpates a protector and states, as a matter of law, that unless otherwise provided in the document, the protector is not a fiduciary? Will that make it so?

We observed earlier that the relevant law of the Cook Islands, one of the first of its kind, states: "Subject to the trust instrument, a protector of a trust shall not be liable or accountable as a trustee or other person having a fiduciary duty to any person in relation to any act or omission in performing the function of a protector under the trust instrument."[46]

In other words, according to the letter of the Cook Islands law, if we say nothing in the trust about the protector being a fiduciary, then he or she is simply not a fiduciary in respect 'to any act or omission' in serving as a protector. And if, in addition, we have language in the trust that states the protector shall not be deemed a fiduciary, then it would appear we would have a double denial of liability and therefore apparent absolute protection of the protector from any liability for a breach of what are unquestionably fiduciary duties. Could it be that simple? Does the statute really mean any act or omission? Surely it would undermine the very foundation of trust law to conclude that it does, when by every common law account and analysis the basic fiduciary duty of a trustee, or of one who is deemed to be akin to a trustee by virtue of his or her relation to the trust and the beneficiaries (eg, a protector), is an inseparable part of the fundamental concept of a trust. As one English justice aptly put it: "There is an irreducible core of obligations owed by the

---

45   See *Thornbrook International Inc v Rivercross Foundation*, Case 03 C1113 (US Dist Ct IL, 2003).
46   Cook Islands International Trusts Act 1984 (as amended), Section 20(4).

trustees to the beneficiaries and enforceable by them which is fundamental to the concept of a trust. If the beneficiaries have no rights enforceable against the trustees, there are no trusts."[47]

Nevertheless, here is the picture we are expected to blindly accept: we have a protector whose only basis for not being treated as a fiduciary is that the trust language says he or she is not; and we also have governing law that says he or she is not; and say there is also governing law that says the trustee is completely exculpated for following the protector's directions (discussed earlier). Clearly, there has to be something wrong with this picture, for if we do accept it, what then do we have? Certainly not a trust, as the judge stated in *Armitage v Nurse*, quoted above, since there would be no liability of any of the fiduciaries to the beneficiaries. And would any experienced trust counsel in any other common law jurisdiction believe that a court would not reach the same conclusion as the English judge in *Armitage v Nurse*, despite governing law and trust provisions that attempted to provide to the contrary? Is there not a public policy issue here?

To make matters worse, it appears that the same fundamentally bankrupt approach is being followed in the United States by several states. Take, for instance, the relevant South Dakota and Idaho statutes (in this part referred to as 'the US statutes').[48] These two US statutes define a trust protector as a "disinterested third party".[49] This in itself is quite interesting, since it immediately suggests a party who has nothing to gain by exercising the powers of a protector, which in turn suggests that such powers are likely to be fiduciary and unlikely to be personal powers. Furthermore, the definition of 'fiduciary' under these US statutes specifically includes a trust protector or adviser "who is acting in a fiduciary capacity." Another section of the respective statutes provides that the powers and discretions of the trust protector "may in the best interests of the trust be exercised or not exercised". Still further, in the definition section, the US statutes define a 'trust adviser' as "the grantor or other fiduciaries" who are given exclusive powers (emphasis added). Thus, the clear inference, if not clear provisions, in the US statutes strongly suggests that the position of protector or adviser by its very nature is a fiduciary position. Unfortunately, and as a sad testimony to the drafters' ignorance of the underlying law, the whole issue is then left to chance and abandonment by a subsequent provision which states that an adviser (which by statutory definition includes a protector) will be considered to be a fiduciary, "unless the governing instrument provides otherwise".[50]

---

47   *Armitage v Nurse* [1998] Ch 241 (CA).
48   Idaho Code, Section 15-7-501 (Michie 1999); South Dakota, Codified Laws, Sections 55-1B-1, 55-1B-4 to
      55-1B-7 (Michie 1997, 2005, 2006); Cook Islands International Trust Amendment Act, Section 3 (1989).
49   Idaho Code Section 15-7-501(1)(g) (Michie 1999); South Dakota Codified Laws, Section 55-1B-1(2)
      (Michie 1997, 2006).
50   South Dakota Codified Laws, Section 55-1B-4 (Michie 1997, 2006); Idaho Code, Section 15-7-501(4)
      (Michie 1999).

The US statutes also contain a new (and disturbing) designation referred to as the 'excluded fiduciary'. An excluded fiduciary is "any fiduciary excluded from exercising certain powers under the instrument which powers may be exercised by a trust advisor or a trust protector".[51] The excluded fiduciary is then expressly exculpated under the statutes from any liability for loss that results from any act or failure to act (by the excluded fiduciary) that is in compliance with the direction of the protector or adviser holding such powers. Typically, the excluded fiduciary will be the trustee of the trust!

Accordingly, under the US statutes it appears that with a few poorly chosen words exculpating both the protector and the trustee, combined with an array of powers granted to a disinterested protector, an uninformed though perhaps well-meaning drafter can totally eliminate all fiduciary duty associated with a trust.[52]

If this were truly possible, we would all be in deep trouble. While it has been observed that the form and content of the offshore protector statutes were largely motivated by concerns of local practitioners and the economic interests of local trustees, this should certainly not be the case for any US statute addressing the subject. As suggested above, I strongly believe that the legally unsound approach taken by the US statutes is uninformed if not embarrassing, and simply would not be upheld under the foregoing circumstances if and when challenged in court.

On the other hand, there are seven US states that, by statute, specifically provide that the protector or adviser is a fiduciary, and in that regard they do not state "unless the trust provides otherwise".[53] In addition, one state's statute provides that "a trust advisor or trust protector shall act in good faith and in accordance with the terms and purposes of the trust and the interests of the beneficiaries".[54] Clearly a breath of fresh air on the issue. Under this statute, it is possible to designate the protector as an excluded fiduciary, but only with respect to powers granted exclusively to other fiduciaries, which means that no fiduciary can be fully exculpated with respect to powers that he or she holds.[55]

This is not at all to say that either a trustee or a protector or both could not be exculpated, so long as they act in good faith and are not motivated by an improper purpose or act with reckless indifference to the interests of the beneficiaries. In fact, we have seen that a trustee can be exculpated within certain guidelines and there is no basis for concluding that a protector who is

51 Idaho Code, Section 15-7-501(1)(a) (2003); see also, South Dakota Codified Laws Section 55-1B-1(5) (Michie 1997, 2006), 12 Delaware Code, Sections 3313(b) and (c).
52 See, for instance, Alexander A Bove, Jr, "The Death of The Trust", *Trusts & Estates Magazine*, February 2014.
53 North Carolina, Mississippi, Michigan, Tennessee, Vermont, Virginia and Wyoming. (The limited exceptions in North Carolina and Michigan do not contradict the fiduciary issue.)
54 New Hampshire Revised Statutes Section 564-B:12-1202(b) (2008).
55 Scott, *op cit* (footnote 2), at Section 222.3.

acting in a fiduciary capacity could not be exculpated to the same extent. Under widely accepted and tested public policy rules, however, neither can be exculpated absolutely, whether by the document or by statute, if we are still to have a trust.[56] In this regard, courts have repeatedly recognised the principle that the law "determines a point beyond which the parties cannot agree to relieve a trustee from liability for breach of a trust duty. For instance, a trustee cannot contract for immunity from liability for acts of gross negligence or for acts done in bad faith. Such contracts are invalid because repugnant to law".[57]

Perhaps one of the most important and significant events that bears heavily on the question of whether the protector is a fiduciary is the recent promulgation of the Uniform Directed Trust Act, adopted by the Uniform Law Commission on 20 July 2017. One of the key tasks of the commission was to review and consider the duties and responsibilities of a 'director' under a trust – specifically meaning a trust protector.[58] The commission concluded that "a trust director has the same fiduciary duty and liability in the exercise or non-exercise of the power....as a sole trustee in a like position and under like circumstances".[59]

Unfortunately, the act does not suggest that this prohibits a state from allowing a settlor to state otherwise, but the encouraging message is that the default position should be that the protector is clearly a fiduciary.

10.   Is the protector subject to court supervision?

If the protector is a fiduciary – which will usually be the case – then it must necessarily follow that he or she will be subject to the supervision of the appropriate court.[60] Such supervision would presumably include the power of the court to surcharge a protector and even to remove or appoint a protector to fill a vacancy under appropriate circumstances. In a milestone 1995 Isle of Man case, that very issue was presented to the court. In that case, *Steele v Paz, Ltd*,[61] a trust provided that the protector of the trust was to consent to the selection of beneficiaries, and was to consent to all distributions to beneficiaries. The problem was that no protector was named; nor was there a provision in the trust to name one. Thus, the very function and purpose of the trust was effectively frustrated by the absence of a protector or a mechanism to appoint one. So a petition was filed by the trustee asking the court to declare the trust invalid. Of course, if the question before the court had been whether the trust would be allowed to continue without a trustee, it is common knowledge that the court would simply appoint a trustee under the well-settled legal maxim that "no

---

56   See *Armitage v Nurse, op cit* (note 47).
57   *Browning v Fidelity Trust Co*, 250 F 321, 325 (3rd cir, 1918).
58   Uniform Directed Trust Act, section 2, comment 9.
59   Uniform Directed Trust Act, section 8(a)(1)(A).
60   *In re Rogers*, 63 OLR 180 (Ontario, 1928).
61   *Steele v Paz, Ltd*, Manx LR 102 426 (High Court, Isle of Man, 1993-95).

trust shall fail for want of a trustee". But what about the case of a trust, the purpose of which is dependent not on the appointment of a trustee but of a protector, which fails to name one or provide for the appointment of one? That was exactly what occurred here, and the court decided that the protector's powers in this case were fiduciary powers, the protector was therefore a fiduciary and it was clearly within the court's power to appoint a fiduciary rather than abandon the trust. Accordingly, the court appointed a protector to carry out the purpose of the trust.

It is interesting to note the widespread international attention and extensive commentary that followed the decision in *Steele v Paz*, which was undoubtedly because a court formally acknowledged the critical role of the protector and viewed the protector as a fiduciary. What may be, or in this case should be even more interesting, at least to US practitioners, is that the United States had its own *Steele v Paz* case 57 years before *Steele v Paz*!

In *Gathright's Trustee v Gaut*,[62] Emma Gathright provided in her will that her executor/trustee could not sell any property or make future investments without the consent of two individuals (in other words, advisers or protectors). If either failed to act, he was to be succeeded by a judge of the local court. One of the named advisers died and none of the local judges wished to be placed in the position of an adviser to a personal estate. On appeal to the Kentucky Court of Appeals, the court first formally acknowledged that all of the judges of the local court declined to act and that the advisers in this case were clearly to serve in a fiduciary capacity, observing that "equity will not permit the trustee or advisory duties specified in the will to fail for want of [an] advisory 'trustee' to exercise [the advisory duties]". Accordingly, the court ordered the appointment of a successor adviser so that the 1938 trust could be carried out, just as the Manx court did in the 1995 'landmark' case of *Steele v Paz, Ltd*.

The *Freiburg Trust* case (*Mourant & Co Trustees Limited v Magnus*) is a further indication of the courts' inherent jurisdiction over a protector who is deemed a fiduciary. In that case the provisions of the trust appointed a protector and provided for his removal, but only in limited situations. The named protector was convicted of stealing from the trust funds and, after serving a prison sentence, he disappeared. Unfortunately, the terms of the trust did not dictate that a vacancy would occur in such a case so, technically, the thief remained as the named protector and, under the terms of the trust, could not be removed. The trustee therefore applied to the court for an order removing the protector. The primary question before the court was whether the court had jurisdiction over the protector and therefore, over the office of protector (and perforce, the related trust provisions).

In its opinion containing an affirmative answer to the foregoing the court

---

62   *Gathright's Trustee v Gaut*, 124 SW 2d 782 (KY, 1939).

stated: "A protector is in the position of a fiduciary and the court must have power to police the activities of any fiduciary in relation to a trust whether he be called a protector or indeed by any other name. Such a jurisdiction is a necessary incident of the duties to protect the interests of the beneficiaries ... and to ensure that the wishes of the settlor are respected."

And further: "It would be quite unconscionable and unthinkable that this court should have no jurisdiction to remove a protector who was thwarting the execution of a trust or who was otherwise unfit to exercise the functions entrusted to him by the trust instrument."[63]

As to the right to surcharge a protector who is regarded as a fiduciary, this would certainly follow if it is agreed that the courts have supervision over protectors as fiduciaries. In the United States, the question has been answered through the courts' treatment of trust advisers – a position used fairly often in that country – and although not normally thought of as a protector, it clearly amounts to exactly that, as presented earlier. Further, the position of trust adviser has almost invariably been held to be a fiduciary position, demanding a duty of "loyalty and impartiality".[64] And as one *Harvard Law Review* commentary observed in addressing the responsibilities of a trust adviser who is not a trustee: "No less care will be expected of an advisor with such [investment] powers than of the trustee himself, and the advisor should be surchargeable for failure to direct investment prudently."[65]

In an illustrative US case, a Florida testator named a bank in Minnesota (his previous home) as 'managing adviser' of his estate, requiring that the Florida executor (also a bank) could act only as directed by the Minnesota bank. This arrangement apparently allowed the Minnesota bank to participate in the estate settlement process as an adviser, even though it was not authorised to act as executor under Florida law. As it happened, the beneficiaries of the estate felt that certain losses incurred by the estate were the result of the failure of the Minnesota bank to act on a timely basis, and they sued the adviser bank for the losses. The federal district court held (and the circuit court of appeals affirmed in principle) that the adviser could be liable for losses resulting from negligent acts committed by the adviser within the applicable period of limitations.[66]

In some respects, it should be reassuring to the settlor and to the beneficiaries that the protector who is a fiduciary will be subject to the review and supervision of the court, despite those situations which purport to dispense with any fiduciary liability. *Rogers*, discussed earlier, is a good example of the value of court supervision, as in that case the protector refused to give the trustee his consent to act in a situation where it was in the protector's (but not

---

63   *(Re the Freiburg Trust) Mourant & Co Trustees Limited v Magnus* (Royal Court of Jersey, 2004), JRC056.
64   Scott, *op cit* (footnote 2), at Section 185.
65   "Trust Advisors", 78 *Harvard Law Review* 1230, at 1231 (1965).
66   *Warner v First National Bank of Minneapolis*, 236 F 2d 853, (8th Cir, 1956), (cert denied) 352 US 927 (1956).

the beneficiaries') best interests to do so. Despite the trust provision giving exclusive powers to the protector, the court overrode the provision by dispensing with the required consent of the protector. And although in *Steele v Paz* the issue was whether the court had the authority to appoint a protector, there should be no question that if there had been a protector who refused to act, the court would have taken it upon itself to remove the protector and appoint another, because in that case no trust distributions could be made to beneficiaries without the protector's consent. Thus, if the court took no action in such a case, the result would have been the same as if there were no protector (or no trustee), and the trust would fail, since its terms could not be carried out. It was quite appropriate, therefore, that the court refused to allow the trust to fail for want of a fiduciary.

11. What are the rights of the protector?

An interesting and important question that necessarily follows the fiduciary issue is whether the protector, if deemed to be a fiduciary, has the rights of a fiduciary; and if the protector is not a fiduciary, whether he or she has any rights at all. If the protector's powers are personal, then although the protector's duties and responsibilities to the trust or to the beneficiaries are practically non-existent, he or she nevertheless will have the right to information necessary to exercise the power knowledgeably, as well as the right to enforce a properly exercised power. For instance, a protector who is given the personal power to appoint income or principal would certainly have the right to obtain a trust accounting showing the income and principal of the trust that is subject to the power. Similarly, if the protector had the (personal) power to add or delete beneficiaries, he or she would have the right to see the trust instrument to determine the nature and extent of all beneficial interests. On the other hand, a protector whose powers are personal clearly should not have the right, for example, to petition the court for fees or expenses, to employ advisers at the expense of the trust or to question a trustee's performance or selection of investments, or a beneficiary's right to distributions, because the power is a personal one and not for the furtherance of the trust.

If, and to the extent that, the protector is considered to be a fiduciary, however, it should necessarily follow that he or she has at least some of the rights of a trustee; but due to the paucity of cases on the subject, the extent of such rights is not entirely clear. Despite this, some rights would have to be implied, and there are a few cases which are helpful and seem to recognise such implied rights. For instance, in *Von Knieriem*,[67] the court considered an action brought by the protector to force the removed trustee to transfer the trust assets to the new trustee appointed by the protector. In a US case, a trust protector was

---

67   *Von Knieriem*, 1 BOCM 116 (Bermuda High Court, 1994).

approved by the court as a plaintiff in an action against a trustee for breach of trust.[68] In neither of these two cases did the court suggest that the protector, since he was not a trustee, had no standing to exercise the right of a fiduciary to petition the court or prosecute a case. Instead, it appeared that both courts readily accepted the fact that the protector, as a fiduciary, had standing to bring the action, even though he was not a named trustee. And if that is the case, then it must follow that the protector, as a fiduciary on behalf of the trust, would clearly have the authority to engage legal counsel at the expense of the trust and also could receive a reasonable fee for his or her own (fiduciary) services.

But how far would the protector's rights extend? For instance, should not the protector (who is a fiduciary) be entitled to seek an order for compensation? Or for indemnification by the trust? For expenses incurred in the performance of his or her duties? To employ agents? To redress a trustee? Once again, to paraphrase the *Von Knieriem* court, it will depend upon the circumstances of the case, the nature of the powers and the language governing the protector. And in one US decision, the court clearly acknowledged the protector's right to remove a trustee and seek an accounting and a possible surcharge of the previous trustee.[69]

There may be some actions that might be beyond the implied powers of a protector in carrying out his or her function (eg, the right, without express authorisation, to institute litigation), but other rights should be apparent. For instance, if a protector is acting on behalf of the trust pursuant to the powers given him or her, there should be little or no question that he or she is entitled to reasonable compensation and reimbursement for reasonable expenses, as would any fiduciary; and although one leading commentator seems to take some issue with this,[70] courts at least in the United States and offshore have unequivocally upheld the right of a non-trustee who was deemed to be a fiduciary to receive compensation for services and expenses reasonably incurred in carrying out his or her duties.[71] In *National Bank of Portland*, for instance, a decedent established a testamentary trust for the benefit of his spouse and child, naming a corporate trustee. In addition, the trust named another bank, not as trustee but as a consultant or adviser (or protector), to approve "all changes in investments or new investments" proposed by the named trustee. One of the main issues of the litigation was whether the consultant bank was entitled to fees and expenses, particularly the expenses of the litigation.

In addressing this issue, the court first examined the nature and extent of the duties of the consultant bank. It observed that, although the bank was not

---

68   *Sheldon v The Trust Company of The Virgin Islands, Ltd*, 535 F Supp 667, at 671 (D Puerto Rico, 1982).
69   *Ibid.*
70   Anthony Duckworth, "Protector – Fish or Fowl Part II", 5 *Journal of International Trust & Corporate Planning* 1, at 24 (1996).
71   *United States National Bank of Portland v First National Bank of Portland*, 142 P 2d 785 (Oregon, 1943).

technically a trustee, the bank's role was expressly "for the protection of the beneficiaries," and therefore the bank was a fiduciary, "having responsibilities analogous to those of a trustee and subject to control of a court of equity". Accordingly, even though the consultant bank was not a trustee, the court affirmed the consultant bank's entitlement to fees and expenses in the performance of its duties as a fiduciary.

It is important to note here that the law regarding a fiduciary's right to reasonable compensation for services rendered on behalf of a trust differs substantially between the United States and the United Kingdom (and therefore the jurisdictions which follow UK law). As explained above, a fiduciary in the United States always has the right to reasonable compensation, while in the United Kingdom, the fiduciary (eg, a trustee) has no right to compensation (with certain exceptions) unless such is specifically provided for in the instrument.[72] Thus, as discussed below in greater detail, appointment of a protector, particularly in the United Kingdom or sympathetic jurisdictions, should always be accompanied by inclusion of all related provisions in the trust, especially including those allowing for compensation and reimbursement of expenses.

Following the above reasoning, and with the possible exception where UK law is strictly applied, unless the protector's powers are purely personal, it would be difficult to argue that an authorised person – especially one characterised by the trust or by the court as a fiduciary– should not be compensated for services and reimbursed for reasonable expenses for acting in furtherance of the trust. Furthermore, as with any fiduciary, whether in an express or implied position, and even under UK law, the court has inherent jurisdiction to award costs and compensation where appropriate. In fact, where the protector is deemed a fiduciary and fees are allowable, it should follow that he or she will have a lien on the trust assets for reasonable fees and expenses.[73]

Nevertheless, the result may depend on the jurisdiction at hand, because there is the question of how familiar the courts in a particular jurisdiction may be with the role and position of the protector. For example, in the landmark cases such as *Von Knieriem*, *Steele v Paz* and *Circle Trust*, discussed earlier, the respective courts accepted the protector's role as fiduciary and therefore attributed certain rights and characteristics to it. Contrast that with *McLean*, the only US case to address the role at length. In *McLean*, the appeals court openly admitted it did not have a clue what a protector was, what the duties of the role entail, if any, and to whom the protector might owe a duty.

---

72   *Lewin on Trusts*, 18th edition, Section 20-01 (Sweet & Maxwell, 2009).
73   Scott, *op cit* (footnote 2), at Section 242.3.

12. What are the tax implications of the role of protector?

12.1 General observation regarding taxes

In most jurisdictions (including the United States) that have a gift tax, income tax and/or estate (inheritance) tax, the taxability in each case often depends upon either the of power reserved by an individual who is making a transfer or given to an individual by the transferor.

In the first case, if the individual making the transfer reserves sufficient power over the transferred property, no gift will be deemed to have been made and the individual who reserved the power will be taxed on the income from the transferred assets. In addition, he or she will be deemed to own the assets at death for estate or inheritance tax purposes. Accordingly, if the transferor names himself or herself as trust protector and therewith holds sufficient powers, the transferor will be considered the owner for tax purposes.

In the second case, similar rules apply, except where the protector/powerholder cannot act in a way that would benefit himself or herself directly or indirectly.

The following explanation of the US tax implications of protectors may serve as an illustration of the foregoing principles which apply in a number of jurisdictions, as many jurisdictions base their tax liability on ownership or deemed ownership of the subject property.

12.2 US tax implications of the protector

First, for an offshore trust, whether or not the settlor is the protector, little if anything will change for the settlor from the standpoint of US income or estate taxes. This is because for income tax purposes, Section 679 of the US Internal Revenue Code causes the offshore trust to be treated as a grantor trust as to the settlor if there are any US beneficiaries. As to estate taxes, in virtually all cases, since the offshore trust is typically irrevocable, the settlor will retain a special testamentary power of appointment over the trust property to avoid making a completed gift on transfers to the trust,[74] which in turn will cause the trust property to be included in the settlor's estate.[75] Thus, the basic tax results from the settlor's standpoint, except as noted below, are that the typical offshore trust is ignored for both income and estate tax purposes.

If the trust is domestic and the settlor is the protector (a bad idea), the extent of his or her powers will determine the income, gift and estate tax consequences; but suffice to say, as a general rule, that anything beyond the power to remove and replace independent trustees or change trust situs will likely cause the settlor to be treated as the owner of the trust for tax purposes.

---

74   Treasury Regulations, Section 25.2511-2(b).
75   Internal Revenue Code, Section 2038.

Of course, if the settlor or a spouse is a discretionary beneficiary, then all trust income and losses will be passed through to the settlor.[76]

When dealing with protectors other than the settlor, the question of whether there will be tax consequences on the granting of powers to a protector depends to a considerable extent upon whether the power is personal or fiduciary, and if personal, whether the power is over income or principal and whether it can be exercised in favour of the protector or for his or her benefit.[77] If the exercise can benefit the protector, and if the power is over principal, the power is likely to be treated as a general power of appointment granted to and held by the protector, and, depending on the remaining provisions of the trust, the protector may be treated as the owner of the property for US estate tax purposes.[78] Note also, however, that if the settlor remains as a beneficiary of the trust, the trust assets will be included in the settlor's estate upon death.[79] In any event (whether or not the power is personal), where a foreign trust is involved, Section 679 of the Internal Revenue Code will treat the settlor as the owner of the trust for income tax purposes.

If the power cannot be exercised in favour of the protector or for his or her benefit, then the power will be treated as a special power and, with limited exception, there will be no gift or estate tax consequences to the protector regardless of whether the power is personal or fiduciary. An exception to this would be where the protector is also a beneficiary of the trust and the power is exercised by the protector in a manner which causes a reduction of benefits that would otherwise be paid to the protector/beneficiary.[80]

If the power is held in a fiduciary capacity but could nevertheless be exercisable in favour of the protector or for his or her benefit, it could result in negative US income and estate tax consequences for the protector, possibly on the death of the protector or after the death of the settlor, unless the power is limited by an 'ascertainable standard'.[81] Note that in the typical case utilising a protector, a settlor will almost never specify a standard, such as 'health, education, maintenance and support', in connection with the protector's powers; therefore, when a power can benefit the protector, there is the risk that the protector could face unwanted tax consequences after the death of the settlor just by holding the power. In addition, if the protector is deemed to have been given a general power of appointment because he or she could name

---

76   Internal Revenue Code, Section 677.
77   For a more detailed discussion of the tax implications of powers of appointment, see Alexander A Bove, Jr, "Powers of Appointment – More (Taxwise) Than Meets the Eye", *Estate Planning*, Volume 28 No 10 (October 2001).
78   Internal Revenue Code, Section 2041(a).
79   Internal Revenue Code, Section 2036(a).
80   Bove, *op cit* (note 75), at 500, and note the exception that would apply in certain jurisdictions where a special power is exercised in a manner that would postpone vesting beyond the applicable rule against perpetuities. See Internal Revenue Code, Section 2041(a)(3).
81   Internal Revenue Code, Section 2041(b); Treasury Regulations, Section 20-2041–1(c)(2), and Internal Revenue Code, Sections 674(b)(5) and 674(d).

himself or herself as sole beneficiary, this would be treated as a completed gift by the settlor to the extent of the funding of the trust,[82] although the income tax consequences would not change during the settlor's lifetime.[83] Nevertheless, I believe that where the power, by both inference and fiduciary duty, could not be exercised in favour of the protector or for his or her benefit, and even though not specifically restricted in its language, the power would not be held to be a general power and adverse tax consequences to the protector would not result.

For instance, as illustrated earlier, if the settlor's attorney or other professional adviser were given the power to add or delete beneficiaries or to amend the dispositive provisions of the trust, this certainly would not suggest that the attorney or adviser could delete the settlor's children and insert his or her own, or amend the trust to give a spouse a power of appointment. Therefore, despite the lack of an ascertainable standard, the protector who is a fiduciary generally should not be deemed to possess a general power of appointment for US tax purposes.[84] (Although it is important to note that it may not reduce the risk to the settlor of mismanagement of the trust assets.)

There could, however, be adverse estate tax consequences to a protector who could not exercise the power for his or her own benefit, but could exercise the power in favour of someone to whom the protector owed a legal obligation of support. In such case the property would be included in the protector's estate for estate tax purposes, unless the power is clearly subject to an ascertainable standard or the equivalent as explained above.[85]

In view of the foregoing, then, for tax purposes one should be cautious about appointing a spouse, children or other close relation as protector with powers to benefit either the protector personally or his or her dependants, because in such cases the inference may well be that the power is a personal one, and the attendant adverse tax consequences would follow.

13. What special drafting issues are brought into play along with a protector?

One commentator has stated that "the strongest criticism of trust protectors is that their involvement complicates the trust administration and makes it more expensive".[86] And materials given to settlors and their attorneys by a Gibraltar trust company include the statement: "Arguably a protector can give greater security but this also creates a greater administrative burden for the trustees,

---

82   Treasury Regulations, Section 25.2511-2.
83   Internal Revenue Code, Section 678(b).
84   See, for example, *Matter of Stillman*, 433 NYS 2d 701 (1980). Further, some states prohibit or restrict the exercise of such a power for the powerholder's benefit: for example, New Hampshire Revised Statutes, Section 564-A:3(IV) (1996), and *Allan v Nunnally*.
85   Bove, *op cit* (note 75), at 500, and note the exception that would apply in certain jurisdictions where a special power is exercised in a manner that would postpone vesting beyond the applicable rule against perpetuities. See Internal Revenue Code, Section 2041(a)(3).
86   See Duckworth, *op cit* (note 15), Part II at 32.

and consequentially increases costs. Use of a protector can also result in some delay in the trustees exercising their powers and discretions whilst the consent of the protector is sought."

Both comments may be correct, but the administrative issue is only one factor in considering a protector in the first place, and any such complication and expense can definitely be lessened by the inclusion of well-thought-out and carefully drafted trust provisions which make clear the protector's rights and responsibilities in dealing with the trustee and the beneficiaries, the rights and responsibilities of the trustee in dealing with the protector and the rights of the beneficiaries in dealing with both. That is to say, if as typically intended, the role of the protector results in avoiding the need for the trustee repeatedly to petition the court for instructions, in avoiding expensive litigation between the beneficiaries and trustees and in expediting important functions of the trust, among other things, then the modest added expense would be well worth it.

Therefore, when the decision is made to include a protector in a trust, that decision should be accompanied by an orderly and focused review of the essential issues surrounding the position. For instance, unless the protector's powers (or any of them) are intended to be purely personal, why complicate matters and generate needless expense by declaring that the protector shall not be a fiduciary? And why leave open the question as to whether a protector (who is a fiduciary) is entitled to reasonable fees and expenses? Or whether the protector can employ agents to help carry out his or her responsibilities? Or whether the protector can seek indemnification from the trust before acting? Or engage tax counsel to determine the consequences of his or her acts? Or whether the protector is entitled to access to all trust records, documents and accounts? Even in cases where the protector's powers are limited, it would seem that consideration of every one of the foregoing issues would eliminate otherwise unavoidable questions and therefore expense. Therefore, they should each be addressed in drafting provisions relating to the protector.

In addition, the more apparent questions must be thoughtfully covered, including appointment of a successor protector in the event that the current protector ceases to serve for any reason, as well as removal of a protector, if desired. The appointer (or remover) could be the former protector, the settlor and/or a spouse (having in mind the tax and asset protection ramifications), the trustee, the beneficiaries, an independent outside party (sort of a protector higher level), or even a committee or a professional protector, as discussed earlier. The appointed protector or successor who accepts the position should either sign the trust or so indicate in writing. A practitioner must always be mindful that some of these choices may have tax and/or fiduciary ramifications. Other drafting issues include what constitutes the protector's consent when such is required and, in the case of a veto power, when the trustee may act if the protector does not respond. Typically, veto provisions allow the trustee to act if a protector does not overtly veto a distribution or transaction, or if the protector does not respond within a specified time (eg, 30 days) after notice to the protector of the proposed distribution or transaction. And should every transaction by the trustee be subject to the protector's veto or consent? Consideration should be given to allowing the trustee to administer the trust without such disruption and to require approval only for larger or significant transactions (eg, over a specified dollar amount or on the sale of certain property or closely held business interests).

With regard to the veto power, one approach that is commonly taken – with which I strongly disagree – is where the trust gives the protector (who has veto or consent power) the authority to give the trustee a blanket consent to all actions taken by the trustee unless and until such carte blanche is withdrawn by the protector. If the power in the protector is a fiduciary power (which it is very likely to be and which would then require the protector to consider whether to veto or give consent in each case), why would such a blanket consent not be a *prima facie* breach of fiduciary duty by the protector? And what would be the trustee's exposure for accepting and acting on a blanket consent? This blanket consent arrangement does little more than render the protector impotent, contradicting and defeating the very purpose of the appointment of a protector by the settlor; and yet it does not seem to stop drafters from including such a provision.

The trust should also contain provisions allowing the trustee to act during any period where there is no protector serving, as could happen where a protector dies or becomes incompetent and a successor is not quickly appointed. Further, the trust should provide (which few trusts do) that a protector may resign the office and how this is accomplished.

This is neither a required list nor an exhaustive review of all drafting issues involved, since the particular circumstances surrounding the trust in question and the reason for having a protector may generate fewer or additional considerations in each instance. Nevertheless, it should be clear that neither the position of protector nor the drafting issues relating to the position should be treated casually; nor should sample language proposed by other attorneys or manuals be blindly accepted, particularly that old familiar (and misleading) language which declares that the protector is not a fiduciary and that neither the protector nor the trustee is liable so long as the trustee follows the protector's direction.

14. The springing protector

It is interesting to note that in many trusts where a protector is appointed, the protector simply stands by, waiting to be called to action. Despite the stand-by position, however, the protector still charges a fee (for standing by), and this very presence invites the question of whether, as a fiduciary, he or she has the responsibility to take some action, such as periodically to monitor the performance of the trustee and the activities of the trust.

For those drafters who wish to avoid exposure to this expense and potential complication, and who therefore do not wish to have a protector presently, but who understand that the need for one may arise in the future, there is a solution. The trust could be drafted omitting the appointment of a protector for now, but allowing for the appointment of one in the future. My firm successfully uses and recommends that a provision be included in the original version of the trust allowing for a 'springing' protector. And if the subject trust is an offshore asset protection trust, the appointment will be restricted to one who is not a person or entity subject to US court jurisdiction.

Such a provision would give the trustee (or some other person) the power to appoint a protector for the trust where none existed previously, thus establishing and filling the position only when needed. The provision could allow for the appointment of a protector for a specified period of time or permanently, or in certain cases give the trustee the power to remove and replace protectors or revoke the appointment. Such a provision should include all the necessary terms and conditions for protector powers, compensation, length of appointment, removal and/or replacement and so on. Attention to all of these issues will enhance the flexibility, integrity and asset protection qualities of the trust, without the need to fill the position before it is necessary.

15. Conclusion

When one considers the reported case law on the subject, the knowledgeable commentary, the history of fiduciary law, and the very purpose of having a protector, the question of the true role of the protector should hardly be a question at all. At the outset, the very choice of the term 'protector', is suggestive. As one justice put it: "It seems to me that it would be wrong to entirely neglect the terminology involved. The word 'protector' seems to me to connote a role for the person holding that position even before one considers the detailed provisions relating to it. A 'protector' is, presumably, one who 'protects'. But what is he to protect?"[87]

And the court stated, in answer to its own question, "It is, therefore, the settlement that he is obliged to protect."[88]

As such, then, the protector can serve a critical function outside the trust, while acting in conjunction with the trustee to enhance the carrying out of the settlor's wishes, but not without responsibility to interested parties if the protector breaches his or her duty. In such a role the protector can introduce flexibility to the trust and respond to future needs and changes that a trustee

---

87   *Steele v Paz, Ltd*, Manx LR 102 426 at 119-120 (High Court, Isle of Man, 1993-95).
88   *Ibid*.

could not do, or would certainly be reluctant to do without first obtaining court permission. In this context, then, the position can be uniquely useful and should definitely be considered in any trust where such flexibility and outside consultation is indicated, especially where the trust is anticipated to extend considerably into the future, including, for instance, dynasty trusts, special needs trusts, purpose trusts (where protectors or enforcers are required by statute)[89] or business succession trusts.

At the same time, however, as legal advisers and drafters we must not be vague about the role of protector or ignorant of the ramifications of the position, as that is often what has proved to be the real source of the problems. Perhaps, then, we should take a lesson from the character Humpty Dumpty when he said to Alice, "When I use a word, it means just what I choose it to mean – neither more nor less."[90] When we decide to utilise the position of a protector in a trust, let us present it in a thoughtful way to ensure that the position is deemed to be just what we choose it to be – neither more nor less.

---

89   See for example, British Virgin Islands Trusts Ordinance (Cap 103) as amended (1993) Section 84(2)(d).
90   Lewis Carroll, *Through the Looking Glass*, Chapter VI (Macmillan, 1871).

The European Union and data protection campaign

Filippo Noseda
Mishcon de Reya LLP

1. Introduction

At the time the fourth edition of this book was published in 2016, my mind was preoccupied by the data protection issues posed by the forthcoming introduction of the Common Reporting Standard (CRS) at the beginning of 2017.

Accordingly, in my chapter I discussed what I then thought was a relatively concise title: "Trusts under attack – privacy, transparency and conflict with the taxman".

Three years on and, if anything, my combative nature has increased.

What is happening out there is a constant struggle over data, pitting governments and the Organisation for Economic Co-operation and Development (OECD) against data protection authorities and data protection campaigners

For three years now, I have been actively campaigning to raise awareness of the privacy and data protection implications of the CRS, as well as the public registers of beneficial ownership, which are the new gold standard of transparency. Originally an EU invention (registers of beneficial ownership were first introduced as part of the Fourth EU Anti-Money Laundering Directive), public registers are now being thrust onto non-EU jurisdictions, with the United Kingdom leading the way (as detailed below).

On 31 July 2018, a formal complaint was brought on behalf of an individual against the CRS in the United Kingdom. The complaint was formally disposed of by the UK Information Commissioner's Office (the UK's General Data Protection Regulation (GDPR) regulator), and the battle on that front continues.

In this chapter, I will provide an update on the current status of transparency and data protection. We are dealing with a fast-moving target and therefore more updates may be necessary at regular intervals.

2. Tax data of a whole nation hacked – recent developments

The OECD's commentary to the CRS (at page 79) reassures us that: "Confidentiality of taxpayer information has always been a fundamental cornerstone of tax systems... the ability to protect the confidentiality of tax information is also the result of a 'culture of care' within a tax administration."

In addition, in response to a recent questionnaire prepared by the European Data Protection Board, the new EU data protection regulator introduced by the GDPR, the finance ministries of 25 EU member states indicated as follows:

- "So far none of the jurisdictions that participate in the questionnaire has reported a data breach or received information according to section 5 of the MCAA" (Question 8).
- "The OECD and the Global Forum have built a secured exchange IT platform (Common Transmission System – CTS) for the exchange of CRS data between jurisdictions. This system was in operation for the first exchanges in 2017."

How surprising, then, that on 17 July 2019 news outlets around the world picked up the story that cybercriminals had gained access to the IT system of the Bulgarian tax administration and stolen the data of "almost every adult" in Bulgaria, causing the Bulgarian finance minister to apologise before the local Parliament amid accusations of sub-standard computer systems. According to reports, the tax data of approximately 5 million taxpayers (includes names, dates of birth and in some cases even their income) was made available online.[1]

Bulgaria is a full member state of the European Union and is subject to the full rigour of EU law. The recent incident shows the pervasive nature of hacking and its effects for the CRS.

3.   Not an isolated incident

Cynics may argue that Bulgaria is not a standard bearer for cybersecurity and more evidence is required to show the dangers of systems of automatic exchange of information for individuals' fundamental rights.

Let's start with the United States, then.

On 20 April 2018, the editorial board of the *Washington Post* published an article in which it reported that the Internal Revenue Service (IRS) still uses software dating back to the 1960s and operates a patched-up legacy system in which taxpayer case records are managed in more than 60 separate systems. In a written testimony before the US Congress, the IRS deputy commissioner lamented that "approximately 64 percent of IRS hardware is aged, and 32 percent of supporting software is two or more releases behind the industry standard, with 15 percent more than four releases behind". Taxpayer files are kept in an archaic 'master file' that operates in a computer language few people still use.[2]

Separately, on 14 November 2018, the US Treasury's inspector general issued

---

1   www.nytimes.com/2019/07/17/world/europe/bulgaria-hack-cyberattack.html; www.bbc.co.uk/news/technology-49015511 and www.zdnet.com/article/bulgarias-hacked-database-is-now-available-on-hacking-forums/.

2   See www.washingtonpost.com/gdpr-consent/?destination=%2fopinions%2fthis-years-tax-day-meltdown-should-be-a-wake-up-call-for-congress%2f2018%2f04%2f20%2fc7e7a056-4412-11e8-ad8f-27a8c409298b_story.html%3futm_term%3d.52160b8dd1de&utm_term=.2e191560eec5.

a report stating that during the 2016 and 2017 tax years, the IRS failed to record and monitor a number of third-party breaches,[3] confirming the data protection problems within and without the OECD.

As part of my advocacy activity on behalf of a client, I was able to identify additional incidents of hacking, data breach and data management issues relating to several other countries, including Australia, Canada, Sweden, the Netherlands, Norway and the United Kingdom.

The case is clear: in the digital world, data is not safe and tax agencies are not immune to the scourge posed by hacking. Therefore, anyone wishing to introduce monitoring systems should consider the inherent data protection risks of transmitting information across borders very carefully.

As many of the data breaches affecting tax authorities date back to the pre-CRS era, the contention is that the architects of the CRS were either conscious or utterly negligent in their quest to copy Foreign Account Tax Compliance Act procedure with a view to rolling it out all over the world.

In reports to finance ministers of the G20, the secretary general of the OECD has advocated accelerating the adoption of the CRS in developing countries: "There is still more work to come. Particular concerns are raised by the fact that developing countries remain behind more advanced economies with respect to the implementation of tax transparency standards and the use of tax cooperation tools... Technical assistance has been offered by the Global Forum to all developing members to address this gap."[4]

In light of the unfortunate state of affairs in the developed world exemplified by the findings of the *Washington Post* and the latest Bulgarian incident, it remains to be seen what the implementation of the CRS across the developing world will bring in terms of data protection.

Anyone looking for answers should look no further than the next sentence in the OECD secretary-general's report to the G20: "As such help becomes more readily available, it is the political will and commitment of domestic leadership that defines the ultimate progress and success."

This may lead to the conclusion that the CRS is quintessentially a system designed by politicians (acting for governments) and implemented by technical agents guided by 'political will' and 'domestic leadership', rather than legal principles.

For almost 20 years, ever since the hideous terrorist attacks of 11 September 2001, governments have assumed that they are right to infringe personal privacy. The problem is that the CRS was developed between 2009 and 2013[5] – that is, before Edward Snowden's revelations made the headlines. After his

---

3 See www.treasury.gov/tigta/auditreports/2019reports/201940010fr.pdf.
4 OECD Secretary-General Report to G20 Finance Ministers and Central Bank Governors, Buenos Aires, Argentina, July 2018, at p21.
5 See the timeline contained in the preamble to the CRS.

interviews at the beginning of April 2013, the world was never the same and his revelations effectively led to the enactment of the GDPR with the stated objective "to give citizens back control of their personal data".[6]

Nowadays, everyone agrees that government should not have unhindered access to our communications. This was made clear to the security services even when their job is to protect the lives of innocent citizens from terrorism. The position was summarised succinctly in a report published by the Intelligence and Security Committee of the UK Parliament at the time of the overhaul of Britain's intelligence services legislation following Snowden's report:[7] "It is the view of this Committee that privacy protections should form the backbone of the draft legislation, around which the exceptional powers are then built."

Also, few people will be surprised at the string of decisions coming out of the Court of Justice of the European Union (CJEU) in relation to data protection. In the most famous case, the CJEU held – uncontroversially – that:[8] "Legislation permitting the public authorities to have access on a generalised basis to the content of electronic communications must be regarded as compromising the essence of the fundamental right to respect for private life."

Why, then, has nobody opposed automatic exchange of information? After all, the CRS provides tax authorities with "access on a generalised basis" to sensitive personal and financial data.

The answer lies in the Panama Papers. Whereas Snowden's revelations dealt with the misdeeds of governments, the Panama Papers focused on the misdeeds of non-compliant taxpayers. The narrative was set: fight governments when it comes to security and allow governments to go after non-compliant tax persons when it comes to tax. This approach has provided governments and the OECD with enough political capital to ram through their 'transparency package' (CRS, but also Base Erosion and Profit Shifting, public beneficial ownership registers and now compulsory disclosures schemes) virtually unopposed.

What the public has not (yet) understood is that the CRS exposes the data of millions of compliant taxpayers to the kind of risks recently seen in Bulgaria, where sensitive personal data of reportedly every adult in the country was stolen.

4.   The numbers are huge

As mentioned above, the hacking of the Bulgarian tax authorities appears to have affected 5 million taxpayers. This number pales in insignificance when compared with the statistics concerning the CRS.

According to the official report on the first round of automatic information

---

6   www.europarl.europa.eu/news/en/press-room/20160407IPR21776/data-protection-reform-parliament-approves-new-rules-fit-for-the-digital-era.

7   Intelligence and Security Committee Report on the Draft Investigatory Powers Bill, published on 6 February 2016, http://isc.independent.gov.uk/committee-report/special-reports.

8   *Schrems v Data Protection Commissioner*, Judgment dated 6 October 2015, Case C-362/14, http://curia.europa.eu/juris/liste.jsf?num=C-362/14.

exchange published by the European Union,[9] in 2018 Bulgaria and the other 27 EU member states exchanged data of over 8.2 million 'high-value' accounts (ie, accounts over $1 million) for an aggregate value of €3 trillion – three times the market capitalisation of Apple (the world's first trillion-dollar company) and more than any private bank in the world has under management.[10]

Table 1. Values exchanged under the CRS

Values exchanged under the CRS (EU)	€2.9 trillion
Bank of America-Merrill Lynch (world's biggest private bank)	$ 2.7 trillion of client assets
UBS (world's second biggest private bank)	$2.6 trillion of client assets
Morgan Stanley (#3)	$2.3 trillion of client assets
Wells Fargo (#4)	$1.6 trillion of client assets
JPMorgan (#5)	$1.2 trillion of client assets
Credit Suisse (#6)	$1 trillion of client assets

The biggest UK bank (Barclays) does not figure on the list, but according to Reuters, in 2017 it had assets under management of roughly £150 billion[11] – one-twentieth of the values exchanged among EU member states, according to the EU report.

5. Democratic deficit

The reader may assume that the CRS received thorough parliamentary vetting, but this would be a wrong assumption.

In the European Union, the CRS was introduced by the second Directive on Administrative Assistance (DAC2),[12] which was adopted by the European Council which is comprised of the leaders of the 28 EU member states.

---

9   Report from the Commission to the European Parliament and the Council on overview and assessment of the statistics and information on the automatic exchanges in the field of direct taxation, 17 December 2018 COM (2018) 844 final.
10   See https://www.forbes.com/sites/greatspeculations/2018/06/01/client-assets-for-the-worlds-largest-wealth-managers-under-pressure-after-years-of-steady-growth/#278a22367f07.
11   See https://www.reuters.com/article/us-barclays-private-bank-exclusive-idUSKBN18I0IO.
12   Council Directive 2014/107/EU of 9 December 2014 amending Directive 2011/16/EU as regards mandatory automatic exchange of information in the field of taxation.

Contrast the position with, say, the Fourth EU Anti-Money Laundering Directive (which introduced the concept of registers of beneficial ownership), which was adopted by the European Council and the European Parliament.[13]

Crucially, DAC2 omits any reference to the opinion of the European data protection supervisor (EDPS), who advises the European Commission on proposals for legislation and international agreements, as well as implementing and delegated acts with an impact on data protection and privacy.

This is perhaps unsurprising, as the EDPS had issued a damning opinion on a bilateral agreement entered by the European Union aimed at extending the CRS to Switzerland. In his opinion, the EDPS held as follows:[14] "The exchange of information on a certain number of accounts on an annual basis confirms our view that the information exchange is independent of the detection of any actual risk of tax evasion, thus questioning the proportionality of the measure itself."

Clearly, therefore, rather than attracting a stain on their shiny piece of legislation, the heads of government of the 28 EU member states must have decided that it was better to ignore the EDPS and advance the implementation of a system of automatic exchange of information designed by OECD officials at the behest of the G20 – the same heads of state who populate the European Council.

6. Public registers of beneficial ownership

The story here is quite similar, in that the EDPS had let it be known that there are serious concerns with the idea of publicly accessible registers of beneficial ownership of companies.

In his opinion dated 2 February 2017, the EDPS held as follows:[15] "The amendments significantly broaden access to beneficial ownership information by both competent authorities and the public, as a policy tool to facilitate and optimise enforcement of tax obligations. We see, in the way such solution is implemented, a lack of proportionality, with significant and unnecessary risks for the individual rights to privacy and data protection."

Unconcerned and undeterred, the European Union pressed ahead and, after a legal wrangle between the European Commission, the European Council and the European Parliament lasting almost a year, at the end of 2017 EU ambassadors (representing local governments rather than citizens) announced the following break-through:[16]

---

13   Directive (EU) 2015/849 of the European Parliament and of the Council of 20 May 2015 on the prevention of the use of the financial system for the purposes of money laundering or terrorist financing, amending Regulation (EU) No 648/2012 of the European Parliament and of the Council, and repealing Directive 2005/60/EC of the European Parliament and of the Council and Commission Directive 2006/70/EC (Text with EEA relevance).

14   Opinion 2/2015 of the EDPS on the EU-Switzerland agreement on the automatic exchange of tax information dated 8 July 2015.

15   EDPS Opinion 1/2017 on a Commission Proposal amending Directive (EU) 2015/849 and Directive 2009/101/EC – Access to beneficial information and data protection implications.

16   www.consilium.europa.eu/en/press/press-releases/2017/12/20/money-laundering-and-terrorist-financing-presidency-and-parliament-reach-agreement/.

> *On 20 December 2017, EU ambassadors confirmed the political agreement reached between the presidency and the European Parliament on strengthened EU rules to prevent money laundering and terrorist financing...*
>
> *The main changes to directive 2015/849 involve...*
> - *public access to beneficial ownership information on companies;*
> - *access based on 'legitimate interest' to beneficial ownership information on trusts and similar legal arrangements;*
> - *public access upon written request to beneficial ownership information on trusts that own a company that is not incorporated in the EU;*

Previously, registers of beneficial ownership of companies could be accessed only by public authorities and people who could demonstrate a 'legitimate interest'.[17] The new rules, which will have to be transposed into domestic law by 10 January 2020,[18] will expose anyone who satisfies the requirement for 'beneficial ownership', at least in the case of companies.

7. Conclusion

In light of the unwillingness of politicians, EU officials and OECD officials to listen to the concerns raised by the data protection community, the only option appears to be to involve the courts.

This opens the doors to a complex debate about fundamental issues such as privacy and transparency and the correct relationship between citizens and governments.

In the author's view, the issue could not be any simpler. In Europe, the fundamental right to privacy was introduced in 1950 (with the adoption of the European Convention on Human Rights), when the continent was reeling from the horrors of totalitarian regimes that killed millions and was engulfed by the struggle between democracy and communism. When the Berlin Wall finally came down in 1989, several Eastern European countries asked to become full members of the European Union. The European Union welcomed these nascent democracies, albeit not before anchoring the fundamental rights enshrined in the European Convention on Human Rights as part of a new EU Charter of Fundamental Rights, which was adopted in 2000 and which amplifies the existing principles of privacy and data protection. Whoever wanted to access the European Union from the East had to sign up to these fundamental rights.

---

17 See Article 30(5)(c) of Directive (EU) 2015/849 of the European Parliament and of the Council of 20 May 2015 on the prevention of the use of the financial system for the purposes of money laundering or terrorist financing, amending Regulation (EU) No 648/2012 of the European Parliament and of the Council, and repealing Directive 2005/60/EC of the European Parliament and of the Council and Commission Directive 2006/70/EC.

18 See Article 4(1) of Directive (EU) 2018/843 of the European Parliament and of the Council of 30 May 2018 amending Directive (EU) 2015/849 on the prevention of the use of the financial system for the purposes of money laundering or terrorist financing, and amending Directives 2009/138/EC and 2013/36/EU.

When the legality of the CRS and the beneficial ownership registers ends up before the courts, participants in the proceedings will be reminded of the fundamental nature of these rights, in the same way as Snowden's revelations reminded the intelligence community and their political masters that privacy protections should form the backbone of legislation, around which the exceptional powers are then built.

It is not about protecting tax evaders; in the same way as the backlash following Snowden's revelations was not about protecting terrorists. It is about protecting compliant citizens from abuses and the excesses of a surveillance state. In my view, the CRS and public registers of beneficial owners represent the biggest threat to data protection since Orwell published *1984*.

I should like to conclude this chapter with the words of the EU attorney general in an opinion rendered in a case concerning the legality of domestic laws in the United Kingdom and Sweden that required telecommunications firms to store the browsing data of customers and make it accessible to the police and security services. The attorney general understood the philosophical dimension of the right to privacy and data protection, concluding his opinion thus:[19]

1. *In 1788, James Madison, one of the authors of the United States Constitution, wrote: 'If men were angels, no government would be necessary. If angels were to govern men, neither external nor internal controls on government would be necessary. In framing a government which is to be administered by men over men, the great difficulty lies in this: you must first enable the government to control the governed; and in the next place oblige it to control itself.'*

2. *The present cases lead us into the heart of this 'great difficulty' identified by Madison. They concern the compatibility with EU law of national regimes which impose on providers of publicly accessible electronic communications services ('service providers') an obligation to retain data relating to electronic communications ('communications data') in relation to all means of communication and all users ('a general data retention obligation').*

3. *On the one hand, the retention of communications data enables 'the government to control the governed' by providing the competent authorities with a means of investigation that may prove useful in fighting serious crime, and in particular in combating terrorism. In substance, the retention of communications data gives the authorities a certain ability to 'examine the past' by accessing data relating to communications which a person has affected even before being suspected of involvement in a serious crime.*

4. *However, on the other hand, it is imperative to 'oblige [the government] to*

---

19   Opinion of Advocate General Saugmandsgaard delivered on 19 July 2016, Joined Cases C203/15 and C698/15, *Tele2 Sverige AB v Post- och telestyrelsen* (C203/15) and *Secretary of State for the Home Department v Tom Watson*.

control itself', with respect to both the retention of data and access to the data retained, given the grave risks engendered by the existence of databases which encompass all communications made within the national territory. Indeed, these enormous databases give anyone having access to them the power instantly to catalogue every member of the population in question. These risks must be scrupulously addressed, inter alia, by means of an examination of the strict necessity and proportionality of general data retention obligations, such as those at issue in the main proceedings.

Beneficial ownership registers in the European Union under the Fourth and Fifth Anti-money Laundering Directives

Paolo Panico
Paolo Panico's Law Chambers

Legislative and regulatory production regarding the fight against money laundering and terrorist financing has significantly intensified in the European Union since 2015. The Fourth Anti-money Laundering (AML) Directive (2015/849) was published in the *Official Journal* on 5 June 2015.[1] Before it entered into force in most EU member states, the European Commission proposed some relevant amendments which became the Fifth AML Directive (2018/843). This directive was published in the *Official Journal* on 19 June 2018[2] and should come into force across the European Union by January 2020. A Sixth AML Directive[3] was published on 18 November 2018, but does not touch on the matters discussed in this chapter.

These far-reaching legislative exercises commenced 10 years after the entry into force of the Third AML Directive (2005/60/EC), which significantly expanded the armoury available to law enforcement agencies in fighting money laundering and terrorist financing.

The mass publication of purloined information from offshore law firms in 2016 and 2017, known as the Panama Papers and the Paradise Papers respectively, contributed to the political discussion which gave rise to the Fourth and Fifth AML Directives. In particular, a political position emerged which focused on achieving greater transparency of the ultimate beneficial ownership of corporate entities and trusts. As a result, the Fourth AML Directive created an obligation for all EU member states to create central registers of the beneficial owners of companies and trusts. The Fifth AML Directive provided for greater public access to these registers.

This chapter begins by reviewing the main principles that underpin the central registers of beneficial owners under Fourth and Fifth AML Directives.

---

1   OJ L 141/73.
2   OJ L 156 / 43.
3   Directive (EU) 2018/1673.

The reason why some elements of confidentiality are preserved in relation to trusts (but not in relation to companies) is discussed in light of an important 2016 ruling of the French Constitutional Court.[4] At the time of writing, the implementation of the provisions relating to beneficial ownership registers across the European Union is quite diverse; some examples of national legislation are then examined. Some final remarks consider certain issues, such as companies controlled by other companies within the European Union, companies controlled by a trust and the particular case of private foundations.

The legislation and regulations relating to beneficial ownership registers across the European Union are still developing at the time of writing. This chapter reflects the situation of the law, in the understanding of this author, as of 15 August 2019.

Although at the time of writing the United Kingdom was still a full member of the European Union, this chapter does not deal with the register of persons with significant control (the PSC Register) which came into force in the United Kingdom in 2016 under the Small Business Enterprise and Employment Act 2015 independently of any EU directives. Similarly, this chapter does not consider the Trusts Register which was enacted in the United Kingdom under the Money Laundering, Terrorist Financing and Transfer of Funds (Information on the Payer) Regulations 2017, which came into force on 26 June 2017 in implementation of the Fourth AML Directive. A specific chapter in this book deals with the United Kingdom in this respect.

1. Beneficial ownership registers under the Fourth and Fifth AML Directives

Articles 30 and 31 of the Fourth AML Directive deal with the creation, updating and maintenance of beneficial ownership registers. Those provisions were significantly amended under the Fifth AML Directive, especially regarding public access to such registers.

This section describes the underlying principles for the creation of such registers and their mechanics under the EU directives.

1.1 Fourth AML Directive and the idea of beneficial ownership registers

The Fourth AML Directive introduced an obligation for all EU member states to create a central register of the beneficial owners of companies and trusts.

(a) Beneficial ownership register of companies under the Fourth AML Directive

Article 30(1) of the Fourth AML Directive reads as follows: "Member States shall ensure that corporate and other legal entities incorporated within their territory are required to obtain and hold adequate, accurate and current information on

---

4   France, Constitutional Court, Decision 2016-591 QPC of 21 October 2016, *Miss Helen S.*

their beneficial ownership, including the details of the beneficial interests held."

Some EU jurisdictions have enforced this provision by obliging all corporate entities to create and maintain an internal register of beneficial owners. The obligation to duly identify the beneficial owners already existed under the Third AML Directive for all professionally managed companies.

In addition, Article 30(3) of the Fourth AML Directive provides for the creation of a central register of beneficial owners: "Member States shall ensure that the information referred to in paragraph 1 is held in a central register in each Member State, for example a commercial register, companies register…, or a public register. Member States shall notify to the Commission the characteristics of those national mechanisms. The information on beneficial ownership in that data base may be collected in accordance with national systems."

Access to such a central register is governed by Article 30(5) of the Fourth AML Directive:

Member States shall ensure that the information on the beneficial ownership is accessible in all cases:

> *(a) to competent authorities and FIUs, without any restriction;*
> *(b) to obliged entities, within the framework of customer due diligence in accordance with Chapter II;*
> *(c) to any person or organisation that can demonstrate a legitimate interest.*

The persons and organisations referred to in point (c) shall access at least the name, the month and year of birth, the nationality and the country of residence of the beneficial owner as well as the nature and extent of the beneficial interest held. For the purposes of this paragraph access to the information on beneficial ownership shall be in accordance with data protection rules and may be subject to online registration and to the payment of a fee. The fees charged for obtaining the information shall not exceed the administrative costs thereof.

Unrestricted access to the beneficial ownership register of companies is therefore granted under the Fourth AML Directive to the authorities in charge of fighting money laundering and to law enforcement agencies. An actual list of competent authorities must be drawn up in the implementing legislation of each individual member state. Unrestricted access is also granted to 'obliged entities' – that is, financial intermediaries, accountants and auditors, as well as legal professionals – when conducting customer due diligence (the activity regulated in Chapter II of the directive).[5] Finally, the directive allows for any natural or legal person to inspect the contents of the beneficial ownership register in relation to a specific entity, provided that a 'legitimate interest' test is passed. The directive does not specify the nature of such 'legitimate interest', but the implementing legislation of several member states has introduced a fairly narrow test which specifically links 'legitimate interest' to the fight against money laundering, some examples of which are discussed in sections 2.2(b) and 2.5.

(b) *Beneficial ownership register of trusts under the Fourth AML Directive*

Article 31 of the Fourth AML Directive introduced an obligation to create a beneficial ownership register of trusts.

As in the case of companies, the first obligation is for trustees to acquire and update adequate information on the beneficial owners of the trust. More precisely:

> *Member States shall require that trustees of any express trust governed under their law obtain and hold adequate, accurate and up-to-date information on beneficial ownership regarding the trust. That information shall include the identity of:*
>> *(a) the settlor;*
>> *(b) the trustee(s);*
>> *(c) the protector (if any);*
>> *(d) the beneficiaries or class of beneficiaries; and*
>> *(e) any other natural person exercising effective control over the trust.*

This obligation was already in place under the Third AML Directive, which expressly introduced it for professional trustees. The Fourth AML Directive thus extended it to all trustees (including lay trustees) of express trusts. The wording was perhaps infelicitous, as it referred to express trusts "governed by the laws" of the member state. The only EU member states which have a domestic law governing trusts are the United Kingdom, Ireland, Malta and Cyprus – that is, the common law jurisdictions. For all other EU member states, a beneficial ownership register for trusts was not mandatory under the directive, even though Article 31(8) provided for an extension of the obligation to similar arrangements: "Member States shall ensure that the measures provided for in this Article apply to other types of legal arrangements having a structure or functions similar to trusts."

Some of these loopholes were closed under the Fifth AML Directive, which significantly extended the bearing of a beneficial ownership register for trusts and similar arrangements, as is discussed in section 1.2(c).

---

5   The definition of 'obliged entities' can be found at Article 2(1) of the 4th AML Directive which covers the following professionals:
> *(1) credit institutions;*
> *(2) financial institutions;*
> *(3) the following natural or legal persons acting in the exercise of their professional activities:*
>> *(a) auditors, external accountants and tax advisors;*
>> *(b) notaries and other independent legal professionals, where they participate, whether by acting on behalf of and for their client in any financial or real estate transaction, or by assisting in the planning or carrying out of transactions for their client concerning the:*
>>> *(i) buying and selling of real property or business entities;*
>>> *(ii) managing of client money, securities or other assets;*
>>> *(iii) opening or management of bank, savings or securities accounts;*
>>> *(iv) organisation of contributions necessary for the creation, operation or management of companies;*
>>> *(v) creation, operation or management of trusts, companies, foundations, or similar structures;*
>> *(c) trust or company service providers not already covered under point (a) or (b);*
>> *(d) estate agents;*
>> *(e) other persons trading in goods to the extent that payments are made or received in cash in an amount of EUR 10 000 or more, whether the transaction is carried out in a single operation or in several operations which appear to be linked;*
>> *(f) providers of gambling services.*

Another condition for trusts to be the subject matter of a beneficial ownership register under the Fourth AML Directive was that they "generate tax consequences". The wording of Article 31(4) is as follows: "Member States shall require that the information referred to in paragraph 1 is held in a central register when the trust generates tax consequences. The central register shall ensure timely and unrestricted access by competent authorities and FIUs, without alerting the parties to the trust concerned. It may also allow timely access by obliged entities, within the framework of customer due diligence in accordance with Chapter II. Member States shall notify to the Commission the characteristics of those national mechanisms."

'Tax consequences' are not defined in the directive and only the United Kingdom and Malta have articulated a definition to this effect. No other jurisdiction will legislate along this line, however, as the Fifth AML Directive has radically amended Article 31 so that the current condition for a trust to be entered into the beneficial ownership register of a member state is that it is managed by a trustee in that member state, not that it is governed by the law of that member state and produces tax consequences there.

Access to the beneficial ownership register of trusts under the Fourth AML Directive was not open to the public. Only the "competent authorities" and "obliged entities" performing customer due diligence could view its information.

1.2 Fifth AML Directive and the extension of public access

The Fourth AML Directive was due to come into force by 26 June 2017, but fewer than half of the 28 EU member states had passed the required implementing legislation on the due date.

One reason for this significant delay was the human rights issues raised by the creation of central registers of beneficial owners which would be partially available to the general public. Articles 7 and 8 of the EU Charter of Fundamental Rights protect the fundamental right to privacy, in relation to both private and family life and to personal data.[6] Public access to the beneficial ownership information of companies may represent a breach of such fundamental right.

Nevertheless, the European Commission pushed through a series of amendments to the Fourth AML Directive which substantially increased the

---

6   EU Charter of Fundamental Rights:
      Article 7 – Respect for private and family life
      Everyone has the right to respect for his or her private and family life, home and communications.
      Article 8 – Respect of personal data
      Everyone has the right of protection of personal data concerning him or her.
      Such data must be processed fairly for specified purposes and on the basis of the consent of the person concerned or some legitimate basis laid down by law. Everyone has the right of access to data which has been collected concerning him or her, and the right to have it rectified.
      Compliance with these rules shall be subject to control by an independent authority.

opportunities for the public to access beneficial ownership information. The European Data Protection Supervisor (EDPS) had expressed some serious concerns about the extension of public access to beneficial ownership information, as outlined in the next section,[7] but the European Parliament overwhelmingly voted for the amendments which led to the Fifth AML Directive.[8]

(a) Beneficial ownership register of companies under the Fifth AML Directive

The new Article 30(5), as amended under the Fifth AML Directive, reads as follows:

> Member States shall ensure that the information on the beneficial ownership is accessible in all cases:
>> (a) to competent authorities and FIUs, without any restriction;
>> (b) to obliged entities, within the framework of customer due diligence in accordance with Chapter II;
>> (c) any member of the general public.
>
> The persons and organisations referred to in point (c) shall be permitted to access at least the name, the month and year of birth, the nationality and the country of residence of the beneficial owner as well as the nature and extent of the beneficial interest held.
>
> Member States may, under conditions to be determined in national law, provide for access of additional information enabling the identification of the beneficial owner. That additional information shall include at least the date of birth or contact details in accordance with data protection rules.

The main difference between this version and the original version under the Fourth AML Directive is paragraph (c): the register is no longer reserved to "any person or organisation that can demonstrate a legitimate interest", but is accessible to "any member of the general public".

It is legitimate to question whether indiscriminate, unrestricted access to the beneficial ownership information of companies in fact breaches the fundamental right to privacy under Articles 7 and 8 of the EU Charter of Fundamental Rights. It is difficult to believe that such publicity will make an effective contribution to the fight against money laundering which justifies the restriction of such a fundamental human right.

It is useful to quote here some relevant passages of Opinion 1/2017 issued

---

7   European Data Protection Supervisor, Opinion 1/2017 on a Commission Proposal amending Directive (EU) 2015/849 and Directive 2009/101/EC. Access to beneficial ownership information and data protection implications, 2 February 2017.

8   On 27 February 2017 the Economic and Monetary Affairs and Civil Liberties Committee of the European Parliament voted by 89 to one (with four abstentions) in favour of unrestricted public access to the beneficial ownership information of companies and trusts, with no need to demonstrate a legitimate interest. A different treatment was eventually granted to trusts where the 'legitimate interest' requirement has remained in place, as discussed in section 1.2(c).

by the EDPS in relation to the European Commission's proposal amending the Fourth AML Directive and making beneficial ownership information available to the general public.

The EDPS first noted that a fundamental principle of data protection – that of purpose limitation – was expressly infringed by the European Commission. In other words: "The Commission is proposing new amendments to the AML Directive in order to put it up to speed with technical and financial innovation and new means to perform money laundering and terrorist financing. At the same time the Proposal aims at improving the transparency of financial markets for a number of purposes that we identify, among others, in the fight to tax evasion, protection of investors and fight against abuses of the financial system."

This led to the following conclusion in the Executive Summary to the Opinion:

Processing personal data collected for one purpose for another, completely unrelated purpose infringes the data protection principle of purpose limitation and threatens the implementation of the principle of proportionality. The amendments, in particular, raise questions as to why certain forms of invasive personal data processing, acceptable in relation to anti-money laundering and fight against terrorism, are necessary out of those contexts and on whether they are proportionate...

Last, and most importantly, the amendments significantly broaden access to beneficial ownership information by both competent authorities and the public, as a policy tool to facilitate and optimise enforcement of tax obligations. We see, in the way such solution is implemented, a lack of proportionality, with significant and unnecessary risk for the individual rights to privacy and data protection.

The EDPS made express reference to the European Court of Justice (ECJ) decision in *Österreichischer Rundfunk*,[9] where it was discussed whether the policy objective "could not have been attained equally effectively by transmitting the information as to names to the monitoring bodies alone". The Fourth AML Directive already provided for unrestricted access to beneficial ownership information by the "competent authorities". It remains to be seen whether its extension to the general public respects the principle of proportionality. A judicial review would be required to this effect, but at the time of writing there appears to be no information of any such initiative in any member state.

The EDPS drafted its opinion at the beginning of 2017, when the European Commission's proposal essentially provided for unrestricted public access to the beneficial ownership information of both companies and trusts. However, the final version of the Fifth AML directive maintains a 'legitimate interest' test in

---

9   ECJ, Judgment of 20 May 2003, joint Cases C 465/00, C 138/01 and C 139/01.

relation to trusts. The French Constitutional Court decision of 21 October 2016[10] played an important role in this respect.

(b) Public access to beneficial ownership information of trusts: French Constitutional Court decision

French residents who are settlors or beneficiaries of foreign trusts, as well as foreign trustees of such trusts and of trusts that include French property, have been subject to a reporting obligation to the French tax authorities since 2011. Law 2011-900 of 29 July 2011 rectifying the Budget Law of 2011[11] introduced this obligation for the first time.

Law 2013-1117 of 6 December 2013 against tax fraud and serious economic and financial crime[12] provided for the creation of a register within the Ministry of Finance based on the information supplied by French taxpayers (and possibly foreign trustees) in compliance with the obligation introduced in 2011. The register was created under a new Article 1649 AB of the French General Tax Code.

The Fourth AML Directive was published in the *Official Journal* on 5 June 2015, and in its original redaction did not directly apply to France as far as trusts are concerned. The original Article 31, as we have seen, provided for the creation of a register of beneficial owners of trusts governed by the law of each member state. France has no domestic trust law apart from the *'fiducie'* introduced into the Civil Code under Law 2007-211 of 19 February 2007,[13] which has its own express system of publicity.

Independently of the debates which led to the Fifth AML Directive, the French minister of finance on 10 May 2016 issued Decree 2016-567, which provided for the trust register to be freely searchable online by the name of the trust or by the name of an individual.[14] This register had been created in 2013 based on information which the French Ministry of Finance had received from complying French taxpayers. In a sense, the decree opened to public inspection a section of those taxpayers' tax returns.

Ms Helen S, an American who lived in France and had organised her succession by way of various trusts, took issue at this indiscriminate publicity and petitioned the French Constitutional Court (*Conseil Constitutionnel*) on the compatibility of the decree creating a public register of trusts with the French Constitution. A first result was obtained on 22 July 2016, when public access to the register was blocked pending determination of the issue.[15]

---

10   *Quoted* supra, footnote 4.
11   France, *Loi 2011-900 du 29 juillet 2011 de finances rectificative pour 2011.*
12   France, *Loi 2013-1117 du 6 décembre 2013 relative à la lutte contre la fraude fiscale et la grande délinquance économique et financière.*
13   France, *Loi 2007-211 du 19 février 2007 instituant la fiducie.*
14   France, *Décret 2016-567 du 10 mai 2016 relatif au registre public des trusts.*
15   France, Constitutional Court, Decision 2016-555 QPC of 22 July 2016.

The decision of 21 October 2016 definitively held that a public register of trusts is unconstitutional and even contrary to the Declaration of the Rights of Man and the Citizen of 1789. More precisely:

(3) The freedom proclaimed by Article 2 of the 1789 Declaration of the Rights of Man and the Citizen implies the right to respect for private life; Owing to this, collecting, recording, keeping, consulting and communicating information of a personal nature shall be justified by general interest and implemented in an adequate and proportional manner.

(6) Listing, in a registry accessible to the public, the names of the settlor, the beneficiaries and the administrator of a trust provides information on the manner in which a person intends to manage his or her estate. The result is an infringement on the right of respect for private life. However, the legislature, which did not specify the quality nor the motives that justify consulting the registry, did not limit the people that have access to the information in this registry, placed under the responsibility of the tax administration. Therefore, these disputed provisions have a clearly disproportionate effect on the right of respect for private life in regard to the objectives sought. As a result, without reviewing other grievances, the second paragraph of Article 1649 AB of the General Tax Code should be declared counter to the Constitution.

To the extent that the Declaration of the Rights of Man and the Citizen is at the basis of most modern European legal systems, the French Constitutional Court judgment had a significant bearing on the shaping of the Fifth AML Directive. As a result, the extensive amendments introduced by the new directive preserved an element of confidentiality in relation to trusts: only persons demonstrating a legitimate interest, and not the general public indiscriminately, are allowed to access the beneficial ownership register of trusts.

(c)   **Beneficial ownership register of trusts under the Fifth AML Directive**

Article 31 of the Fourth AML Directive was significantly amended under the Fifth AML Directive. The amendments encompassed the definition of trusts and other legal arrangements which are the subject matter of a beneficial ownership register, as well as the conditions to access such register.

The new Article 31(1) reads as follows:

(1) Member States shall ensure that this Article applies to trusts and other types of legal arrangements, such as, inter alia, fiducie, certain types of Treuhand or fideicomiso where such arrangements have a structure or functions similar to trusts. Member states shall identify the characteristics to determine where legal arrangements have a structure or functions similar to trusts with regard to such legal arrangements governed under their law.

Each Member State shall require that trustees of any express trust administered in that Member State obtain and hold adequate, accurate and up-to-date

> *information on beneficial ownership regarding the trust. That information shall include the identity of:*
>
> *(a) the settlor(s);*
>
> *(b) the trustee(s);*
>
> *(c) the protector (if any);*
>
> *(d) the beneficiaries or class of beneficiaries; and*
>
> *(e) any other natural person exercising effective control over the trust.*
>
> *Member States shall ensure that breaches of this Article are subject to effective, proportionate and dissuasive measures or sanctions.*

Express trusts "administered" in a member state, as opposed to "governed under its law", are now the subject matter of the beneficial ownership register under the Fifth AML Directive. This expands the application of Article 31 to virtually all EU member states, including those which do not have a domestic trust law. Some civil law member states – Italy, the Netherlands and Luxembourg – recognise trusts under the Hague Convention of 1 July 1985 on the Law Applicable to Trusts and on their Recognition.[16] Other member states – such as Belgium[17], Romania[18] and the Czech Republic[19] – recognise trusts under express provisions in their private international law. In any case, a trust may be administered in a member state even though its domestic law does not recognise it as a legal arrangement, provided that a trustee is based in that jurisdiction or the trust fund includes property situated there.[20]

Furthermore, all EU member states have in their domestic legal systems "other types of legal arrangements, such as, inter alia, *fiducie*, certain types of *Treuhand* or *fideicomiso* where such arrangements have a structure or functions similar to trusts". Each member state should therefore determine which of its domestic legal arrangements are similar to trusts for the purposes of creating a register of their beneficial owners. Private foundations, which are a substitute for trusts under the laws of certain member states (Austria, Belgium, Estonia, Germany, Malta, the Netherlands and more recently Hungary) tend to be treated in the same way as companies, as is discussed in section 3.3 – a circumstance which, if confirmed, would create a clear disadvantage for them in terms of confidentiality.

The international experience of trusts shows that most trustees are based outside of the European Union. A new Article 31(3a) deals with this case and extends the obligation to register the beneficial owners of trusts administered outside the European Union, but with certain connections to a member state:

---

16   The United Kingdom, Malta and Cyprus have also ratified the Hague Trusts Convention, but in their case a trust register would also have been a requirement under the Fourth AML Directive by virtue of their domestic trust law.

17   Belgium, Code of Private International Law of 16 July 2004, Chapter XII (Articles 122 to 124).

18   Romania, New Civil Code (in force since 1 October 2011), Articles 2659–2662.

19   Czech Republic, Law 91/2012 on Private International Law (in force since 1 January 2014), § 73.

20   The UK Supreme Court confirmed this principle in *Akers v Samba Financial Group* [2017] UKS 6, in the case of a trust of shares in a Saudi Arabian company.

Member States shall require that the beneficial ownership information of express trusts and similar legal arrangements as referred to in paragraph 1 shall be held in a central beneficial ownership register set up by the Member State where the trustee of the trust or person holding an equivalent position in a similar legal arrangement is established or resides.

Where the place of establishment or residence of the trustee or the trust or person holding an equivalent position in similar legal arrangement is outside the Union, the information referred to in paragraph 1 shall be held in a central register set up by the Member State where the trustee of the trust or person holding an equivalent position in a similar legal arrangement enters into a business relationship or acquires real estate in the name of the trust or similar legal arrangement.

Where the trustees of a trust or persons holding equivalent positions in a similar legal arrangement are established or reside in different Member States, or where the trustee of the trust or person holding an equivalent position in a similar legal arrangement enters into multiple business relationships in the name of the trust or similar legal arrangement in different Member States, a certificate of proof of registration or an excerpt of the beneficial ownership information held in a register by one Member State may be considered as sufficient to consider the registration obligation fulfilled.

In other words:

- a trust with a single trustee based in an EU member state must publish the information of its beneficial owners (as defined under the Fifth AML Directive) in the trust register created in that member state;[21]
- a trust with more than one trustee, based in different EU member states, may register in the trust register of one member state only; and
- a trust with a trustee based outside of the European Union must be recorded in the trust register of the EU member state where the trust "enters into a business relationship or acquires real estate".

While the acquisition of real estate in an EU member state creates a clear condition for a trust to publish its beneficial ownership information in the trust register of that member state, the directive does not define the concept of a 'business relationship'. Various interpretations have been advanced, but it is up to the implementing legislation of each EU member state to specify the circumstances under which a trust administered by a non-EU trustee must be entered in the local trust register.

Not only has the definition of 'trusts' been significantly expanded by a shift from the governing law to the place of administration; access to the beneficial

---

21 Although trusts have no legal personality, some short-cut expressions are used in this chapter as they appear to be easier than sentences referring to the fact that the trustee must perform the corresponding actions in the name of the trust.

ownership information of trusts is now determined by the new Article 31(5) of the Fifth AML Directive:

> *Member States shall ensure that the information on the beneficial ownership of a trust or a similar legal arrangement is accessible in all cases to:*
>
> > *(a) competent authorities and FIUs, without any restriction;*
> >
> > *(b) obliged entities, within the framework of customer due diligence in accordance with Chapter II;*
> >
> > *(c) any natural or legal person that can demonstrate a legitimate interest;*
> >
> > *(d) any natural or legal person that files a written request in relation to a trust or similar legal arrangement which holds or owns a controlling interest in any corporate or other legal entity other than those referred to in Article 30(1), through direct or indirect ownership, including through bearer shareholdings, or through control via other means.*
>
> *The information accessible to natural or legal persons referred to in points (c) and (d) of the first subparagraph shall consist of the name, the month and year of birth and the country of residence and nationality of the beneficial owner, as well as nature and extent of beneficial interest held.*

Trust registers remain fully accessible, with no restrictions for the competent authorities or for financial intermediaries and other regulated professionals performing customer due diligence, as was the case under the Fourth AML Directive. In addition, the new paragraph (c) extends access to "any natural or legal person that can demonstrate a legitimate interest". This was originally the condition for access to the beneficial ownership register of companies under the Fourth AML Directive and is now extended to trusts. 'Legitimate interest' is still not defined under the Fifth AML Directive and it may be expected that the same criteria which were set out for companies in the legislation of those EU member states that have enacted the Fourth AML Directive will henceforth apply to trusts.

The new paragraph (d), which was inserted under the Fifth AML Directive, is more puzzling. It provides for unrestricted public access (the only condition is a written request) to the beneficial ownership information of trusts which hold a controlling interest in a company outside of the European Union. It is difficult to understand the rationale for this provision. A literal construction appears to lead to the following cases:

- A trust administered by a trustee in an EU member state with no shareholdings in any companies will have its beneficial ownership information accessible only to people who can demonstrate a legitimate interest.

- A trust administered by a trustee in an EU member state with a shareholding in a EU company will have its beneficial ownership information accessible only to people who can demonstrate a legitimate interest. In addition, the information of persons who qualify as 'beneficial owners' of the underlying EU company will be accessible to the general public in the corresponding beneficial ownership register of companies (for the determination of these persons, see also section 3.2).

- A trust administered by a trustee in an EU member state with a controlling interest in a company outside the European Union will have its beneficial ownership information accessible to any member of the general public who makes a written request.
- A trust administered by a trustee outside the European Union with a shareholding in an EU company may have its beneficial ownership information published in the trust register of the EU jurisdiction where the underlying company has its registered office, if such a shareholding qualifies as a 'business relationship' under the legislation of that member state. The beneficial ownership information of that trust will be accessible only to people who can demonstrate a legitimate interest. In addition, the information of persons qualifying as 'beneficial owners' of the underlying EU company will be accessible in the corresponding beneficial ownership register of companies.
- A trust administered by a trustee outside of the European Union with shareholdings in one or more companies outside the European Union is outside the scope of the EU directives.

The beneficial ownership information of all these types of trusts (except those which are outside the scope of the EU directives) will also be available to the competent authorities, as well as to financial intermediaries performing customer due diligence.

It is difficult to understand the rationale for this difference of treatment, particularly in relation to a trust holding a controlling interest in a non-EU company. Unrestricted public access to the beneficial ownership information of trusts is an infringement of the fundamental right to the respect of private life under the Declaration of the Rights of Man and the Citizen of 1789, as was discussed in section 1.2(b). It appears unlikely that a trust holding a controlling interest in a company outside the European Union represents an inherently higher money-laundering risk justifying such an infringement than a trust holding a corresponding shareholding in a EU company or not holding any shares in any company. The implementing legislation of the individual member states may clarify this provision or possibly ignore it altogether.

2. Implementation of the Fourth and Fifth AML Directives: some national experiences

The enactment of beneficial ownership registers of companies and trusts (or similar legal arrangements) across the European Union was very diverse across member states. Not only were most EU member states late in passing the required implementing legislation by the due date of the Fourth AML Directive (26 June

2017), but the approaches adopted in different states varied significantly, giving rise to a situation which is highly diversified and far from homogeneous.

From an anecdotal review of some national legislative experiences, the following approaches can be detected:

- implementation of a fully public register of beneficial owners of companies and trusts under the Fourth AML Directive (Portugal);
- implementation of a beneficial ownership registers of both companies and trusts accessible only to people demonstrating a legitimate interest (Germany and Austria);
- implementation of a beneficial ownership register of companies accessible only to people demonstrating a legitimate interest (France);
- implementation of a beneficial ownership register of companies by the introduction of an obligation to publish beneficial ownership information in companies' annual accounts (Spain);
- implementation of a beneficial ownership register for companies accessible to people demonstrating a legitimate interest and a beneficial ownership register of trusts available only to the competent authorities and financial intermediaries performing customer due diligence (Malta);
- implementation of the Fourth AML Directive under enacting legislation, but the ministerial decrees to let it come into force are pending (Italy, Cyprus); and
- implementation of a fully public beneficial ownership register of companies directly under the Fifth AML Directive (Luxembourg).

This is just an anecdotal selection of the implementation of the Fourth and Fifth AML Directives in some EU member states. The jurisdictions were selected because of their size and relevance within the European Union, as well as with a view to considering the main financial centres in the region. Different approaches may have been followed in other member states which are not covered in this chapter, or the same approaches discussed here may also have been followed by other member states.

As the implementation of the Fifth AML Directive was still underway at the time of writing, particularly in relation to the beneficial ownership register of trusts, additional approaches may be recognised in the near future.

2.1 Portugal: a fully public beneficial ownership register under the Fourth AML Directive

A Central Beneficial Ownership Register (*Registo Central do Beneficiário Efetivo*) was enacted in Portugal under Law 89/2017 of 21 August 2017.[22]

---

22 Portugal, *Lei n° 89/2017 Aprova o Regime Jurídico do Registo Central do Beneficiário Efetivo, transpõe o Capítulo III da Diretiva (UE) 2015/849, do Parlamento Europeu e do Conselho, de 20 de maio de 2015, e procede à alteração de Códigos e outros diplomas legais.*

It expressly concerns corporate entities, both Portuguese and foreign, that exercise a business activity in Portugal and have a Portuguese tax identification number to such effect. It also concerns "fiduciary management instruments registered in the Madeira free zone (trusts)".[23]

Portugal, as a civil law jurisdiction, does not have a domestic trust law. However, Decree-Law 352-A/88 allows for the registration of offshore trusts governed by any foreign law in the free zone of Madeira. A register of trusts was created under the same decree-law to that effect.

The Central Beneficial Ownership Register was expressly designated as a fully public register.[24] In relation to trusts, the following persons are listed as beneficial owners:[25]

- the settlor or creator:
- the fiduciary administrator or administrators and, if applicable, the respective substitutes if they are natural persons;
- the legal representatives of the fiduciary administrator or administrators, if these are legal persons;
- the protector, if applicable;
- the beneficiaries and, if applicable, their substitutes; and
- any other person exercising effective control.

The extent of information available to the general public in relation to Madeira trusts is quite significant. Not only all parties who have a connection to the trust must be registered (ie, the settlor, the natural persons acting as trustees or as directors of a corporate trustee, the protector and the beneficiaries) but also their 'substitutes' (*substitutos*) – which may mean persons designated to hold the office of trustee or protector in case of a vacancy, but does not appear to be immediately clear in relation to beneficiaries (eg, contingent beneficiaries? Members of a class of beneficiaries?).

The Portuguese register came into force under Implementing Regulation (*Portaria*) 233/2018 of 21 August 2018 and provided for a deadline of 31 October 2019 for commercial companies and 30 November 2019 for all other entities to publish their beneficial ownership information.

The final implementation deadlines are consistent with the due dates of the Fifth AML Directive; but it is interesting to note that the Portuguese register was originally conceived under the Fourth AML Directive with the extent of public access (and, in the case of Madeira trusts, even a broader one) as under the Fifth AML Directive.

---

23 Portugal, *Lei 89/2017 Anexo, Art. 3(1)(d) Os instrumentos de gestão fiduciária registados na Zona Franca de Madeira (trusts)*.
24 Article 19 of the Annex to Law 89/2017 provides that the information of beneficial owners is "publicly available online".
25 Portugal, Law 89/2017, Annex, Article 8(2).

2.2 Germany and Austria: beneficial ownership registers of companies and trusts open only to people with a legitimate interest

The implementing legislation of the Fourth AML Directive in both Germany and Austria provides for the introduction of beneficial ownership registers available only to people who can demonstrate a legitimate interest. In both countries no distinction is made between companies, foundations and trusts. All domestic (or domestically administered) entities and legal arrangements are listed in the same register and access is granted to those who can pass a legitimate interest test.

(a) Germany

A *Transparenzregister* was created in Germany under the law implementing the Fourth AML Directive and amending accordingly the local AML Law. The register came into being on 26 June 2017, the due date for the Fourth AML Directive, and access was granted starting from 27 December 2017.[26]

Paragraph 23(3) of the German AML Law (*Geldwäschegesetz*) provides that access shall be granted to those who can prove to the registrar that they have a legitimate interest in accessing the information of a certain entity.

At the time of writing, draft legislation was being discussed whose effect would be to lift the beneficial interest test for access to the *Transparenzregister* as of 1 January 2020. Nonetheless, access would be subject to registration and payment of a fee. This is consistent with paragraph 5a of the Fifth AML Directive, which reads as follows: "Member States may choose to make the information held in their national registers referred to in paragraph 3 available on the condition of online registration and the payment of a fee, which shall not exceed the administrative costs of making the information available, including costs of maintenance and developments of the register."

This is a minimum element of protection of the personal information of beneficial owners of the entities listed in the register. The registrar will therefore know who has accessed the beneficial ownership information of any entity at any time, and that such information may be used in case of abuses. It is unfortunately possible that unrestricted public access to beneficial ownership information may lead to some abuses.

The German *Transparenzregister* concerns companies, foundations and trusts. The definition of 'beneficial owners' of "foundations and legal arrangements under which assets are managed and distributed in a fiduciary capacity" (*rechtsfähigen Stiftungen und Rechtsgestaltungen, mit denen treuhändersich Vermöghen verwaltet oder [..] verteilt wird*) under paragraph 3(3) of the German AML Law includes the following persons:

---

26   Germany, *Verordnung über die Einsichtnahme in das Transparenzregister* (*Transparenzregistere-insichtnahmeverordnung*, TrEinV).

- every natural person acting as settlor (*Treugeber*), trustee or protector, if applicable;
- every natural person who is a member of the management board (*Vorstand*) of a foundation;
- every natural person who has been appointed as a beneficiary;
- the group of natural persons for whose benefit the assets are managed or distributed, insofar as the natural persons who shall be the beneficiaries of the managed assets have not yet been determined; and
- every natural person who exercises on any other grounds a direct or indirect controlling influence on the administration of the assets or the distribution of the results.

Although Germany is not a signatory to the Hague Trusts Convention, this article underpins the possibility of a trust administered in Germany. The German legal arrangement functionally equivalent to a trust, the *Treuhand*, is not expressly mentioned in the legislation implementing the Fourth AML Directive. It remains to be seen whether the *Transparenzregister* will be extended to such arrangements under the Fifth AML Directive.

It is also remarkable that the settlor of a trust[27] is listed as a beneficial owner. On the other hand, the founder of a foundation (*Stifter*) is not. Only the members of the management board and the beneficiaries of a foundation, or the group of persons for whose benefit the foundation is managed, qualify as beneficial owners for the purposes of the *Transparenzregister*.

When the *Transparenzregister* becomes available to the general public in 2020, Germany will have achieved a degree of transparency beyond the standards prescribed by the Fifth AML Directive. Not only the beneficial ownership information of companies, but also that of foundations and trusts, will be available to any member of the public. Although the case of a trust administered in Germany is probably purely academic, the same is not true for family foundations, which are regulated under the German Civil Code and the individual legislation of each German federal *Land*. Family foundations have been the German domestic equivalent of trusts since the mid-19th century and accompanied the country's industrial revolution. Nevertheless, the beneficial ownership information of the directors and beneficiaries of German foundations will be in the public register, alongside that of any other corporate entity.

(b) *Austria*

A beneficial ownership register (*Wirtschaftliche Eigentümer Register*) (WiERe) was enacted in Austria under the Beneficial Ownership Register Law (*Wirtschaftlicher*

---

27 The word used in the German legislation is *'Treugeber'*, the term designating the creator of a German *Treuhand*.

Eigentümerregistergesetz, WiERG), which was gazetted on 15 September 2017 and came into force on 15 January 2018. The register became accessible to people and organisations demonstrating a legitimate interest on 1 June 2018.

The Austrian WiERe lists all Austrian corporate entities, including private foundations regulated under the Private Foundations Law of 1993 (*Privatstiftungsgesetz*). Significantly, the register also encompasses trusts that are administered in Austria. An express mention of such trusts is in paragraph 1(17) of the law creating the beneficial ownership register, which clarifies that a trust is administered in Austria when the trustee is resident or has its registered office in the country. Similar to Germany, Austria is a civil law jurisdiction that did not sign the Hague Trusts Convention and as such it does not recognise trusts. Nonetheless, for the purposes of the beneficial ownership register, an Austrian statute now expressly mentions the case of a trust administered in Austria.

The definition of 'beneficial owners' under Austrian law is in some respects different from the corresponding definition in Germany.

In relation to private foundations, the founder (*Stifter*) is a beneficial owner alongside with the directors and the beneficiaries, while in Germany he or she is not. A specific category of beneficiaries is also included under Austrian law: so-called 'one-time beneficiaries' (*Einmalbegünstigte*), who receive a distribution in excess of €2,000 in a certain calendar year. Such beneficiaries are listed as 'beneficial owners' in the WiERe for the calendar year in which they receive the distribution. In January 2019 some regulations were issued in this respect, clarifying that such beneficiaries will not be listed in the subsequent year if they do not receive another distribution.[28]

Access to the register is regulated in detail under paragraph 10 of the Beneficial Ownership Register Law, which reads as follows (in the English translation by this author):

(1) Natural persons and organisations may make a written application to the registrar to access the information of the beneficial owners of a specified entity by mentioning its registration number. In the request a legitimate interest must be demonstrated in the context of the fight against money laundering and terrorist financing in relation to that entity. The registrar, if a legitimate interest exists, must communicate to the applicant an extract in compliance with paragraph 2. A rejection by the registrar must be duly notified. An appeal against the registrar's decision may be made to the Federal finance court...

(3) A condition for the existence of a legitimate interest in the context of the fight against money laundering and terrorist financing is in any case that the petitioner has an obligation to the fight against money laundering and terrorist financing under its articles of incorporation or in a mission-statement, can demonstrate actual successful activities in the fight against money laundering

---

28   Austria, BMF 24 January 2019, BMF-460000/0002-III/6/2018.

or terrorist financing or is an obliged entity under Directive (EU) 2015/849. Furthermore, it must be demonstrated what actual contribution can be provided by the requested extract to the fight against money laundering or terrorism financing.

The definition of 'legitimate interest' which allows access to the WiERe is specified in a very narrow way, with a direct reference to the fight against money laundering and terrorist financing. The applicant must not only be active in this field under its constitutive documents, but must also prove some actual successful activities in this respect. Access to the register can be requested only for one particular entity at a time, and the application must clarify the advantages to the fight against money laundering which may result from the applicant's access to the beneficial ownership information of that particular entity.

The Austrian system appears to strike an adequate balance between the two competing aims of transparency in the beneficial ownership of corporate entities and the protection of the fundamental right to privacy.

At the time of writing, there was no draft legislation for the enactment of the Fifth AML Directive and the lifting of the legitimate interest test to access the register. If Austria followed the German example, the beneficial ownership information of all corporate entities – companies and foundations – as well as that of trusts administered in Austria (if any) would become accessible to the general public. That would be a degree of transparency exceeding the requirements of the Fifth AML Directive, which expressly preserves the legitimate interest test for trusts and "similar arrangements".

2.3 France: a beneficial ownership register for companies accessible subject to a judicial review of the legitimate interest

The beneficial ownership register of trusts has existed in France since 2013. Pursuant to the Constitutional Court decision of 21 October 2016 discussed at section 1.2(b) above, such register is internal to the French Ministry of Finance and cannot be accessed by the general public.

A beneficial ownership register of companies was introduced in France under Ordinance 2016-1635 of 1 December 2016 transposing the Fourth AML Directive,[29] whose provisions were complemented by Decree 2017-894 of 12 June 2017 of the Ministry of Economics.

The beneficial ownership register was enacted by the insertion of new articles into France's Monetary and Financial Code (*Code Monétaire et Financier*). The Fourth AML Directive was carefully transposed, with Article R 561-57 of the Code providing a detailed list of the competent authorities that can inspect the

---

29 France, *Ordonnance n° 2016-1635 du 1er décembre 2016 transposant la Directive EU 2015/849 du 20 mai 2015.*

register without restriction. Article 561-58 introduces the mechanism for obliged entities to access the register. In essence, an obliged entity must designate in writing the person authorised to inspect the register and must submit a written request to access the beneficial ownership information of one or more entities, expressly specifying the due diligence activities in progress in relation to such entity or entities.

Members of the public can access the beneficial ownership information of a particular entity subject to a judicial review of their legitimate interest. An application must be submitted to the president of the commercial court at the place where the registered office of the company which is the subject matter of the inquiry is located. Pursuant to Article R 561-59 of the Monetary and Financial Code, the judge may hear all parties who can provide information or whose interests may be affected by the decision (*"Il a la faculté d'entendre sans formalités les personnes qui peuvent l'éclairer ainsi que celles dont les intérêts risquent d'être affectés par sa decision"*). The decision takes the form of an ordinance and may be appealed either by the applicant or by the concerned beneficial owner. The court of appeal's decision on the matter is definitive and if the application is approved, the applicant is authorised to inspect the beneficial ownership information of the relevant company.

France's judicial review of the existence of a legitimate interest appears to be unique within the European Union. Some other jurisdictions, such as Austria and Malta, have introduced an administrative control by the registrar in charge of the beneficial ownership register. France's judicial review has the additional advantage of allowing the concerned beneficial owner to be heard. The beneficial owner of the relevant company appears to be covered by default by the definition of a person whose interests may be affected by the judicial decision.

This mechanism will have to be lifted when France implements the Fifth AML Directive. Nevertheless, it is hoped that it will be maintained in relation to the beneficial ownership register of trusts and similar arrangements, which France will have to enact under the same directive.

2.4 Spain: a beneficial ownership register by publication of beneficial ownership information in companies annual accounts

Spain's implementation of the Fourth AML Directive, which could easily achieve the degree of publicity demanded under the fifth, is unique in Europe.

Ministerial Order JUS/319/2018 of 21 March 2018 introduced a new obligation for all Spanish companies and other corporate entities that publish their annual accounts in the Register of Commerce (Registro Mercantil). A new section was introduced into the annual financial report with an indication of the company's beneficial owners. This information had to be provided for the first time in relation to the accounts for the year 2017.

Under the ministerial order, Spanish companies must provide details of their beneficial owners at least once a year when they file their annual accounts. This will guarantee that the beneficial ownership information is "adequate, accurate and current" as is prescribed under Article 30(1) of the Fourth AML Directive.

The inclusion of this information in the annual accounts was intended to facilitate the creation of a beneficial ownership register (*Registro de Titularidade Reales*) of all Spanish corporate entities. To the extent that Spain does not recognise trusts in any manner, no trust register exists for the time being.

A company controlled by the Spanish Chamber of Notaries (*Consejo General del Notariado*) submitted a petition against the ministerial order of 21 March 2018 in relation to the new obligation to include information on beneficial ownerships in the annual accounts. The Spanish Upper Administrative Court (*Audiencia Nacional*) rejected the petition on 26 June 2019, essentially on the grounds that the petitioner lacked standing. At the time of writing, the Chamber of Notaries has announced that it will appeal the decision to Spain's Supreme Court (*Tribunal Supremo*).

A background to this petition may be the circumstance that Spain's Chamber of Notaries already maintains an important database of the beneficial owners of corporate entities. The *Base de Datos de Titularidad Real* was created on 24 March 2012. To the extent that most important activities in a Spanish company's life require a notarial deed (incorporation, capital increase or reduction, merger or demerger, liquidation), Spanish notaries are in a privileged position to collect beneficial ownership information for all companies that carry out such activities.

It would have been easy for this central database to become Spain's beneficial ownership register in accordance with Article 30(3) of the Fourth AML Directive. Nonetheless, a political decision was made to create an independent register within the system of Spain's Register of Commerce. The most expedient way for the new register to be created and populated with the required information was to oblige all companies to include the details of their beneficial owners when they file their annual accounts.

A peculiarity of Spain's implementation of the Fourth AML Directive was that the relevant ministerial order pre-dated the legislation which transposed the directive, which is Royal Decree-Law 11/2018 of 31 August 2018.

One of the criticisms made by the Spanish Chamber of Notaries is that the inclusion of beneficial ownership information in a company's annual accounts would breach those individuals' human right to privacy, insofar as the registrar has an arbitrary power to decide who can access such information.

This criticism may be even more pertinent when such information becomes public under the Fifth AML Directive. It will be important to see how Spain's Supreme Court treats the appeal.

2.5 Malta: beneficial ownership registers in accordance with the Fourth AML Directive

Of the jurisdictions discussed in this chapter, Malta appears to have implemented the Fourth AML Directive in the way which is most faithful to its original terms.

A beneficial ownership register of companies was introduced under the Companies Act (Register of Beneficial Owners) Regulations 2017, which came into force on 1 January 2018.

The register is maintained by the Malta Financial Services Authority and is available to a list of competent authorities, to Maltese service providers conducting customer due diligence and to members of the public (under Regulations 7(2) and (3)):

(2) Any person or organisation that upon a written request can satisfactorily demonstrate and justify a legitimate interest shall, in accordance with data protection requirements, be granted access to the name, the month and year of birth, the nationality, the country of residence and the extent and nature of the beneficial interest of the beneficial owners of a company.

(3) A legitimate interest to have access to information on the beneficial owners of a particular company in accordance with sub-regulation (2) shall be satisfactorily demonstrated if the person or organisation requesting such access can satisfactorily demonstrate that the interest specifically and solely relates and will contribute to the prevention, detection and combating of money laundering or the associated predicate offences or the financing of terrorism and shall be justified on the basis of previous activities and a proven track record of actions in that field by means of relevant documentary evidence.

(4) A legitimate interest shall be conclusively determined by the Registrar, and for this purpose the Registrar may request information or seek guidance from or consult with any person or authority as he may deem necessary.

The criteria for identifying whether a legitimate interest exists and access to the beneficial ownership information of a particular entity can therefore be granted are similar to those introduced under Austrian law. Applicants must:

- demonstrate that they have a "proven track record of actions" in the fight against money laundering and terrorist financing; and
- justify that their access to that specific information "will contribute to the prevention, detection and combating of money laundering or the associated predicate offences or the financing of terrorism".

A beneficial ownership register of trusts was created under the Trusts and Trustees Act (Register of Beneficial Owners) Regulations, 2017. The register is available only to competent authorities and professionals performing customer due diligence.

Possibly because it is one of the few EU member states to have its own domestic trust law, Malta has created two separate registers: one for companies, which is accessible to the public subject to a legitimate interest test; and one for trusts, which is not open to public inspection. These were the exact requirements of the Fourth AML Directive and few other jurisdictions appear to have implemented it in such an accurate and faithful way.

The Fifth AML Directive will remove the legitimate interest test as a condition for access to the beneficial ownership register of Maltese companies and possibly, as discussed in section 3.3, foundations; but it will have to be preserved for trusts.

2.6 Italy and Cyprus: enactment of legislation implementing the Fourth AML Directive, where the register is not yet in force as the implementing regulations are pending

Italy and Cyprus are examples of EU member states where the legislation implementing the Fourth AML Directive was enacted in a timely manner, but no beneficial ownership register is yet in place because the ministerial regulations for its implementation are still pending.

(a) Italy

Italy was one of the few EU member states to implement the Fourth AML Directive within its due date. Legislative Decree 90 of 25 May 2017 was gazetted on 19 June 2017 and created a beneficial ownership register for companies and one for trusts. These registers will be maintained by Italy's Register of Commerce (*Registro delle Imprese*).

This legislation was enacted under the Fourth AML Directive and as a result the beneficial ownership register of companies is open to competent authorities, to obliged entities performing customer due diligence and to persons who can demonstrate a legitimate interest. The definition of 'legitimate interest' under Italian law is interesting. Article 21(2)(f) of the legislative decree reads as follows:

> *Access to the information shall be granted to:*
>
> ...
>
> *(f) upon the payment of secretarial duties under article 18 of the Law of 29 December 1993 n. 580, private persons, including those representing collective interests, who hold a relevant and distinct legitimate interest, in the cases where knowledge of the beneficial ownership is necessary to protect or defend, in a judicial procedure, an interest corresponding to a situation that is legally protected, when they have actual and documented reasons to suspect that the beneficial ownership is different from the legal ownership. The interest must be direct, concrete and actual and, in the case of entities representing collective interests, it must not coincide with the interests of the individuals belonging to the class which is so represented.*

Thus, 'legitimate interest' is very narrowly defined. One of the elements in the provision above, which does not appear in the laws of any other member states considered in this chapter, is that the existence of a legitimate interest appears to be related to some judicial procedure.

Despite these legislative provisions, no beneficial ownership register is operative in Italy thus far. The legislative decree refers to ministerial regulations to implement it, which have not been issued at the time of writing.

It is likely that Italy will directly implement the Fifth AML Directive and therefore lift the legitimate interest test for access altogether.

Trusts have been recognised in Italy since the entry into force of the Hague Trusts Convention on 1 January 1992.[30] There is a significant practice of Italian domestic trusts where all elements apart from the governing law are Italian. A register of trusts administered in Italy (ie, where the trustee is Italian and possibly including trusts where the trust property includes Italian assets) will have to be created under the Fifth AML Directive. It will be a separate section of Italy's Register of Commerce, and it remains to be seen whether the definition of 'legitimate interest' under Article 21(2)(f) of the Legislative Decree of 25 May 2017 will apply to trusts or whether a new definition will be enacted.

(b) Cyprus

Some amendments to the Prevention and Suppression of Money Laundering Activities Law 2007–2016 came into force in Cyprus on 3 April 2018. They provided for the creation of beneficial ownership registers for companies, other legal entities and trusts.

No ministerial regulations had been issued at the time of writing and as a result the actual functioning of the Cypriot registers remains unclear.

2.7 Luxembourg: fully public beneficial ownership register of companies under Fifth AML Directive

Luxembourg had partially implemented the Fourth AML Directive under the Law of 13 February 2018, which amended the Law of 12 November 2004 on the fight against money laundering and terrorist financing.[31] Chapter III of the directive, comprising Articles 30 and 31, was temporarily omitted.

A beneficial ownership register of companies (*Registre des Bénéficiaires Effectifs*, RBE) was created under the Law of 13 January 2019 which came into force on 1 March 2019. The law was complemented by the provisions of the Grand-Ducal Regulation of 15 February 2019 relating to the registration procedure, the payment of administrative duties and access to the information

---

30   In fact, Italy was the second signatory country to ratify the Hague Trusts Convention, after the United Kingdom and before Australia.
31   Luxembourg, *Loi du 12 novembre 2004 relative à la lutte contre le blanchiment et contre le financement du terrorisme*.

contained in the beneficial ownership register;[32] and by several circulars and guidelines issued by the registrar of the RBE itself.

All Luxembourg companies and other corporate entities had a six-month timeframe in which to publish details of their beneficial owners, with a deadline of 31 August 2019. The RBE became fully accessible to the general public on 1 September 2019.

Although some draft legislation had been advanced by the Luxembourg government in 2017 with a view to creating a beneficial ownership register under the Fourth AML Directive, the definitive legislation directly provided for the unrestricted public access demanded by the Fifth AML Directive.

Trusts have been recognised in Luxembourg since 1 January 2004, when the Law of 27 July 2003 relating to trusts and fiduciary contracts[33] came into force. The same law reformed the regulation of a domestic 'similar arrangement', the fiduciary contract. To this effect, some due diligence obligations were introduced in relation to fiduciary contracts under the Law of 10 August 2018 relating to the information to be obtained and filed by fiduciaries and transposing Article 31 of the Fourth AML Directive.[34] This appears to be an unnecessary piece of legislation to the extent that only qualified financial intermediaries can act as fiduciaries (*fiduciaires*) in a Luxemburg contract.[35] The duty to identify the beneficial owners of the arrangements they enter into is thus already applicable under general AML rules. A beneficial ownership register of fiduciary contracts and trusts must be created under the Fifth AML Directive, but no legislation has been enacted to this effect at the time of writing.

3.   Particular issues

The beneficial ownership registers under the Fourth and Fifth AML Directive have been implemented through different approaches and on different timeframes. Some of these differences were highlighted in the preceding section, with no pretence of completeness in relation to any jurisdiction.

Some particular issues appear to have been omitted from the laws of most EU member states. Practitioners and their professional associations may potentially fill the gaps in some cases. For this reason, three issues are discussed in this final section:

- the case of EU companies controlled by other EU companies;
- the case of EU companies controlled by trusts; and
- the case of EU private foundations.

---

32   Luxembourg, *Règlement grand-ducal du 15 février 2019 relatif aux modalités d'inscription, de paiement des frais administratifs ainsi qu'à l'accès aux informations inscrites au Registre des bénéficiaires effectifs.*
33   Luxembourg, *Loi du 28 juillet 2003 relative au trust et aux contrats fiduciaires.*
34   Luxembourg, *Loi du 10 août 2018 relative aux informations à obtenir et à conserver par les fiduciaires et portant transposition de l'article 31 de la directive (UE) 2015/849.*
35   Luxembourg, *Loi du 28 juillet 2003 relative au trust et aux contrats fiduciaires*, Article 4.

3.1 EU companies controlled by other EU companies

The rules on the beneficial ownership registers of all EU member states require each company or corporate entity to identify the natural persons who are its beneficial owners and to publish their personal details.

It does not appear to matter whether a company is directly held by individuals or by one or more parent companies in a corporate chain. In both cases the relevant company must publish the information of its beneficial owners.

This situation is differently handled for the purposes of the PSC Register in the United Kingdom. If a UK company – which is defined to this effect as a 'registrable legal entity' (RLE) – is held by another UK company (ie, another RLE), it must indicate just the details of that RLE in the PSC Register. In the case of a corporate chain of RLEs, only the last RLE at the top, which is directly controlled by individuals, will publish the names of the individuals qualifying as its controlling persons in the PSC Register.

To the extent that all EU member states are due to enact beneficial ownership registers under the Fourth and Fifth AML Directives, a notion equivalent to the RLE in the United Kingdom would be useful in order to avoid duplications. This is especially true given the requirement under Article 30(10) of the Fifth AML Directive that beneficial ownership registers be interconnected within the European Union.

The directors of different companies within the same EU member state may have different views as to who their beneficial owners are. Different views may be held by the directors of different companies with their registered offices in different EU member states. The fact that each company in a corporate chain must publish the information of its beneficial owners may lead to different information being filed by different companies within the same group.

A rule establishing that only the last company at the top of a corporate chain must publish the information of its beneficial owners, while all other companies below make reference to their immediate parent(s), would avoid duplications of filings and potential discrepancies.

This problem may be exacerbated by the fact that no precise rules exist for companies to provide the detail of the corporate chain in which they are embedded. In other words, companies belonging to the same group and based in different Member States (or even in the same Member State) may publish the details of certain individuals as their beneficial owners with no evidence of the corporate interests linking one to the other. In principle they should publish the details of the same individuals, but different interpretations may lead to different and equally legitimate filings of who the ultimate beneficial owners are.

The equivalent of the UK RLE rule should apply only to the extent that all companies in a corporate chain have their registered office in the European Union and possibly in the European Economic Area (EEA).

Nevertheless, no provisions to this effect appear to have been passed in the legislation of any of the EU member states considered in this chapter.

3.2   EU companies controlled by trusts

Another issue which does not appear to have received the attention of most EU legislatures is that of a company where a trust holds a controlling interest, or at least a participation in excess of 25%.

A potential source of confusion appears to result from the definition of 'beneficial owners' under the Fourth AML Directive. The definition, which was slightly amended under the Fifth AML Directive, can be read at Article 3(6):

> 'beneficial owner' means any natural person(s) who ultimately owns or controls the customer and/or the natural person(s) on whose behalf a transaction or activity is being conducted and includes at least:
>
> (a) in the case of corporate entities:
>
>   (i)   the natural person(s) who ultimately owns or controls a legal entity through direct or indirect ownership of a sufficient percentage of the shares or voting rights or ownership interest in that entity, including through bearer shareholdings, or through control via other means, other than a company listed on a regulated market that is subject to disclosure requirements consistent with Union law or subject to equivalent international standards which ensure adequate transparency of ownership information.
>
>   A shareholding of 25% plus one share or an ownership interest of more than 25% in the customer held by a natural person shall be an indication of direct ownership. A shareholding of 25% plus one share or an ownership interest of more than 25% in the customer held by a corporate entity, which is under the control of a natural person(s), or by multiple corporate entities, which are under the control of the same natural person(s), shall be an indication of indirect ownership. This applies without prejudice to the right of Member States to decide that a lower percentage may be an indication of ownership or control. Control through other means may be determined, inter alia, in accordance with the criteria in Article 22(1) to (5) of Directive 2013/34/EU of the European Parliament and of the Council;
>
>   (ii) if, after having exhausted all possible means and provided there are no grounds for suspicion, no person under point (i) is identified, or if there is any doubt that the person(s) identified are the beneficial owner(s), the natural person(s) who hold the position of senior managing official(s), the obliged entities shall keep records of the actions taken in order to identify the beneficial ownership under point (i) and this point;
>
> (b) in the case of trusts, all following persons:
>
>   (i)   the settlor(s);
>
>   (ii) the trustee(s);

> (iii) *the protector(s), if any;*
>
> (iv) *the beneficiaries or where the individuals benefiting from the legal arrangement or entity have yet to be determined, the class of persons in whose main interest the legal arrangement or entity is set up or operates;*
>
> (v) *any other natural person exercising ultimate control over the trust by means of direct or indirect ownership or by other means';*
>
> (c) *in the case of legal entities such as foundations, and legal arrangements similar to trusts, the natural person(s) holding equivalent or similar positions to those referred to in point (b).*

In this definition, which was enacted virtually unchanged in the AML legislation of all EU member states, two different standards are adopted for companies and trusts.

The beneficial owners of companies are determined following either a quantitative test (ie, people who hold more than 25% of the company's shares or voting rights) or a qualitative test (ie, people who can exercise control "via other means").

The beneficial owners of trusts are all persons who have a role in relation to the trust – that is, the settlor, the trustee, the beneficiaries (or class of beneficiaries), the protector and any other person who can exercise "ultimate control over the trust by means of direct or indirect ownership or by other means". The 25% threshold, above which persons are identified as beneficial owners of companies, does not apply for the beneficiaries of trusts. Foundations and other "legal arrangements similar to trusts" are treated in the same way with reference to the corresponding functions.

This general definition of 'beneficial owners' applies to all fields covered by the AML Directive, from customer due diligence (to which effect it indicates which persons must be identified by financial intermediaries and other professionals subject to the AML rules) to the creation of beneficial ownership registers.

A literal construction of the directive suggests that the beneficial owners to be published in the register of companies are those indicated at Article 3(6)(a), whether or not the company is controlled by a trust. On the other hand, all parties listed in Article 3(6)(b) must be indicated as beneficial owners of a trust in the trust register.

A difficulty which professionals face in most jurisdictions is how to apply the definition of Article 3(6)(a) in the total absence of guidance in the legislation and the implementing regulations enacting the beneficial ownership register.

STEP Benelux published a position paper on 18 July 2019 in relation to the case of a Luxembourg company controlled by a trust.[36] The conclusions of the

---

36   The Position Paper, which is in French, can be freely downloaded from https://benelux.step.org/branch-news/position-paper-18-july-2019.

position paper may also be of general relevance for other jurisdictions and are summarised as follows. If a company is 100% controlled by a trust, a case-by-case analysis must be conducted in order to identify the natural persons who qualify as 'beneficial owners' following the definition under Article 3(6)(a) of the directive. Different conclusions can be reached based on the actual nature of the trust. At least three cases can be identified:

- Case 1 – a revocable trust (or a bare trust or an equivalent arrangement such as a nominee agreement or a fiduciary contract): The beneficial owners of the company held in such an arrangement are:
  - the individual(s) acting as trustee(s) or nominee(s) or as managing director(s) of the corporate trustee(s) or nominee(s); and
  - the settlor (or beneficial owner of a nominee agreement), to the extent that he or she has the power to put the arrangement to an end by revoking the trust or terminating the nominee agreement.
- Case 2 – an interest in possession trust (or 'fixed trust') where the beneficiaries have vested interests in the trust fund: The beneficial owners of the company held in such an arrangement are:
  - the individual(s) acting as trustee(s) or nominee(s) or as managing director(s) of the corporate trustee(s) or nominee(s); and
  - the beneficiary or beneficiaries who hold a beneficial interest in excess of 25% of the company.
- Case 3 – an irrevocable and discretionary trust: The beneficial owners of the company held in such an arrangement are:
  - the individual(s) acting as trustee(s) or nominee(s) or as managing director(s) of the corporate trustee(s) or nominee(s); and
  - the settlor or the protector or any other officer (or the natural person(s) acting as managing director(s) of any company holding such offices), to the extent that he or she has reserved the power to revoke the trust or to replace the trustee or to appoint and revoke beneficiaries.

In all these cases the individuals acting as trustees or as managing directors of a corporate trustee must be indicated as beneficial owners with the express mention of their capacity. This allows the readers of the beneficial ownership register to distinguish the case where a person holds shares in a company directly from that where the shares are held via a trust or a similar arrangement.

In the absence of a specific statutory provision to this effect, listing all parties to a trust mentioned under Article 3(6)(b) of the directive as beneficial owners of the company controlled by that trust is not correct. It may also expose the company directors who made that choice to risks under data protection legislation. The General Data Protection Regulation came into force across the European Union on 25 May 2018 and imposes serious sanctions on unauthorised data leaks. Publishing personal information of persons who are not beneficial owners of a company (eg, the objects of a discretionary trust or a trust settlor who qualifies as an 'excluded person' under the terms of the trust) may trigger significant sanctions for anybody who unwarily does so.

The beneficial ownership information of trusts is broader than that of companies under Article 3(8)(b) of the Fifth AML Directive, but that information is not meant to be available to the general public. The directive itself, in its Recital (34), provides some balance between transparency and the respect of personal information:

> *In all cases, both with regard to corporate and other legal entities, as well as trusts and similar legal arrangements, a fair balance should be sought in particular between the general public interest in the prevention of money laundering and terrorist financing and the data subjects' fundamental rights. The set of data to be made available to the public should be limited, clearly and exhaustively defined, and should be of a general nature, so as to minimize the potential prejudice to the beneficial owners. At the same time, information made accessible to the public should not significantly differ from the data currently collected. In order to limit the interference with the right to respect for their private life in general and to protection of their personal data in particular, that information should relate essentially to the status of beneficial owners of corporate and other legal entities and of trusts and similar legal arrangements and should strictly concern the sphere of economic activity in which the beneficial owners operate.*

France appears to be the only jurisdiction among those considered in this chapter to have expressly stated that all the parties relating to a trust (ie, the settlor, the trustee, the beneficiaries and the protector, or the beneficial owners of any companies holding any such offices) must be listed as beneficial owners of a company where such trust or equivalent legal arrangement holds a controlling interest.[37]

Nevertheless, the beneficial ownership register of French companies is not open to the public. Article R 561-59 of the French Monetary and Financial Code provides for a judicial review of the legitimate interest of anybody applying to inspect the beneficial ownership information of a particular company, as is discussed in section 2.3.

It is to be expected that the provision under which all persons with a relationship to the trust as beneficial owners of a French company controlled by that trust must be listed will be amended when the Fifth AML Directive comes into force in France, and the details of the beneficial owners of all companies will be available to the general public.

---

37   France, Monetary and Financial Code, Article R 561-3-0.

3.3 Private foundations

Private foundation legislation has been enacted in several EU member states, where they are used as alternatives to trusts, such as Austria,[38] Belgium,[39] Estonia,[40] Germany,[41] Malta,[42] the Netherlands[43] and recently Hungary.[44]

Private foundations, as opposed to charitable foundations, may be created for the benefit of specified beneficiaries or for a class of beneficiaries to whom appointments may be made at the discretion of the board of directors.

A significant difference between a private foundation and a trust is that the former is a legal person, whereas the latter is just a 'legal arrangement' where the only 'person' is the trustee. Legal personality has the consequence that private foundations are registered in the companies register or commercial register of the jurisdiction where they are incorporated.

Accordingly, they have been equated to companies in the implementation of beneficial ownership registers under the Fourth AML Directive which, under Article 30(1), applies to "corporate and other legal entities incorporated within [the member state's] territory". The consequence is that the beneficial ownership information of foundations has been subject to the same publicity regime as that of companies, and has been available to persons demonstrating a legitimate interest.

Under the Fifth AML Directive, the beneficial ownership information of companies and other incorporated entities shall be available to the general public. At the same time, the new redaction of Article 31 provides for a register of "trusts and other types of legal arrangements, such as, inter alia, *fiducie*, certain types of *Treuhand* or *fideicomiso*, where such arrangements have a structure or functions similar to trusts". The information in such register will be available only to persons and organisations that can demonstrate a legitimate interest.

It would appear natural for all EU member states with private foundation legislation and practice to conclude that private foundations are arrangements which have 'functions similar to trusts', and as such their beneficial ownership information should continue to be available based only on passing the legitimate interest test.

On the contrary, it appears that in many EU member states the structural approach prevails over the functional approach. In their words, to the extent that private foundations are incorporated entities, their beneficial ownership

---

38   Austria, Private Foundations Law 1993.
39   Belgium, *Loi du 27 juillet 1921 sur les associations sans but lucratif etc.*, reformed as of 1 July 2003 under the *Loi 2002-05-02/51 sur les associations sans but lucratif et les fondations*.
40   Estonia, Foundations Act 1995 (in force since 1 January 1996).
41   Germany, Civil Code, Sections 80 and following, reformed under the Modernisation Law as of 1 September 2002 and complemented by the foundation legislation of each federal *Land*.
42   Malta, Second Schedule to the Civil Code, Title III (in force since 2007).
43   Netherlands, Civil Code, Book 2, Part 6.
44   Hungary, Law of Asset Management Foundations of 2019.

information will be treated in the same way as that of companies and will be made available to the general public without restriction.

This approach is dangerous and appears to be contrary to the letter and spirit of the Fifth AML Directive, where some degree of confidentiality was expressly reserved for trusts and 'similar arrangements'. Most private foundations are prevented from carrying on business activities and as such are much more similar to trusts than to commercial companies.

If the beneficial ownership information of private foundations will be made public under the Fifth AML Directive, private foundations will be the real losers in this AML exercise. Either convoluted drafting techniques will have to be adopted in order to avoid publication of beneficiaries' details or trusts will prove to be a superior estate planning arrangement, if anything because of the higher degree of confidentiality made available under the directive.

To the extent that Liechtenstein is a member of the EEA, it will have to enact equivalent legislation to that of the European Union. It remains to be seen how Liechtenstein will treat private foundations to this effect. It would be very surprising if the Liechtenstein legislation equated private foundations to commercial companies and thus made the details of beneficial owners accessible to the public.

At the time of writing, the legislation enacting the Fifth AML Directive was at best in draft form in most EU member states. It is hoped that the functional nature of private foundations, as legal arrangements similar to trusts, will prevail in the versions which will be eventually enacted by the national parliaments.

Trust information disclosure

Simon Gibb
McDermott Will & Emery

1. Introduction

1.1 Overview

A significant trend in the trust world in the past decade – one which is highly likely to continue with gathering pace in the next decade – is the dramatic increase in the transparency and accessibility of information concerning trusts in the modern world. A wide range of initiatives – unilateral and multilateral – have increased the regulatory burden of trusts, resulting in the compulsory disclosure of important information about the trust, its assets and beneficiaries to government taxing authorities or company registrars. These new initiatives have a common framework: complex and at times inconsistent rules to identify living individuals who have actual or deemed control over or economic interests in a trust's assets.

To provide a comprehensive statement of these various initiatives would require several volumes, so this chapter seeks to provide the reader with an overview of the main regimes and contextualise their development over recent years. Inevitably, as the trust is a creature of English law, the UK government has been at the vanguard of these developments and so this chapter focuses not just on multilateral initiatives, but also on the United Kingdom's own regimes which are, in some respects, more advanced and wide ranging than those of other jurisdictions. However, the United Kingdom's regimes are derived from EU law anti-money laundering rules. These rules apply in the other member states and the same outcomes are intended to be achieved there as well.

Following the global financial crisis of 2007–2008, high-tax jurisdiction governments implemented a wide range of measures to protect their tax bases. An early, long-established – and obvious – hurdle in these efforts was the inability to independently obtain sufficient information about a taxpayer's assets and affairs without relying on cooperative exchanges with taxpayers themselves. In addition, obtaining relevant information about trusts established outside high-tax jurisdictions could be hard, to say the least.

There is a long tradition of granting taxing authorities extensive information-gathering powers, ranging from requests for documents to the ability to seize relevant information, within the confines of the home jurisdiction. However, the general legal principle that State A would not use its own domestic tax compliance apparatus to assist State B in enforcing the domestic tax rules of State B created considerable hurdles to effectively investigating and taxing taxpayers not resident in the jurisdiction and the assets and income of resident taxpayers which were located outside the jurisdiction. Efforts have been made to ameliorate these issues in bilateral tax treaties. Then contemporary information exchange arrangements were in large measure reactive: information could be requested by one taxing authority under a double tax agreement if it contained mutual assistance provisions, but there was no general cooperation no information exchange. The effectiveness of these provisions could be further curtailed if the jurisdiction receiving the request had limited domestic powers to gather the pertinent information in the first place. Furthermore, such 'on request' provisions could (and can) be challenged in courts if the requests were considered mere 'fishing expeditions' where there was no clear reason why the information was relevant to the requesting authority's investigations.

In the immediate aftermath of the financial crisis, the inadequacy of these arrangements became a focal point for policy and, ultimately, treaty and legislative change: enough countries' tax authorities wished to know where their taxpayers' assets were and how much they had to build the infrastructure for a true revolution in information exchange. An initial flurry of tax information exchange agreements (TIEA) were signed after the Organisation for Economic Co-operation and Development (OECD) compiled a 'black list' of non-cooperative jurisdictions. A jurisdiction could be removed from such list if it entered into the required number of TIEAs and cooperated effectively with information requests, thereby encouraging the establishment of ever more TIEAs. However, this expansion of the tax information treaty network has been substantially augmented (indeed, in some regards, overtaken) by developments concerning the multilateral automatic exchange of information between jurisdictions. A series of initiatives were developed to procure the automatic exchange of information concerning taxpayers which have added a new battery of acronyms to the tax and trust lawyers' lexicon: the Common Reporting Standard (CRS), the Foreign Account Tax Compliance Act (FATCA), persons with significant control (PSC) and the UK Trust Registration Service (UK TRS), to name those most common to UK and offshore practitioners. Each of these regimes has application beyond the realm of trusts which is not the topic of this chapter. Of immediate relevance is the fact that each poses a significant challenge to the conventional wisdom that trusts provide individuals and their family with confidentiality around such assets and investments by adding the substantial caveat that confidentiality no longer extends to the trust's existence.

The common approach of these regimes is to treat a trust as though it were a legal entity in its own right and then provide a definition of deemed 'controlling persons' or 'beneficial owners' of the trust. The regimes then require one to pierce the trust relationship and look behind the titular owner of the trust's assets – the trustee – to find living individuals who fall within these regulatory fictions: commonly, the settlor, fixed interest beneficiaries, discretionary beneficiaries and protectors will be identified and disclosed, along with their deemed interest in the trust's assets. Regrettably, no single definition or analytical approach has been used to define 'control or ownership' in the context of trusts. This may be a pragmatic policy response to so flexible a concept as a trust, but certainly has the concomitant drawbacks of difficulty in application and the gathering of much irrelevant – and at worst, potentially misleading – information.

An important distinction between these regimes is whether the information disclosed under them remains confidential between the disclosing entity and the recipient. In the case of the regimes which have arisen principally as a tax compliance exercise (FATCA, the CRS and the UK TRS) the information is not publicly accessible[1] and so remains confidential. However, under regimes which have arisen, at least in part, to address anti-money laundering concerns (eg, the UK PSC regime and the EU Fifth Money Laundering Directive (MLD5)), considerable amounts of sensitive information are publicly accessible.

1.2 MLD5

MLD5 is of particular note as it is the most developed instrument requiring the collation of extensive information regarding trusts and carries the possibility that the information may become public in the future. On 19 April 2018 the European Parliament voted to adopt MLD5, having been agreed by EU member states in December 2017. It came into effect on 9 July 2018 and is part of the EU anti-money laundering and counter-terrorist financing framework. MLD5's objective is to increase financial transparency and address the ways in which terrorist groups finance and conduct their operations by amending the provisions of the existing Fourth Money Laundering Directive (MLD4). The provisions of MLD5 must be transposed by member states by January 2020, but may be implemented prior to this date. MLD5 will require all member states (although not their satellite territories) to keep a publicly available register of company owners and a database of company and trust owners. It will also require trustees of all existing and new express registerable trusts to register details of the beneficial ownership of the trust assets on a central national register.

---

1   In the case of the UK TRS it is expected that some of the information on this system will be made publicly available in order to comply with the Fifth Money Laundering Directive, which despite Brexit the United Kingdom has stated it will implement in full.

The term 'beneficial ownership' is not redefined in MLD5 and under MLD4 is considered to be any natural person who ultimately owns or controls a corporate or legal entity and/or on whose behalf the entity is conducting its activity. In the case of corporate entities, this relates to a natural person who ultimately holds a shareholding/controlling interest or ownership interest of 25% plus one share or ownership interest. In the case of trusts, the beneficial owner is deemed to be the settlor, beneficiary, trustee, protector and any individual exercising effective control of the trust. The information required to be registered will cover a beneficial owner's name, month and year of birth and country of residence and nationality, as well as the "nature and extent of beneficial interest held".

MLD5 also extends the registration requirements to non-EU resident trustees of express trusts (or vehicles with a structure or effect similar to a trust) which form a business relationship or acquire real property in a member state. The definition of what constitutes a 'business relationship' was not provided within MLD5, but is defined in MLD4. It is expected to be defined broadly and is likely to include engaging the legal or financial services of advisers in member states which are anticipated to last for some time. By way of example, this could include a trustee who engages a firm of solicitors to provide ongoing legal advice in relation to the issues arising in that member state

The rest of this chapter considers the main regimes and their interactions with trusts. As is to be expected with such regimes, the rules are highly technical and the precise facts of any situation should be considered with specific advice. This chapter seeks only to illustrate in outline the structure of the main disclosure regimes and their general implications for trusts. It is not a guide to compliance with the regimes.

2.   Foreign Account Tax Compliance Act

2.1   Overview
The first out of the blocks in 2010 was FATCA and is consequently the template for many of the subsequent developments. In brief, FATCA requires non-US entities to undertake due diligence to identify whether their 'accounts' (ie, interests in the entity, deemed to include beneficial interests in trusts) are held by or deemed to be owned by US persons. The principal sanction for non-compliance is that US persons are required to operate a 30% withholding tax on some payments to non-compliance foreign financial institutions and some other entities. The most pertinent forms of payment are US source dividends and interest.

The FATCA compliance obligations of a non-US entity turn in part on whether the entity is subject to one or more FATCA intergovernmental agreements (IGAs) or to the US Treasury Regulations. In general, the compliance obligations of an entity under an IGA are less onerous than under the Treasury

Regulations. There are two forms of IGAs: the Model 1 IGA and the Model 2 IGA. The Model 1 IGA is by far the most common of the two forms.[2] If a non-US entity is subject to the IGA of a FATCA partner jurisdiction that has adopted a Model 1 IGA, information about certain US owners of the entity may be reported to the government of the partner jurisdiction and then automatically transmitted to the United States under information sharing agreements. If an entity is subject to the IGA of a jurisdiction that has adopted a Model 2 IGA, information about certain US owners of the entity may need to be reported directly to the Internal Revenue Service by the entity or by a FATCA 'sponsor'. At the time of writing, the United States has signed IGAs with 113 jurisdictions, including major EU jurisdictions and offshore centres.

2.2 Basic architecture

An IGA may apply to entities that are organised under the laws of a particular jurisdiction or to entities that are resident in the jurisdiction. Because an entity might be organised under the laws of a jurisdiction that adopts the 'organised under the laws of' approach for its IGA and resident in a jurisdiction that adopts the 'resident in' approach, an entity may be subject to more than one IGA.

Once the entity has determined which jurisdictions' IGA apply to it, it must be categorised to determine its reporting obligations. For FATCA purposes, every non-US entity is either a 'foreign financial institution' (FFI) or a 'non-financial foreign entity' (NFFE). For FATCA purposes, a trust is an 'entity'. NFFEs are defined as non-US entities that are not FFIs. The classification of an entity as an FFI or an NFFE determines how the entity is required to comply with FATCA, it being the case that NFFEs have neither registration nor reporting requirements, whereas FFIs may have such requirements under certain circumstances.

The Treasury Regulations and the IGAs provide that FFIs include custodial institutions, depositary institutions and investment entities. The 'investment entity' category is the most relevant for purposes of classifying trusts. The Treasury Regulations and the IGAs define the term 'investment entity' slightly differently, though many countries with IGAs allow an entity to choose to use either definition. For example, in its original FATCA guidance (the UK Guidance Notes), the United Kingdom adopts the definition of 'investment entity' that is found in the Treasury Regulations, even though the UK IGA itself contained a slightly different definition. The UK Guidance Notes defined an 'investment entity' to include:

> (i) an entity that "'conducts as a business', for or on behalf of a customer (for example an account holder) one or more of the following activities: trading in

---

2   There are two forms of Model 1 IGA, but the principal difference between them is whether the United States also undertakes to provide reciprocal automatic exchange of information. However, given that the United States lacks an equivalent domestic legal framework to gather information, this point is of limited practical implication at the time of writing.

money market instruments (cheques, bills, certificates of deposit, derivatives etc.); foreign exchange; interest rate and index instruments; transferable securities and commodity futures trading; individual and collective portfolio management; otherwise investing, administering or managing funds or money on behalf of other persons. The entity will be regarded as conducting these activities as a business if the entity's gross income attributable to such activities is equal to or exceeds 50 percent of the entity's gross income during the shorter of (a) the three-year period ending on December 31 of the year preceding the year in which the determination is made; or (b) the period during which the entity has been in existence.

or

(ii) an entity that is managed by a Financial Institution and the gross income of which is primarily attributable to investing, reinvesting, or trading in financial assets (defined to exclude non-debt direct interests in real property or land). An entity's gross income will be considered to be "primarily attributable" to the activities listed above if its "gross income attributable to such activities is equal to or exceeds 50 per cent of the entity's gross income during the shorter of: (x) the three-year period ending on December 31 of the year preceding the year in which the determination is made; or (y) the period during which the entity has been in existence.

It is this second limb which will result in a professionally managed trust being an 'investment entity'. The definition of an 'investment entity' is extensive, but is consistent between the Treasury Regulations and IGAs. An entity will be an 'investment entity' if 50% or more of its gross income over the shorter of the previous three calendar years or the period during which it has been in existence was from investing, reinvesting or trading in financial assets and it is managed by an entity that is also an investment entity. However, this can depend on whether the assets of the trust are 'financial'. Under this definition, an entity that does not hold 'financial assets' – for example, a trust solely owning holding real estate – should not be an 'investment entity', even if it is managed by a financial institution and does not fit into the definition of any other type of FFI.

Whether a trust is professionally managed will be clear if, for example, the trustee is a company and that company runs or is part of fiduciary business and charging a fee. Where a fee is not directly charged, but the trustee entity is part of a wider group obtaining income from activities connected with the trust, it is still expected that the trust will be treated as professionally managed. The case of private trust companies is less clear; but provided that such company charges a fee, it is generally accepted that a trust with a private trust company as trustee will be treated as an FFI.[3] Consequently, non-US trusts managed by individuals

---

3   For further discussion, see the STEP guidance note "FATCA: Trusts under a Model 1 Intergovernmental Agreement (IGA): Jurisdiction X"; www.step.org/sites/default/files/ Policy/model1-intergovernmental-agreementv3.pdf, 15 September 2014.

(rather than a company) are generally not FFIs, but are instead NFFEs, which are subject to much less onerous requirements under FATCA.

2.3 Trust FATCA compliance

Trusts are generally not treated for FATCA purposes as owned by other entities that will themselves comply with FATCA as FFIs. Accordingly, trusts may have their own reporting obligations in relation to their US reportable accounts. The rules for when a trust will have US reportable accounts differ under the Model 1 IGA on the one hand and the Model 2 IGA and Treasury Regulations on the other hand. Under the Model 2 IGA and the Treasury Regulations, a trust will have US accounts in reasonably limited circumstances. Generally, only US beneficiaries who actually receive trust distributions in a particular year are considered to have US accounts in the trust. Under the Model 1 IGA, a trust may have US accounts in broader circumstances than under the Model 2 IGA and the Treasury Regulations. First, under the Model 1 IGA, a US discretionary beneficiary of a trust who may receive a distribution from the trust in a given year is considered to have a US account in the trust, even if the beneficiary does not actually receive a distribution. This said, some governments of Model 1 IGA jurisdictions have released guidance specifying that, in spite of the IGA language, a discretionary US beneficiary will be treated as having a US account in a trust only in a calendar year in which the beneficiary actually receives a distribution from the trust.

Where reporting is required because the trust is an FFI, the reported information will include the following:

- the name, address and taxpayer identification number (TIN) of each individual account holder that is a specified US person or, if the account is held by a US-owned foreign entity, the name of the foreign entity and the name, address and TIN of each substantial US owner of that entity;
- the account balance or value; and
- the gross amount of all distributions during the year.

Where a trust is an NFFE, such reporting is not required. Rather, to comply with FATCA and ensure that withholding is not applied, the trust will certify to the payer that it does not have any substantial US owners or identify such substantial US owners.

3. Common Reporting Standard

3.1 Overview

Following the United States' implementation of FATCA, the OECD accelerated work on a multilateral automatic exchange of information regime which resulted in the CRS: the Standard for Automatic Exchange of Financial Account

Information developed by the OECD. CRS is a minimum standard for jurisdictions (through their taxing authorities) to obtain information from their financial institutions and automatically exchange that information with other jurisdictions on an annual basis. The CRS specifies:

- which financial institutions must report;
- which accounts such financial institutions must report on;
- what due diligence procedures such financial institutions must apply; and
- what information on such accounts such financial institutions must collect and report.

Participating jurisdictions must translate the CRS into domestic law as well as base the automatic exchange of CRS information with counterparty jurisdictions on some international agreement (eg, a bilateral agreement such as a double tax treaty or a tax information exchange agreement, or a multilateral agreement). To facilitate the international information exchange contemplated by the CRS, a multilateral agreement pursuant to Article 6 of the Convention on Mutual Administrative Assistance in Tax Matters has been created (Multilateral Competent Authority Agreement).[4] At the time of writing, there are 106 signatories to the Multilateral Competent Authority Agreement,[5] including major European countries and offshore centres.

3.2   Basic architecture

The CRS is primarily based on the Model 1 IGA for the implementation of FATCA discussed above. As with FATCA, trusts are considered 'entities' in their own right, but their compliance will be effected by the trustee of the trust. A trust is resident in the jurisdiction in which it is considered tax resident or where its trustees are resident.[6] Broadly, an entity will have to determine whether it is a 'financial institution'. If it is not, it will be treated as a 'non-financial entity'. These definitions broadly track the definitions in the Model 1 IGAs.

A financial institution which is resident in a CRS jurisdiction will have to report accounts that it maintains for residents in counterparty CRS jurisdictions. This reporting is made to the financial institution's local taxing authority, which will then exchange this information on an annual, automatic basis with the taxing authority where each particular account holder is tax resident. A non-financial entity will have to certify to financial institutions with which it maintains accounts as to its 'controlling persons' – under current guidance, its

---

4   For exchanges between EU member states, the European Union has transposed the CRS by virtue of the amended EU Directive on Administrative Cooperation (DAC2).
5   www.oecd.org/tax/automatic-exchange/international-framework-for-the-crs/crs-mcaa-signatories.pdf
6   The OECD's CRS Implementation Handbook, 2nd edn para.249 and 250.

25% direct or indirect equity owners who are natural persons, or, if none, the natural person who otherwise exercises control over the management of the entity – to any financial institutions with which it maintains accounts. Any direct debt or equity interest in a financial institution will be treated as an account (which, if held by a tax resident of a jurisdiction that is a CRS counterparty, will be reportable). If the interest is held by an entity that is not a resident of a jurisdiction that has adopted CRS, then the controlling persons of such entity will have to be identified.

Trusts receive special treatment under the CRS guidance. A trust may qualify as either a financial institution or a non-financial entity. The circumstances in which a trust is likely to be treated as a financial institution are those in which it derives at least one-half of its income from passive sources and a professional trust company or fee charging private trust company serves as trustee.[7] Where a trust is a financial institution, it is required to report annually its reportable accounts. The debt and equity interests in a trust are reportable accounts if held by a person who is resident in another CRS participating jurisdiction. The CRS deems settlors, fixed interest beneficiaries, discretionary beneficiaries who receive distributions in a reporting period and individuals exercising ultimate effective control over a trust to have an equity interest in a trust (which concept includes, at least, individual trustees and protectors). Where such persons are non-financial entities, they must be looked through and the controlling persons of such entity must be identified. The information disclosed about each person is as follows:

- Settlor – the total value of all the trust property and all payments made to him or her;
- Fixed interest beneficiary – the total value of all the trust property and all payments made to him or her;
- Discretionary beneficiary receiving distributions – all payments made to him or her;
- Discretionary beneficiary not receiving distributions – nothing; and
- Individual exercising effective control – the total value of all the trust property and all payments made to the settlor.

Where a trust is treated as a non-financial entity, it must be able to provide details of its controlling persons to a reporting financial institution. A trust's controlling persons mirror those persons deemed to have an equity interest in a trust which is a financial institution: the settlor, trustee, beneficiaries, protectors and any other individual exercising ultimate effective control over

7   For further discussion, see the STEP guidance note 'CRS and Trusts' – www.step.org/sites/default/files/Policy/Guidance_note_CRS_and_trusts.pdf – 8 March 2017 as well as the OECD's CRS Implementation Handbook, 2nd edn para 244

the trust. The consequence of this mirroring is that the only substantive difference in the CRS guidance between the reporting required of trusts that are treated as financial institutions and those treated as non-financial entities is that the latter would identify as their controlling persons all beneficiaries (not just those receiving distributions in a given year).

4. UK Trust Registration Service

The origins of the UK TRS are different from FATCA and the CRS. This is not a UK initiative to share information with third parties, but to gather information on trusts which have or are expected to have UK tax liabilities. It is part of the United Kingdom's implementation of MLD4. It is not a public database, but under MLD5 (which the United Kingdom intends to implement despite Brexit), the information will need to be made available to those with a legitimate interest in the information. What amounts to a legitimate interest has not been defined at the time of writing, but the UK government's expectation is that this must be linked to combating money laundering and terrorist financing.[8]

Under the UK TRS, a trust is registrable if either it is UK tax resident or the trustees are directly liable for UK taxes (mainly income tax, capital gains tax, inheritance tax and stamp duty land tax). The trustees of taxable relevant trusts must provide Her Majesty's Revenue and Customs (HMRC) with the following information:

- the full name of the trust;
- the date on which the trust was set up;
- a statement of accounts for the trust, describing the trust assets and identifying the value of each category of the trust assets at the date on which the information is first provided to HMRC (including the address of any property held by the trust);
- the country where the trust is considered to be resident for tax purposes;
- the place where the trust is administered;
- a contact address for the trustees; and
- the names of any paid legal, tax or financial advisers.

The trustees must also register information about the beneficial owners of the trust. Beneficial owners include the settlor, the trustees, the beneficiaries and any individual who has control over the trust. For these purposes, 'control' includes anyone with the power to make dispositive decisions, amend the trust, revoke the trust, alter the beneficial class, change the trustees or direct/veto any of these decisions.

---

8   See UK consultation paper "Transposition of the Fifth Money Laundering Directive: consultation", https://assets.publishing.service.gov.uk/government/uploads/system/uploads/attachment_data/file/795 670/20190415_Consultation_on_the_Transposition_of_5MLD__web.pdf, 15 April 2019.

In the case of beneficiaries two circumstances merit attention. First, where the beneficiaries are a class all of whom have not been or cannot be determined, the trustees can simply identify the class without naming all individuals. However, where a beneficiary has in fact received a distribution, he or she must be individually identified and the information listed below provided. Second, the concept of 'beneficiary' includes a potential beneficiary. This concept is ill defined, but is expected to catch persons named in letters of wishes who are anticipated will receive a benefit at some stage. However, if the circumstances in which they are expected to benefit are contingent, disclosure is expected only when such contingency is met.

Once a person has been identified as a beneficial owner, the trustee must provide HMRC with the following information:

- the person's full name, date of birth and role regarding the trust; and
- the person's national insurance number or taxpayer reference, failing which his or her residential address. If there is no UK address, the trustee must provide the individual's passport number or identification card number.

In 2020 the UK TRS is expected to be expanded to apply to all express trusts established in the United Kingdom and all non-UK express trusts which own land in the United Kingdom or have a business relationship with a UK obliged entity, including legal advisers. Similarly, while this chapter addresses the UK response to the EU directive, these obligations apply in all other EU member states and so extensive trust information will be reported to and centralised in all these countries.

5.   UK persons with significant control regime

As part of the UK government's drive to establish greater transparency over the ownership of UK companies and in compliance with MLD4, it established the PSC regime. This regime was introduced to compel the directors of UK companies to identify people controlling more than 25% of a UK company or who in fact or otherwise have the right to exercise significant influence or control over a UK company. Each UK company must create and maintain a register identifying their PSCs and include information such as the name of the individual, date of birth, nationality, service address, country or state of usual residence and the nature of his or her control over the company. The majority of the information on the register is publicly available, subject to some key omissions, and the entire register is available to UK government agencies. The only permitted reason for an identified PSC not to appear on the register is by court order on the basis there is a real risk of physical harm to the individual or persons living with him or her. Failure to comply is backed up by criminal penalties both for the UK company directors and for individuals who ought to have known they were PSCs, as the latter have an obligation to notify the company of their status.

Where trusts are direct or indirect owners of UK companies, the PSC regime requires an analysis of the trust relationship to determine whether any participant in the trust is a PSC. The definition of a PSC is any individual who:

- holds (directly or indirectly) more than 25% of the shares in the company;
- holds (directly or indirectly) more than 25% of the voting rights in the company;
- has the right or ability to replace more than half the board of the company;
- has the right or does in fact exercise significant influence or control over the company; or
- has the right or does in fact exercise significant influence or control over trustees, where such trustees meet one of the foregoing criteria.

It is this final category, category 5, which is of concern here. Where the trustees themselves meet one of the other conditions, the PSC regime mandates an inquiry into the terms of and actual operation of the trust relationship to ascertain whether there is 'significant influence or control' over the trustees. What is meant by significant influence or control is not defined in the legislation and is the subject of government guidance. At the time of writing, the material part of this guidance stated:[9]

A person has the right to exercise "significant influence or control" over a trust or firm if that person has the right to direct or influence the running of the activities of the trust or firm, for example:

    (a) Right to appoint or remove any of the trustees or partners, except through application to the courts, or as a result of a breach of fiduciary duty by the trustees;

    (b) Right to direct the distribution of funds or assets;

    (c) Right to direct investment decisions of the trust or firm;

    (d) Right to amend the trust or partnership deed; or

    (e) Right to revoke the trust or terminate the partnership.

A person is likely to exercise significant influence or control over a trust or firm if they are regularly involved in the running of the trust or firm, for example a person who issues instructions, which are generally followed, as to the activities of the trust or firm to the trustee(s) or members of the firm. This may be a settlor or beneficiary who is actively involved in directing the activities of the trust.

As will be self-evident from this extract, most holders of settlor reserved

---

9   https://assets.publishing.service.gov.uk/government/uploads/system/uploads/attachment_data/file/675104/psc-statutory-guidance-companies.pdf.

powers or beneficiaries who also are involved with investment policy are therefore potentially within the PSC definition, whether or not they are involved in the trust's activities. This is an evolving area, but the fact that non-compliance with the PSC regime carries criminal sanctions for both the company directors and individuals who ought to have known they could be PSCs is a strong indicator of the UK government's expectation that people will err on the side of caution and disclose their PSC status.

The suitability of these definitions for analysing information concerning the tax profile of a trust are open to debate. Two common issues are illustrative:

- Corporate trustees: Insufficient consideration appears to have been given to the relevance of analysing/disclosing corporate ownership above a corporate trustee while also reporting any individuals who have the right to or do in fact wield significant influence or control by virtue of the terms of the trust relationship. The PSC regime's analysis and guidance are focused on ascertaining effective ultimate control of companies. However, where there is a trust, the category 5 analysis appears to be focused on effective control of the trustee or the trust's key dispositive decisions. There is therefore a tension between an analysis of the corporate ownership of the trustee entity (eg, its shareholders) and the analysis of the trust relationship. At the time of writing, there is no authoritative guidance on how to resolve this tension. It remains to be seen whether the fiduciary duties of a corporate trustee would be considered paramount by the directors and consequently disclosure/analysis of the shareholders of a corporate trustee not to be required and, indeed, could produce a misleading impression of involvement in the trustee duties of the corporate trustee which should not exist (especially where the parent of the trust company is a regulated/listed professional service provision business).
- Trust beneficiaries: PSC category 5 is, in practice, often difficult to apply. The statutory guidance of the right to control/influence extracted above appears focused on the ability to rewrite the trust, 'direct' the trustee in the exercise of his or her powers or replace the trustee. While these rights assist in identifying abilities to influence a trust, they may have little relevance to who actually enjoys a trust's assets – the matter which one may argue is far more relevant when considering a trust situation generally and certainly in a tax analysis. In many situations, a trust has a wide class of people who may and do benefit such that implying or attributing ownership or rights to individuals who hold but do not use powers can often be arbitrary or misleading.

At the time of writing, the UK government has stated that it intends to extend this PSC obligation to non-UK companies which own UK land, requiring them to keep registers of their PSCs, using the same PSC definitions listed above. Therefore, trusts which indirectly own UK land through non-UK companies will also be caught by this disclosure regime. The register is intended to be held at Companies House and will need to be updated annually. The register will be the first of its kind in the world with the potential to directly affect all legal entities (including but not limited to companies, partnerships and trusts) that hold or intend to hold UK property. Under current proposals, there will also be serious practical repercussions stemming from failure to register beneficial ownership. Without a registration number, the entity will be unable to register as the owner of property at the Land Registry, which could prevent the sale or lease of land as well. Additionally, as an anti-avoidance measure, it is proposed that the purchaser will not receive the full legal property interest in the land.

6. Conclusion

As will be clear from this brief discussion, there is already an extensively developed network of overlapping disclosure regimes whereby previously confidential information regarding the value of trust property and the identity of trust settlors and beneficiaries will be made known automatically to those individuals' taxing authorities. Furthermore, the collation of trust registers in the United Kingdom (and other EU member states) will be available to other government agencies and those who can demonstrate a 'legitimate interest' in that information. While the UK government appears to be taking a sensible approach in defining this terms as tied to the anti-money laundering activity, it remains to be seen whether this will be the full extent of the provision or whether other unforeseen interests will be granted access to the extensive information held by tax authorities. The direction of travel has been clear: drastically enhanced disclosure regarding trusts to governments to assist them in assessing and collecting tax and combating crime. Can it be safely concluded that only government authorities have – or will ever have – a legitimate interest in accessing these databases?

About the authors

Moses J Anahory
Partner, Hassans
moses.anahory@hassans.gi

Moses Anahory joined Hassans in 1994 before returning to London in 1996 to join global law firm Baker & McKenzie, specialising in advising on tax planning strategies for resident, non-resident and non-domiciled individuals, and on inheritance and probate matters. He returned to his native Gibraltar and rejoined Hassans in 2000.

Mr Anahory is one of the firm's leading lawyers in setting up, administering and advising on offshore trust structures. He advises on issues concerning the formation and validity of complex trust structures, and on the ongoing operation of trusts across jurisdictions. He also provides active management and control for major investors in UK real estate.

Mr Anahory qualified as a barrister in 1994 and qualified as a solicitor in 1997. He became a member of the Society of Trust and Estate Practitioners (STEP) in 2005. He has contributed chapters and articles to several publications on the law, formation and administration of trusts, and has spoken on the same subject at a number of trusts conferences.

Makoto Arai
Professor of law, Chuo University
makotoar@guitar.ocn.ne.jp

Makoto Arai is a professor and the dean of the Graduate School of Law at Chuo University in Tokyo. His research interests include the use of the trust system in an ageing society and the encouragement of better utilisation of adult guardianship. His major works include *Trust Law* (4th edition, 2014), *Visions of the Trust Law System* (co-author, 2011) and *Visions of the Adult Guardianship Law System* (co-author, 2011). He has also authored numerous articles and is particularly noted for his work in comparative law.

Professor Arai received the Humboldt Research Award in 2006 and the Officer's Cross of the Order of Merit of the Federal Republic of Germany in 2010. He is also the president of the Japan Adult Guardianship Association and a standing director of the Japan Association for the Law of Trust. He also serves as chair of the Agency for Cultural Affairs' Religious Juridical Persons Council.

Daniel Bader
Partner, Bär & Karrer AG
daniel.bader@baerkarrer.ch

Daniel Bader provides national and international tax, social security and legal advice to individuals and corporate clients. He advises private clients, executives and entrepreneurs on tax and legal-related questions, including succession planning, compensation plans and private wealth structures.

Mr Bader develops solutions, particularly relating to cross-border structuring and to corporate and private relocations to and from Switzerland. He assists clients with questions regarding income and wealth tax, estate and gift taxes, real estate tax and social security.

Mr Bader is a frequent speaker at national and international tax and private client conferences, and acts as a board member of family offices. He is president of the Swiss branch of the International Fiscal Association. He is listed as a leading lawyer by *Chambers*, *Legal 500* and *Citywealth*. Furthermore, *Who's Who Legal 2018* recognised him as expert in the practice areas Private Client and Corporate Tax.

Stanley A Barg
Partner, Kozusko Harris Duncan
SBarg@kozlaw.com

Stanley Barg practises in the areas of tax and estate planning, with an emphasis on planning for international families, including US income, estate and gift taxation, the use of trusts, expatriation and other related matters.

Mr Barg is a member of STEP's Worldwide Council and was previously the chairman of STEP USA. In addition, he is a member of the American Bar Association's taxation and real property, probate and trust law and international sections; the International Bar Association; and the International Tax Planning Association. He has also been recognised by Citywealth as a member of its leaders list in private wealth management for North America.

Mr Barg is admitted to practise in New York, the District of Columbia and Pennsylvania, and is also a member of the Israel Bar Association qualified to practise in Israel as a foreign lawyer.

Allan Blaikie
Senior tax counsel, Clayton Utz
ablaikie@claytonutz.com

Allan Blaikie formerly headed up the Clayton Utz national taxation team. With over 40 years' experience, including over a decade as a chartered accountant, Mr Blaikie advises leading Australian and international companies and high-net-worth individuals on a broad range of international and domestic tax matters. He has been involved in the successful conduct of several landmark Australian tax cases, particularly in the area of tax treaty interpretation. He has also led large multi-disciplinary teams in the conduct of Australian and international tax audits and reviews. Mr Blaikie also provides oversight on large taxation engagements undertaken by corporate tax departments, auditors and so on. His practice also extends to undertaking sensitive matters for governments and government authorities in the area of taxation.

Rachel Blumenfeld
Partner, Aird & Berlis LLP
rblumenfeld@airdberlis.com

Rachel Blumenfeld is a partner in Aird & Berlis LLP's estates and trusts group and tax group. Her practice focuses on trusts and estates, personal tax planning and charities and not-for-profit law. She advises on tax, trusts, estate planning and administration, preparation of wills and powers of attorney documents, business succession and insurance planning.

Ms Blumenfeld advises on tax and estate planning for families with children with special needs. She has significant experience with cross-border planning for clients who have US or other foreign connections. She is an active member of STEP Canada, serving as national secretary from 2014–2019, and is currently deputy chair of STEP Canada. Ms Blumenfeld was awarded the 2018 STEP Canada Volunteer of the Year award. She is recognised in *Chambers HNW: The World's Leading High Net Worth Advisers* for her expertise in private wealth law and *The Canadian Legal Expert Directory* as a leading practitioner in Estate & Personal Tax Planning and Charities and Not-for-Profit Law.

Alexander A Bove, Jr
Partner, Bove & Langa Law Firm
bove@bovelanga.com

Alexander Bove is an internationally known and respected trust and estate attorney with over 35 years of experience. He is admitted to practise in Massachusetts and as a solicitor in England and Wales. In addition to a JD and LLM, Mr Bove earned his doctorate in law from the University of Zurich Law School.

Mr Bove frequently serves as an expert witness in matters requiring extensive knowledge and experience in the field of trusts, wills and probate. His practice encompasses domestic and international estate planning, and he is regularly consulted by US attorneys and other professionals on issues relating to cross-border estate planning in such jurisdictions as the United Kingdom, Italy, Germany and France.

He has published seven books, including three law books. His latest book, *Trust Protectors – A Practice Manual with Forms*, is available through Juris Publishing.

Bernadette Carey
Partner, Carey Olsen
Bernadette.Carey@careyolsen.com

Bernadette Carey is a partner in Carey Olsen's Cayman Islands office. She has a broad private client practice advising on wealth structuring and estate planning matters, including the administration, restructuring and termination of trusts, as well as probate and testamentary issues. She also has significant experience in trust litigation, regularly appearing before the Grand Court of the Cayman Islands on multi-party contentious trust disputes, estate litigation and other cross-border private client disputes. She is a member of STEP and an international fellow of the American College of Trusts and Estates Counsel. Ms Carey is recognised for her trusts and private client work by *Chambers, Who's Who Legal* and *Legal 500*, with market sources describing her as "incredibly hard-working" and "really first class".

Nina Clift
Senior associate, Carey Olsen (Guernsey) LLP
nina.clift@careyolsen.com

Nina Clift is a senior associate in Carey Olsen's trusts and private wealth group, and advises individual fiduciaries as well as trust companies and commercial clients. She drafts bespoke trust instruments and advises on contentious and non-contentious trust matters. Her practice also includes estate planning for local and international clients, the drafting of wills and codicils, and the administration of estates, together with advising on probate issues.

Lyat Eyal

Partner, Aronson, Ronkin-Noor, Eyal Law Firm
lyat@are-legal.com

Lyat Eyal manages the firm's private client practice with a focus on multi-jurisdictional estate planning, including trusts, wills, durable powers of attorney and pre-immigration planning for international families. She also provides services in connection with probate and estate administration matters.

Ms Eyal was admitted to the New York State Bar in 1998 and practised law at New York law firm Faust Oppenheim, LLP. She was admitted to the Israel Bar in 2005 and practised law at Alon Kaplan Law Firm until 2015, when she founded Aronson, Ronkin-Noor Eyal Law Firm together with her partners.

Ms Eyal is a member of STEP, the New York State Bar Association Trusts and Estates Law and International Sections and the International Tax Specialist Group. She is also a fellow at the American College of Trust and Estate Counsel and an academician at the International Academy of Estate and Trust Law.

David Faust

Partner, Gallet Dreyer & Berkey LLP
DIF@gdblaw.com

David Faust represents US and non-US individuals and public and private entities on commercial, corporate, real estate, trust, estate and tax matters, including cross-border corporate, tax, estate planning and trust issues.

His practice includes estate planning for clients with assets and/or family in more than one country. He has prepared a wide variety of charter documents, contracts, financial instruments, wills and trusts for asset protection, charitable giving and business continuity, providing for heirs with special needs and general estate planning. He has also probated, challenged and defended wills and trusts in various US and non-US courts.

Mr Faust has participated in numerous programmes in the United States and internationally on trust law and other legal topics. He was qualified as an expert witness in international trusts by the Supreme Court, Westchester County in an international asset protection trust litigation.

Mathew Fenwick

Lawyer, Clayton Utz
mfenwick@claytonutz.com

Mathew Fenwick is a lawyer in the Sydney tax practice of Clayton Utz. He practises in matters involving domestic and international tax laws, with a focus on the taxation of trusts. He advises generally on tax structures, direct and indirect taxation, tax disputes, securitisation, corporate tax, cross-border transactions, tax residence and the taxation of trusts. He also has broad experience in administrative law and litigation.

Wayne Fortunato

Partner, Hassans
wayne.fortunato@hassans.gi

Wayne Fortunato is a partner of Hassans, specialising in all aspects of trusts, from their legal drafting to their management and administration.

Educated in Gibraltar, he received an honours degree in accounting and finance from Teesside University before going on to complete a postgraduate diploma in law, along with the Bar Vocational Course, at the University of Northumbria in Newcastle. He was called to the Bar of England and Wales in 2002, as a member of the Middle Temple, followed shortly after by admission to the Gibraltar Bar.

Mr Fortunato also holds a Diploma in International Trust Management from STEP and has contributed chapters and articles to several publications on the law, formation and administration of trusts.

Michael W Galligan
Partner, Phillips Nizer LLP
mgalligan@phillipsnizer.com

Michael W Galligan, PhD, JD, TEP, is a partner in the trusts and estates department of New York law firm Phillips Nizer LLP, where he practises primarily in the areas of domestic and international estates and trusts, US and cross-border estate and income tax planning, private international law and immigration. A former chair of the International Section and recent member of the executive committee of the New York State Bar Association, Mr Galligan is a fellow of the American College of Trust and Estate Counsel and an academician of the International Academy of Estate and Trust Law. He is a graduate of the Columbia University Law School (JD 1985) and was an editor of the *Columbia Law Review*. He also holds a PhD in religious studies from the Yale University Graduate School and an MA in international affairs from Columbia's School of Public and International Affairs.

Simon Gibb
Partner, McDermott Will & Emery
sgibb@mwe.com

Simon Gibb is a partner in the law firm of McDermott Will & Emery, based in its London office. He focuses his practice on tax advice, trust and estate planning for UK and non-UK resident and domiciled individuals, including

on the protection and devolution of trust assets. While he advises on all aspects of personal taxation and structuring, his practice has an emphasis on the structuring of family businesses through trusts and foundations. Mr Gibb is regularly involved in both non-contentious and contentious tax work.

Mr Gibb also advises individuals, family offices and trustees of offshore settlements on trust law matters and UK tax matters.

Maggie Gonzalez
Partner, Buzzacott LLP
gonzalezm@buzzacott.co.uk

Maggie Gonzalez is a tax partner in the private client team at Buzzacott, based in London. She has over 25 years' experience within the international private client field, specialising in the UK taxation of offshore trusts, their settlors and beneficiaries and non-UK domiciled individuals generally. She helps her clients to navigate the complexities of the extensive UK anti-avoidance legislation as it applies to internationally mobile clients and their structures, providing practical solutions to the many challenges they encounter. This includes advising on residence, domicile and the operation of the remittance basis. She is a chartered accountant and chartered tax adviser. She is a member of the Chartered Institute of Taxation's technical sub-committees covering succession taxes, capital gains tax and the taxation of investment income.

Justin Harvey-Hills
Partner, Mourant Ozannes
Justin.Harvey-Hills@mourantozannes.com

Justin Harvey-Hills has been a partner in the international trust and private client group and the litigation group in the Jersey office of Mourant Ozannes since 2010. He specialises in banking, financial services, corporate and trust litigation. He has particular experience of investment and employee fraud, asset recovery, anti-money laundering legislation, regulatory investigations and trust disputes.

Mr Harvey-Hills qualified as an English solicitor in 1997 (currently non-practising). He then spent six years with Simmons & Simmons in London before joining Mourant Ozannes in 2003. He was admitted as a Jersey advocate in 2005.

Mr Harvey-Hills has been counsel in a number of the most important Jersey cases of recent years, and appears regularly in the Royal Court and Court of Appeal. He also appeared in the Judicial Committee of the Privy Council in *La Générale des Carrières et des Mines SARL v FG Hemisphere Associates LLC.*

Barbara R Hauser
Independent family adviser
brhauser@gmail.com

Barbara Hauser has combined extensive experience advising families, family businesses and family offices first as a private client lawyer and later with a focus on governance. Ms Hauser has helped families to develop their unique governance process, which may include a family constitution, a family council and a holding company board. She is a sought-after speaker and prolific writer, and is often referred to as a true thought leader in the family office field.

Her books include *International Family Governance, International Estate Planning, Trusts in Prime Jurisdictions* (advisory editor, Globe Law and Business), *"Mommy, are we Rich?"*: *Family Offices Handbook; Talking to Children about Family Money* (co-author); *Never Ask Where You Are; Saudi-Girl Barbara;* and *Selling Dog Food in Japan.*

Her articles include "The Family Office: Insights into Their Development in the US, A Proposed Prototype and Advice for Adaptation in Other Countries", "Family Office Trends: Lessons from Dubai?" and "The Family Office Landscape: Today's Trends & Five Predictions for the Family Office of Tomorrow". Ms Hauser is also the editor of Globe Law and Business's *International Family Offices Journal* and is listed in the *Spears 500.*

Ying Hui
Associate, Withers LLP
ying.hui@withersworldwide.com

Ying Hui is an associate in the private client and tax team of Withers Hong Kong. She advises high-net-worth individuals and trust corporations on a broad range of private client matters, with a particular focus on trusts, wills, estate and succession planning, as well as establishment of charitable organisations. Ms Hui is admitted as a solicitor in Hong Kong and England and Wales and as an attorney at law in New York State, United States. She is also a qualified trust and estate practitioner.

Raoul Jacobs
Senior policy adviser in financial supervision
raoul.jacobs@bafin.de

Raoul Jacobs' professional background is in law, which he studied in Gottingen, Vienna and Manchester, United Kingdom. He also obtained a PhD from Gottingen University on "Mandate and Trusteeship in international Law". He worked in corporate law firms in Hamburg and Dubai before joining the government service in Germany. He has been active in international policy-making organisations such as the European Securities and Markets Authority, the International Organization of Securities Commissions and the Financial Action Task Force (FATF), dealing with a wide range of different topics.

Dominique Jakob

Professor of private law; director of the Center for Foundation Law, University of Zurich; independent adviser
dominique.jakob@rwi.uzh.ch

Dominique Jakob is a professor of private law at the University of Zurich. Of German origin, he was appointed as a full professor at the University of Zurich in 2007, where he established the Center for Foundation Law in 2008. Alongside his university work, he has developed a successful national and international private practice. His main fields are all aspects of foundation law (with a focus on Swiss, Liechtenstein, and German relations), as well as international estate and wealth planning (including trusts).

He is the author of numerous publications, a sought-after speaker at international conferences and a board member of various institutions, and acts as independent counsel to governments, financial institutions, companies, foundations, associations, families and private clients. Professor Jakob is a member of the International Academy of Estate and Trust Law and has been elected in the Private Client Global Elite since 2017.

Alon Kaplan

Founder and managing partner, Alon Kaplan Advocate & Notary
alon@alonkaplan-law.com

Alon Kaplan, PhD, TEP, was admitted to the Israel Bar in 1970 and appointed a notary in 1989. He was admitted to the New York Bar in 1990 and became a member of the Frankfurt Bar in 2010.

Mr Kaplan was among the founders of STEP Israel and currently serves as its president. He is an academic coordinator and lecturer on the STEP diploma programme. He was also an adjunct lecturer at the law faculty of Tel Aviv University and lectured on its LLM programme.

Mr Kaplan is an academician of the International Academy of Estate and Trust Law and of the American College of Trust and Estate Counsel, and has advised the Israeli Tax Authority on trust legislation.

He obtained a PhD from Zurich University in 2014. His doctoral dissertation was titled "Trusts in Israel: Development and Current Practice".

Natasha Kapp

Partner, Carey Olsen (Guernsey) LLP
natasha.kapp@careyolsen.com

Natasha Kapp is a partner in Carey Olsen's trusts and private wealth group in Guernsey. She deals with all aspects of contentious and non-contentious trust matters. She advises professional trustees, family offices and ultra-high-net-worth families and individuals on the establishment, administration and restructuring of complex trusts and foundations and underlying structures. She has acted on the establishment of and continues to advise some of the largest family offices and philanthropies established on the island.

Ms Kapp has recently appeared before the Royal Court of Guernsey in applications regarding the interpretation of trust powers, the variation of trusts, the doctrine of mistake, the application of the Rule in *Hastings Bass* under Guernsey law, Beddoe applications, rectification of trusts and a significant breach of trust case. She is a member of the Association of Contentious Trusts and Probate Specialists

Vanessa King
Managing partner, O'Neal Webster
VKing@onealwebster.com

Vanessa King is managing partner of O'Neal Webster and heads the firm's corporate and commercial department. She is based in the firm's BVI office and specialises principally in BVI trusts, estate planning and private client wealth management, but enjoys a diversified practice which includes banking and finance, corporate and commercial law. Her client base covers the major financial centres of the world, domestic and international financial institutions, leading onshore law firms and trust companies.

Ms King serves as the current chair of the BVI branch of STEP and as deputy chair of STEP's Caribbean and Latin America region. In October 2017 she was elected to serve a three-year term on BVI Finance's board of directors and she is also a member of the administrative committee of the Financial Services Institute.

Hein Kötz
Emeritus director, *Max-Planck-Institut für ausländisches und internationales Privatrecht*;
International Academy of Comparative Law
koetz@mpipriv-hh.mpg.de

Hein Kötz is emeritus director of the *Max-Planck-Institut für ausländisches und internationals Privatrecht*; and of the International Academy of Comparative Law. He represented Germany for the Hague Trust Convention and was a member of the German Federal Commission on the Reform of the Civil

Law of Obligations. He is a fellow of the British Academy, a member of Academia Europaea and of the International Academy of Comparative Law. Until 2004 he was president of the International Association of Legal Science.

Daniel Leu
Partner, Bär & Karrer Ltd
daniel.leu@baerkarrer.ch

Daniel Leu advises private clients and family offices on wealth and succession planning, the handling of estates, foundations and trusts, and questions connected to place of residence. Other areas of work include advising clients who buy or sell real estate in Switzerland and advising on art law.

Dr Leu is a certified Swiss Bar Associaton inheritance law specialist and publishes regularly in the field of inheritance law. He frequently lectures on trust and estate matters in Switzerland and abroad. In addition to his practice, Dr Leu is a lecturer at the University of Muenster, Germany (Master of Law in Inheritance Law & Corporate Succession).

Dr Leu is recommended by *Chambers and Partners, Who's Who Legal, Legal 500* and the *Legal Week Private Client Global Elite Directory*.

James Levy
Senior partner, Hassans
james.levy@hassans.gi

James Levy, CBE QC, is the senior partner of Hassans, specialising in corporate and international tax law. He was appointed Queen's Counsel in October 2002 and, in 2013, was awarded a CBE for his services to the community of Gibraltar and for his work in helping to grow and develop its economy.

Mr Levy advises large public companies on

mergers and acquisitions and property companies on acquisitions throughout Europe. He is often called upon by high-net-worth individuals from around the world to advise on complicated commercial and family dispute resolution. He assisted the government of Gibraltar on its development of the jurisdiction as a finance centre.

Mr Levy is consistently ranked as a leading individual by the *Legal 500* and has been awarded Star Practitioner status by *Chambers and Partners* every year since 2007. *Chambers and Partners* also conferred the highly prestigious Lifetime Achievement Award upon Mr Levy in May 2008.

Meytal Liberman

Associate attorney, Herzog, Fox & Neeman
libermanm@hfn.co.il

Meytal Liberman, LLB (Bar-Ilan), LLM (Tel Aviv), TEP, was admitted to the Israeli Bar in 2013. She advises private clients from Israel and overseas on trusts and estate planning as an associate advocate at the law office of Herzog Fog & Neeman, after acquiring expertise in her field of practice over the course of her employment with Dr Alon Kaplan, Advocate & Notary. Ms Liberman has been a member of STEP since 2015, after she completed two years of studies and earned a diploma in international trust management. She is the general editor of, and a contributor to, the book *Trust in Israel: Theory and Practice* by Dr Alon Kaplan, published in 2017 (Hebrew), and has also authored articles published in publications such as *Trusts & Trustees, The International Family Office Journal* and the *STEP Journal*.

Dietmar Loretz

Lawyer, David Vogt & Partner
dietmar.loretz@dvp.li

Dietmar Loretz is a specialist with over 25 years' experience, providing expert legal, tax and financial advice and assistance with regard to the formation and administration of foundations and trusts; the incorporation and management of companies; trust and estate planning; wealth preservation and protection of assets.

He obtained his law degree from the University of Vienna and an MBA in international wealth management from the Swiss Banking School on a joint programme of the University of Geneva and the Tepper School of Business, Carnegie Mellon University, Pittsburgh, United States. He is a member of STEP and the International Tax Planning Association.

Jacqueline Marxer-Tschikof

Lawyer, David Vogt & Partner
jacqueline.marxer@dvp.li

Jacqueline Marxer-Tschikof obtained her law degree from University of Bern. After practising at the Liechtenstein court and working for the Liechtenstein government, she spent several years at a Liechtenstein law firm. In 2016 she was admitted to the Liechtenstein Bar Association. She joined David Vogt & Partner in 2018.

Paul Matthams

Partner, Stonehage Fleming
paul.matthams@stonehagefleming.com

Paul Matthams is a partner at Stonehage Fleming, having joined the multi-family office group in 2018. Prior to that, he was a lawyer in private practice in Jersey for over 30 years, specialising in non-contentious trusts and estates law and pensions, acting for high-net-worth individuals and families, family offices and private trust companies. He has particular skills in drafting technical trusts and foundation documentation tailored to meet client needs.

Mr Matthams is a graduate of Cambridge University and was called to the Bar of England and Wales in 1981. He qualified as an English solicitor in 1988 and a notary public and an advocate of the Royal Court of Jersey in 2001. He is a long-standing member of STEP.

Christopher McKenzie

Partner, O'Neal Webster
CMcKenzie@onealwebster.com

Christopher McKenzie is a partner in the London office of leading BVI firm O'Neal Webster. He was the founding chair of STEP in the British Virgin Islands and served as one of the two council members for STEP's Caribbean and Latin America region from 1999 to 2010 (and then as chair of the region for a further three years). He is also a former vice-president of the BVI Bar Association. Mr McKenzie is generally regarded as the British Virgin Islands' foremost trusts and estates expert; and from 1997 to 2012 and since 2018 has chaired the committee whose proposals led to most of the jurisdiction's most significant trust and estate reforms, including both the original Virgin Islands Special Trusts Act legislation and the equally highly regarded private trust company regulations. He is also the author of most of the British Virgin Islands' leading texts on trusts and estates, and is a frequent speaker at international trust conferences.

Priscilla Mifsud Parker

Senior partner, Chetcuti Cauchi Advocates
askpmp@cclex.com

Priscilla Mifsud Parker is a private client lawyer heading the firm's corporate trusts and fintech practices, as well as the families and wealth practice. Through her extensive knowledge in the field of corporate and trusts, she can advise on wealth structuring and wealth preservation strategies for ultra-high-net-worth individuals. She is also well versed in the process of setting up corporate structures for individuals and successful families, finding the optimal structure for businesses to protect high-value assets and reorganise complex structures. Having participated in various forums for Malta's Fintech Legislative Framework, Dr Mifsud Parker can also advise clients seeking to enter the fintech industry.

Philip Munro

Partner, Withers LLP
philip.munro@withersworldwide.com

Philip Munro is a partner in the private client and tax team. He has worked for the firm in London, Hong Kong and Singapore. His practice focuses on succession planning for international families. As well as implementing estate planning arrangement for individuals, Mr Munro frequently acts for trustees and financial institutions in relation to trust planning matters. He has been involved in recent years in a number of matters involving the administration of cross-border estates.

Ravi Nath

Partner, Rajinder Narain & Co
ravi.nath@rnclegal.com

Ravi Nath is one of India's leading lawyers and

has been recognised as such several times by *Legal 500, Chambers* and *Who's Who*. He served as president of the Inter Pacific Bar Association; chair of the Aviation Committee of the International Bar Association; and Senior Vice President of the Society of India Law Firms. The chief justice of India and the law minister conferred on him the highest honour of the Bar Association of India.

The well-known clients he advises include Boeing, Bechtel, BMW, United Technologies, Lego, Airbus, UBS, US Exim, Hermes, Deutsche Bank, BNP Paribas and Barclays. His clients also include some of India's well-known families and high-net-worth individuals. He frequently addresses international conferences and has delivered talks and lectured at various chambers of commerce and lawyers' gatherings and universities in Oxford, Hamburg, London, Zurich, New York, Chicago and Vancouver.

Filippo Noseda

Partner, Mishcon de Reya LLP
Filippo.Noseda@Mishcon.com

Filippo Noseda is a partner at Mishcon de Reya and a visiting lecturer at King's College in London. He is qualified in the United Kingdom and Switzerland, and is also admitted in the British Virgin Islands.

Mr Noseda has appeared before the European data protection authorities as an expert on the human rights and data protection implications of systems of international exchange of information and registration.

He is particularly well known for his publishing and speaking activities in his areas of expertise. His ability to tackle complex international issues in a pragmatic way has won him praise in the legal community – he has been recognised as one of the United Kingdom's Top 50 Influential Private Client Lawyers by *e-private client* and is ranked as a leading individual in both *Legal500* and *Chambers High-Net-Worth Guide*. Peers say: "Filippo Noseda has a tremendous reputation" and "stands out for his broad range of expertise" (*Legal 500*).

Mohammad Abu Obied

Judge of the High *Sharia* Court of Appeal, Jerusalem
mabuobied@yahoo.com

Mohammad Abu Obied has been judge of an Islamic court in Israel since 2005. Dealing with family law concerning Muslims, this court has powers over inheritance cases and the establishing of *Waqf* (the trust). As a part of his responsibilities as *Qadi*, he has the power to supervise the lawful management of *Waqf*s established in courts.

Mr Obied is a graduate of Essex University Law School in England and has a second BA in Islamic studies. He also has an LLM in criminal law from Haifa University. He is a member of the Israeli Bar and worked as a lawyer for six years in various fields such as company law, banking law and civil litigation. He has also provided legal advice for Bank Leumi in Israel and has worked as a director of the al-Meezan human rights group. He is a member of the High *Sharia* Court of Appeal and chairman of the *Sharia* Counsellor Ethics Board.

Paolo Panico

Partner, Paolo Panico's Law Chambers
paolo.panico@privatetrustees.net

Paolo Panico is an *avocat à la cour* in Luxembourg, a Scottish solicitor and an advocate in Romania. He is also chairman of

Private Trustees SA, an independent trust and corporate service provider in Luxembourg. He has an academic interest in the law regarding trusts and foundations and teaches courses at the University of Luxembourg and the University of Liechtenstein. He has published, among other works, *Private Foundations. Law and Practice* (Oxford University Press, 2014) and *International Trust Laws* (2nd edition, Oxford University Press, 2017). He is an academic of the International Academy of Estate and Trust Law, deputy chairman of the International Tax Planning Association and chairman of the STEP Europe Region.

Marilyn Piccini Roy
Partner, Robinson Sheppard Shapiro LLP
mpicciniroy@rsslex.com

Marilyn Piccini Roy is a partner and the head of the wealth management group at Robinson Sheppard Shapiro LLP in Montreal, practising in the areas of estates, trusts, regimes of protective supervision and elder law. She is an adjunct professor at the Faculty of Law of the McGill University. She has written numerous articles and presented seminars and conference papers on successions, trusts and elder law, and is currently a member of the editorial board of the *Estates, Trusts & Pensions Journal*. She is an academician and the secretary of the International Academy of Estate and Trust Law, an active member of STEP, an international fellow of the American College of Trust and Estate Counsel and a past president and now honorary member of the Canadian Bar Association national wills, estates and trusts executive. She is ranked in *Chambers HNW, Who's Who and Best Lawyers*.

Peter Georg Picht
Director, Center for Intellectual Property and Competition Law, University of Zurich
peter.picht@rwi.uzh.ch

Peter Georg Picht studied law at Munich University and Yale Law School, did his PhD at Munich University/the Max Planck Institute for Innovation and Competition, and holds a master's degree from Yale Law School.

He has been working with the European Commission's Directorate General for Competition, as a senior research fellow with the Max Planck Institute for Innovation and Competition and with two international law firms.

Professor Picht now holds a chair for Economic Law at the University of Zurich and is head of the University's Center for Intellectual Property and Competition Law. He remains affiliated to the Max Planck Institute as a research fellow and is of counsel with Schellenberg Wittmer. His further affiliations include board memberships in the Academic Society for Competition Law, the *Association Européenne du Droit Économique* and the Munich IP Dispute Resolution Forum. He is now a visiting professor at King's College, London.

Michael Reynolds
Managing director, Resolution Trustees Limited
mike.reynolds@resolutiontrustees.com

Michael Reynolds has specialised in corporate and trust structuring and administration for over 25 years and now provides fiduciary and corporate services via his New Zealand trustee company Resolution Trustees Limited.

He is a foundation member of the New Zealand Trustees Association (NZTA) and received the New Zealand Trustee of the Year award from the NZTA in 2000. He is also a member of STEP, which he was instrumental in introducing into New Zealand.

Ziva Robertson
Partner, McDermott Will & Emery
zrobertson@mwe.com

Ziva Robertson is a partner in the law firm of McDermott Will & Emery, based in its London office, where she heads the private client team. She specialises in dispute resolution, including complex trust disputes, contested estates and commercial disputes containing fiduciary elements. Her practice involves both the conduct and the avoidance of disputes, and she has extensive experience in cross-jurisdictional and international litigation. Many of her cases, both in England and offshore, have been reported and include milestone cases such as *Dawson-Damer v Taylor Wessing*, the leading case on beneficiaries' right to information under the Data Protection Act. Ms Robertson is a frequent lecturer on issues concerning trust structuring and disputes, and has contributed to a number of publications on such aspects.

Keith Robinson
Partner, Carey Olsen Bermuda Limited
keith.robinson@careyolsen.com

Keith Robinson is a partner in the trusts and private wealth and dispute resolution practices of Carey Olsen Bermuda. He has over 20 years' experience in non-contentious and contentious trust and private wealth matters. He has particular expertise in high-value trust litigation and court-approved trust restructurings, often with a multi-jurisdictional element. He has represented trustees, beneficiaries, settlors and protectors in a range of cases before the Supreme Court of Bermuda, and has been involved in many major trust cases in Bermuda. He advises on a wide range of non-contentious Bermuda trust matters and also acts as a protector.

Mr Robinson is an active member of STEP. He is also an elected member of the International Academy of Estate and Trust Law, and serves on the Trust Focus Group and the Trust Law Reform Committee of the Bermuda Business Development Agency.

Gideon Rothschild
Partner, Moses & Singer LLP
grothschild@mosessinger.com

Gideon Rothschild is a partner with the New York City law firm of Moses & Singer, where he co-chairs the private client group. He focuses his practice on domestic and international estate planning techniques for high-net-worth clients and is a nationally recognised authority on wealth preservation and offshore trusts.

Mr Rothschild is a past chair of the Real Property Trust & Estate Law Section of the American Bar Association, a fellow of the American College of Trust and Estate Counsel, an academician of the International Academy of Trust and Estate Lawyers and a past chair of the New York Chapter of STEP. Mr Rothschild is a member of the editorial advisory boards of *Tax Management* and *Trusts and Estates*, a former adjunct professor and a frequent lecturer on asset protection and estate planning to professional groups.

Nicola Saccardo

Partner, Maisto e Associati
n.saccardo@maisto.it

Nicola Saccardo is admitted to the Italian Bar (he is also qualified as Italian chartered accountant). He is a member of the International Academy of Estate and Trust Law, as well as its vice president for Europe and chair of its Tax Committee. He is an international fellow of the American College of Trust and Estate Counsel. He is a member of STEP and a member of the International Client Global Special Interest Group Steering Committee of STEP. He is ranked as a leading expert in several legal directories, including *Chambers High Net Worth, Legal Week Private Clients Global Elite* and the *Citywealth* Leaders List. He is the author of many publications on Italian tax matters and is a frequent speaker at conferences. He leads the EU tax law course on the LLM at King's College in London. His areas of expertise include taxation of trusts and estates, estate planning and international and EU tax law.

Susan R Schoenfeld

Chief executive officer and founder, Wealth Legacy Advisors LLC
schoenfeld@wlallc.com

Susan R Schoenfeld, JD, LLM (Taxation), CPA, MBA, is CEO and founder of Wealth Legacy Advisors LLC. She is an award-winning thought leader to families of wealth and public speaker to the financial services professionals who serve them – or want to! – on the human issues that keep families of wealth up at night. Based in New York City, she is a 'recovering' attorney and certified public accountant with deep experience as an adviser to families and family offices on the human issues of wealth.

Ms Schoenfeld's passion is giving families (and their provider organisations) the tools to take them to their full potential.

After practising law in both tax and trusts and estates, Ms Schoenfeld was fiduciary counsel at Bessemer Trust for over 14 years. She then served as a family ambassador for a private single family office, before launching her consulting practice to ultra-high-net-worth families and family offices.

Yehuda Shaffer

Independent consultant
yshaffer@riskbasedconsultancy.com

Yehuda Shaffer is a consultant specialising in risk and wealth management in the private and governmental sectors, with extensive worldwide expertise in both implementing and evaluating the FATF standards on anti-money laundering and counter-terrorist financing, as well as in the investigation and prosecution of financial crime and confiscation of assets.

He served as the Israeli deputy state attorney (financial enforcement) from 2009 to 2018, and as the director and founder of IMPA – the Israeli financial intelligence unit in the Ministry of Justice – from 2002 to 2009.

He received his LLB (1987) and LLM (1989) from the faculty of law at the Hebrew University in Jerusalem (where he has also taught), and an MPA from the Kennedy School of Government at Harvard University (2000).

Rahul Sharma

Partner, Miller Thomson LLP
rsharma@millerthomson.com

Rahul Sharma advises Canadian and international clients on a variety of tax, trust and estate planning matters. He is experienced with cross-border and international trust and estate matters and matters involving offshore or non-resident trusts with ties to Canada. He also counsels clients in the areas of corporate income tax and business succession planning.

Mr Sharma is co-author of chapters on tax and estate planning-related topics. He is a co-editor of Thomson Reuters' *Taxes and Wealth Management* publication and the assistant editor of *Miller Thomson on Estate Planning*, a comprehensive guide to tax and estate planning in Canada. He is also the editor-in-chief of Thomson Reuter's *Personal Tax and Estate Planning Journal*, as well as the author of several papers and articles on tax, trust and Canadian estate matters. Mr Sharma is a regular presenter on Canadian and cross-border tax and estate planning topics.

Geoffrey Shindler

Director, Old Trafford Consulting Limited

geoffrey@oldtraffordconsulting.co.uk

Geoffrey Shindler OBE is a director of Old Trafford Consulting, a Manchester-based trust advisory company. He specialises in wills, trusts, capital taxation and estate work.

Mr Shindler has a degree and postgraduate degree in law from the University of Cambridge and is a registered trust and estate practitioner. He was a founder member of STEP and its chairman between 1994 and 1998. He was chairman of its Education Committee when its diploma examination was developed and introduced; and was its president from 2006 to 2016.

He is also a member of the UK-based Trust Law Committee and has sat on various committees studying the working of inheritance tax legislation in the United Kingdom. He is the consulting editor of *Trusts & Estates Law & Tax Journal* and a member of the editorial board of *Wills & Trusts Law*

Reports. He is a joint author of *Practical Inheritance Tax Planning, Trust Drafting and Precedents* and *Aldridge Powers of Attorney*.

Christian Stewart

Managing director, Family Legacy Asia (HK) Limited

cstewart@familylegacyasia.com

Christian Stewart is the founder of Family Legacy Asia, a process consulting firm based in Hong Kong. He assists family enterprises around Asia with family governance, succession, learning and development.

Mr Stewart originally qualified and practised as a solicitor in South Australia from 1990 to 1994. He moved to Hong Kong in late 1994, joining PricewaterhouseCoopers, and became a partner and head of its trust and private client group. In July 2002 he joined JPMorgan Private Bank to head the bank's wealth advisory team for Asia, where he worked for six years. He founded Family Legacy Asia in July 2008 to provide independent advice to Asian families on family and family business governance issues. In addition, from May 2016 he became an associate with Wise Counsel Research, a non-profit think tank and boutique consultancy based in Massachusetts, United States, focused on matters of wealth and philanthropy.

Mark Walley

Chief executive officer, STEP

Mark Walley joined STEP as chief executive in January 2019. Prior to joining STEP, he worked as managing director, Europe, Middle East and Africa (EMEA) at the Royal Institution of Chartered Surveyors, where he was responsible for ensuring growth in the EMEA region and led on the organisation's development of global sales, marketing and customer service strategies. Prior to this, he was director of corporate development for the IFS School of Finance, responsible for take-up of its professional qualifications and executive education programmes; and before that, regional director EMEA for Cohen Brown Management Group. He started his career with Barclays, where he spent 25 years – the latter part as sales director and then chief operating officer of Barclays Wealth's International Personal and Premier Banking Division. He holds a BSc (Hons) in banking and finance and is a fellow of the Institute of Directors

Emily Yiolitis
Partner, Harneys Aristodemou Loizides
Yiolitis LLC
emily.yiolitis@harneys.com

Emily Yiolitis is a graduate in jurisprudence from Trinity College, Oxford, a founding partner of the Harneys Cyprus office, global head of Harneys' tax and regulatory practice and head of the Cyprus fiduciary practice. Her work includes international tax structuring and planning and her clients include professional intermediaries around the globe as well as high-net-worth individuals.

Ms Yiolitis is the chair of the Cyprus Electricity Authority and has served on a number of public boards, including that of the Cyprus Telecom Authority. She is a founding committee member of STEP Cyprus and served as its chair for three consecutive years. She is a regular speaker at international tax conferences and her work is frequently published in Cyprus and international tax periodicals.

Ms Yiolitis is consistently ranked as one of the leading corporate lawyers in the jurisdiction for her expertise in tax planning matters.